D0379715

THE JEDBURGHS

THE
JEDBURGHS

The Secret History of the
Allied Special Forces, France 1944

LT. COL. WILL IRWIN,
U.S. ARMY (RET.)

PUBLICAFFAIRS
NEW YORK

Copyright © 2005 Wyman W. Irwin

Published in the United States by PublicAffairs™, a member of the Perseus Books Group.

Printed in the United States of America.

Book Design by Janet Tingey

Library of Congress Cataloging-in-Publication Data
Irwin, Will, 1950-
The Jedburghs : The secret history of the Allied Special
    Forces, France 1944 / Will Irwin.—1ˢᵗ ed.
p.   cm.
Includes index.
ISBN–13 978–1–58648–307–4
ISBN–10 1–58648–307–2
1. World War, 1939–1945—Secret service—France. 2. World
    War, 1939–1945—Campaigns—France—Normandy. 3.
    World War, 1939–1945—Underground movements—
    France. 4. Special forces (Military science) 5. Special
    operations (Military science) 6. Normandy (France)—
    History, Military. I. Title.
D810.S7I79 2005
940.54′86′0944—dc22
2005050917

First Edition

10 9 8 7 6 5 4 3 2 1

This book is dedicated to the Jeds lost in the campaign for France.

"For always, no matter how powerful one's armies, to enter a conquered territory one needs the good-will of the inhabitants."

Niccolò Machiavelli, *The Prince*, 1513

"Any nation that uses [partisan warfare] intelligently will, as a rule, gain some superiority over those who disdain its use."

Karl von Clausewitz, *On War*, 1833

"The difficulties [for an invader] are particularly great when the people are supported by a considerable nucleus of disciplined troops. The invader has only an army: his adversaries have an army, and a people wholly or almost wholly in arms . . . even the noncombatants have an interest in his ruin and accelerate it by every means in their power."

General Baron de Jomini,
A Treatise on the Art of War, 1838

CONTENTS

A NOTE ON MILITARY UNITS

The following table gives readers an idea of the organization and typical authorized strength of the various ground force units—both Allied (American, British, Canadian, and Free French) and German—referred to in the book. The "composition" column in the table shows only the major combat elements at each level of organization; in addition to these, organizations at the division level and above also had additional artillery, engineer, signal, medical, or other specialty units. As the weeks and months passed following D-Day, virtually all units operated below their authorized strength, even with replacements. Many German units, in particular, were at a fraction of their authorized strength by the late summer of 1944.

Throughout the book, specific unit designations are shown following conventional U.S.-European practice: Arabic numerals for divisions, regiments, battalions, and platoons (*e.g.*, 2nd SS Panzer Division, 16th Infantry Regiment); spelled-out numbers for field armies (*e.g.*, French First Army, Third U.S. Army); Roman numerals for corps (*e.g.*, VII Corps); and letters for companies (*e.g.*, Company B).

CHART 1

Organization	Typical Composition	Typical Strength
Army Group	Two or more field armies	200,000–300,000
(Field) Army	Two or more corps	100,000–150,000
Corps	Two or more divisions	25,000–50,000
Division	Three or more regiments, brigades, or combat commands	10,000–15,000
Regiment, Brigade, or Combat Command	Two or more battalions	1,000–3,500
Battalion or Squadron	Four to six companies	400–1,000
Company or Troop	Three to five platoons	100–250
Platoon	Two to four squads	16–50
Squad		8–12

PROLOGUE

A lone bomber climbed slowly into the darkness from the airfield in Northamptonshire, in central England. It was a little more than an hour before midnight on July 8, 1944, a warm Saturday night. To anyone outside at that hour in the nearby village of Harrington, the B-24 Liberator looked like hundreds of others based throughout Britain; but residents of Harrington knew that nothing at this particular airfield could be taken at face value. Something strange went on there, though no one could say exactly what. Planes took off at about this time—or even later—almost every night, and they always returned before dawn. Nearly always, the planes were silhouetted against a moonlit sky and bore no telltale running lights. Anyone who'd paid any attention at all during the past two years knew that the Americans stationed at every other base in England flew only daytime bombing missions.

The young airmen of the U.S. Eighth Air Force who worked at the base—they called themselves "Carpetbaggers"—were friendly enough. They often spent their free time drinking the weak wartime beer in local pubs, and many had accepted invitations from villagers to come by for a home-cooked meal. But if asked about what they did, the young men grew tight-lipped and evasive. Once it became clear that their work was a military secret, people stopped asking—as if they knew of some flaw in your family's past, but liked you and respected you enough not to bring it up.

Closer examination of the bomber lifting off at 2240 hours that night would have revealed that it was no ordinary Liberator. This B-24 was cloaked in a non-reflective black paint. Gun turrets had been removed from the nose, waist, and belly of the fuselage, leaving two gun mountings—one in the top of the fuselage and one in the tail. The crew had been reduced from the standard ten men to eight. Bomb racks had been stripped from the aircraft and replaced by specially designed racks for carrying supply containers; both the racks and the containers were of British manufacture. A plywood trapdoor had been fitted over the hole in the floor where the belly gunner's turret usually was—a hole meant to allow parachutists to exit the aircraft, one at a time. The air force called it the "Joe hole," referring to their universal name for jumpers.

Advanced avionics had been added to the plane, as well as a primitive "friend or foe" identification system. There also was advanced radio equipment and an early radar device designed to help prevent the plane from hitting the ground when flying at low altitudes. Oxygen bottles had been removed; this plane wouldn't be flying high enough to need them. The only light left to burn continuously once a mission was underway was a small one in the navigator's compartment that gave off an eerie green glow, providing just enough illumination for the navigator to read his charts.

Seated on the airplane's plywood floor were three young men—parachutists who would jump on the first pass over the drop zone. The leader of the team was a tall, handsome twenty-nine-year-old American army captain, an aircraft armaments officer before volunteering for duty with the Office of Strategic Services. Bernard Knox, a naturalized citizen of the United States, was a native Briton, a Cambridge graduate, and a veteran of the Spanish Civil War. His second-in-command, a French captain named Paul Lebel, had come from a Free French infantry regiment in North Africa, and the third member of the team, Sergeant Gordon Tack, was a British army radio operator assigned to that country's Special Operations Executive. All three men wore battledress uniform with a winged patch on the upper sleeve. In the center of the patch's spread white wings was a red circle with the letters SF, for Special Forces, in light blue.

Their equipment was an odd mixture—British radios, American M1 carbines and .45-caliber pistols, and British compasses. The men wore canvas money belts stuffed with hundreds of thousands in French francs and a smaller amount of American dollars. Over their uniforms they wore standard British jump smocks, their pockets crammed with code books and radio crystals. On their heads they wore British parachutist helmets, on their feet American jump boots.

Positioned above the bomb bay were twelve Type C containers—man-sized tubular-shaped canisters filled with weapons and other equipment for the resistance fighters. These would be dropped during the aircraft's second pass over the planned drop area, followed by twelve more from a second B-24. The containers were stamped from sheet metal, with reinforcing ribs on the surface. Each had an opening which ran the length of the container and was fastened closed with three latches. A small compartment at one end held a parachute. Protruding from a hole in the compartment was a static line that was fastened to a bar in the aircraft's interior; when the container left the aircraft the line would pull out the parachute. Carefully packed in the larger main compartment was a standard load of submachine guns, ammunition, grenades, explosives, radios, boots, and other gear—the impedimenta of guerrilla warfare.

The drop zone was a field two miles north of the town of Briec, near the westernmost tip of the Brittany peninsula—that dog-ear-like appendage of northwestern France that points into the North Atlantic. The field was ideal for receiving a parachute drop of men and equipment—a rolling, pastoral stretch of countryside with no high-tension wires or other obstacles on the field itself or along the plane's approach path.

The previous evening's French-language news broadcast by the BBC had been followed, as it was every evening, by coded "personal messages" intended for various French resistance groups. Nonsensical phrases that were pointless to anyone but those who knew their hidden meanings: "Jacques has a tall brother," or "The first snow fell in November," or some other such silliness.

One such message had meaning for members of the Finistère resistance, which picked up the BBC broadcast on a hidden radio in defiance of an edict by the German occupation authorities. One of the personal messages informed the members of the impending arrival of the three-man team and had directed that the reception committee—the men and women who would await the parachutists at the drop zone—should use a light to flash a pre-arranged letter in Morse code as the aircraft approached, indicating that the drop zone was secure—that no Germans were in the immediate vicinity.

Monsieur Arzel, deputy police chief of Quimper, a large market town to the southwest, organized the reception committee. Around midnight, members of the resistance from nearby villages converged on the drop zone and began preparation for the team's arrival. A small truck and a few horse-drawn wagons were pulled out of sight into the nearby woods, partly to remain hidden from anyone who might pass by and partly to keep the horses from being frightened by the low-flying aircraft. Armed men took up positions on approaching roads and trails to provide security against possible German patrols. Other men broke up into small groups for retrieving the metal containers packed with arms and ammunition and loading them onto the wagons—it usually took four to handle each container. Still others prepared three small bonfires; these were arranged to form the corners of a large triangle to mark the drop zone and were not to be lit until the aircraft could be heard approaching from the expected direction.

When all was ready, the reception teams hid along the edge of the woods. Shortly before one o'clock in the morning, the drone of the plane was heard and the bonfires were lit. Once the unmistakable shape of the Liberator loomed in the pale moonlit sky, a man standing on the drop zone aimed a flashlight skyward, with a tubular attachment to hide its beam from anyone but those in the bomber. He blinked the appropriate dashes and dots to indicate the pre-arranged letter.

Aboard the Liberator, an air corps sergeant—called the dispatcher—stood near the Joe hole. Only minutes earlier he had removed the plywood trap door in the floor of the bomber. The pilot, however, unable to spot any lights marking the drop zone, circled for twenty minutes searching for the triangle of small bonfires, the center of which would be his target. While the triangle lighting system of marking drop zones was common, it was only one of four methods used during the war.

Special operations piloting was something more than an acquired skill, and it demanded the very best pilots. It was low-level, seat-of-the-pants flying in a ponderous heavy bomber designed for formation flying at high altitudes. The B-24 could be cumbersome at these lower altitudes; the machine had to be manhandled. After circling for a time, the pilot informed the dispatcher that he had finally spotted the fires. Then the pilot leveled the plane off and began his run in—at an altitude of around six hundred feet above ground level—lowering the flaps halfway and slowing the bulky plane to about 125 miles per hour, barely above stall speed.

For everyone aboard the airplane, nervous tension rose in proportion to the slackening of the engines. With the bomber on final approach, the sergeant shouted, "Running in!" loudly enough to be heard over the groan of the four huge Pratt & Whitney engines. The dispatcher then busied himself re-checking the static lines leading from the men's parachutes, which he had moments before hooked to an anchorage in the floor just behind the Joe hole. Within seconds, a red light above the seated men came alive with a dim ruby glow. And, on its cue, the sergeant yelled, "Action stations!" Captain Knox scooted to the edge of the opening, dangling his feet in the slipstream below the plane, watching the grayish green patchwork that defined the ground some six hundred feet below. Only seconds later, a green light came to life as the red one died, and the dispatcher screamed, "Go!" In prearranged order, Captain Knox, then Sergeant Tack, and finally Captain Lebel dropped through the hole and were swallowed up by the darkness.

Thus began the mission of an Allied special forces team in German-occupied France, one of dozens carried out by these three-man units known as "Jedburghs." The secret Jedburgh project entailed dropping up to one hundred hybrid special forces teams into occupied France—hundreds of miles ahead of conventional ground forces. The men, commonly referred to as Jeds, were a mix of

British, American, and French operatives. Only about one team in ten, however, included a member of each of those nationalities; on most teams, two of the men were from the same country. But all teams included at least one Frenchman. The Jeds' mission was to organize, arm, and train groups of French resistance guerrillas.

But, more importantly, these teams were to orchestrate the sabotage and guerrilla warfare activities of these resistance groups to ensure that they complemented operations of the advancing Allied ground forces. The bands of underground partisan fighters with whom they worked were commonly called maquis (pronounced mah-kee)—named for a scrub brush that thrives in the hills of Corsica much as the partisans thrived in the more remote terrain of mainland France. Such maquis bands were initially formed by young men, many of them teenagers, who'd fled to the hills to avoid German labor drafts.

American Jeds belonged to the Office of Strategic Services (OSS); their British counterparts were from the Special Operations Executive (SOE). They were joined by men of General Charles de Gaulle's Free French organization. Espionage agents they were not. They all were military officers and noncommissioned officers who jumped and worked far behind German lines, most often in uniform. Joining them in this effort, and usually working hand in hand with them in the field, were other uniformed special forces, particularly the British and French Special Air Service (SAS) and the American Operational Groups.

The Jedburghs, along with a few other British and American special forces created at about the same time, were the first such units in history. Never before had nations institutionalized a uniformed military force organized, trained, and equipped to rally and direct the operations of irregular partisans deep in enemy territory. These units functioned in much the same way that their descendants—the U.S. Army Special Forces* (the Green Berets), Britain's SAS, and France's Premier Régiment Parachutiste d'Infanterie de Marine—do today.

But how and for what purpose were such units initially formed?

* Throughout this volume, references to special forces in general are lowercased. The capitalized term "Special Forces" specifically refers to the U.S. Army Special Forces, a standing organization added to the U.S force structure in 1952.

The original concept for such special forces in World War II Europe was to support British Prime Minister Winston Churchill's idea of engaging the people of occupied Europe in a guerrilla war against the Germans. In this way, Churchill hoped to tie down enemy forces by compelling them to engage in counter-guerrilla operations far from the front lines. Guerrillas could also sabotage railways and ambush enemy columns, delaying reinforcements from reaching the front and improving the prospect for Allied victory and a reduction in Allied casualties.

Unconventional warfare, as conducted during the Second World War, was unprecedented in its scope and methods. New technologies allowed for methods of clandestine and irregular warfare never before even imagined. The airplane provided a means for delivering not only intelligence agents and special forces teams, but also the ordnance and supplies to sustain the men in the field. Modern short-wave communications equipment made it possible for these elements to receive instructions from headquarters in friendly territory, hundreds of miles away. In turn, soldiers operating deep behind enemy lines could use such equipment to report enemy activity and to request supplies or reinforcement from the base station.

The Jedburgh concept was born in the minds of political and military leaders at the highest levels and developed by a small group of dedicated, imaginative Allied army officers (both regulars and soldier-civilians). It was supported with varying degrees of enthusiasm by Allied field commanders and executed by a few hundred highly motivated and adventurous soldiers. The British had devised a strategy of supporting partisan forces in occupied Europe as early as February 1941, and the Jedburgh plan had been first proposed the following year. Planning and preparation began almost in isolation. But over the next three years, with the backing of Churchill and General Dwight D. Eisenhower, it became more and more an integral part of the plan for Operation Overlord—the return of Allied forces to France.

The ideas and efforts of these men of imagination, however, would have counted for little without the remarkably capable young men who were selected and trained to carry out these missions. It took a special type of man to fight the unconventional war;

the work required extraordinary nerve. Once on the ground in German-occupied territory, there was no falling back when things got hot. Retreat or withdrawal was out of the question; there was no rear area to fall back to. And if a member of a Jedburgh team was killed or seriously wounded the loss represented a 33 percent reduction in the unit's strength and capability. Unlike in an infantry battalion, where units could eventually expect a replacement for such a loss, field replacements in the Jeds were almost unheard of and certainly were not expected.

In conventional combat units, men drew strength from the very nearness of large numbers of their comrades. In the Jedburghs, on the other hand, men had only their inner strength and that of a couple of teammates to pull them through some extraordinarily terrifying experiences.

These men were asked to parachute hundreds of miles behind enemy lines and establish contact with battle-hardened resistance fighters who had grown leery of strangers as a result of German infiltration ploys. The Jeds' task was to gain the confidence of these underground leaders and work with them to support the Allied ground campaign. It was work that left little margin for error, and it called for top-drawer men.

So who were these men and where did they come from? Some were army regulars, but many more came into the military from civilian life after the war began. And they were a tremendously mixed lot, coming from all walks of pre-war life: brewery worker, scholar, Hollywood stuntman, lawyer, silver polisher, business executive, whiskey taster, stockbroker, physical therapist, bank auditor, lumberjack, musician, restaurateur, foundry worker, French nobleman, grocery deliveryman, chemical lab assistant, photoengraver, politician, tennis pro, oil executive, and cattle rancher. There were engineers, radio repairmen, newspaper reporters, college undergraduates, medical and law school students, taxi drivers, university lecturers, high school teachers, and athletic coaches.

They hailed primarily, and in roughly equal numbers, from France, Britain, and the United States. Into this mélange were sprinkled, as if for flavoring, a Belgian, a Canadian, a handful of Dutch, and a South African. Just under three hundred men in all.

But, as diverse as their backgrounds were, they also had much in common. They all were men of adventurous spirit—not inclined to shrink from a challenge or to look for the easy way out. And they were men who liked to think for themselves.

The Americans among them could recall the anti-war movement in the United States in the pre–Pearl Harbor days—a movement whose sentiments some of them shared at the time—but since their country's entrance into the war these men were anxious to do their part. The British had seen the devastation and withdrawal of their army from France in 1940, and the costly German bombing of their cities and the evacuation of children and whole families to the countryside. The French had seen firsthand the theft of their country and the humiliation of its population. All the men were products of the Depression—a bleak and fearful time for most, regardless of nationality. And, as a result, most of them had become accustomed to risk, austerity, and hardship.

Then, as these men were finishing high school or college—generally during the late 1930s and early 1940s—their world started coming apart. Nations had once again failed to resolve their differences short of going to war. And, characteristically, these young men chose a most challenging and atypical way in which to help put the world right again.

These were the few men who remained in their seats at OSS and SOE recruitment briefings, even after hearing of the risks involved. Their motives for volunteering may have differed, but self-confidence was a common trait. They stayed because, regardless of what else they were, they were men of action—athletes, travelers, adventure seekers—tough guys, both physically and mentally.

The officers were graduates of some of the best colleges and universities in the world. Even the Jedburgh radio operators—noncommissioned officers (although the French made a practice of commissioning theirs just prior to deployment)—often had completed one or two years of college. And this was at a time when the average soldier had but two years of high school. Despite their tender ages, the noncoms were catapulted in rank, promoted at a pace unheard of in conventional units.

If you walked into a room full of Jeds, you could likely find someone with whom to discuss Greek tragedy or epidemiology or tort law or bel canto opera. Any number of them, as a result of their radio training, might get you in over your head on the subject of electromagnetic wave propagation—and many of them could do so in two or more languages. But, given cause, they could also knock you on your ass.

Although they were brassy, cocksure, boundlessly self-confident, these men were not without human emotion. In the field—hunted like wild animals by the Germans—some knew fear so strong that they clearly recalled it more than forty years later. But they never let that fear overcome them; they prevailed in spite of it. Some felt a need to prove something. But most were simply determined to serve with only the best—in other words, with men like themselves. In doing so, they formed a lifelong brotherhood.

General Eisenhower himself, supreme commander of Allied forces in Europe, recognized the special forces' contribution in the campaign for France when he said, "In no previous war, and in no other theater during this war, have resistance forces been so closely harnessed to the main military effort."[1]

Details of their activities were not widely known at the time because the operations were classified, and remained so until well after the war. As records emerge through declassification efforts begun in the 1980s, however, it is clear that these special forces, and the resistance movements they supported, did a great deal to help drive Hitler's army from France in the summer of 1944. Eisenhower praised their actions on numerous occasions, according to his naval aide, Captain Harry C. Butcher. As Butcher noted in his wartime diary, Ike considered the maquis to have been "far more effective than many doubting Thomases thought before D-Day."[2] And the Jedburghs contributed significantly to their success.

Fewer than three hundred men deployed on Jed teams—a third the strength of an American infantry battalion of the time;[3] indeed, only half again the size of a rifle company. Yet, this group of men earned an impressive number of decorations. Of the eighty-three American Jeds, for example, no less than fifty-three were decorated. The awards include twelve Distinguished Service Crosses, two Navy Crosses, eight Silver Stars, six Legion of Merit medals, and fourteen Bronze Star Medals;[4] and more than three dozen men earned the French Croix de Guerre.

If postwar careers of Jedburgh veterans are any indication, those who ran the exhaustive recruitment, assessment, and selection process did a remarkable job. Many of those chosen for the Jedburghs went on to become successful statesmen and diplomats, military and intelligence professionals, doctors and lawyers, scholars and educators, journalists and authors, businessmen and tradesmen. The French, British, and American contingents each included future generals (a dozen in all) and statesmen of cabinet, minister, and ambassadorial rank. Two would become members of Britain's parliament. There was a future director of the Central Intelligence Agency, a top columnist for *The Saturday Evening Post* and *Newsweek*, an acclaimed scholar and professor of Hellenic studies, and a world-renowned cardiac surgeon. The Jeds also produced an Episcopalian priest and a Benedictine monk, a cotton plantation manager and a wine grower, an artist and a novelist, and a public relations agent for Princess Grace of Monaco. One former Jed would become a television producer, another a psychiatrist, and still another an accomplished chef. Quite a showing for a group of roughly two hundred and eighty men. And all were true heroes—in a day when that label was not carelessly applied.

It is an unfortunate irony that most of these self-sacrificing heroes have lived unnamed and uncredited among us for decades. They taught us in school, they treated our illnesses, they sold us insurance, they saw to our legal affairs, but few ever spoke of their wartime experiences. Many of their immediate family members told me that they had no idea of the part their father or husband or brother had played in the war. The majority of them remained silent because they had been ordered to do so. Their role in the war was classified, and they were sworn to secrecy by their respective governments. In most cases, even family and friends only learned of their wartime deeds when the CIA began declassifying the relevant records in 1985. Wide exposure came even later in Britain, where the Official Secrets Act delayed declassification until more recently. And, until now, there never has been a complete account of how these men were selected and trained and how they operated in the field.

Ernie Pyle, the great war correspondent, wrote in 1944: "The story of the French underground, when the day comes for it to be written, will be one of the most fascinating stories in all history."[5] And the Jedburghs and other Allied special forces who did so much to help the resistance are an important part of that story.

Space restrictions compel me to limit this account to a representative half-dozen teams, allowing their stories to be told in greater detail. But the reader should keep in mind that for each Jedburgh team whose story is told here a dozen more were engaged in similar operations. I also should caution readers against comparing the Jedburghs to elite infantry strike forces such as the British Commandos or the U.S. Army's Rangers. The Jeds were not organized or equipped as those units were because the Jeds had a different and much broader mission. The Jedburghs were fighters, but they also were teachers and advisors, counselors and advocates, combat leaders, negotiators—the first diplomat-soldiers.

1

CALL TO ACTION

THE alert came on a clear and sunny Friday morning. The date was June 2, 1944, and Sergeant Bob Kehoe and his teammates were on a training exercise in central England. Unknown to the men, the long-awaited cross-channel invasion of occupied France, called Operation Overlord, was scheduled to begin on Monday morning, the fifth. In military planners' terminology, that gave June 5 the designation "D-Day."

The coming weeks were to bring adventure beyond anything that Kehoe, a young GI from New Jersey, ever had expected. More than six months of training ensured that he possessed the necessary skills and that his body was in peak condition. But no training could prepare young men like Kehoe for the human dimension of combat—especially behind enemy lines. He and his Jedburgh teammates soon would experience firsthand the deadly and unpredictable—yet exhilarating—war of the partisan. The men would come to know its inconceivable treachery, its unsung valor, its abrupt and unanticipated violence—its unimagined fear and excitement.

That spring, with D-Day drawing near, Allied rehearsals of all types had been stepped-up throughout Britain—everything from amphibious landings, with naval forces supporting infantry and armor as they splashed ashore on unchallenged Devon beaches, to

1

mass parachute landings by the airborne regiments. And to fine-tune the unconventional part of the grand scheme, the Jedburgh training staff had staged a series of field exercises. The Jeds were one of three special forces elements which General Eisenhower planned to drop throughout occupied France to sever German communications and to delay the movement of enemy reinforcements to the Normandy beachhead. They would do so by stiffening the French resistance and by relaying operational direction to the partisans from Eisenhower's headquarters.

Formal training for the multinational three-man Jedburgh teams, some six to eight months of it, was complete by the first week of June. The final and most extensive Jedburgh war game, Exercise Lash, put the teams in the hilly picture-postcard terrain of the Charnwood Forest, in Leicestershire.

For the past few days, Jeds had been lurking about the wooded upland, through its secluded valleys and up its rocky summits, organizing and controlling surrogate partisan groups. The field exercise required the men to put six months of guerrilla warfare lessons into practice—stealth, sabotage, clandestine communications, ambush. Fit young men worked at becoming shadows. Bodies had hardened, wits sharpened—they were ready. Lash was, in a sense, their final exam. It had kicked off on the last day of May under unsettled skies and occasional rain showers and was to continue until June 8.[1]

Kehoe had enlisted in the U.S. Army Signal Corps in September 1942. Less than two years later, he was the radio operator for—and the youngest member of—one of the few Jedburgh teams that was tri-national in makeup. All teams had at least one French officer; in some cases, the radio operator also was French and the third member was either an American or a British officer. On most other teams, the French officer was accompanied by an officer and radio operator who were both either American or British. Only about one team in ten featured an American-British-French combination. At twenty-one years of age, Kehoe looked much younger—too young, by appearance, to be served alcohol, and much too young to be in this deadly business. He was a good-looking kid, with a head of hair that the older Jeds must have envied, and sharp-nosed in a way that gave him a distinguished look, like the mature Joe DiMaggio, underwriting his youthful innocence with a no-nonsense image.

Friday had begun warm and clear, a perfect early summer day, and Sergeant Kehoe's team was in the middle of the Lash exercise. Then, without much in the way of a sensible explanation, Kehoe and the two officers he was teamed with were ordered to return to the country estate that served as the Jedburgh training center. By afternoon, they were back at the sprawling brownstone mansion known as Milton Hall—a seventeenth-century Elizabethan, set amidst sporadic hardwood groves in an otherwise pastoral flatland. The men saw that another team, led by a Frenchman, Captain Erard, and an American, Captain Cyr (pronounced "sear"), had also been called back. Kehoe had seen Captain Cyr before and knew who he was, but he had never really gotten to know him. Both teams were told to pack for a five-day exercise with the British Special Air Service (SAS). The men were forewarned that, just in case the exercise extended beyond five days, they should pack thoroughly. In fact, they should prepare as they would for combat. The teams were to be ready to depart on Sunday morning, June 4, 1944.

Leading Kehoe's team was Captain Adrian Wise of the British army. Wise had come to the Jedburghs from the Royal Warwickshire Regiment, was a graduate of the Royal Military Academy at Sandhurst, and was a veteran of two commando raids on the coast of Norway early in the war. Kehoe liked Wise and admired the captain's command of French, which he was told had been cultivated during the summers Wise had spent with his family in Normandy. The twenty-six-year-old Wise, with his beaming, handsome face and his dark, wavy hair, looked as if he'd been picked for the role of guerrilla leader by a Hollywood casting director. More to the point, though, his experience as an infantry officer in combat was invaluable.

Kehoe found himself agreeing with Wise's hunch that this "exercise" story was just that—a cover—and that what lay ahead was the real thing. Many soldiers currently engaged in field exercises throughout England, after all, had noticed the steady increase in convoys of troop-laden trucks and trains carrying military vehicles southward. Such activity only added to the nationwide speculation that the big invasion was near. Two other teams that had returned to Milton Hall over the last couple of days now were nowhere to be seen. Plus, being withdrawn from one exercise to be carted off to another just sounded too phony; they must have been pulled out for a real mission. They were sure of it. Still, anything was possible in the army.

The third member of the team, a French officer and Wise's second in command, was skeptical about the prospect that the team was embarking on anything other than another exercise. A moon-faced Parisian with deep-set eyes and a high forehead, the amiable Lieutenant Paul Aguirec was a bit older than Wise and Kehoe. He was an experienced army officer, having been activated from the reserves in the late 1930s, and, like many of the French Jeds, he had been recruited for the secret special forces project in North Africa. Wise and Kehoe enjoyed the company of the fun-loving Frenchman, despite his limited command of English. In keeping with a practice followed by all French men and women taking part in the shadow war, the lieutenant had adopted a nom de guerre to protect his relatives still in France in the event of his capture. His real name was, in fact, Paul Bloch-Auroch. But Aguirec was the only name Kehoe and Wise knew him by.[2]

Kehoe had first met the two officers when he was teamed with them on a recent exercise, and they had asked him to permanently join them a week later. He'd come to like both officers and was delighted to become their radio operator, and in the ensuing weeks he grew to appreciate their sense of teamwork. Although his job was communications, nothing on Captain Wise's team was the exclusive domain of the officers. During the exercises in the weeks since their team had been formed, Kehoe helped with the planning right alongside them.[3]

But, on the chance that this might be more than just another exercise, the two teams packed their gear carefully with an eye toward the prospect of months of combat rather than a week or two of training. The next day, all six men and their equipment were inspected and deemed ready. That afternoon, gloomy skies descended over southern England.

★　★　★

On the Channel coast that Saturday night, rain, driven by a howling wind, hammered General Eisenhower's tent camp. The great Allied invasion, Operation Overlord, was about to be launched from staging bases throughout southern England, and the supreme commander and a few senior members of his staff had left their London headquarters on May 29 and established an advanced command post at Southwick, seven miles north of Portsmouth.

Tucked away in a patch of woods atop a bluff, it was a GI tent and trailer affair, spread along trails in the manner of a tourist campground. Not far away, amid manicured lawns and gardens, sat a mansion called Southwick House which served as the headquarters of Admiral Bertram Ramsay, Eisenhower's naval commander in chief. The view from the house overlooking Portsmouth harbor showed it to be crowded with naval vessels—battleships, destroyers, landing craft, and transports and tenders of all types.

Eisenhower held a special meeting in the library of the big house for his senior commanders at two o'clock on Sunday morning, June 4. Because of the terrific storm raging outside, he announced a postponement of the invasion for at least twenty-four hours, pushing D-Day from June 5 to June 6.[4]

Later that morning, the six Jeds threw their gear on the back of a truck, climbed aboard, and began the two-hour drive to London. At about eleven o'clock, the truck turned into Devonshire Close, an attractive side street just south of Regent's Park, and stopped in front of a handsome row house, just a few blocks east of Madame Tussaud's wax museum in north London. The house, the men were told, would be their home for the next few days. Oddly, there was no sign of security in the area; it was a typical London residential street. But such tedious benignity provided its own kind of security. The British Special Operations Executive (SOE) and the American Office of Strategic Services (OSS) had taken over many such flats and houses in the Marylebone district of the city. The buildings were used as temporary quarters and briefing rooms for agents and special forces teams awaiting transport to the Continent. This one was less than half a mile from Special Operations Executive headquarters on Baker Street and Special Force Headquarters in nearby Montagu Mansions.[5]

A British officer from the London Jedburgh staff arrived at the Devonshire house and introduced himself as Major Horton. He would be the teams' escort and briefing officer. And yes, there was a real mission. No more exercises.

The Jeds soon learned that they would be jumping into Brittany, but also that they would not be going in alone. In the months leading up to the invasion, as it turned out, there had been heated debate at the highest levels about the role Britain's Special Air Service was to play. In the end, it was decided that SAS parties would parachute deep behind enemy lines and establish bases of operation from which to perform their mayhem. In North Africa, the SAS had made good use of heavily armed jeeps during raids on German air bases. Current plans called for these same jeeps to be dropped by parachute, or landed by glider, to allow similar mobile raiding parties in France. By the spring of 1944, the SAS had grown to brigade size with more than two thousand men organized in two British regiments, two French parachute infantry battalions, a Belgian parachute squadron, and supporting signal units.[6] In Brittany, the 4th French SAS was to be used. The 4th included many native Bretons, and their mission would be to arm and train the local maquis there, while adding their own firepower and leadership.

Unfortunately, there had been little coordination or planning between the SAS and the Jedburghs, and there were important differences in their approaches to unconventional warfare. Where the Jedburghs had been taught the importance of mobility in guerrilla warfare, constantly moving and never remaining long in one place, the SAS insisted on establishing and operating from fairly permanent and sizable bases deep behind enemy lines. While operating from such bases is a reasonable procedure in some parts of the world and against less capable enemies, plans which called for special forces and guerrillas to defend such bases in occupied France against attacks by the highly mechanized Wehrmacht at least should have raised some eyebrows.

The French SAS was to establish two bases in Brittany. One, code-named Samwest, would be in the Forêt de Duault, a forest west of the medieval cathedral town of St-Brieuc on Brittany's north coast. The other would go farther south, where the SAS would set up a somewhat larger base under the code name Dingson.

Captain Wise's Jed team, assigned the code name Frederick, was to accompany the Samwest party and, at least initially, operate under the command of the SAS leader, Captain André Leblond. Being subordinated to the SAS rankled Wise and Kehoe, but they bit their tongues, knowing that the mission would, at least, soon get them into France. On the eve of D-Day, the men learned, the SAS would drop two officers and sixteen soldiers as a lead element to find a site for a camp and prepare for the arrival of the remainder of the party. That remainder amounted to about one hundred men to be dropped over two consecutive nights. Jed team Frederick was to jump with the first contingent of forty-five SAS troopers on Friday night. They were to be dropped just southwest of the crossroads town of Guingamp, about a dozen miles in from the coast, west of St-Brieuc, in the department known as the Côtes-du-Nord (today called the Côtes d'Armor), one of five administrative departments that made up the region of Brittany. It was an area of farmlands and scattered hilly woodlands, with charming villages and towns that, like Guingamp, featured cobblestone streets and granite buildings with gray slate roofs.

The other team, with Captain Erard and Captain Cyr, was codenamed George. This team would be attached to the Dingson SAS party and would jump with them into an area near Redon in the department of Morbihan in southern Brittany.

Once on the ground, the Jeds were to contact local resistance elements, about which very little was known, and enlist their aid in defending the SAS camps. Any additional arms and supplies needed were to be delivered by airdrop arranged by the Jeds. The teams also were to provide London an assessment of the resistance potential in their respective areas. Additionally, if circumstances warranted it they were to request the deployment of additional Jedburgh teams and designate suitable drop zones for their delivery.

At one point, a communications expert arrived at the house and took Sergeant Kehoe to a separate room and went over communications procedures with him.[7] All radio messages, to and from the field, would be via wireless telegraphy and would be kept secure through the use of a cipher system known as the one-time pad. This pad of eight-inch-square sheets provided a key for enciphering and deciphering messages and was matched by an identical pad at the receiving station. Each sheet, different from all the rest, was used only once and then was destroyed, enabling the rendering of a brief message in a cipher that was unbreakable to anyone not possessing an identical pad.

For added security, Kehoe and the other radio operator memorized security checks. These were code words or letters or numbers which served as danger signals—to either be included in a message or omitted from it, according to the individual operator's instructions—to indicate to London that the operator had been captured and was transmitting under duress. Sergeant Kehoe was grilled until he and the briefer were certain that he had the codes down cold. For obvious reasons, they could not be written anywhere.

Security also could be enhanced by keeping messages as brief as possible. To assist in this, Kehoe was issued a twenty-inch-square piece of silk—which would outlast paper in the field—printed with four-letter brevity codes designed to replace often-used phrases in all messages. He also received a schedule of radio contacts to be made. The schedule designated times for both sending and receiving messages.

Next, the teams learned about German forces known to be in the area. Every scrap of available information was provided—unit designations and locations, and sites of headquarters and supply depots. Brittany had been vital to the German naval war, providing bases for the U-boat wolf packs that had decimated Allied shipping in the North Atlantic. Some fifty thousand German troops occupied Brittany, intent on defending those strategic bases. There were first-rate parachute divisions, other units comprised largely of Russians captured on the Eastern Front and thrown into German uniform, and everything in between. Intelligence estimated that the Germans could move three divisions from Brittany to reinforce front-line units in Normandy once the Allied landings began. They had to be delayed or stopped, and that responsibility fell largely to the resistance and Allied special forces.

The men were also reminded of German intelligence and security measures and units, including the Abwehr (military intelligence) and the Geheime Staatspolizei (secret state police). Normally referred to by the abbreviated term Gestapo, the latter was already well known for its brutal interrogation methods. Rumor had it that the Gestapo could be either ruthlessly efficient or bungling idiots.

Working hand in hand with the Germans, and equally detested by the French, was the collaborationist police force called the Milice—composed of Frenchmen who had been enticed to aid and abet the occupation forces. This militia had been created by the Vichy government in January 1943 to assist the German intelligence and security agencies in their campaign against the French resistance, and had become, in essence, a "French Gestapo." Some said that its ranks included convicted criminals whom the Germans had released under the condition that they work faithfully for the occupiers—work which included tracking down members of the resistance and anyone who supported them.

Maps were issued, and the men were briefed on the topography of the area. One map, in a scale of 1:50,000 (meaning one inch on the map represented fifty thousand inches on the ground), covered the area where they were to jump. A series of Michelin road maps, though, would prove best for daily use and for identifying drop zones for Special Force Headquarters in London. Each man also received a map printed on silk, to be tucked away in the bottom of a pocket so that it would be available, if needed, in survival or escape situations.

Finally, the Jeds were shown a list with names and descriptions of Allied agents known to be operating in the area. The names, of course, were pseudonyms, and the list was to be memorized, not carried.[8]

After remaining in the house all afternoon, the men were taken out to dinner by Major Horton. Decked out in their assorted field uniforms, the small group walked through London's eerily quiet streets. Men in a wide variety of military uniforms, so prevalent throughout the city only a few days before, were few in number on this night. The small group of men finally settled on a restaurant that was nearly empty and enjoyed their first good meal of the day.

The night seemed long in coming. With wartime Britain on double daylight saving time (standard time plus two hours) it remained light until half past ten.

*   *   *

Many Londoners who were not on the streets that night were listening to the nine o'clock BBC news broadcast, where they learned that troops of General Mark Clark's Fifth U.S. Army had entered Rome earlier that day. Following the news, as it did every night, the French-language BBC service aired the "personal messages" that provided coded signals to the French resistance.

At nine-thirty, in the library at Southwick House, Group Captain John Stagg of the Royal Air Force, chief meteorologist at Supreme Headquarters, Allied Expeditionary Force (SHAEF), briefed General Eisenhower and his senior commanders on the near-term weather prospects. Brass and braid filled every easy chair and couch in the small room. Outside, the storm had been gathering strength throughout the day and seemed to threaten disaster if the operation proceeded as scheduled. Every man in the room understood the implications of another postponement. If the landings could not take place on the morning of June 6, as then scheduled, the tide and moon conditions—tides coming in at just the right time to aid the landings and moonlight enough to aid the airborne divisions— would not be favorable again for nearly two weeks. Months of planning and training and waiting were taking their toll on troops as well as commanders. The strain was palpable. But Stagg predicted that a break in the storm would arrive in time for the landings scheduled for the morning of June 6. The commanders would meet again at four-fifteen in the morning for a final update and decision on whether the invasion would be launched.

Early on Monday morning, June 5, through gusting winds and a cold, driving rain, Eisenhower drove the mile from his tent to Southwick House. His staff and subordinate commanders were waiting there for him. Group Captain Stagg once again gave the general the latest weather forecast, which continued to call for a slight break in the storm—probably no more than twenty-four hours. Eisenhower asked each of his subordinate commanders for their recommendation. After each had spoken, Ike thought for a moment, surveying the assembled group through brisk blue eyes, and then gave his decision.

"O.K., let's go."[9] Eisenhower had just ordered the launching of history's greatest military invasion.

General Eisenhower would spend the day visiting British and American units as they prepared to depart. As the day progressed, the sky over southern England remained gray, but the wind began to die down. There was still a distinct chill in the air, while only days before it had been hot.

Throughout that Monday, the two Jedburgh teams sequestered in the row house on Devonshire Close pored over maps and worked on memorizing code names and other details. To Sergeant Kehoe, Captain Cyr seemed a bit edgy, constantly asking questions. But it wasn't just Cyr; all of the men were pretty nervous.[10]

Again, that evening, Major Horton escorted the Jeds to a local restaurant. Unknown to the men as they enjoyed their meal that night, five thousand ships and ten thousand airplanes were preparing to carry nearly two hundred thousand troops across the channel to the beaches of Normandy.

In the very early hours of Tuesday, June 6, light sleepers in London and throughout southern England were aware of endless formations of aircraft passing overhead in a southerly direction. Beginning around midnight, the continuous drone of more than ten thousand Allied planes—bombers, fighters, and troop carriers loaded with fifteen thousand American and eight thousand British paratroopers—caused a vibration that could be felt in the buildings below. Some planes circled over London for nearly two hours as groups formed up before heading toward Normandy. The din continued until after dawn—and by then, tens of thousands of Allied soldiers were fighting to gain and hold a sixty-mile-wide beachhead on the coast of Normandy.

At the Devonshire Close house that Tuesday morning, the Jeds woke to a clear, warm day. An hour before noon, the BBC announced that the invasion of occupied France was under way. By day's end, the Allies would have fifty-five thousand men ashore. All that day and into the following morning, the six Jeds kept the radio on, following the latest updates from the Normandy beachhead.

On Wednesday morning, Major Horton arrived in a Dodge truck stenciled with U.S. Army markings. The men had been issued weapons—American .30-caliber carbines and Colt .45-caliber automatic pistols—radios, frequency crystals, and cipher materials. They threw their gear in the truck, boarded, and were off to the SAS camp.

About fifty miles northwest of London, they came to the medieval city of Oxford, and Major Horton stopped long enough for the men to enjoy a stroll through the university grounds. After hours of sitting through briefings and memorizing details of the mission—as if cramming for the greatest of final exams—the pause at Oxford was like stepping into another world. The Americans, especially, seeing it for the first time, were enchanted with the majestic spires, and the medieval residence halls and academic buildings. Bob Kehoe appreciated the peaceful interlude. Strolling through the manicured gardens of an institution in its eighth century of existence, the oldest university in the English-speaking world, took him away from the war for a time. Much information had been thrown at the Jeds over the past few days—code names, order-of-battle data, cipher procedures, danger signals, evasion methods, agent identities. It could be mind-numbing; the brain needed a break from it all. But the respite ended too soon.[11]

Leaving Oxford, the truck wandered along narrow English roads until it came to the quaint old town of Fairford, in Gloucestershire. South of the town, the truck pulled into a camp that was adjacent to an airfield. In May, the SAS brigade had moved here to be close to the airfields used by their transport, the Royal Air Force's No. 38 Group. They ran a secure camp, meaning that it was enclosed by a double barbed-wire fence and no one was allowed to leave without specific orders.

Kehoe's first impression of the French SAS men was that they were itching for action. "Wild" was a word he used to describe them. They certainly appeared fit, and had obviously trained hard and well. Not surprisingly, both the Jeds and the SAS were uncomfortable with the relationship that had been forced upon them. The redundancy in their missions was obvious to the dullest of military minds, and both groups were uneasy with it. The SAS seemed to regard the Jedburghs as interlopers. Who were these six guys, seemingly just along for the ride? The SAS men were confident of their ability to handle the mission at hand, and they could see little of value that the two Jed teams might add. The men joked and made small talk, feeling one another out, as if the Jeds were new kids in a tough school.

That evening, the two Jedburgh teams were taken to meet the leader of the French SAS contingent that was going into Brittany, thirty-six-year-old Commandant (Major) Pierre-Louis Bourgoin. He was a brawny six-foot-three, with a jowly face that featured a long, broad nose and intense, narrow-set eyes. A thick shock of brown hair sprouted from the widow's peak above his forehead. Commandant Bourgoin would be called handsome only by very close family members. But he was clearly not a man to be trifled with, and the absence of an arm did nothing to diminish that impression. An Algerian-born teacher, he had received his lieutenant's commission in a reserve regiment in 1928, had distinguished himself in battle in North Africa early in the war, and the second of two wounds had cost him the arm. He had taken command of the 4th SAS Battalion in England in November 1943.

Bourgoin met each of the Jeds and, upon greeting Bob Kehoe, remarked how young the sergeant looked. He then directed the Jeds to attend a meeting that he planned to hold in the officers' mess at the evening meal. This, unfortunately, caused a stir. How was Sergeant Kehoe to accompany his teammates to a meeting in the officer's mess, an area off limits to enlisted personnel?

Special Force Headquarters had instructed the Jeds to remain together at all times while on the SAS base. But, like all European armies, France's observed many age-old traditions, including that of a distinct class barrier between officers and enlisted men. The Jeds soon found that the French SAS was no different. Irritated at the thought of having to exclude Sergeant Kehoe from the meeting, Captain Wise convinced their hosts to dispense with custom and to allow Kehoe to join them for dinner and to attend the war council. The French radio operator on team George, Kehoe noted, had just been made an officer.

Thursday—which was Captain Cyr's twenty-third birthday—was spent studying maps with the SAS and sitting through more of Commandant Bourgoin's chalk talks. The Algerian spoke and carried himself with authority, and his men loved him. In the evening, the Jed teams mingled with the SAS officers, and the drinks flowed freely, and as the Jeds learned more about these Frenchmen, their respect grew. Many of them had trained and fought with the British SAS in North Africa. Then they had all gone through commando training in Scotland, as well as parachute training. As the hours passed, the frost on the SAS began to thaw.

Some last-minute promotions came through for the Jeds. Wise was raised to the rank of major and Kehoe to technical sergeant, the rank known today as sergeant first class. But Aguirec's promotion to full lieutenant, the equivalent of first lieutenant, wasn't to come until later.

On Friday, the men packed their gear and prepared for the jump. Kehoe, who had the most to carry, was allowed to make use of a container for the two radios, each of which weighed nearly forty pounds. His carbine went into another container, but he kept his pistol with extra loaded magazines on his belt. Adding to his bulky load were eight cipher books, another book-sized box containing his transmission crystals, and extra dry-cell batteries for the receiver.

The officers each carried a carbine and a rucksack which contained all equipment not otherwise worn or strapped to the body. Like Kehoe's, the officers' rucksacks carried ammunition, rations, and a few extra items of clothing. In a canvas money belt, each officer carried the standard Jedburgh issue of one hundred thousand French francs and fifty U.S. dollars; Kehoe carried another fifty thousand francs and fifty dollars. Each man wore the standard grayish-green British parachute smock over his uniform. The smock would be discarded along with the parachute upon landing. Lastly, the parachute was strapped on.

When all equipment had been checked, the Jeds and the SAS men headed out to the airstrip, where a row of majestic four-engine British Stirling bombers awaited them.[12]

2

INTO THE HORNET'S NEST

THE long, blunt-nosed Stirling had a wingspan of ninety-nine feet, which proved barely adequate; the plane was difficult to get off the ground and ponderous once it was airborne. Because it was so inferior in performance to the next generation of bombers—the American B-24s and B-17s, for example—Britain's Bomber Command had stopped using the Stirling in early 1943. The black planes which now stood before the Jeds had been relegated to the shadow war; they belonged to two squadrons from 38 Group, which flew primarily for the SAS.

Both Jed teams prayed that the mission would be a go. So many missions were scrubbed at this stage because of bad weather over the target area or a last-minute message from the field warning that German activity near the drop zone made it too risky. Some unfortunate teams took off and made it nearly to the drop area before the mission was aborted and the team had to turn back.

It was a pleasant enough evening, with only a slight cloud cover. Special operations air missions like these depended on moonlight, both to provide jumpers some ability to see the ground below them and to aid the reception committee in its work. Cloud cover increasing to the point of obstructing the moon could cause a postponement of the mission. This night was near the end of the moon phase—a half-moon lingered low in the sky—so an uncomfortably long delay was possible.

Containers packed with weapons, explosives, and other gear for the maquis were first stowed aboard by the aircrew. These would be dropped after the parachutists had all jumped. Two of the containers held Bob Kehoe's carbine and the team's two radios. The men checked each other's parachutes to ensure that the harnesses were in good condition and fastened correctly.

The aircrews had planned a late-night departure. In early June days were long, and the crews wanted the added security that a takeoff in darkness provided. Brittany was not far away; it would be a relatively short flight. At 2330 hours (or eleven-thirty PM) the heavily laden men of the Samwest SAS party and Jed team Frederick lined up to board three Stirlings from 620 Squadron. Each plane would carry about fifteen jumpers, along with the dispatcher and the crew. All told, the three planes' cargo included fifty men, twenty-three containers, and five smaller parcels.

Not far away, Jed team George and the Dingson SAS detachment began climbing aboard two Stirlings from 299 Squadron. The same load of men and containers that the Samwest group had put into three planes in this case was loaded into only two. The Stirling's fuselage was long but narrow and, with space taken up by the containers, it was a tight fit for the jumpers. They were packed in like travelers on a cheap bus. At twenty-six minutes past midnight, team Frederick's plane lifted off. Nine minutes later, team George was airborne.[1]

On team Frederick's plane, the pilot steered low along a prescribed route, one that would become familiar to the crew in the coming week. The Jeds were seated in the middle of a row—known in paratrooper jargon as a stick—of SAS troopers. Kehoe's position in the stick determined that he would be the fourth man to jump. Four husky Bristol engines pulled the big plane over the Channel at just over two hundred miles per hour. In the bomber's dark interior, the steady grind of the Bristols was oddly comforting—if you let it, it could put you to sleep. At times, the plane bucked or jigged, or suddenly shifted direction ever so slightly, as the pilot sparred with the wind and attempted to dodge antiaircraft fire when they crossed over the French coastline. Slightly more than an hour into the flight, the dispatcher shouted the "Running in!" alert. The plane passed over the drop zone once and circled back; the SAS and Jeds would be ready to drop through the open bomb bay on the second pass.

Any fear of jumping had been forced to the deepest recesses of Bob Kehoe's mind by the thoughts of what might happen once the men left the aircraft. Two of the three possibilities that coursed through his consciousness were not attractive. Machine gun and small-arms fire could greet them as they hung helplessly under canopy. Worse, the Gestapo could be on the ground waiting to police them up as soon as the jumpers touched down. The third prospect, of course, was that all would go as planned. Then the men were standing, with their static lines hooked to the overhead cable, and almost without realizing it, Bob Kehoe found himself reciting the Twenty-third Psalm.[2]

When the dispatcher shouted, "Go!" the Stirling emptied its human load faster than seemed possible. The jump procedure on the Stirling was new to the Jeds. Like commuters hurrying to make a subway connection, the men raced toward the rear of the aircraft, scrambling as fast as their load and the bear-hugging parachute harness would allow. Reaching the gaping bomb bay opening, they spilled through into the moonlit Breton sky.

Kehoe's mind was jolted back to mission awareness by the shock of the parachute opening—but the euphoria that an air-filled canopy evokes in every jumper was followed sooner than expected by a bone-jarring landing. Although the pilot had tried to drop the men at an altitude of between six hundred and eight hundred feet, Kehoe was sure that they must have jumped from less than five hundred feet. There had barely been time for the parachute to open.

Kehoe got up from the ground and began rolling up his chute. He looked around but saw no sign of the other Jeds. Not far away, fires were burning. He was startled at first when two figures approached in the dark from a nearby woods. Kehoe's first reaction was to reach for his pistol, but the two men greeted him warmly and told him that they would take care of his parachute. They told the young American to follow them, and Kehoe was led to one of the fires. Other jumpers filtered in, and soon he was reunited with Major Wise and Lieutenant Aguirec.

The SAS men quickly conducted checks to account for everyone and to determine whether anyone had been injured. One SAS trooper, Kehoe quickly learned, had been killed upon landing because he had ignored standard safety procedure that called for detonators to be packed separately from explosive charges. That accounted for the odd, muffled explosions that the Jeds had heard during their descent. The SAS man had gambled and lost.

The reception committee was large—much larger than it needed to be or should have been with Germans not far away. Normally, reception committees were formed and assigned to mark the site for the pilot and then to quickly clear it of parachutes, containers, and other debris after the drop. Jumpers were to be whisked off to a safer location. All of this was to be done as rapidly as possible—before the Germans could react.

But the Jeds found themselves in the midst of something more like a celebration—a community event. People of all ages crowded around them in the glow of the fire. Excited children scampered about as if they were on a school outing. Women thrust mugs of bitter apple cider into the Jeds' hands, or gave them Brittany's version of Calvados, an apple brandy which has been called the "White Lightning" of Normandy (potent stuff—as much as 140 proof—you could use it for lantern fuel). They also offered the men bread and butter and cheese.

People questioned the French SAS about their families. Where were the men from? How had they gotten to England? The local people were intensely interested in Bob Kehoe, the man in the strange olive-drab uniform. While the French were familiar with the tan British battledress worn by Major Wise and Lieutenant Aguirec (the latter with French insignia), no one from these parts had seen an American uniform in more than twenty years. And he was so young!

Word spread through the crowd that this was the advance party for a major Allied landing to come on the shores of Brittany, and so the Jeds were pumped for details of the presumably imminent operation. And the bonfires—they were enormous. The whole thing had a high school pep rally quality to it.[3]

The team had come down in farmland south of the town of Guingamp in north-central Brittany, amid a patchwork of hedgerow-bordered fields with narrow and often sunken one-lane trails.[4] The scantily populated countryside was rugged and rocky, with traces of forest and scattered farmsteads and grasslands supporting small cattle herds.

The SAS detachment which had jumped in here on the eve of D-Day had organized the reception committee from local resistance workers—but had done a poor job of it. Security on the drop zone was a joke. German troops occupied a town barely two miles away. Seemingly oblivious to the danger, this large crowd of men and women had gathered to watch the spectacle. Cigarettes burned in the night, not that it mattered much with the large bonfires still ablaze, fires which should have been much smaller and should have been extinguished the minute the planes departed. The Jeds were appalled.

In fact, the SAS advance party—the handful of men who had formed the reception committee—could not have done a better job of *violating* security rules if they'd worked from a checklist. Noise and light discipline was nonexistent. And the throng that had gathered to watch indicated that far too many people knew far too much about things that they had no business knowing. There were even reports of the SAS men dining in local restaurants. It all seemed headed toward a bad end. You just didn't carry on like that in the enemy's backyard.

Eventually, the drop zone was cleared, and Sergeant Kehoe found that his carbine had not survived the jump. The container it was in had been smashed on impact. Both radios, however, were all right. Someone handed Kehoe a Sten submachine gun for his personal use.

With the equipment accounted for, the Jeds followed the SAS advance party to the base camp southwest of Guingamp. The camp was well concealed, about a mile into the Forêt de Duault, a modest-sized vestige of the conifer forests that once covered inland Brittany. There were many hardwoods now, and thick growths of a dense, spiny shrub called gorse. The camp was fairly high up on the side of a rather steep hill, where boulders were crowded in amongst a thick stand of trees. It was a good site, difficult for the Germans to spot, even from the air.[5]

Late on their first day in camp, the Jeds stumbled onto an ugly scene. Groups of partisans had been filtering into camp throughout the day, anxious to benefit from the distribution of arms that had accompanied the Jeds and SAS. While walking about the camp late that evening, the Jeds came upon a small crowd gathered around three people in civilian clothes. One of the three, a man, was sprawled on the ground, his face battered to a pulp from numerous beatings. The other two were women. The maquis had accused the trio of spying for the Germans.

The recruiting of resistance fighters, the Jeds had learned back at Milton Hall, was one of the most dangerous of guerrilla activities. Over the past few years, the Germans had become adept at infiltrating Vichy loyalist French into resistance groups to act as spies for the Germans. An alternate, and often more effective, method was to quietly capture a known resistance member and, through the threat of harm to his family, turn him into an informer. And in the spring of 1944, the Germans had stepped-up their efforts to penetrate the maquis in the hope of learning details of the expected invasion.

Ideally, when new recruits joined a maquis group, they underwent a period of probation while background checks were conducted. Candidates were kept under surveillance and did not meet other members of the group until each check had been accomplished. Whether these three people had survived such a vetting was not clear, but something had tipped off the maquis as to their true allegiance.

Questioning was quickly followed by guerrilla justice. The maquis inquisitors shot one of the women and stabbed the man to death. According to author Roger Ford, Captain Leblond later reported that, as a result of the interrogations, two people—a man and woman—were determined to be spies, infiltrators working for the Germans. The man had contradicted himself three times and was found to have a plan of the camp on him, and the woman was carrying a list of nearby villages. Leblond reported that he had ordered that both of them be shot.[6]

Perhaps fear of appearing too soft for the partisan war prevented the Jeds from intervening. Among the things at which special forces men had to be adept was the ability, when the situation called for it, to mind their own business. After all, they were newcomers and had yet to prove their value to the group. Prudently, they accepted that this was not their concern, and they were careful to stay out of it.[7]

Sergeant Kehoe was to make radio contact with London as soon as possible; the operations staff there would be anxiously awaiting word of the team's safe landing and recovery by the maquis. But London would not receive such a message on this day. Try as he might, Kehoe's first attempts at making contact failed. The seriousness of this was not lost on him. Indeed, all of the Jeds knew that the "wireless" man was key to their success and their survival. He was their lifeline, their sole means of gaining and maintaining contact with London. Kehoe would try again the next day.

Britain's Special Operations Executive, which early in the war had depended on the Secret Intelligence Service for radios, had begun developing its own in mid-1942. After a couple of early less-than-adequate models, the SOE introduced the Type B Mark II set, more commonly called the B2, in 1943. This radio proved to be highly effective and popular with users. In the version designed for agents who operated in civilian clothes, the transmitter, receiver, power supply, and accessories were all housed in a common-looking suitcase not much larger than an attaché case. Completely equipped with headset, aerial wire, and other accessories, the set weighed thirty-two pounds and had a range of more than five hundred miles. A modified version of the B2, carried in a compartmented canvas backpack, was developed for use by the Jedburghs and came to be called the Jed Set.

Whereas the B2 was designed to work from the main power supply found in houses or other buildings, or from a six-volt battery, the Jed Set was capable of operating in the countryside, away from main power supplies. It included a receiver which operated on dry-cell batteries and a transmitter powered by a small, tripod-mounted hand-cranked generator. The entire Jed Set was packed in five small canvas-web satchels and weighed thirty-seven pounds.[8]

Radio contacts were to be made according to a pre-arranged schedule. That schedule also determined the frequency to be used, and this varied according to the time of day, because optimum signal propagation varied throughout the day. Setting the frequency was accomplished by inserting the proper crystal, a fragile postage-stamp-size slice of quartz in a small rectangular Bakelite (plastic or resin) housing, with a pair of plug-in prongs. The precisely cut thickness of the quartz determined the signal's wavelength.

The next day, June 11, Sergeant Kehoe moved farther up the hill to make another attempt at sending his message. Finding what appeared to be a good spot, he laid out the hand-cranked generator and his transmitter and sending key and strung up his aerial wire. He then took out the message he had prepared based on Wise's instructions, written out and enciphered for transmission to London. When all was ready, someone turned the generator for him and Kehoe tapped out the message. In its deciphered form back in England, the message read: "ARRIVED SAFELY WITH ALL CONTAINERS AND EQUIPMENT. HAVE CONTACTED LOCAL GROUPS. GREAT POSSIBILITIES COTES DU NORD AREA. SEND JED TEAM AND ARMS FOR THEM. ADVISE SOONEST POSSIBLE DROPPING GROUND."[9] When he was finished, Kehoe destroyed the written message and packed up his radio.

Bob Kehoe had been a nineteen-year-old lab assistant in a chemical plant, with two years of college under his belt and no firm plans for the future, at the time of the bombing of Pearl Harbor. Anxious to enlist in response to that attack, like countless others, Kehoe had first tried joining the air corps with the intent of going to flight school. His nearsightedness, however, had closed that door. He had been taking a course in radio mechanics in civilian life, so he decided to enlist in the army Signal Corps, and was sent to Camp Crowder, Missouri, for basic training and radio operator training.[10] Near the town of Neosho, in the Ozarks of southwest Missouri, Camp Crowder had been established as a U.S. Army Signal Corps Training Center early in 1942. And Neosho, like so many other small communities of the time, saw its population more than double almost overnight with the camp's construction. Averaging a military population of forty thousand, the camp generated something of an economic boom for the town that had been the boyhood home of both Thomas Hart Benton and George Washington Carver.

By the fall of 1943, Kehoe was deep into the Morse code training course at Crowder. The Signal Corps began to strike him as pretty dull, however, and he kept his ears open for an opportunity to get closer to the war. Just such an opportunity arrived at lunchtime one day, with an announcement that came over the camp's loud-speaker. There was to be a briefing for any qualified radioman who spoke a foreign language or was interested in hearing about a special mission offering immediate overseas assignment.

Kehoe attended the talk given by a Captain Al Cox, a stranger to Camp Crowder. As details of the assignment emerged, soldiers began to get up and leave; and the longer Cox spoke, the more the audience thinned out. Men with two years of college were most desired, the captain said. Kehoe had that. It would be helpful if volunteers had some knowledge or training in a European language, particularly French. And then the kicker that sent most men scurrying for the door: Parachute training would be required and the prospects for hazardous duty were very good. Still not deterred, Kehoe volunteered, was interviewed, and was among those selected for the project.

For a time, he heard nothing else of the enigmatic assignment, and Kehoe's friends assured him that he had made a foolish mistake. But he noted a tinge of envy when they said it; such secrecy excited young minds. It also drove domineering first sergeants up a wall. Nothing riled a "top kick" more than having to ship good men off to God-knows-where on secret orders that he couldn't even question. God-knows-where, in this case, turned out to be a high-society country club outside Washington, D.C., and a remote camp in the Maryland mountains, both of which had become training areas for the Office of Strategic Services—the OSS. After nearly two months of training and psychological assessment at those locations, the men selected to remain in the unit boarded a train for Fort Hamilton, New York, a port of embarkation for the European Theater.

During his brief stay at Fort Hamilton, Sergeant Kehoe found time for a quick trip home to New Jersey. Under strict security restrictions, he was only allowed to tell his puzzled family that he was about to go overseas. His parents tried to make sense of the sudden change in Bob's status and of his unexpected embarkation. Why was he shipping out so soon, when his two older brothers, both of whom had served longer than he had, remained stateside?

It just didn't make any sense. But Bob could say nothing of his unit or the nature of his work, and it was all a little unsettling to the family.[11]

After having met some of the local maquis and witnessed the manner in which informers were handled, Major Wise, Lieutenant Aguirec, and Sergeant Kehoe began to settle into their work. They were somewhat disconcerted, though, by the way the SAS was feverishly arming the maquis—with little thought to training or security measures. And, soon, the inevitable happened.

On Sunday evening, June 11—the same day that Bob Kehoe had earlier made his first radio contact with London—a small group of patriots gathered at a farm about two hundred yards from the camp. They were freshly armed young men, but were untrained and untested—combat virgins—as green as week-old apples. Having been invited for supper, they were enjoying their meal when a car pulled up to the farmhouse. Two German officers got out and approached the house, unaware of the danger inside.

Upon entering, the Germans politely asked for directions to the nearby town of Carhaix. One of the officers stepped into the room where the young maquisards were eating. Repeating the request for directions, the German was completely unprepared for the burst of submachine gun bullets that ripped open his abdomen. Miraculously, the officer was able to stagger back to the car, all the time containing his ruptured belly with one hand. One of the Germans then pulled out a hand grenade and threw it at the house.[12]

Men at the SAS camp heard the Sten gunfire and the grenade explosion and prepared for action, but nothing more happened that night. At dawn, trucks delivered forty members of a nearby German parachute division, and the paratroopers burned the farm—in retribution—killing everyone there.[13]

The SAS outposts located nearest to the farm opened up on the Germans with every weapon they had, but a quick radio call by the enemy brought help. By mid-afternoon, reinforcements had arrived and an estimated four hundred enemy paratroopers were attacking the maquis outposts. In June 1944, the parachute divisions were probably the best combat troops Germany had in France—so this was no slouch outfit. The enemy paratroopers fanned out and began a slow but steady advance through the forest, directly toward the SAS base.

Sergeant Kehoe, as he was sending another message to London, became aware of the attack when he heard rifle shots coming from the north and west. He immediately broke off the radio transmission and packed up the radio.

Kehoe attributed the German assault to the reckless manner in which the SAS reception committee had behaved, advertising their presence with large bonfires and crowds. He feared that the trigger-happy maquis would generate a mass uprising, which, he knew, the local resistance was in no way strong enough to carry out. They needed time—time to build up arms and ammunition, time to be trained, time for the Allied armies to draw nearer. The best that the Jeds and SAS could hope to do now was to escape with as many men as possible, kill as many Germans as they could in the process, and regroup to fight another day.

The situation rapidly worsened for the maquis and their Allied benefactors, including the Jeds. The isolation of the guerrilla war struck home to them; the nearest Allied combat division was nearly two hundred miles away, in Normandy. There, American and British forces had just linked up to form a sixty-mile long beachhead, but it would be more than a month before sufficient forces were ashore to launch a breakout toward Brittany. So help would be a long time in coming. In the meantime, the Jeds and the SAS had their wits and little else to see them through.

As the minutes passed, the fighting steadily approached the SAS command post. Although another fifty SAS men had jumped in, as planned, raising the total strength of SAS and Jedburghs in the Duault forest to a hundred and fifteen, they were still badly outnumbered. The SAS, along with a few dozen maquis, put up a terrific fight, reportedly killing at least fifty-five Germans and wounding close to twice that number, at a cost of seventeen SAS casualties.[14] But, by late afternoon, the sputtering of British-made Stens and Bren guns steadily gave way to the distinctive belch of German Schmeissers and the occasional jackhammer drill of MG42 machine guns. Kehoe and the others had spent hours familiarizing themselves with German weapons at Milton Hall, and the authoritative voice of the precision-engineered guns was unmistakable.

When Captain Leblond of the SAS judged their position untenable, he ordered a withdrawal southward to the SAS Dingson base, some ninety miles away. Sergeant Kehoe thought it a stupid decision but was in no position to argue.[15] The Jeds hurriedly packed up their gear, taking only that which they considered necessary to fight their way out and survive. Weapons and ammunition. Maps. Medical aid kit. A small amount of food. They decided to take one radio and hide the other in hopes of retrieving it later; that would lighten their load by nearly forty pounds. And, because Kehoe expected that the Germans would thoroughly search the command post site, he quickly decided to hide the radio some distance away. Shots cracked over his head as he ran down the hill in the direction that the enemy fire was coming from. He recognized that most of the German fire was concentrated on the SAS positions at the edge of the woods. As soon as Kehoe found a spot in a depression—out of sight of the enemy—he hid the radio under a large boulder, covered it as well as he could, and took careful notice of the trees and rocks nearby, as they would have to serve as landmarks when he was able to return.

By this time, SAS troops were leaving in small groups, and those fighting so hard to hold the perimeter would soon have to bolt as well. Intent on avoiding capture (or worse), the Jeds broke out to the east. They had been joined by a British Royal Air Force officer who was serving in a liaison capacity with the SAS, a squadron leader (major equivalent) named Smith. He was a tall man in his forties with a spidery build, and he had jumped in with the follow-up SAS contingent the previous day.

Kehoe couldn't help but notice how Smith's bright blue RAF uniform stood out. None of the Jeds knew Smith, but it was clear that the man preferred to stick with them. Clearly unprepared for such action, though, he quickly proved to be a hindrance, and the Jeds wondered how anyone could send such an ill-prepared man on a mission behind enemy lines. Kehoe also noticed Smith's obvious lack of ground tactical training when, as the others crept along at ground level, Smith walked along the crest of the hedgerows.

Known as "bocage," these embankments of earth, trees, and

shrubbery—anywhere from three to twelve feet in height—had bordered the fields of Normandy and Brittany for centuries, serving as fences. Moving along the tops of the embankments, Smith was silhouetted like a tin rabbit in an arcade shooting gallery. Worst of all, though, was the slowing effect he had on the team. Determined to keep up, he probably did better than most men his age would, but he was not in shape for this. They were literally running for their lives, and he was like a flat tire on a getaway car. Kehoe would never understand how the man survived.

At first, they headed north, following an old forest road. Then German rifle and machine gun fire from the west forced the men to turn eastward and they scampered into some brush, expecting to shortly be overrun by the enemy. They also expected the Germans to begin pumping mortar rounds at them, but that didn't happen. The Jeds then made a desperate decision. The way ahead of them to the east—the only direction they could go to have any chance of breaking out—was thick with brush and hedgerows. To shed all the weight they possibly could, to make better time and put more distance between themselves and the enemy, the team agreed to hide the remaining radio. Hurriedly, the men placed it behind a boulder near the road, although it was not well hidden.

Breaking through the dense growth of vegetation as quickly as they could, the Jeds eventually came to some cultivated fields. Kehoe noted how speedy Squadron Leader Smith had become since he'd been motivated by German gunfire. The small group continued on, using the cover of the woods and brush as much as possible, until it came to a hard-surfaced road and prepared to cross it.

Just then, a fighter plane roared overhead on a strafing run. Although the Jeds couldn't see what it was firing at, they assumed that the plane was German and that they were its intended targets. But when the fighter rolled around for another pass, the men identified it as a British twin-engine Beaufighter; and then they saw what it was targeting.

A German motorcycle patrol was heading north on the same road the Jeds were about to cross. Sustained bursts of fire from the Beaufighter's wing-mounted .303-caliber machine guns discouraged further pursuit by the patrol, and the Germans abruptly reversed direction and disappeared. Had the Jeds just been lucky?

Kehoe recalled that the attack on the command post had come during his radio contact with London earlier in the day, and that he had been forced to break off right after transmitting the signal for imminent danger. Perhaps this fighter had been dispatched as a result of that call. Whatever the reason, luck seemed to be with team Frederick.

The men pressed on, staying in the forest as much as possible and skirting fields when necessary. They had learned their lesson about avoiding roads. As they made their way, they were occasionally seen by local people. The careful Bretons, though, aware of the assault on the Duault Forest, ignored the small group. Germans had posted notices throughout France, warning of the price to be paid for helping Allied parachutists. Men would be shot, women sent off to concentration camps. One such warning issued by the German high command bluntly explained: "Whoever on French territory outside the zone of legal combat is captured and identified as having participated in sabotage, terrorism, or revolt is and remains a bandit or franc-tireur [guerrilla] and shall consequently be shot, whatever his nationality or uniform."[16]

As dusk approached, the Jeds looked for a place to rest but consciously kept their distance from villages and farmhouses—for the Germans surely would be conducting searches. Finding at last what appeared to be an isolated drainage ditch, well-concealed by a thicket of the dense, spiny gorse, the four men crawled in and collapsed. After eating some bread, they let exhaustion overtake them and slept, with no lookout posted, until dawn. When they awoke the next morning, early rays of sunshine revealed that the drainage ditch they had spent the night in was not as isolated as they had believed. Not fifty yards away was a small farmhouse.

Hungry and chilled to the bone, the men decided, despite the potential danger, to see if anyone was in the house and to try to obtain some food. Lieutenant Aguirec approached the house while the others waited in the ditch. A woman answered the door, but when Aguirec greeted her, she responded in a strange language. Aguirec nearly panicked, thinking she might be speaking German. But then he recalled that many people in the area spoke only Breton. A younger woman, who spoke French, appeared. She told the lieutenant that she had heard of the fight in the forest and that she was willing to help the team. She instructed Aguirec to return to the ditch while she gathered some food to bring to the men. Thirty minutes later, the Jeds were enjoying their first real meal in twenty-four hours—potatoes and gravy and bread and boiled milk.

The young woman introduced herself as Simone Le Göeffic. She explained that she was a schoolteacher from a nearby town called Trémargat, but that school had been suspended at the time of the Allied invasion. Of more importance at the moment, though, was the fact that she was involved in the resistance. A woman of disarming charm, with light-brown neck-length hair and an attractive figure, she now took charge of the situation. She instructed the men to remain where they were. She would be back in the evening with instructions and a guide. Then she was off on a bicycle. All day, the Jeds remained in the ditch, speculating on the trustworthiness of Simone Le Göeffic and bothered only by occasional visits from inquisitive cows.

Simone returned that evening, as promised, and with her was a muscular, ruddy-faced young man with light hair named Marcel Queinnec, who was to be their guide. They would have to wait until dark before moving, however, Simone and Marcel cautioned, because the Germans were on a high state of alert. Patrols had been combing the area all day.

After nightfall, Marcel led the team southward toward a town where the Jeds were to be handed off to another guide. But the guide did not show, and so the men remained hidden in the woods outside of town.

During the night, Simone arrived on her bicycle and told the Jeds of three SAS men, two officers and a corporal, who had been severely wounded in the previous day's battle and who'd been taken to a deserted farm near the forest. Major Wise decided that the team should return and see what they could do for the SAS men.

The farm lay at the end of a winding path, not far from the village of Peumerit-Quintin. When the Jeds arrived, they found Marcel's wife, Louise, and another woman from the village, Madame Le Moigne, attending to the wounded men. The SAS casualties, they learned, had been brought in on stretchers under the direction of an SAS sergeant by the name of Jean Robert, who was also present. A doctor had arrived (by bicycle) from Guingamp and performed life-saving surgery on the two officers under austere conditions.

All three of the wounded men appeared to the Jeds to be near death, although the corporal seemed to be in slightly better condition than the officers. Moving the wounded men obviously was out of the question. The two women would look after the SAS men and shelter them from the Germans until they were fit to rejoin their unit. Louise Queinnec—an attractive, smooth-complexioned woman with long, dark hair—and her husband Marcel were schoolteachers at Peumerit-Quintin and had two small children. For the remainder of this summer of 1944, however, the Queinnec children would be under the care of family friends. Marcel's time largely would be spent with Jed team Frederick, and Louise would be occupied with looking after the wounded SAS men.

After seeing that the wounded men were being taken care of, the Jeds made contact with the departmental resistance chief for the Côtes-du-Nord, a man called Marceau. As it turned out, Marceau was a close friend of Marcel Queinnec, who was quickly becoming a valuable asset to team Frederick, being both resourceful and reliable. Marceau had grown up on Brittany's south coast in a Breton-speaking home, only learning French when he began school. He had fought with a division in northeastern France in June 1940, but when his unit was decimated and demoralized to the point of surrendering, Marcel had left and made his way back to Brittany.

Major Wise was faced with a decision. Would the team continue to make its way to the Dingson SAS base, or instead stay and work with Marceau? When an operation has not worked out as planned, or the situation has changed, as indeed this one had, a good leader will remember the higher commander's intent and adjust the plan in accordance with it. Adrian Wise knew what had to be done. The Jedburghs had been formed and trained for months to carry out guerrilla warfare with the maquis, not to scamper from one SAS base to another. Team Frederick would get on with it from right here.[17]

3

AN ALTERNATIVE FORM OF WARFARE

THE genesis of the Jedburghs lay in events that unfolded more than four years before the first teams jumped into France. In September 1939 Hitler's army and air force invaded Poland, an unprovoked mauling that brought Britain and France to declare war on Germany. Then, in May 1940, after long months of what journalists called the "sitzkrieg" or "phony war," the Nazi war machine launched a blitzkrieg invasion of the Low Countries (comprised of Belgium, Luxembourg, and the Netherlands). Within forty-eight hours of crossing the Belgian border, German tanks broke through the Ardennes forest and entered France by outflanking the Maginot Line, the expensive string of concrete gun emplacements and fortifications along the republic's eastern frontier. Panzers, as the German tanks were called, brushed aside the sparingly armored French forces in the region, forced the British to evacuate their army from the beaches at Dunkirk, and muscled their way on toward the capital.

By June 10, the streets of Paris were strangely empty and quiet; many of her citizens had joined the pitiful exodus of refugees fleeing the city. Cars and horse-drawn wagons, handcarts and wheelbarrows, bicycles and baby carriages, and people on foot filled all roads leading westward or southward from Paris. All forms of transport were loaded down with family possessions—clothing, mattresses, heirloom furniture—anything that could be salvaged or that could ease the transition to the unknown life and dangers that lay ahead. Among the crowds of refugees were the members of the French government, which was abandoning Paris to regroup in Bordeaux on the Atlantic coast to the southwest.

British Prime Minister Neville Chamberlain—naive champion of a failed policy of appeasement—resigned soon after the Germans entered Belgium, and King George VI asked Winston Churchill, then first lord of the Admiralty, to form a new government. From 1933 until 1939, Churchill had been a lonely voice speaking out against Nazi Germany, decrying the appeasement policies of the governments of Stanley Baldwin and Chamberlain. When war came in 1939, Churchill was returned to the post of first lord of the Admiralty and, as the Germans overran Western Europe, was seen as the one man capable of leading Britain through the crisis.

Even though more than three hundred thousand British and French troops had been saved at Dunkirk, virtually all of their weapons and equipment had to be abandoned on the beaches of France. There were not a hundred tanks left in all of Britain, and it would take months—or even years—to build the war machine needed to liberate the fallen countries of Europe. Until such time, the people of France would simply have to hold on, suffering as best they could the humiliation and hardships of occupation. But there were other ways to continue the fight.

Churchill and a few others in government began to talk of an armed resistance movement within France, and Churchill was hardly unfamiliar with the subject. Thomas Edward "T. E." Lawrence, the "Lawrence of Arabia" who had raised the Arabs in revolt against the Germans and Turks in the First World War, was a friend and had been a frequent visitor to Churchill's home at Chartwell in the inter-war years.[1] As Hitler's armies swept over Western Europe in the early summer of 1940, the new prime minister and others considered such an armed resistance movement as a method by which the occupied countries could continue the fight against Germany while the British army was being rebuilt. Plans also were made for an organized force to conduct guerrilla warfare against the Germans on home soil should Hitler succeed in invading the British Isles.

On June 11, Churchill and his top military advisors flew to France to talk with the leaders of the country, who were then en route to Bordeaux. Churchill urged his plan for guerrilla warfare on the French cabinet and senior military leaders, but such ideas generated little enthusiasm, and the French were angered that this was all the British could offer at a time when they were asking for fighter squadrons. Only one among the French agreed with Churchill, the newly appointed under-secretary of state for national defense, the tall and sensitive Brigadier General Charles Joseph de Gaulle. The day after Churchill's first meeting with the French leaders, the young general departed for Brittany, boarded a plane for London, and a week later delivered a radio address calling for all free Frenchmen to stand together in defiance of the German occupation.

France fell soon after Churchill returned to London. The French declared Paris an open city on June 13, and the following day German soldiers paraded arrogantly and triumphantly down the Champs-Élysées. Two days later, Paul Reynaud resigned as premier and Marshal Philippe Pétain, the aged hero of Verdun, took over direction of the French government and sued for peace.

Under the terms of an armistice signed on June 25, Germany occupied three-fifths of France and annexed the regions of Alsace and Moselle. Pétain and his cohort Pierre Laval established a collaborationist government at the sleepy spa town of Vichy to rule over the unoccupied southeastern portion of the country. French divisions were demobilized, though Vichy France was allowed to keep an "Armistice Army" of limited size and capability, and Hitler hauled more than a million and a half French prisoners of war to Germany to be held as virtual hostages, hoping thereby to ensure French cooperation. Pétain's government broke off diplomatic relations with the British and sentenced de Gaulle, in absentia, to death as a traitor.

Men and women of France, humiliated and angered by German occupation policies that led to the systematic plundering of their country to the Reich's benefit, searched for solace in organized opposition. Almost immediately, small and unrelated pockets of resistance began to emerge throughout France. And as summer gave way to autumn, and the initial shock of defeat wore off, those isolated pockets grew and coalesced, like a nascent cancer in the growing body of the Third Reich.

Several senior British government and military officials had foreseen the likelihood of war with Germany as early as 1938 and, like all the war-scarred people of Britain and France, they were apprehensive of another conflict. Both countries had spent much of their youth and treasure on the war of 1914–18 and were fearful of another such costly ordeal. Aside from the astronomical financial cost of that conflict, Britain had lost nearly a million men dead, more than two million wounded, and almost two hundred thousand missing, leaving Churchill to observe that the victory had been "bought so dear as to be indistinguishable from defeat."[2] In March 1938, the Secret Intelligence Service had formed a new branch whose job it would be to study "alternative forms of warfare,"[3] in an effort to avoid losing another generation to barbarous trench warfare.

Churchill and others believed that the people of occupied Europe, through organized underground resistance movements, should have a large role in their own liberation. And Britain, they agreed, needed an organization capable of nourishing and directing such movements. So, in July 1940, the War Cabinet approved the charter for a new organization to be called the Special Operations Executive, or SOE. To its newly appointed director, Dr. Hugh Dalton, the serving Minister of Economic Warfare, Churchill offered succinct instructions: "And now, set Europe ablaze."[4]

To carry out its work in France, the SOE created F Section, one of a number of country sections to deal with resistance movements in occupied Europe. Soon F Section began parachuting agents throughout France with the mission of organizing "circuits" of trained and equipped saboteurs. These were not to be intelligence networks; rather, the business of the circuits would be special operations, and particularly sabotage. Intelligence would remain the business of the Secret Intelligence Service.

Typically, F Section's circuits were set up and run by three agents—an organizer, a lieutenant, and a radio operator. Some were military people, others civilians, and while most were men there also were some women. All potential agents were put through a lengthy and demanding selection and training regimen that weeded out all but those best suited to the work. All spoke French fluently—most without a foreign accent—and they performed their duties in civilian clothes while carrying forged papers to conceal their true identities. Some agents had lived in France as children, others had lived there for many years before the war for business purposes. All of F Section's agents, though, had to be British citizens, or at least hold dual citizenship. For SOE also supported another section—RF Section—which served General de Gaulle's Free French organization; and, by agreement, all agents of French citizenship were allotted to RF Section. In time, F Section would also employ American agents.

Across the Atlantic, President Franklin D. Roosevelt took the first step in establishing an American special operations capability in the spring of 1941. On May 27, primarily due to an increasing threat from German naval actions in the Atlantic, the president declared a limited state of national emergency in the United States.

One of the many emergency measures that the president invoked was the creation of a service responsible for secret intelligence and special operations. In July, he named fifty-eight-year-old William Joseph Donovan to be director of the office of Coordinator of Information, an organization established for that purpose. The stout, white-haired, blue-eyed Donovan had commanded a New York National Guard cavalry troop that rode with Pershing's 1916 expedition into Mexico in pursuit of Pancho Villa. He later earned the Medal of Honor—as well as the Distinguished Service Cross, the Distinguished Service Medal, and the French Croix de Guerre— while leading a battalion of the famed "Fighting 69th" Infantry Regiment in World War I, then went on to become a successful Wall Street attorney and a millionaire.

Roosevelt had long admired Donovan, whom he had first known as a fellow law student at Columbia, and, in spite of his political affiliation—Donovan was a Hoover Republican—the president put

Donovan's talents to work during the 1930s, sending him around the world on secret fact-finding missions.[5] Donovan met with Benito Mussolini in Rome in 1935 and joined Generalissimo Francisco Franco's army in the field in 1939, during Spain's civil war, to get a firsthand look at new German and Italian weapons. He had even observed German army maneuvers near Nuremberg on behalf of the War Department, and visited France, Belgium, Holland, Germany, and Scandinavia.

Arguably, though, Donovan's most important excursion as an agent for the president came when he visited England in July 1940. There, he met with King George VI and discussed British war preparations with Prime Minister Churchill. He also talked with the War Cabinet, the British chiefs of staff, and their commanders in chief.

The meetings which influenced Donovan most, however, were those with Colonel Stewart Menzies, head of Britain's intelligence service, and with Colonel Colin Gubbins of the newly formed Special Operations Executive. Gubbins, a gifted artillerist who was fluent in French and German, had written two pamphlets on the subject of irregular warfare—*The Art of Guerrilla Warfare* and *Partisan Leaders' Handbook*—and he was to figure prominently in the development and approval of the Jedburgh concept. He brought Donovan up to date on work being done to develop resistance movements in occupied territories. Both Menzies and Gubbins were unusually generous with the sensitive information they shared with Donovan, as Churchill had directed them to be.

Shortly after the December 7, 1941, Japanese attack on Pearl Harbor and Germany's declaration of war on the United States a few days later, Churchill sailed to Washington to confer with Roosevelt on an Anglo-American war strategy. The prime minister wasted no time in presenting his proposals—he introduced them during a White House dinner party, which William Donovan attended, on his first evening in Washington. Churchill envisioned landings in western and southern Europe by the armies of Great Britain and the United States, and a simultaneous uprising by the populations of the occupied countries.[6] Although Roosevelt and Donovan were intrigued by Churchill's plan, the more traditional American chiefs of staff were not.

Donovan, like Gubbins in Britain, was left to advocate an irregular warfare strategy to a General Staff which did not understand it or believe in it. Indeed, many senior army leaders of both countries shunned such unorthodox thinking, considered it distasteful and ungentlemanly, and viewed Donovan and Gubbins as adventuristic mavericks. Fortunately, some of the more open-minded Allied generals would later be in positions to see that irregular warfare did have a part in the grand strategy.

In May 1942, Colin Gubbins, by then a brigadier, met with senior British army officials to discuss Special Operations Executive's potential role in the liberation of Western Europe. The discussion centered around a paper which had been drawn up by SOE's regional director for France and the Low Countries, Robin Brook, and a member his staff, Lieutenant Colonel Peter Wilkinson. Among the concepts outlined in the paper was that of a uniformed special forces unit—purely military—which would work with the French resistance. Wilkinson, principal author of the concept, proposed dropping three-man teams of highly trained soldiers behind enemy lines with the purpose of supporting guerrilla resistance groups and coordinating their operations with those of the Allied ground forces taking part in the cross-channel invasion and liberation of Europe.[7]

In early July, Gubbins wrote the chief of SOE's security office, suggesting that the code name "Jumpers" be applied to the project. But the security chief rejected that name; the new group would be code named "Jedburghs."[8]

In the years since World War II, Jedburgh folklore has produced several explanations for the project's code name. The one most often repeated cites the Scottish town of Jedburgh, where, according to the story, the Jedburgh operatives took their training. There is indeed a Scottish Borders town called Jedburgh, but it sits roughly two hundred and fifty miles north of Milton Hall, near Peterborough, England, the Jedburghs' actual training site. A variation on this story notes that the village of Jedburgh was the scene of guerrilla warfare during twelfth-century border wars between England

and Scotland; hence its appropriateness as a name for special forces. Still another version places Jedburgh in South Africa, where British forces were on the receiving end of guerrilla tactics used by the Boers at the close of the nineteenth century. One explanation claims the name comes from the Jedburgh radio sets used by the teams. And, finally, a French version has it that the code name Jedburghs was chosen because it begins with the letter "J" as in "J-Jour," the French translation of "D-Day."

More likely, the name was simply taken at random from a list of pre-approved code names. All of the above explanations ignore the fact that code names used by the British and Americans throughout the war were, for the sake of security, supposed to have no connection whatsoever with the nature of the operation, project, or unit the names represented. Churchill paid attention to this dictum. He had a fascination, almost an obsession, with code names, and he insisted on personally reviewing and clearing for approval all code names, as he reminded General Sir Hastings Ismay, his military deputy, in early August 1943. After reviewing a list of proposed code names and crossing many of them out, Churchill explained what he considered to be characteristics of suitable code names: that they not be frivolous, boastful, or sentimental and that they not reveal the nature of the operation. He noted that proper names (such as those of towns or cities) made particularly good code names.[9]

All British code names during the war came from an approved list maintained by an office in Whitehall called the Inter-Services Security Board. And in the case of "Jedburgh," it was likely the next name available on the list.[10]

On November 8, 1942, British and American forces landed in North Africa to begin their campaign against Germany's Afrika Korps. In response, German forces marched into unoccupied France and ordered the Vichy Armistice Army disbanded. Many of its officers and noncommissioned officers took their training and experience with them into the resistance.

Germany further, and unwittingly, swelled the ranks of the

French resistance with its next move. In need of workers to provide muscle and sweat for its war industry, Germany, in February 1943, demanded laborers from the Vichy government. To satisfy this injunction, Vichy obligingly passed a compulsory labor service law called the Service du Travail Obligatoire, a program designed to send young Frenchmen into forced labor in Germany. An almost immediate result was that hundreds of young men, to escape the labor draft, took to the mountains and forests to join the resistance. By the end of 1943, they would number in the thousands, but they could hardly be called a fighting force. Compelled to live as outlaws in the most remote rural areas, for these young Frenchmen survival was the main concern. They were sustained through clandestine support from local people or from captured German supplies, but these pockets of potential resistance fighters were unorganized. Weapons were scarce, and most of the men who had them were untrained in their military application. These were the men—many of them only teenagers—who would come to be called the maquis.

Meanwhile, in the United States, Bill Donovan's organization had, in June 1942, assumed a new name—the Office of Strategic Services, or OSS. In December the OSS was activated as a military organization under the direction of the Joint Chiefs of Staff, with responsibility for the conduct of both secret intelligence and special operations. In January 1943, Donovan's staff completed a formal agreement with SOE, gaining access to the SOE's training facilities and giving OSS the opportunity to begin fielding its own language-qualified special forces.

The Americans rushed to catch up to the British in their special operations capability. Personnel authorization increases for OSS were approved by the War Department, and two squadrons of B-24 bombers (later expanded to a full group) were allocated to fly special operations missions. Aircraft modifications were begun, American crews were trained by their experienced British counterparts, and construction began on an airfield at Harrington. An American packing station, where supply canisters and packages would be prepared for air drops to the resistance, was established at Holme, eighty miles north of London and located conveniently near Harrington.

The next step was to find the men who would comprise the Jedburgh teams. For the American contingent, this task fell to Major Franklin Canfield, an OSS special operations staff officer in London, who immediately arranged for a recruiting effort in the United States. Canfield primarily sought volunteers who were physically athletic, and especially any who were familiar with the French language. He hoped to find at least fifty officers and fifty enlisted radio operators who showed a sufficient degree of confidence, self-reliance, maturity, and stability.

Military skills were also important, and so men who already knew how to handle weapons, could apply small unit tactics in the field, were familiar with explosives, and were already parachute qualified would be a step ahead of the rest. The radiomen were required to be capable of sending and receiving Morse code at a speed of at least fifteen words per minute.

OSS headquarters in Washington helped Canfield organize the recruiting effort and provided officers to do the recruiting. In September 1943, the recruiters began drawing a dragnet through an army that was in the middle of unprecedented expansion. Nearly fifty new army camps had been built from scratch across the country, and older installations had been greatly expanded to accommodate the millions of men who had entered the service since the beginning of the war. Jedburgh recruiters were most likely to find the type of officers they sought at camps with large populations of paratroopers: Fort Benning, in Georgia, and Fort Bragg and Camp Mackall in North Carolina. They also would sweep through other camps throughout the South.

Radio operators were to be found at three schools run by the U.S. Army Signal Corps—the High Speed Radio Operator School at Fort Monmouth, New Jersey; the Morse Code School at Camp Crowder, Missouri; and the air force Radio Operator and Mechanics School at Scott Field in Illinois. Radio operators from the U.S. Navy also were trained at these schools, and one sailor volunteered and served on a Jedburgh team.

The routine was the same at each camp. Recruiters began by reviewing personnel records to identify any men who spoke French. Notices appeared on unit bulletin boards announcing a briefing for anyone interested in overseas duty. When those enticed by the notice had assembled, the recruiter explained that the assignment called for volunteers who would undergo parachute training, and that there would be danger involved. Those who were still interested were then individually interviewed by the OSS recruiter. At no time during this process, however, did the recruiters mention OSS or the Jedburgh project by name. Volunteers were simply told that, if they were selected, orders would follow.

Shortly after the recruiters completed their rounds, about one hundred prospective Jedburgh officers and more than sixty radio operators received orders to report to Washington, D.C., in October. Surprisingly few of them spoke or understood French at anything above an elementary level.

Meanwhile, Britain's Special Operations Executive was looking for British Jedburgh candidates, and it was mainly from the armored regiments that the recruiters sought radio operators in September 1943. Before long, more than sixty men had been chosen to undergo testing at a camp near Oxford, and from that screening about fifty men went on to Special Training School No. 54, west of London, in October. The school—which doubled as a receiving station for messages sent by SOE agents already operating throughout Europe—occupied a country house called Fawley Court, just north of the town of Henley-on-Thames. The Jedburgh recruits were housed nearby in a Victorian house called Countess Gardens, and by Christmas their group's number had been cut to forty-five candidates.[11]

In late October, the search for British officers began. Notices on unit bulletin boards throughout England beckoned the curious and the adventurous. Those who responded were sent to a hotel on Northumberland Avenue in London for an interview. Among the interviewers was Wing Commander Forest Yeo-Thomas, an officer who had parachuted into occupied France for SOE in early 1943 to encourage the unification of resistance organizations. He knew what to look for in a man, and he didn't hesitate to turn away those who, in his opinion, failed to display the necessary degree of discipline. Of eight officers he interviewed in one day, Yeo-Thomas rejected six, convinced that a few of them "had volunteered merely in order to obtain a free railway voucher to London."[12]

Following the interviews, the men were told to pack gym shoes and a few other items of clothing, and they were hauled to a country house for two days of physical and psychological testing. There, according to volunteer Stanley Cannicott, they were subjected to strange interviews with a psychiatrist. Cannicott, a future psychiatrist himself, was convinced that "they were crazy."[13] Two weeks later fifty-five selectees were taken to a mansion called Milton Hall, near Peterborough.

The Jedburgh plan also called for French officers and radio operators, and in July 1943 a request for such men was sent to de Gaulle's Free French General Staff in Algiers. French combat arms officers in North Africa at that time were particularly susceptible to the Jedburgh recruiting pitch. Vichy French forces there had thrown in with the Allies after the 1942 Anglo-American invasion of North Africa, and Free French divisions were in the process of being rearmed by the United States.

Many combat units were scheduled to be restructured as service and support units, however, and infantry, armor, and artillery officers in those units were anxious to find a means of joining the war against Germany in more active roles. Even those soldiers who were fortunate enough to remain in the rearmed combat units feared sitting out the rest of the war in North African garrisons. Many of these men decided to volunteer and take a chance with this new offer, and those who did were sent in small groups to Maison Blanche airfield, near Algiers, in November. There they boarded Royal Air Force planes to Great Britain. Most of those selected were regular army—career officers—and most were combat-experienced platoon leaders and company commanders.[14]

Another handful of French officer volunteers came from the French Military Mission in the United States. Among them was seventeen-year-old Lieutenant Michel de Bourbon, the Prince de

Bourbon-Parma, a descendent of the family which once provided France's monarchs. He and the other volunteers from the French Military Mission joined the American Jedburgh candidates who were then gathering in Washington.

The officers and men who had been selected in the stateside recruiting effort began arriving in Washington in October. Most arrived by train at the busy Romanesque Union Station and stepped out into a vibrant city, crowded and full of energy. Radio operators arrived in small groups—one of the larger ones came from Camp Crowder, nine men came from Scott Field, and a few arrived from Fort Monmouth. Officers arrived individually or in twos or threes, most coming off a leave that had been granted en route.

As with any military assignment there was some administrative processing, and then the men found themselves in a taxi or a bus or an army truck (depending on how large a group had reported in) and they were driven off into the Maryland countryside northwest of the city. After about a thirty-minute ride, the vehicle turned left off River Road and followed a long, shaded driveway which eventually curved around to the main entrance of the clubhouse at the Congressional Country Club.

When the club had opened in 1924 it was seen as a place where leaders of government and business could relax in style, and it became known as the Playground of Officialdom. For nearly twenty years it had hosted countless golf tournaments, dinner dances, weddings, tennis matches, horse shows, and other gala events. But the Depression years had had an impact—membership and revenues had fallen, operating costs had risen, and, by early 1943, the club was on the verge of bankruptcy. Then, in March of that year, the Office of Strategic Services had obtained a government lease on the property for use as a training area for the duration, with a guarantee of restoration after the war. Like the rest of wartime Washington, the Congressional Country Club had been called to serve. And to the OSS, the club became known simply as Area F.

In peacetime, the impressive four-story early-Italian clubhouse featured a grand ballroom, a Presidential Suite, an indoor swimming pool, a two-story gymnasium with a basketball court, and bowling alleys. But OSS had transformed the club into something resembling a military installation. The ballroom had become an oversized classroom, complete with folding chairs and blackboards. An army mess hall replaced the main dining room, the bar was now the officers lounge, and the indoor swimming pool had been boarded over to provide office space for the staff.

Dozens of Quonset huts and pyramidal tents with wooden floors littered the lawns and the tennis courts, which had been covered with a layer of crushed cinders. The fairways and greens of the rolling 406-acre golf course had become an obstacle course, a confidence course, and other training areas. And across River Road to the north were pistol and machine gun ranges.

Shortly after their arrival, the newcomers were assembled in the club's ballroom for an orientation. When the men had taken seats on folding chairs, a colonel made some welcoming comments, stressing the secret nature of their assignment, and provided some insight into the purpose of their stay. They had all volunteered for hazardous duty; and this, he said, would entail working with European resistance groups in occupied territory—well behind enemy lines. The staff at Area F was charged with evaluating the candidates to ensure that each met the requirements for the assignment. The men would undergo physical tests and psychological assessments, and those judged to be unsuited for the work would be reassigned to regular duty.

The assessments began at once, and over the next few days the men underwent an endless succession of interviews and completed many questionnaires. An assessment staff of psychologists and psychiatrists hoped to expose the troublesome, the inept, the lazy, the misfit.

Bernard Knox, who'd volunteered for the Jeds from his army air corps station in England, later wrote of what the assessment staff were looking for:

The problem in choosing men for such an operation, of course, is that once they are landed in enemy territory, you can no longer control them. They may do the obviously sensible thing: go to ground in a safe hiding place, do nothing to attract attention to themselves, and wait for the arrival of friendly troops. The psychological and psychiatric tests the Jeds were subjected to had one basic objective: to select men psychologically incapable of remaining quiet—troublemakers, in fact; people who could be relied on to upset applecarts.[15]

Knox felt the assessment team "delivered the goods," noting, "I have never known such a bunch of troublemakers in my life."[16]

But the days were not filled with interviews alone. There was a training agenda as well, and the men tackled it with gusto. "When they arrived at Area F," instructor Roger Hall later recalled, "they were a rough-and-tumble gang of two hundred hellions, paratroopers from Fort Benning, for the most part, who had volunteered for secret missions. They didn't know the exact nature of their future assignments, and they couldn't have cared less."[17]

The training, patterned after that of the British commandos, was seldom dull. Training days normally began at the crack of dawn and often lasted until midnight. Mornings would start with physical training, usually with runs as long as five miles, rope climbing, chin-ups, pushups (sometimes while wearing a backpack), and crossing the nearby Cabin John stream on a rope tied between trees on opposite banks.

Sometimes the training would continue long after sunset, with challenging night compass runs which tested a man's stamina and map-reading ability while at the same time giving instructors the chance to teach orienteering skills. Night exercises in raids and ambushes and stealthy infiltration techniques added an element of excitement.

The men also learned to use some new weapons and learned new ways to use old weapons. They learned how to fight empty-handed or with a knife, and they learned a little about explosives. They also made a good impression with the staff at Area F. In the eyes of instructor Roger Hall,

the Jedburghs flew high. Their three prime requisites were guts, brains, and *savoir-faire*. Training them was a breeze, they did all that was expected and more with a nonchalant ease. They also did it with a flourish whenever possible, and usually with a laugh. Most of them had all the basic military stuff down cold, so the instructors were able to concentrate on the specialized hoop-la which dotted the training agenda. The Jeds stayed three hectic weeks, and things were never quite the same after they left.[18]

By early November the roughly one hundred Jedburgh officer candidates had been whittled down by about half. Added to this were the remaining radio operators. After dark one evening, all those selected to remain in the Jedburgh program were loaded onto army trucks, the canvas cargo compartment covers were buttoned down, and the vehicles headed north into the Maryland countryside.

They drove up Highway 15 toward the town of Thurmont, located about sixty miles northwest of Washington in the Catoctin Mountains. Not far from town, the trucks turned onto a dirt road, and moments later stopped just before a wooden sentry box. A Marine guard emerged and raised the log gate which blocked the road. The trucks continued up the narrow road, through a thick forest of chestnut and dogwood, hemlock and red oak and pitch pine, to a place which had been known as Catoctin Mountain Park. They stopped at an area of the park known as Camp Greentop, which had been a camp for handicapped children. It was part of a vast complex built as a Works Progress Administration project in the late '30s, and before the war it had been known as the Catoctin Recreational Demonstration Area, a retreat for federal employees and their families.

But now Greentop had transformed into another training area of the Office of Strategic Services. The park had been closed to civilians in early 1942, and the War Department had moved in and taken over part of it, an old Civilian Conservation Corps camp at a spot called Round Meadow, that summer. Soon after that, OSS had occupied the Greentop site about half a mile to the northeast, and it soon became a training area for specialized instruction in hand-to-hand combat, surreptitious infiltration, specialized shooting, and demolitions. It was christened Area B, with subdivisions called B–1 and B–2. Headquarters was in a large log cabin with a covered porch, surrounded by a log railing. The trucks deposited the Jedburgh trainees at Area B–1.

The army and the OSS, however, were not the only residents at the Catoctin Mountain Park. Farther up the road to the east was another camp—which had been called Hi-Catoctin—often used in the past for Boy Scout and Girl Scout outings. By the time the Jedburgh volunteers arrived in the area, though, a ten-foot fence with a barbed-wire overhang surrounded the compound. There were sentry booths at regular intervals, equipped with telephones, and floodlights and patrolling Marines with guard dogs.

Upon America's entry into the war, President Roosevelt's staff had selected this portion of the park as a weekend retreat for the chief of state, similar to his retreat at Warm Springs, Georgia, but only sixty miles and two hours driving time from Washington. Roosevelt had begun going there in July 1942 and was to spend much time there during the war. He named the site Shangri La, but a later president named Eisenhower would change the name to Camp David. The existence of the presidential retreat was to be kept secret, but just a fortnight before the Jeds arrived in the Catoctin mountains, the *Chicago Daily News* had run an article on Roosevelt's hideaway and given away its location.[19]

At Area B, the Jeds found comfortable, if rustic, quarters and good food. With the growing November chill, the trainees were glad to move out of the tents of Area F into cabins with indoor plumbing and stone fireplaces. Separate buildings housed a mess hall and classrooms.

As at Area F, training days in the mountains began at sunup and continued until after dark, and the hours were filled with classes on explosives and demolitions, communications, first aid, hand-to-hand combat, tradecraft, weapons, map reading, and cross-country navigation.

At Area B the Jeds met one of the most unforgettable instructors they would ever have—a wiry, bespectacled British major named William Ewart Fairbairn. One of the things that made him so unforgettable was the fact that, at five feet ten, one hundred and seventy pounds, and fifty-eight years of age, Fairbairn could throw around any of the Jeds (who were all thirty years or more his junior) with ease. The little man with the craggy features and the horn-rim glasses exuded strength and self-confidence. Under his close-cropped graying hair were a bulbous nose and dark eyes that seemed to look in all directions at once, missing nothing. Fairbairn had spent thirty years as a Shanghai policeman, rising to the level of assistant commissioner. And after years of riding herd over a water-front population of gangsters and pirates and cutthroats, Fairbairn knew how to take care of himself. He had been schooled in the ori-ental arts of self-defense and silent killing, and he was here to teach what he called the "Fairbairn method" of unarmed combat.[20]

Martial arts, as developed and practiced in the Orient, were not widely known in the United States at that time, and the Jedburgh trainees marveled at Fairbairn's techniques. He introduced the men to the body's nerve centers and pressure points, and he showed them countless ways of using fists and elbows and knees and fin-gers as weapons to attack those sensitive areas. He taught them the principles of joint manipulation and techniques for silently taking down sentries, and he urged them always to follow every maneu-ver with a swift kick to the opponent's groin, just for good meas-ure. One student recalled how Fairbairn would hand a stiletto to a trainee and invite him to stick it into the instructor. "You would find yourself looking up at the sky when he got done with you."[21]

Major Fairbairn's curriculum included knife fighting, and he taught the men how to use the Fairbairn-Sykes fighting knife, which he and a colleague named Eric Sykes had designed. It was a foot-long stiletto with a high-grade steel blade, diamond-shaped in cross-section and razor sharp on both edges, making it suitable for both slashing and stabbing. And Fairbairn showed the Jeds all the places on the human body where vital organs or arteries could be most easily reached.

Whenever a weapons class appeared on the day's training sched-ule, Fairbairn was the instructor. Dressed in his usual coveralls and tan army garrison cap, he taught his instinctive pistol shooting method, quickly stepping forward with one foot to shoot from a semi-crouch position, and he drilled the men in his method of quickly changing magazines in the .45-caliber pistol. Then he would send students with loaded weapons down trails through the woods, and spring-loaded silhouette targets would jump up from behind bushes. He had even had a facility built that came to be called "the mystery house" or "the spook house." Students would enter the darkened building armed with a .45-caliber pistol and two magazines of six rounds each. As the trainee stepped carefully down the narrow passages inside, with Fairbairn following behind whispering instructions, cardboard German soldiers would suddenly pop out from behind a wall or around a corner, and the student would have to react and shoot.

Demolition classes included practical exercises—blowing up trees and walls and old cars. And nights were often spent patrolling through the moist autumn foliage. Physical training continued, with the men setting and breaking personal records in pushups and tearing through the obstacle course. The tough training and the Spartan mountain living had the desired affect, and the men grew hard.

Food was plentiful at Area B and was always well prepared, and for Thanksgiving the men were served a five-course feast with all the trimmings. Afterward cigars were passed around. But entertainment was harder to come by, and after the fourth viewing of a film on the Incan civilization the men had the dialogue memorized. And, from time to time, they had to sit through wearying talks given by officials visiting from Washington.

By most accounts, it was during just such an occasion at Area B that a Jedburgh tradition was born. Its origin was Fort Benning's parachute school, where an officer trainee had reportedly been dropped for fifty pushups, and in counting out the final few repetitions, had said, "forty-eight . . . forty-nine . . . fifty," then jumped to attention and muttered, half under his breath, "Some shit!" Most of the Jedburgh officers, of course, had gone through Fort Benning and had heard the story.

In his autobiography, *Hazardous Duty*, Jedburgh veteran John Singlaub described the origin of the tradition that grew from this incident. A guest speaker's oratory had exceeded the bounds of Jedburgh patience when "a bizarre chant rose in the rear ranks of our formation. 'Forty-eight,' a man called. 'Forty-nine,' two more replied." As the speaker puzzled over the meaningless catcalls and continued his talk, another shouted "Fifty!" Then, in unison, all roared "Some shit!"[22] The target of the outburst was left speechless, and the ritual became a Jedburgh trademark, to be used on many such occasions in the future.

By early December, the days became easier and the men relaxed, enjoyed some passes, and played some football. They were issued .45-caliber pistols, Fairbairn knives, wristwatches, and some special cold-weather clothing.

One night the Jedburgh officers enjoyed a steak dinner and a few drinks and went to bed. They were mustered at two in the morning, told to put on their newly issued cold-weather gear, loaded onto trucks, hauled to a railroad siding, and put aboard a northbound train. The men were told to keep the window curtains in the railroad cars drawn.

They jolted to a stop at New York's Grand Central terminal a couple of hours before noon, but the men were ordered to remain in the cars with the curtains drawn. The cold-weather gear was becoming unbearably hot by the time they were told to fall out, about two hours later, and were warned not to speak to anyone. They marched with packs and full combat gear across to Forty-second Street, where they climbed aboard army "deuce-and-a-halves." The big trucks snaked through Manhattan's urban canyons, crossed a bridge to Brooklyn, and delivered the Jeds to Fort Hamilton in the Bay Ridge section, just across from Staten Island. Fort Hamilton was an embarkation center where troops were prepared for overseas shipment, a place where shots were given, dollars were exchanged for English pounds, and booklets that told of the country and people of Great Britain were issued. The Jedburgh radio operators would arrive about a week later.

On a cold and overcast Monday night, the Jedburgh officers boarded a ferry which took them up the Hudson River to Manhattan's West Side passenger ship terminal, to the Cunard line's berths at Pier 90 at the foot of Fiftieth Street. And the men stared up at the largest ship that any of them had ever seen.

Early in the war, Winston Churchill, as one means of consummating the Atlantic Alliance, had offered up two of the greatest ocean liners in the world—the Cunard-White Star line's *Queen Mary* and *Queen Elizabeth*—for service as troop ships to bring

American servicemen to the British Isles. The giant ships, each more than a thousand feet long, had been stripped of their peacetime splendor, the luxuriant furnishings and carpeting put into storage, though much of the Art Deco styling remained. Each ship still featured an immense map of the North Atlantic on a wall of the First Class Dining Room, where the progress of peacetime voyages had been tracked.

Now every available space, including the drained swimming pools, had been fitted out with rows of wooden or metal bunks stacked three or four high, and more than twelve thousand fold-down canvas bunks called "standee" berths had been installed on each ship. Additional lavatories and showers had been added. Each of the Queens, originally designed to carry slightly more than two thousand passengers and a crew of a thousand during peacetime, could now carry fifteen thousand troops—a full division—even though the lifeboats would barely hold half that. And in the warmer months they carried another two thousand, with additional bunks placed on deck. Portholes and windows, roughly two thousand on each ship, had been blacked out, and the ships had been painted entirely in dreary gray, covering for the war's duration the elegant satin black hulls, the white upper works, the red funnels. Because the Queens made such prestigious targets for the enemy, anti-aircraft guns and cannons, deck guns, and rocket launchers had been installed.

As the Jedburgh officers lined up to board the Queen Elizabeth, each was issued a mess card and a card with his berthing assignment. Red Cross volunteers doled out coffee and donuts. And the men, loaded down with field gear and barracks bags, filed up the gangplank from the pier, under an overcast sky, and were met at the top by the British crew, all Cunard employees. The men worked their way through the maze of passages and stairways to find their assigned berths, and soon the Jeds were scattered throughout the ship.

Those in the rank of captain might get a stateroom, which held fewer men but was still crowded. A cabin which in peacetime accommodated two people now held six or eight men in steel cots stacked two high, and barracks bags and other gear consumed most of the remaining space. Other cabins held as many as twelve men, and two Jed lieutenants found themselves sharing a sixteen-bunk cabin with a detachment of army chaplains. Many of the men aboard the ship, the Jeds noticed, were airmen.

It was cold and threatening rain as tugboats pushed the liner back into the Hudson at high tide in the early morning darkness of December 14, 1943. Smoke billowed from her funnels as she turned and crept downstream, past Ellis Island and the Statue of Liberty on the starboard side, through The Narrows and into the Atlantic.

As wartime trans-Atlantic crossings went, this run by the *Queen Elizabeth* was uneventful and, aside from daily evacuation drills, the officers were left to pass their time as they wished. A recreation room remained thick with cigarette smoke and laughter and the clatter of dice. Some men preferred the smaller room which doubled as an officers' lounge and library. But the Jeds were clannish and tended to stay together when not in their quarters; and each night the men set their watches ahead an hour.

Meals on both *Queens* were served almost continuously, with six shifts resulting in two meals a day for each passenger, breakfast in the morning and dinner in the late afternoon. With so many men to feed, the seemingly endless chow lines for one meal often didn't wind down until the next meal was beginning. Even when a soldier finally got his food, he might have to eat it standing up if he couldn't find a spot to sit. The mess cards the Jed officers had been issued told them where and when to eat, such as: "Officers' Dining Room, 'R' Deck Aft, Third Sitting." Officers ate well, under the circumstances, with dinners including such entrees as fillet of haddock, Florentine roast duckling, and Pear Mont Blanc.

The greatest defense for each of the *Queens* against submarine attack was a cruising speed of around twenty-eight knots—more than twice the surface speed of a U-boat and four times its speed submerged—and they were safer traveling alone, rather than in convoy with ships that could average no more than ten knots. The ships steamed in a zigzag pattern as an additional defense, changing course about every eight minutes, and at full cruising speed such a turn could send food trays scurrying off the table. There were no storms during the *Elizabeth*'s crossing, but the North

Atlantic was always rough and the ship rolled and pitched constantly, enormous dark-gray waves showering the deck with salt spray.

As the *Queen Elizabeth* neared the British Isles she picked up a destroyer escort, and those topside spotted Northern Ireland off to the right. She steamed up the Firth of Clyde, and the men, most of whom had never been outside their native land, caught their first glimpses of Scotland. They drifted past rolling pasturelands and thatch-roofed houses and patchwork fields lined with stone fences. Then the great ship slowed to a stop and dropped anchor off the city of Gourock, at the mouth of the great estuary which feeds the port of Glasgow.

On that cold afternoon of December 20, the fifty-five American Jedburgh officers went ashore and found the drab Scottish port town packed with men in a wide variety of uniforms. At first the Jeds were tucked away in a warehouse. Then, when darkness came, two trucks picked them up and hauled them to a railroad station. Three trains and a day later they arrived at a commando training area near Arisaig on the northwestern coast of Scotland, where the men were comfortably billeted in three spacious old homes used by Special Operations Executive to house trainees—Garramoor, Inverie, and Traigh House. The beautiful but barren countryside which surrounded the Americans had more in common with Wyoming than with the lush greenness of England.

Three days after the American Jedburgh officers arrived in Scotland, the American radio operators sailed from New York aboard the *Queen Mary*. War voyage number 30E for the great ship began at dawn on the clear and cold morning of Thursday, December 23, with just under twelve thousand troops and a crew of more than a thousand aboard. Among the troops sharing the cramped ship with the Jed radiomen were those from an anti-aircraft searchlight battalion and a combat engineer battalion, and there was a general service engineer regiment aboard which was composed entirely of black soldiers.

Like those of her sister ship *Elizabeth*, the *Queen Mary*'s twelve decks were divided, for troopship purposes, into three areas—the Red Area, comprising the forward third of the ship; the White Area, the midships; and the Blue Area, the aft third. As troops boarded the ship they were issued colored buttons corresponding to the area in which they would be berthed, and signs on the bulkheads directed the men to their berthing areas with red and white and blue arrows. Most of the sixty-two Jed radio operators were berthed as a group on the promenade deck, in what had been the liner's tobacco shop and gift shop.

Troops on the Boat Deck, seventy-five feet above the waterline, watched as America slipped beyond the horizon. Many of them were seeing it for the last time. Men wandered about the three acres of deck space or leaned on the wooden rails, covered with initials and graffiti carved by troops of earlier shuttles, and watched the great ship's wake as it remained visible in the distance for as much as a mile. Because German U-boats were known to patrol the east coast of the United States, an escort of four or five destroyers stayed alongside the liner throughout the first day, until she was well out to sea.

But the crossing of the *Queen Mary* which brought the American Jedburgh radio operators to England would prove to be nothing like what the officers had experienced on the *Elizabeth*. Shortly after leaving New York a violent storm began, with gale-force winds and giant waves that tossed the ship for the duration of the crossing. It was an absolutely miserable experience for all, with most of the men aboard being on a ship for the first time in their lives; and virtually everyone got seasick at some point, some remaining so throughout the wretched voyage.

The Jed radio operators were appointed military police (MPs) for the duration of the crossing. Some of them guarded prisoners in the ship's brig, but many had to rotate through shifts on an even less pleasant detail. The ship's large First Class Dining Room, with the map of the North Atlantic on one wall, served as the enlisted men's mess hall. And it was the job of the Jed MPs to station themselves at the doors to the mess hall and help men as they tried to make it from the serving line to a table. Bob Kehoe was on the detail, and he later recalled trying to keep men "from being tossed across the deck, which was covered with several inches of seawater, food, and vomit."[23] Once seated, troops tried to eat unappetizing meals of overcooked pork chops, bully beef, boiled cabbage, brussels sprouts, or lamb stew from trays intent on sliding down the long table with each roll or pitch of the ship. Men were then faced with the challenge of retaining the meal on their way back to their bunks. Many failed to do so.

The mess hall was a constant mass of moving lines and unending noise—queues to get food served in army mess kits and eaten at crowded tables, lines to dip the emptied kits in a barrel of greasy water, all to be done at the rate of forty-five minutes per man. Before one group had even cleared the dining area, a loudspeaker summoned the next group from the block-long lines that snaked through the ship. Many men came to find the ship's nine canteens preferable. Here they could buy twenty-five-cent candy bars for a dollar, or live on crackers and Cokes.

Long lines, however, didn't just lead to the mess hall. Men had to stand in line just to get to one of the lavatories, each of which was shared by about sixty men and usually consisted of open rows of urinals and toilets. The floors were continuously awash in an inch-thick mixture of water and vomit, leaving a nearly permanent stain line on the men's boots.

Aisles were jammed full of duffel bags and gear, and men had baggage lost or stolen. There was no place to change clothes, so men stayed in the same uniform during the entire voyage, and the limited supply of fresh water and an overtaxed ventilation system resulted in a ship's interior that was stuffy and rank with the odors of cigarette smoke, vomit, and unwashed men.

Days became an endless routine of boredom and misery. Aside from the daily evacuation drills, troops played poker, tossed dice, tried to read or sleep, or went to see the movies that were shown nightly. But most of the men spent most of their time standing in chow lines. At sunset each night, blackout time was announced over the loudspeakers, the black-painted porthole windows had to be closed, and smoking no longer was allowed on deck.

December on the North Atlantic was cold, and men on the *Queen Mary* sometimes spotted icebergs. And then it was Christmas Day. When writing of the experience later, Bob Kehoe would recall how an effort was made to serve a special dinner, but I am not sure many could enjoy it. Religious services held in the mess hall were well attended; a combination of loneliness, fear, and general misery made men extra-conscious of traditional ties. Standing guard duty, I shared the feelings of fear and separation. The hymns, even at a distance, were reassuring.[24]

On the morning of December 29, the *Queen Mary* arrived in Scotland, though a thick fog prevented the Jeds from seeing much of it.[25] Later, the weather grew clear and warm, and the Jedburgh radio operators debarked and were immediately escorted to a station and put on a southbound train to join the British Jed radiomen at Henley-on-Thames. There, the men were taken to the country house called Fawley Court, where they were billeted in Nissan huts, a British version of the Quonset. The first contingent of French radio operators arrived at about the same time. The men were all introduced to the Jedburgh radio set which they would be using in the field, and they trained with it until reporting to Milton Hall in the first week of February.

The French Jedburgh volunteers had begun arriving in Scotland in November, and those who passed a session of physical and psychological testing had been sent to the offices of General de Gaulle's intelligence organization at 10 Duke Street in London, where each was interviewed by a board of four officers. After a week, those selected were sent to a large house in the country—and if they asked where they were they were told that they didn't need to know.

One of the first instructors to meet the French officers was Captain Bernie Knox, an Englishman who wore an American army uniform and spoke faultless French. So fluent, in fact, that one of the Frenchmen, Lieutenant Paul Aussaresses, was certain that Knox must be French, as he had a trace of accent similar to that of the poor working class in the eastern districts of Paris.

Another of the American instructors was an engineer lieutenant who would eventually join the Jeds, a paratrooper who had twenty-six jumps to his credit and who used one four-letter word so often

in the first few minutes that Lieutenant Aussaresses, who understood no English at the time, assumed it to be an English form of
punctuation. Aussaresses, who would go on to become a general in
the French army, would later claim to have learned 50 percent of
the American military vocabulary in his first five minutes at the
base.

After about two weeks of physical training and an introduction
to explosives, the French officers moved on to a place called Gumley Hall, where they remained until the last week of January. Then
they were sent through parachute training and on to Milton Hall.[26]

The training areas and country houses that hosted the Jedburgh
trainees were part of an elaborate network of schools that Special
Operations Executive had developed since the early years of its
existence. Never before and, arguably, not since has such a vast and
complex factory for the development of special operators existed.
The various country sections, including the French Section, used
this machinery of training and assessment to produce the agents it
sent to occupied Europe, and at the close of 1943 it was serving the
needs of the Jedburghs.

The American officers remained at Arisaig, under constantly
dreary and overcast skies, for about two weeks. The short winter
days were filled with basic commando training—long cross-country hikes with heavy rucksacks on their backs, obstacle courses,
hand-to-hand combat drills, and pistol firing. Then, beginning
December 28, the men were sent in three groups through another
psychological assessment, this time in the south of England, at a
place the men began to call the "booby hatch."

Apparently not satisfied with the results of the American Jedburgh assessment conducted in Washington, the British had insisted that all Jedburgh candidates, Americans included, be evaluated
by SOE's Student Assessment Board.[27]

Again, each of the officers sat through a few days of various written psychological tests—intelligence tests, word-association tests,
ink blot tests, and more—and interviews with psychiatrists. But
they also went to a small training area outside, where they were
subjected to hands-on situational exercises designed to reveal an

operative's tolerance for frustration, his ability to think quickly and clearly and reasonably in difficult situations. The men might be told to complete a task with materials that were ill-suited to the purpose, or with "assistants" who were purposely more of a hindrance than a help.

Lieutenants with little notebooks followed the Jeds around, occasionally jotting down their findings, noting how a man adapted to a situation, overcame obstacles, improved solutions, and coped with stress and disappointment. There were even ways of measuring the time of hesitation that a candidate showed prior to attempting an obstacle. Other tests determined a man's faculty for memorizing details of a room, a face, or a map or other document. There was much that the assessment personnel needed to learn about a candidate's character in a very short time, and the staff became quite adept at it.

Aside from the obvious requirement for moral and physical courage, the Jeds should display confidence and self-reliance, good judgment, a degree of controlled aggressiveness, and discretion with secret information. The men had to be highly resourceful in order to complete their mission—even when communications and support were disrupted; they had to be able to adapt to rapidly changing situations.

Their work required an alert mind, capable of a quick appreciation of a situation—one that was decisive and inventive. Mental stamina was no less important than physical endurance; and maturity, emotional stability, and self-discipline would be needed for the men to hold up under stressful situations or during periods of prolonged isolation. And because of their international make-up and the nature of their work, their willingness and aptitude for working with other nationalities was an absolute must. As advisors, they needed to be perceptive, persuasive, assertive when necessary, and diplomatic—capable of interacting with others with no thought to class distinctions.

The assessment staff looked for men with an above-average intelligence and a desire for self-improvement. And each man selected would possess all of the physical and mental qualities that would enable him to accomplish his mission alone, if necessary, but which at the same time would make him a cooperative team player.

The last group of American Jedburgh officers completed the assessments in early January 1944. Only thirty-seven of the fifty-five American officers evaluated were selected for further training.[28] French officers experienced a similar rate of attrition.

The upshot, of course, was that all this weeding out resulted in a shortage of American and French officers. So a search for additional American officers from among the thousands of men assigned to U.S. divisions in England, especially the 9th Infantry and the 101st Airborne, began in January and was completed by late February. To make up the shortage in French officers, SOE and OSS each sent an officer on a recruiting mission to the Middle East, where seventy more French officer volunteers were found. They arrived at Milton Hall in late March.

Rather than sending the sixty-two American radio operators to the Student Assessment Board, a team of three psychiatrists visited Special Training School 54 and interviewed each candidate. Forty-six of the sixty-two American radio operators were chosen to continue training.[29]

The buildup of invasion forces in the British Isles was well underway, and American divisions and support units poured in from the States. By the end of May 1944, there would be more than one and a half million American troops in Britain, occupying one hundred thousand buildings in more than eleven hundred locations.[30] All, of course, required billeting, training and medical facilities, supply depots, and airfields. The result was an intense competition for real estate.

The British and American special operations staffs in London had begun searching for a site to serve as the Jedburgh training school and holding area in the fall of 1943. In October they settled on a large country estate known as Milton Hall, located about ninety miles north of London and just west of Peterborough. The property included an expansive Elizabethan brownstone house at the end of a half-mile-long driveway through well-kept grounds, the ancestral family home of the Earl Fitzwilliam. Special Operations Executive gained permission to use the estate and began the necessary renovations. Many of the oak-paneled rooms in the seventeenth-century house were transformed into billeting and classroom space, lecture halls, supply rooms, and administrative offices. The surrounding grounds, including a golf course on the property, became training areas.

The Jedburgh training center was to have been ready for occupation and the commencement of training on New Years' Day, 1944, but material shortages and construction delays prevented occupation until early February. In the interim, temporary arrangements were made. The officers were divided into three groups and sent to three different Special Operations Executive training schools, one at Fairford, Gloucester, another at Gumley Hall, in Lancashire, and the third at Walsingham, in Surrey. At these sites the officers received most of their preliminary training, and in the first days of February they reported to Milton Hall.

On February 5 the radio operators arrived, forty-six Americans, forty-five British, and twenty French.[31] And from the time they arrived, they were included in all general training along with the officers, although they would also continue to receive specialized training in wireless telegraphy.

Prior to the commencement of training at Milton Hall, though, all Jedburgh trainees had to complete an abbreviated SOE parachute training course at Ringway, near Manchester—even those who had completed the parachutist course at Fort Benning. Beginning on the first of February the men were sent for the three-day course in groups of fifty. American paratroopers had been trained to jump from slow twin-engine C-47 cargo planes, exiting the aircraft through a side door. They would now have to learn the SOE method: dropping through a hole in the bottom of the fuselage of a faster, four-engine bomber.

The British cadre at times must have found the Americans a challenge at times. One aspect of the training that was new to the Americans was jumping from a large basket suspended from an airship, a huge football-shaped balloon. Groups of four would be taken up and, one at a time, the men would be given the command to sit at the hole in the floor of the basket and then to jump. On one occasion, while a group was waiting for a man to position himself at the hole, one of the American Jeds, Captain René Dussaq—a former

Hollywood stuntman who had once done a handstand on a ledge at the top of the Empire State Building—stunned the instructor by doing a swan dive over the side of the basket.[32]

The really disconcerting thing about the balloon jump was the amount of time it took for the parachute to open. When jumping from an airplane, a parachute normally opened when the jumper was within sixty to ninety feet of the plane, and the slip-stream helped to rapidly inflate the canopy, usually within a few seconds. But when jumping from an anchored balloon floating some six hundred feet above the ground, a parachutist's body fell uninterrupted for a hundred and fifty to two hundred feet before the parachute opened.

The Fort Benning graduates would jump and then count "one thousand, two thousand, three thousand . . ." as they had been taught to in their Stateside training, but instead of feeling the opening shock as expected, they were still falling—and were sure that they had "bought it." Then the canopy would open with a slight tug. Such feelings of dread were not confined to the Americans. A British Jedburgh officer, James Hutchison, later wrote that he felt a "curious detached feeling" on his first balloon jump. "I became an onlooker on my own fate," he recalled, "as though thinking 'I wonder if that man's parachute is going to open.'"[33]

Shaggy, fat sheep and bored cows still roamed freely about the lawns of Milton Hall, but the dairy barn had become a Morse code classroom, complete with female instructors from the First Aid Nursing Yeomanry. Several huts stood on the grounds, serving as barracks, and the large sunken garden was a weapons training area. The golf course was a demolition range, and the quadrangle behind the mansion had sprouted a boxing ring and other exercise equipment.

Inside the old mansion were many classrooms, and a large room on the ground floor had been fitted with a movie projector and screen. But little of the old house's charm had been lost in the transition. Suits of armor still stood stoically by, and many large portraits hung on ornately furnished walls. British Captain Stanley

Cannicott later described how "eminent, be-wigged gentlemen looked down on us in a faintly disapproving and questioning manner as we trained with our explosives."[34]

The Jedburgh training school at Milton Hall was administered by an Anglo-American staff. The first commandant was British Lieutenant Colonel Frank Spooner—a regular army officer, formerly of the Indian army—who had previously served as commandant of SOE's finishing school at Beaulieu, the final training stop for F Section agents. But Spooner's style of leadership, according to one of the French officers, "had a sense of formal discipline, maybe narrowly minded," and was not best suited for heading a special forces training camp.[35] The staff included twenty-five instructors, seventeen British and eight American.[36]

The first morning at Milton Hall began early, and when British batmen arrived to greet the officers with morning tea they were roundly cursed for their efforts. It was dark and damp and raw outside as the men fell out for muster, taking fifteen minutes to get squared away while a sergeant major barked in vain at men from half a dozen countries. Stanley Cannicott, in his memoir *Journey of a Jed*, described the men's reaction as Colonel Spooner then tried to call the formation to attention: "The dutiful Brits sprang to attention, the French raised their eyes and their hands and said 'We do not understand,' the Americans looked the other way and I will not print what they actually said."[37]

For the next few months, the Jeds followed a training program designed to sharpen old skills and at the same time familiarize the men with techniques and equipment that were totally new to them. As always, days began with calisthenics, but the hikes became more demanding, twenty to twenty-five miles over rough terrain, and there were difficult night compass courses.

Survival training included fieldcraft and how to live off the land—even the fine art of poaching. After one long cross-country march, recalled Captain Cannicott, the trainees bivouacked in a wooded area. Soon, a truck drove up and stopped. A live sheep and a bag of flour were thrown out of the back and someone shouted, "That's your supper."[38]

Just as important was another kind of survival skill, the kind that involved knowledge of Continental customs and mannerisms, ignorance of which would mark one as an outsider. Conditions might call for Jeds to wear civilian clothes and eat in French restaurants. So the men had to learn to dress like Frenchmen, and the Americans had to learn to keep the knife in the right hand and the fork in the left hand when eating, and not switch the fork to the right hand after cutting meat, as they would at home. The Brits had to unlearn the habit of putting milk into a cup before pouring the tea.

Language instruction continued, and there was observation and memory training. And the men were introduced to tradecraft skills—how to establish and operate intelligence networks, use forged papers, and conduct surveillance; how to follow someone without being detected or, more important, how to discern when one is being followed—and what to do about it. They learned of curfews being enforced in occupied territory and of the enforcement methods used by police and security forces. They were introduced to codes and ciphers for clandestine communications, and officers were given limited training on the wireless equipment and Morse code, just in case the radio operator got "knocked off."

From time to time, the men would assemble in the old mansion's Great Hall to hear guest speakers talk of the geography of France, or of the French resistance movement, its history and organization, and its most effective methods. And always, if a speaker began to lose his audience, he would hear the growing chant: "forty-eight . . . forty-nine. . . ." But the speakers who held the Jeds' attention were those who had been to occupied France on a mission with one of F Section's circuits, and the men would listen intently as the agent described what life was really like behind enemy lines.

Additionally, because the Jeds would be living among the enemy they had to know the organizations and uniforms and ranks of not only the German military, but also of the various German and Vichy police units.

In weapons classes, the men became familiar with British, American, French, and German small arms—pistols, rifles, shotguns, submachine guns, and light machine guns—including not only their operation, but also the disassembly and assembly of each weapon. They learned how to employ anti-tank mines and how to neutralize booby traps, and they became proficient with hand grenades. Major Fairbairn was there to drill the men in his "instinctive shooting" technique—firing a pistol from a crouch position with two hands or from the hip with one hand—and he taught them to always fire two shots in rapid succession. The old Shanghai policeman also continued to teach hand-to-hand combat, knife fighting, and silent killing.

Demolition training included learning to use plastic explosives—malleable enough to be molded into any form and stable enough to take considerable abuse without exploding. The stuff was powerful and hot-burning, capable of bringing down trees or cutting through steel. The Jeds also were introduced to primacord (a flexible explosive detonating cord), time pencils (devices used for initiating explosions after pre-determined time delays), and to a variety of other fuses and igniters. Bridge and railway demolition were studied, along with the sabotage of power stations, factories, canals, electrical transformers, high-tension-wire pylons, dams, and reservoirs.

Probably every Jedburgh trainee, no matter what his background, learned new skills at Milton Hall—from driving a motorcycle to picking a lock to paddling a boat without making a sound.

One important detail which remained was the formation of the three-man Jedburgh teams. And, as with everything else, the Jeds found an unconventional way to accomplish it. Around the middle of March, the commandant instructed the Jeds to begin seeking out their own teammates—men with whom they felt they could work best in the field. To operate effectively, the men making up a team had to be physically, emotionally, and temperamentally compatible—matched like a team of horses in harness. The men were more apt to find their own best mates, reasoned the Jedburgh staff, instead of having mates chosen for them. The only criteria was that each team must have a British or an American officer, another officer of French, Belgian, or Dutch nationality (which would determine the country that the team would operate in), and a radio operator of any nationality. By this time, of course, the officers had all gotten to know one another somewhat, and friendships had formed.

Over the next two weeks, officers paired off and began a trial period known as the "engagement." If this "courtship" period proved satisfactory to both parties, the "marriage" was officially recognized by a posting on the bulletin board, and the couple either chose or was assigned a radio operator. Regrettably, some engagements were broken and an occasional marriage would end in divorce, in which case the process was started over again. By the first of April, however, most of the teams had been formed, and the men would go through all remaining training events as teams. And so they gelled—men who, in civilian life, might have met on the street and never taken notice of one another.

The newly formed teams found many opportunities to train together on field exercises called "schemes." These drills, usually forty-eight to seventy-two hours in duration, gave the Jeds a chance to perform under clandestine circumstances. Teams might be dropped by parachute into Scotland or Wales and have to make their way back to Milton Hall without being caught. The men would be armed and in uniform, and police and even the Boy Scouts along the way would be alerted and given descriptions of the men. One team reportedly beat the others back by hijacking a train.

On another survival scheme, the team of Major Wise, Lieutenant Aguirec, and Sergeant Kehoe had been making its way across the Yorkshire moors all day. At day's end, the men—who were supposed to be living off the land—decided to cheat a little by stopping at a farmhouse and asking if they could buy some food and perhaps sleep in the sheepfold. But the farmer and his wife, who had a son in the service, fed the men a hot meal and gave them a warm bed to sleep in. Other schemes might require teams to contact resistance members, tail a subject, or give the slip to someone following them.

In March the Jeds began taking part in a series of major field exercises—the first a six-day affair called Spill Out, then another called Sally, and then one called Levee. In April there was Exercise Spur and, finally, in late May, came the exercise called Lash, which was still ongoing when D-Day arrived.

*   *   *

Formal planning for Operation Overlord, as the cross-channel invasion was called, was, for the most part, completed by the end of March. The assault would take place over a sixty-mile frontage of Normandy beaches. British divisions, coming ashore on the easternmost beaches, would capture Caen as quickly as possible and push south. The Americans would land to the west and at the base of the Cotentin peninsula. The British would thereby be in a position to provide some protection for the U.S. troops as they pushed out to capture the port at Cherbourg and those in Brittany.

The first phase of the operation was the establishment of the beachhead and the subsequent expansion and buildup of a lodgment area as follow-on forces and supplies continued to come ashore. Of critical importance to this plan would be the protection of the area from enemy counterattack. It was projected that it would be weeks before a large enough force could be brought ashore to allow the Allies to break out of the lodgment area and go on the offensive.

Eisenhower himself thought that the first five or six weeks would be critical in getting forces ashore and keeping them ashore. As late as three weeks before the invasion Eisenhower's chief of staff, Lieutenant General Bedell Smith, was only giving fifty-fifty odds that the Allies would be able to stay ashore. Eisenhower's naval aide had his own doubts after sitting through a briefing, held just two weeks before the invasion, and hearing that the latest intelligence estimates numbered the German forces in France at fifty-eight divisions, some three-quarters of a million troops in all.[39] Overlord's success was far from certain.

General Smith, like Eisenhower, recognized how badly the Allies would need support from the French resistance. Smith complained that the American and British chiefs of staff were tying Eisenhower's hands by not allowing him to be more open with the French in planning for the invasion.[40] Because the French were considered a security risk, the supreme commander was not even allowed to share the planned invasion date and landing sites with General de Gaulle.

Even if the initial Allied landings were successful, the plan only called for putting seven divisions ashore in Normandy on the first day. Eisenhower's planners sought every means possible to buy time for the subsequent expansion of the beachhead and the buildup of forces. As it then stood, they calculated, the ratio of landing forces to defending forces in the immediate invasion area would be marginally in the Allies' favor. But this could change dramatically if additional German divisions were hastily moved into the Normandy battlefield as reinforcements.

In their calculations, Overlord planners judged that the Allied landing force could be successful so long as German mobile reserves on D-Day did not exceed twelve divisions. Any more than that and the advantage in forces might go to the Germans. Of the twelve-division reserve, planners further reasoned, no more than three could be allowed to approach within striking range of Caen on D-Day. This number could increase to five on the second day following D-Day (D+2) and to nine by D+8. No more than fifteen German divisions could be allowed to move into the area within sixty days of the landings.[41]

But how many divisions would the Germans be capable of moving to Normandy if they recognized the landings as the main Allied invasion and reacted accordingly? Eisenhower's intelligence staff crunched the numbers and concluded that by D+25, the Germans might be able to move as many as thirty-one divisions, nine of them panzer (tank) divisions, to the Normandy battlefield. Such a force could overwhelm the Allied invaders. Somehow, the Allies needed to prevent this from happening, and the final Overlord plan, along with some highly classified supporting plans, spelled out how it would be done.

Three means were to be used to deter or delay the movement of German divisions to the beachhead area. The first was an elaborate and, in the end, highly successful deception operation called Fortitude. The object of Fortitude was to reinforce Germany's belief that the cross-channel invasion would come in the Pas de Calais area of the French coast near the Belgian border. The deception would prove successful and would accomplish its objective of persuading the German high command to keep the bulk of its highly mobile Fifteenth Army—eighteen divisions strong—tied down between the Seine and Holland, waiting for Allied landings which never came.[42]

A second means of thwarting German troop movement was the Transportation Plan, which called for the bombing of key bridges and rail yards throughout France and the Low Countries by the Allied air forces.

The third instrument to be used in delaying German reinforcements was the French resistance. An early version of the Overlord plan had been completed by an Allied staff in London in 1943, and British and U.S special operations planners had been asked in June of that year for their concept for employment of the French resistance in support of the operation.[43] In April 1944, with the final Overlord plan completed, General Eisenhower's operations officer, Major General Harold R. Bull, asked for an updated and detailed review of the special operations plan.[44]

The plan, laid out in Appendix P of the preliminary Overlord plan, remained essentially unchanged in the final version. In the first phase of Overlord, the resistance would contribute to the Transportation Plan by cutting rail lines and obstructing road movement by ambush and sabotage.[45] The support of the resistance would become crucial in the event of bad weather, which often grounded aircraft in the European theater. Additionally, in areas where civilian populations in the immediate vicinity of targets might be threatened, partisans could be more precise in their attacks. They were, in a sense, the "smart bombs" of their day.

Once the lodgment area was secure, the resistance would shift to a general campaign of guerrilla warfare—sabotaging communications; attacking enemy supply depots, command posts, and road and rail traffic; and, where necessary, preventing enemy demolition of bridges or other structures that were needed by the Allies.

General Eisenhower was convinced by this time that the French resistance would play a key role in supporting Overlord, and he was equally sure that he needed some means of controlling and directing and encouraging them. He and his British counterpart in the Mediterranean, General Sir Henry Maitland Wilson, both recognized that the most important function of the Jedburgh teams would be as a means of providing such direct influence over the resistance fighters.[46]

Eisenhower had known of the Jedburgh concept since September 1942, when he was commander of U.S. troops in Britain. An early draft of the concept had been tabled at a meeting of joint planners in Washington in late August of that year. War Department officials had agreed with the concept, with the proviso that the Jeds be employed under the direct control of the theater commander. Before giving the concept their official endorsement, however, they had decided that they needed Eisenhower's opinion, and in September the concept had been forwarded to him in London for his recommendation.

On September 11, 1942, Sir Charles Hambro, chief of Britain's Special Operations Executive, met with Eisenhower in the general's second-floor corner office at Grosvenor Square. It was not Hambro's first visit to Eisenhower's office. He and General "Pug" Ismay, Churchill's military deputy, and a colonel representing the special operations branch of OSS had met with Eisenhower back in July, shortly after his arrival in London.

Major General Bill Donovan, director of the OSS, was present at Hambro's second meeting with Eisenhower, and Donovan would meet separately with Ike two days later. It was during these meetings that Eisenhower first learned of the Jedburgh project, and immediately after their conclusion Donovan informed the Joint Chiefs of Staff in Washington of the general's recommendation. Eisenhower followed up with his formal and favorable endorsement of the Jedburgh concept in a message to the War Department on September 16, 1942, adding his agreement that the Jeds should operate under the theater commander's control. He also suggested that planners reconsider the idea of the Jeds being dropped in uniform.[47]

Clarification of the chain of command for directing the unconventional warfare campaign in support of Overlord came in May 1944. Special Operations Executive and the Special Operations Branch of the Office of Strategic Services had been working essentially as a combined headquarters in London since January. With D-Day approaching, and in recognition of the role it would be playing, it was decided that the headquarters needed a designation which could be used for open dissemination. In other words, one which did not identify SOE, the name and existence of which was still classified at the time. So, on the first day of May, General Smith, Eisenhower's chief of staff, issued a directive naming the organization Special Force Headquarters (SFHQ). It would be directly subordinate to Eisenhower's Supreme Headquarters Allied Expeditionary Force (SHAEF).[48]

With their formal training program completed, the Jeds continued to participate in field exercises, but they also had more time to relax as they awaited the coming invasion and their deployment to the field. There were games of soccer and rugby and softball. And in the evenings men might catch a ride into Peterborough for drinks at the Bull Hotel or one of the local pubs. Some enjoyed dances held at the Peterborough town hall. But others found Peterborough a bit dull, and preferred a visit to the "Fox & Hound," a pub within walking distance of Milton Hall in the opposite direction from Peterborough.

Music lovers tuned radios in to the Armed Forces Network or to German propaganda stations, which played all the current hit songs along with the equally entertaining propaganda messages of British expatriate Lord Haw Haw.

Weekends often meant passes to London. The Jeds found that, for all the bombings and hardships imposed on Londoners during the war, many of the city's pre-war attractions managed to carry on; some even flourished as a result of the war. Shows at theaters such as the Windmill and the Prince of Wales featured chorines wearing smiles, and perhaps some form of military headgear, and little else.

Streets were a colorful showcase for military garb from all over the world. Even war correspondents were often in uniform. Some of the men found time to visit the more traditional tourist attractions such as Trafalgar Square, Buckingham Palace, the Tower of London, and Westminster Abbey. They could stop by the American PX on South Audley Street and stock up on candy bars, cigarettes, gum, soap, and razor blades, or grab the latest issue of *Yank* for threepence or the *Stars and Stripes* for a penny. The Jeds often frequented the clubs run by the American Red Cross, such as the Eagle on Charing Cross Road and the Washington on Curzon Street. The Red Cross's Rainbow Corner (on Shaftesbury Avenue near Piccadilly Circus) had American flags flying outside and the army, navy, and air corps emblems on the façade, and offered a café with good food, jukeboxes and a game room, a barber shop, a library, and even a bed for the night. Some of the men enjoyed dancing with "nice girls" at the Palladium Ballroom or the International Room, where the dance floor was large enough to accommodate three hundred couples.

The men might rendezvous at Piccadilly Circus, under giant ads strutting from Edwardian buildings: "Wrigley's—for Vim and Vigour"; "Guinness is Good for You—Gives You Strength"; "Bile Beans—for Radiant Health & Lovely Figure." The bustling crowds and the lively commercialism and the big-city grime might have reminded some of the Americans of Times Square, save for the bright red double-decker busses and the colorful horse-drawn ale wagons pushing through the circling traffic. After dark prostitutes would congregate at the Circus. The girls came to be called "Piccadilly Commandos" and "Hyde Park Rangers," the latter known to ply their trade in the open air.

Lieutenant Colonel Spooner remained commandant at Milton Hall until early April, when he was succeeded by another British officer, Lieutenant Colonel G. Richard Musgrave. But operational control of the Jeds transferred at that time to the British and American co-directors of the Jedburgh section at Special Force Headquarters, which was located in the Montagu Mansions near Baker Street in London.

It had been two years since the Jedburgh idea had been conceived. After making it through a rigorous assessment and selection process and months of training, the Jeds were ready and restless—thoroughbreds eager to break from the starting gate. On the third of June, the first teams were alerted for their mission briefings in London.

4

"SITUATION HOT"

"**4**000 PARTISANS MUST RECEIVE HUNDRED BRENS, 1000 STENS, 1000 BATTLEDRESS. SITUATION HOT WILL EXPLODE IF ARMS NOT RECEIVED."[1] So began the wireless telegraph message informing Special Force Headquarters in London on June 11 that Jedburgh team George was safely on the ground and operating. In a second message later that day, the Jeds added an order for anti-tank weapons, carbines, and equipment for an additional two thousand men.

Before the reception committee had cleared the drop zone of parachutes and bundles from team Frederick's landing near Guingamp, Jed team George had jumped roughly ninety miles to the southeast. The two Stirlings carrying team George and the Dingson SAS party dropped their jumpers from a higher altitude than those carrying the Samwest party had, a little more than eight hundred feet. Captain Paul Cyr, the American member of team George, was anxious to leave the overcrowded bomber, and when the green light glowed the Jeds and the SAS men spilled out as fast as the gaping bomb bay would accommodate them.

Floating under a full parachute canopy, Cyr watched for signs of activity on the ground below. The moonlight, dim as it was, offered just enough illumination to see the field and a few trees. From about a hundred feet above the ground, he noticed a group of fifteen to twenty people running toward the area where he and some near-by jumpers would land. Cyr hit the ground and rolled. Then, as he tried to stand, he was mobbed, people tugging and pulling, grasping at harness buckles, until they had freed him from the parachute. And all the while they were laughing and shouting to one another—they were having a ball.

Cyr was sure that these mad Bretons had no idea of the danger they risked by making such a racket, and he asked them to keep it down. But the people assured him that there was no danger. The closest Germans, they explained, were quite far away—two kilometers away. That was slightly more than a mile, and the news didn't make Cyr feel any safer.

When the parachutes had been gathered up, Cyr and the other jumpers followed the reception committee to the rendezvous point in the middle of a field. There they found about seventy-five more people, apparently local members of the resistance. They waited just long enough for the SAS men to join them and then they were off. Captain Cyr hurried along with the crowd, keeping an eye out for his Jed teammates.

The team and the SAS party had jumped into an area of scattered forests and isolated farms in the southeastern part of the Brittany peninsula. The Jeds and the SAS left the drop zone—a large field surrounded by a high hedge—and walked to a nearby farm, just west of the hamlet of St-Marcel. The farm was called La Nouée, and it was to serve as the Dingson SAS base. La Nouée was the home of an elderly farmer named Pondard, his wife, and their seven children—five daughters (the oldest was twenty-three) and two sons.[2]

Near the farmhouse, Cyr was reunited with his two French teammates, Captain Philippe Erard and Lieutenant Christien Lejeune.* Erard, a twenty-six-year-old Orléans native and the designated leader of team George, was a graduate of Saint-Cyr, France's military academy. He had been mobilized with his infantry regiment in 1939 and had fought in the desperate battles of June 1940 that had ended in France's defeat. But Erard, like others, had refused to capitulate. Rather than lay down his arms, he deserted

* Philippe Erard's real name was Philippe Ragueneau; that of Christien Lejeune was Pierre Gay.

and joined the resistance, organizing sabotage and propaganda work first in Toulouse and later in Lyon. He had been picked up by the Germans in August 1941 and was sent to prison by a Vichy court but, through the efforts of influential resistance leaders, he was released after three months. Erard had then made his way to Algeria, where he was eventually recruited for the Jedburghs in 1943.

It was three in the morning when they reached the farmhouse, a two-story stone affair with a steep gray slate roof and a long, attached barn of similar construction extending from one side. But the partisans of the St-Marcel maquis, who made their headquarters in the barn, were in a festive mood. Girls showered the men with kisses and poured them wine and handed them bouquets of flowers. And everyone—men, women, and children—acted as if liberation had already come. Some laughed, others cried with joy, as though it were a done deal: all that remained was to march down the road, give the Germans a quick thrashing, and send them on their way back to the Fatherland. And these feisty Bretons, from adolescents to old men, were ready, it seemed, to go and do just that—this very night.

But rational heads prevailed, and the people worked through the remaining hours of darkness to bring the containers in from the drop zone. Finally, the Jeds got two hours of sleep.

Cyr was a small-town New Englander from the picturesque Green Mountain town of St. Johnsbury in Vermont, where he had worked on the town newspaper, the *Caledonian-Record*, before the war. Despite his being underage, he had managed to join the National Guard out of high school in June 1938—one week after his seventeenth birthday. His unit, the 172nd Infantry Regiment, had been called up for one year of federal service in late February 1941, but after the attack on Pearl Harbor the one year had been extended to "the duration." So Cyr accompanied his regiment to Camp Blanding, Florida, to undergo initial training. The regiment was assigned to the 43rd Infantry Division, a New England National Guard outfit that would go on to see action in the South Pacific—but which would go there without Paul Cyr.

In April 1942, Cyr had left the regiment to enter Officer Candidate School at Fort Benning, and had received a commission in the infantry in June of that year. He also found himself attracted by the lure of the new airborne force then being created at Fort Benning. Cyr volunteered for parachute training but had the misfortune of breaking a leg on one of his first jumps. His leg had fully healed by September 1943, and he was back training troops at Camp Blanding when the OSS recruiter arrived there in search of Jedburgh candidates. Cyr hadn't hesitated to volunteer.[3] Nearly a year later, Captain Cyr found himself on French ground with the task of putting months of training to good use by forming an effective combat force out of this mob of Breton patriots.

Partisan warfare was particularly effective in certain regions of France, and for somewhat different reasons in each area. In the south, for example—from the Pyrénées that defined the Spanish border, across the great and rugged Central Plateau, to the Alps on the Italian and Swiss frontiers and even on northward into the Jura and Vosges mountain ranges—the terrain was ideal for guerrilla warfare. Steep, heavily wooded mountains provided relatively safe bases from which the maquis could operate, a sanctuary into which they could retreat after dealing a blow to the Germans. Railroads and highways followed the valleys in between—valleys so confining in places that God might have had ambush on his mind when he laid them out.

But in Brittany—a land so rough in character and so damp in climate that the Romans had largely ignored it two thousand years earlier—it was the people that made things work. The clannish Bretons were as sturdy as the land they lived on, and they shared the same rustic charm. Celtic in heritage (their ancestors had emigrated from Britain in the fifth century), many of the Bretons still spoke a language that was closer to the native tongues of Ireland, Scotland, and Wales than to French. The Bretons—fiercely independent, and accustomed to looking out for themselves and living off the land—were barely tolerant of the mainland French and were not at all accommodating to the Germans.

They made their living from the sea and the soil, for the most part. Each year, schooners sailed from Brittany's ports to bring back cod from the Newfoundland banks, often battling brutal North Atlantic storms to do so. The home waters provided rich harvests of sardines and oysters and mussels. The local farmers spent a lifetime breaking the veneer of sod that hid the granite not far below, and were surprisingly adept at coaxing impressive potato and cereal crops from the poor, loamy soil.

Like many country folk, Bretons could initially be as cold and reserved to strangers as the great stone megaliths that have dotted the Morbihan landscape since Neolithic times. But in that same tradition of country folk, they could also warm to an uncommon friendliness. In happier times, their Celtic spirit was evident in their passion for festivals, with bagpipe music and folk dances, and women dressed in traditional costumes that included colorfully embroidered ankle-length aprons and tall, white-lace headdresses known as coiffes. Rarely, though, did their enemies ever see this festive and genial side of the Bretons. And the people of Brittany were not the least bit intimidated by the Wehrmacht units occupying their land. For four years they had waited for the opportunity and the tools with which to fight back. Clearly, team George had much to work with.

On their first day at La Nouée, the Jeds met resistance leaders and got a feel for the local situation. In the daylight they could see that the farm was surrounded by forest. There was a large field, about five hundred yards in length, and other smaller fields, each cleared out of the forest. The large field served as the drop zone where the Jeds had landed the night before. A long lane reached from the main road to the farm buildings, and the SAS had posted a sentry on the lane.

The Jeds also met a young-looking British agent called Fernand, whose real name was André Hue. The product of a British mother and a French father, he worked for the Special Operations Executive and had jumped in with the initial small SAS team on the eve of D-Day to help organize the resistance in the St-Marcel area.[4]

At about two in the afternoon, a farmer arrived in a horse-drawn cart. In the cart were the packages containing the Jed radios, which had been dropped near the farmer's house—nearly two miles from the drop zone. This was a stroke of luck; the Jeds would now be able to get their first message off to London.

Over the coming days, Captain Cyr grew to admire the French SAS. The men were out every night on demolition operations, cutting telecommunications lines, blowing up railroads, ambushing Germans on the roads, and generally making life difficult for the enemy. Every night they mixed it up with the Germans and then returned to camp with their dead and wounded.

And the Jeds marveled at the efficiency of the SAS resupply system. Planes arrived for eight consecutive nights—anywhere from five to thirty per night—dumping arms and ammunition and explosives. Just three nights after team George had arrived, thirteen Stirlings dropped eighty-seven more SAS men and 249 containers.[5] Still more men arrived five nights later, when thirteen planes dumped another forty-eight SAS, nearly two hundred more containers, and a jeep. The local resistance members hustled night after night to clear the drop zone before dawn. Even though the Jeds also arranged arms drops from London, theirs paled in comparison to those of the SAS. Most of the weapons that arrived in the containers for the maquis were Sten submachine guns, and each of them came with a handful of loaded magazines.

In the make-do world of the guerrilla, the Sten was an engineering marvel. To provide the resistance fighters with a dependable submachine gun in the numbers required, the British had developed in the Sten what was arguably the cheapest, simplest weapon of its kind ever made—and the ugliest. But it worked. The seven-pound Sten proved to be uncomplicated to operate, and the gun held up well under the rigors of combat and rustic living conditions. It was a no-frills version of the more sophisticated German MP40—easy to disassemble and assemble and with parts that were easily concealed. Built with the partisan in mind, it was weapons design at its most elementary level. It required little in the way of maintenance and could operate for months without being oiled. The Sten had a simple stamped-metal tubular design with a thirty-two-round box magazine protruding from its left side. It looked more like a bicycle pump than a weapon. And, although ammunition for it could be air dropped, it could also be found in abundance in German stocks or harvested from the battlefield. (It used the same 9mm Parabellum round used in German Lugers.) But the Sten had two drawbacks: it was prone to jam and it had an unwelcome tendency to fire when dropped on the ground, with results that could be hilarious or tragic. From a technological standpoint, though, it was scarcely more complicated than a socket wrench. The dumbest man in France could master the gun in ten minutes.

By the fifteenth of June, SAS Dingson and Jed team George had armed some twenty-three hundred patriots, forming two large battalions—one east of the harbor town of Vannes, located on Brittany's southern coast, and one about thirty miles north of Vannes.[6]

The Dingson base was running magnificently, and with each successful patrol, the SAS men grew more confident, felt more secure—almost invulnerable. Their aggressive, in-your-face approach to behind-the-lines warfare was effective, and the Jeds couldn't help but marvel at their efficiency.[7] But, inevitably, the Germans came to know all about the farm called La Nouée and what went on there. The very success of the Dingson SAS enterprise, with the nightly airdrop activity and the endless radio communications that made it all possible, was, in the end, its undoing.

As the Jeds of team George had been taught back at Milton Hall, a lengthy stay at any one base location was to invite disaster. And the Germans would soon be ready to strike.

Meanwhile, sabotage operations carried out by resistance groups throughout France, organized—and in some cases led—by agents of Special Operations Executive's circuits, were proving more successful than many had thought possible. By D-Day there were more than twenty F Section circuits in operation throughout France, and they had already armed tens of thousands of guerrillas in maquis groups in every region.[8] In the weeks leading up to the invasion, the groups had been attacking their assigned pre-D-Day targets, mostly industries critical to the German war machine.

But the targets which the resistance groups had been most anxious to strike were their D-Day targets—roads and railway lines, telecommunications sites and command posts. These, they had been told, were not to be attacked until pre-arranged signals were received from Special Force Headquarters just before the invasion, signals which would be aired by the British Broadcasting Corporation (BBC) on certain designated nights following its French news program.

On the first day of June, the BBC had broadcast a secret message which served to alert circuit organizers and resistance leaders that the invasion was only days away. Resistance groups had then listened every evening for their second pre-arranged message, which would be their execute order. Plans had called for D-Day targets to be struck forty-eight hours after receipt of this second message.[9]

At nine-fifteen on the evening of June 5, following the BBC's French news broadcast, the seemingly meaningless personal messages, the execute orders—306 in all—had gone out over the air. And out of a planned 1,050 rail cuts all but 100 had been successfully carried out that night.[10]

The British and American air forces, too, had begun their attacks on the transportation system in France, and by the night of the fifth they had destroyed eighteen of the twenty-four bridges over the Seine and knocked out more than five thousand locomotives. This was after the resistance had already destroyed or damaged more than seven hundred locomotives in the four months leading up to D-Day.[11] As a result, on the eve of D-Day rail traffic nationwide in France was running at 30 percent of its January level.[12]

Jedburgh teams were beginning to arrive throughout France to help the growing resistance continue the sabotage campaign and to delay the German reinforcements trying to reach the Normandy battlefields. Major Adrian Wise and his Jedburgh team Frederick were in position in northern Brittany—and were ready to begin.

5

SURVIVAL

L ATER in the campaign for northern France, after the Allies had broken out from Normandy and begun their fairly swift advance toward Germany, some Jedburgh teams were inserted too late to be of much use. A few teams were overrun by the advancing Allied ground forces only days after jumping, having had little time to effectively perform their missions. But that was not the case with the thirteen Jed teams deployed throughout France during the month of June, or even for the dozen more dropped the following month. For these teams, mission completion often came only after weeks of perilous, nerve-racking raids and manhunts conducted by German troops and Gestapo agents.

Several German divisions were on the move toward Normandy as reinforcements, intent on helping defeat the Allied invaders on the beaches. Many more German units remained in place throughout France as reserves, though, and to maintain security in the rear. And until the ground war came to them, these units could devote much of their time and energy to hunting down guerrillas and Allied special forces. Eluding such units was the challenge now facing Jedburgh team Frederick.

★   ★   ★

Major Wise and team Frederick were ready to begin helping the resistance leader Marceau organize and arm his maquis groups throughout the department of Côtes-du-Nord in northern Brittany. At first, all they could do was give Marceau some badly needed cash to use for feeding and paying his maquisards, most of whom still had families to support. Before they could begin arranging air-drops of arms and supplies, the Jeds first had to retrieve the radios which Sergeant Kehoe had hidden in the forest during the attack by German paratroopers four days earlier.

On Friday, June 16, the Jeds enjoyed dinner at a small café in a village a few miles northeast of their campsite. Later, they sat around the table with Robert, the French SAS sergeant who had brought the wounded men to the barn the day of the attack. Sergeant Robert was a seasoned veteran of the French army. Quiet by nature, tall and slim, he carried himself with the dignity and bearing of the professional soldier he was. Bob Kehoe judged him to be in his early thirties. The Jeds were working on a plan for recovering the radios from the Duault forest, and Robert offered to help. The Frenchman indicated that he thought he knew how they could do it.

Sergeant Kehoe's understanding of French, though limited at first, had been improving since his arrival in Brittany. Even when listening to spirited conversation among a group of Frenchmen he was able to follow the gist of the dialogue, while missing some of the detail, rather like listening to a radio program intermittently interrupted by static.

As he listened to Robert's plan, Kehoe grasped enough of the conversation to realize that the plan called for speedy movement. Much more speed, it seemed to him, than men on foot could accomplish. What Kehoe didn't catch was the reason for the urgency. The maquis had learned that the Germans were planning a major operation of some sort in the area; the radios were desperately needed and time was of the essence. In fact, Robert planned to go after them that very night. If all went well, the radios would be safely back in the hands of the Jeds before dawn. Kehoe knew that executing the operation on foot would take at least two days. He soon found out where the necessary speed would come from.

Hidden in a nearby shed was a 1934 automobile which had been up on blocks since the German occupation began. The car belonged to a mechanic who had clandestinely kept it in working order. Employed in a St-Brieuc factory over the past four years, the mechanic had smuggled a considerable amount of fuel out of the factory—one cup at a time. The wheels were re-mounted, the car was pushed from the shed, the hand crank was turned, and the engine roared to life. Kehoe, Robert, and two young maquisards climbed aboard, and they drove off down the road toward the forest some ten or twelve miles away.

With a teenager at the wheel, Sergeants Kehoe and Robert rode with their weapons at the ready. Another teen had come along to help guard the car while Kehoe and Robert searched for the radios. Headlights remained off and the journey was made in complete darkness. They had to avoid detection, and they would be passing through two or three villages which would be observing wartime blackout ordinances. As the car crept along the winding country road, Kehoe and Robert watched for German patrols or for any sign of an enemy roadblock ahead. At the entrance to each village the driver pressed the accelerator, and Kehoe and Robert scanned the buildings and kept their weapons pointed out the windows as they rolled past.

During the German attack four days earlier, team Frederick had hastily abandoned the maquis camp in the forest and, to move faster, had hidden both radios. Sergeant Kehoe had buried one under a boulder in the immediate vicinity of the camp, and the second had been quickly stashed behind a boulder along the forest trail that the Jeds had taken while being chased. Kehoe and Robert planned to search for both sets, but they knew nothing of the current situation at the former campsite. Were there any Germans still in the area? Had the enemy planted mines around the abandoned encampment? Or along the trails leading to it?

Uncertain as to what lay ahead, the two sergeants knew that they had to approach the area using extreme caution. As they neared the forest, they directed the young driver to pull down a side road so that the engine would not be heard from the campsite. Ensuring that the car was well hidden in a thick stand of gorse and guarded by the two teenagers, Kehoe and Robert set out for the camp.

Only a sliver of moon remained in the mid-June sky, and the countryside was quiet and dark. The two men carried flashlights but dared not use them except in an emergency. They made good progress through the woods, even without illumination, and in less than an hour they found the old forest road which led to the camp. Sergeant Kehoe led Robert along the trail until he recognized the spot where he'd stashed the second radio, but when he searched behind the boulder he found no radio there. German patrols had apparently discovered it. Though disappointed, Kehoe was not really surprised; he had not had time during the chase to hide the radio well.

Time was passing quickly and it would soon be daylight. Sergeant Robert had hoped to also be able to look around for remnants of the SAS force in the area—dead or alive—and find out if stockpiles of weapons had survived enemy searches. So he and Kehoe agreed to split up, conduct separate searches, and rendezvous later. Sergeant Kehoe then proceeded directly to the abandoned campsite.

The Samwest camp had been spread out over an area of about five hundred yards by two hundred yards, and Kehoe soon recognized the general area. He had hidden the radio under a boulder not far from the SAS command post and near the center of the camp. Without much trouble, he found the boulder which he had used as a landmark. But, when he crept down the hill to find the boulder under which he had hidden the radio, Kehoe found that, in the darkness, many boulders looked similar to the one that he sought. For nearly an hour he went from one to the next, digging underneath, only to find nothing. Finally, just as dawn approached, his relentless excavating paid off and he uncovered the complete Jed set, unharmed.

Kehoe shouldered the forty-pound radio pack and scrambled up the hill. He found an anxious Sergeant Robert waiting at the rendezvous point, and the two set off for the car at a brisk pace. With the coming daylight, their return drive was relatively quick.

The young American and the experienced Frenchman had gotten a difficult job done under dangerous conditions and, in the process, they developed a new-found respect for one another. The taciturn Robert, despite an occasional show of arrogance, had proved himself to be a natural and resourceful leader. He still needled Kehoe (perhaps a dozen years his junior) about his youthful inexperience—often chiding that the American surely must have lied about his age to enter the army—but Kehoe knew that he had passed muster in the eyes of the older man.[1]

The maquis' sense of urgency for the radio recovery proved well-founded. On Sunday, barely twenty-four hours after Kehoe and Robert returned with the radio, an estimated four thousand Germans moved on the Duault forest and the surrounding area. After throwing a cordon around the area with roadblocks, motorized and foot patrols ravaged the countryside, raiding farms and torching homesteads. Civilians were taken into custody for interrogation. Troops combed every inch of the forest during the well-planned operation.

With radio in hand, team Frederick could begin arming and organizing the maquis of the Côtes-du-Nord. First, they moved south to a more secure area, establishing a camp about five miles east of the Duault forest, not far from the barn where the wounded SAS were being cared for. The campsite was in a rugged pasture where the prickly, yellow-flowered gorse shrubs were particularly tall and thick, providing good concealment. For added security, contact with members of the resistance was kept to a bare minimum, and was nearly always made through the network of female schoolteachers.

The new camp was more than a mile from the nearest paved road and was reached by following narrow footpaths used by the farmers whose cows grazed throughout the area. The Jeds erected no tents or shelters of any kind, opting to sleep in a ditch with only blankets, provided by the French, to give some small measure of warmth during the wettest of Junes that any of the locals could remember. It was an animal's existence—damp, cold, dirty—but it was also a secure one. There was little in such an austere camp that could be spotted by a German plane flying overhead or by the occasional patrols passing on the nearby roads. Gunfire was heard from time to time, and the men never doubted the immediacy of the German presence.

They were also positioned well from a logistical standpoint. They were less than a mile from the old barn where the wounded SAS men lay. Marcel, Simone, and the other local patriots caring for the SAS men would be able to carry food to both the wounded men and the Jeds on the same trip. But the team also knew that, for security reasons, it could not remain at the site for long.

Anxious to get their radio into operation and let London know that they were back in business, Kehoe made his scheduled contact on June 18, the same day the Germans swept through the Duault forest just a few miles away. Kehoe's cryptic message told Special Force Headquarters of the attack on the SAS camp and of the dispersion of the Samwest SAS party, of the care being provided the three wounded SAS men nearby, and of the Jeds' successful contacts with resistance leaders.

Special Force Headquarters had not heard from team Frederick since the twelfth, and it gratefully acknowledged the contact at once. Questions would arise at SFHQ of the authenticity of a transmission from the field after so many days of missing scheduled contacts. Had the team been captured? Was it transmitting under duress to aid the Germans in manipulating London's operations? But Sergeant Kehoe was careful to include his safety signal in the message, as instructed during the briefing back in London, to signify that he was transmitting freely and securely.

Meanwhile, Allied forces continued to come ashore in Normandy—fifteen divisions by June 12, another five by the nineteenth—building up to the day when the Allies would be strong enough to break out of the lodgment area.

On Monday, the nineteenth, SFHQ sent a message to team Frederick confirming the location of drop zones which the Jeds had identified. Headquarters also congratulated Peseta (Bob Kehoe's code name) on his promotion to the rank of first sergeant.[2] It was his second promotion in ten days, and it put him, at age twenty-two, at a rank typically held by older and much more seasoned veterans. It also meant that, in less than two weeks, his monthly pay had gone up from ninety-six dollars to one hundred and thirty-eight dollars. Virtually all of the Jedburgh radio operators were enjoying the same accelerated advancement, and many of the Americans became first sergeants by the time their missions were completed.[3]

With the team separated from the SAS and on its own in a relatively secure location, Kehoe could begin following a standard communications routine. Both SFHQ and the field operators took every precaution possible to limit transmission times to reduce the likelihood of enemy detection by radio direction-finders. For its part, SFHQ sent messages to the field in one-way broadcasts during the late-night hours, typically during the first few hours after midnight. These nightly broadcasts began with a list of stations, or operators, that were the intended recipients of the messages. Once all of the messages had been broadcast the entire series was repeated. If Kehoe received a message, he copied it down and then deciphered it—all by flashlight.

Operators in the field sent messages to London during scheduled contact times, usually during the day. And, whenever possible, they would move some distance from the camp to transmit, thereby reducing the chance of radio direction-finders locating the campsite. The Jed set could receive messages with power provided by the dry cell battery, but the hand-cranked generator was needed when transmitting, and local maquisards would often assist by turning it. Such a schedule was tiring, and enemy signal jamming or inclement weather only made it more demanding. Luckily for Kehoe, the Germans' enthusiasm for patrolling and radio direction-finding searches was dampened by the rainy weather.

Marceau, the resistance leader with whom team Frederick was working, turned out to be a key man in this part of Brittany. His real name was Yves Le Hegarad, and he was the FFI chief for all of the Côtes-du-Nord. The FFI had been created by General de Gaulle in early 1944 and was intended to accomplish a merger of all indigenous resistance movements in France, including the maquis. The organization was called the Forces Françaises de l'Intérieur (French Forces of the Interior), and was nearly always referred to as the FFI.

One of the most active elements of the French resistance, though, was the leftist Francs-Tireurs et Partisans (Irregulars and Partisans), or FTP, and it was particularly strong in Brittany. The FTP was the paramilitary arm of France's Front National political movement, which was dominated by socialists and communists and often, at least early in the war, took its directions from Moscow. As was the case throughout France, maquis leaders at all levels in Brittany shared the common military goal of driving the Germans from their country. But they also had political agendas, and these were not always the same. Quite naturally, in a country which had been occupied for four years, resistance leaders were concerned with the form of government France would adopt upon liberation. And while FTP leaders were socialist-oriented, most of the FFI supported de Gaulle, who was intent on keeping the socialists and communists from gaining power in post-war France.

The FTP had agreed to fight under de Gaulle's FFI organization, but the relationship was always tense and tenuous. Some FTP leaders in other parts of France flatly refused to recognize de Gaulle as their leader, but in Brittany they cooperated with the Gaullists. It was because of leaders such as Marceau that they did so.

Marceau's real authority over the many small maquis groups was limited, with each group primarily loyal to its immediate leader. Although Marceau was nominally the departmental chief of the FFI he also had strong links with the FTP. His leadership qualities enabled him to maintain the support and cooperation of maquis groups throughout the department, regardless of political ideology. He also maintained daily contact with the Jeds, normally by courier, and visited the camp as often as possible.

To be effective in their work, it was important for the Jedburghs to distance themselves from the internal politics of the resistance, and Sergeant Kehoe was finding that this was perhaps easiest for him to do. As an American, he was more inclined to be viewed by the locals as truly unbiased when it came to French politics. But such was not the case with the French Jedburgh team members, and remaining wholly impartial was not always easy for them to do. At times, Major Wise fretted that Lieutenant Aguirec engaged in too many political discussions with resistance people.[4]

Once contact with London had been re-established, the Jeds began arranging air drops, bringing in the arms and supplies and money so desperately needed in the area. On the night of June 23, sixty containers floated under parachute to a field northwest of Guingamp, about twenty-one miles north of team Frederick's camp. In the process of arranging a reception committee and marking the field to be used as a drop zone, the Jeds were careful to train the guerrillas to perform such work on their own.[5]

Team Frederick found the maquis to be not only willing but enthusiastic fighters, often erring on the side of rashness in their eagerness to take the fight to the enemy. And no matter how risky a planned operation was, the Jeds were never short of volunteers.

Sometimes the enemy responded with reprisals and atrocities visited on the local people, usually in the form of burning houses and other buildings. The Germans were aided in this by the Milice, the collaborationist Vichy constabulary whose members betrayed their own countrymen for a pat on the back and a fistful of francs from the occupier. If the maquis loathed the Germans, it was nothing compared to what they felt for the Milice. Major Wise would later report, "I personally witnessed the ill treatment and execution of five Milice and none of us felt the least pity for them."[6]

The last half of June was a busy time for the Jeds. Supply drops continued and more German targets were struck, including an ammunition dump. Sometimes, though, Bob Kehoe would have to hastily send a message asking London to postpone a drop because of enemy activity near the planned drop zone. On June 24, however, he was able to report: "REGION HUMMING WITH ENEMY ACTIVITY. SUCCESSFULLY CARRIED OUT ATTACK ON COMMUNICATIONS. BOCHE* COMMUNICATIONS IN BRITTANY IN CHAOS. WILL TRY AGAIN [to receive another parachute drop] AFTER AMMUNITION DUMP. OUR MORALE TERRIFIC." And on the following day the Jeds asked that their next drop include: "BATTLEDRESS AND CIGARETTES, SOAP, TOBACCO, PIPE AND RATION FOR TWO WEEKS FOR JED TEAM ALSO BATTERIES FOR RECEIVERS."[7] On the twenty-eighth the Jeds confirmed their ability to accept another Jedburgh team, but warned that two days advance notice would be prudent because the area was crawling with Germans. They also asked London to send one million francs for team Frederick, to be carried in by the new arrivals.

More arms and supplies arrived on the night of June 29, when

---

* Pronounced "Bosh," a contemptuous term used by the French in referring to the German occupiers.

four Halifaxes—British bombers converted for special operations use—dropped thirty containers and sixteen packages to a field ten miles south of Guingamp.

Things were heating up. The Germans were stepping up efforts to search out and destroy the maquis. They also were making it clear that parachutists who gave material support and encouragement to the maquis were considered outlaws, just like the guerrillas, whom the Germans called "terrorists." In the last week of June, Germans began posting notices on buildings and fences throughout Brittany. The handbills warned citizens that Allied parachutists were nothing but spies and terrorists, and if captured such men would be shot immediately, along with anyone found to be helping them.

But such threats had little effect on maquis operations, and the tempo of team Frederick's work continued to accelerate. On July 6, Kehoe sent another message requesting delivery of weapons, grenades, and explosives, as well as for boots for a hundred men. Boots were especially important for the men of the maquis, many of whom came from rural France, where people often wore wooden shoes because they provided much better insulation from the dampness and the mud than did leather shoes. But wooden clogs— called *sabots* by the French—were ill-suited for guerrilla warfare, where one had to be prepared to run.

Kehoe's message also told of an attack on a maquis group near Guingamp a few days earlier, a fight which had cost the lives of seventy German soldiers and ten maquisards.

The Germans, however, were not the only ones turning up the heat. Special Force Headquarters began pushing to rapidly expand operations in Brittany in preparation for an Allied breakout from Normandy. By the second day of July the Allies had slightly less than a million men in France. That day, London radioed team Frederick that arms and supplies, as well as additional Jedburgh teams, were to be dropped as fast as the men on the ground could accept them and arrange for their security and dispersal. Headquarters asked the Jeds to identify as many dropping grounds as possible.

Reinforcements coming from London would find plenty of work waiting for them. Maquis groups were growing constantly and were critically short of weapons, explosives, and equipment. As the arms arrived and stockpiles grew, though, Wise's team found it impossible to keep up with the necessary training. There were simply too many small groups scattered far and wide across the department, and so maquis leaders with military experience had to pitch in and conduct most of the weapons and tactics instruction. It was still necessary, however, for the Jeds to train the maquis on the use of specialized explosives and demolition equipment sent from England.

Relief began arriving on the night of July 8, when Jedburgh team Felix jumped and was met by a reception committee arranged by team Frederick. Team Felix would take over responsibility for the eastern half of the Côtes-du-Nord department, leaving the western half to team Frederick.

That same night, Captain Bernie Knox's Jedburgh team Giles parachuted in to the rough department of Finistère at the westernmost tip of Brittany, where the peninsula's most important port, Brest, lay. On the following night two more teams were dropped to the southern Finistère, and another two arrived a week later. In the northeast corner of Brittany, two teams dropped to the Ille-et-Vilaine department on the night of the eleventh.

For a fortnight, team Frederick and the maquis ambushed German patrols and truck convoys, attacked enemy fuel dumps, and blew rail lines. They sabotaged German communications by blowing high-tension power lines and transformers and cutting the underground cable connecting Brest with Paris. Map coordinates for a German general headquarters and for infantry and artillery unit locations were radioed to SFHQ for handoff to the air force for bombing missions. Although the Jeds and Marceau tried to maintain control of all maquis operations by designating or approving targets and tactical plans, they were not able to prevent some FFI bands from acting on their own. These uncoordinated attacks, while usually successful, were risky and often resulted in costly enemy counterattacks or reprisals. German commanders were increasing their efforts to move eastward to help check the swelling Allied lodgment area in Normandy, but German units remaining in Brittany continued their ruthless counter-guerrilla campaign.

Three times in one week the Germans had fired on maquis elements on the road just behind the Jeds' camp, and so Major Wise decided it was time to move. The Jeds struck camp on July 9 and relocated about nine miles to the east.

On a rocky, wooded hillside just above the hamlet of Canihuel stood a deserted one-room cottage. It was on a rough, single-lane country road which appeared to be used only for livestock and horse-drawn vehicles. The Jeds decided to set up their command post in the cottage. Accessibility to the place was good enough to facilitate the direction of FFI operations throughout their area of responsibility. Clearly, though, it would not be as secure as their previous camp. Here they would be in a building, out in the open, with some major roads not far away, and the tiny cottage would be crowded. But at least they would be out of the weather.

Sergeant Kehoe reported the team's new location to London that same day, and in the message he also passed on Major Wise's recommendation for a promotion to captain for Lieutenant Aguirec. Special Force Headquarters would signal back two days later that Aguirec had been made an acting captain.[8]

Team Frederick's new camp soon became a fully functional command post. The Jeds and Marceau, who had become a fairly permanent part of the team, established a courier system to maintain contact with maquis groups throughout the region. Their stable of couriers included two gendarmes, in their official blue and black uniforms, who were sympathetic to the resistance, and five local girls who got around by bicycle. In the case of the gendarmes, travel throughout the area on bicycle or moped was part of their everyday job, providing a convenient cover for their courier work. Greater risk was involved for the girls, but women of all ages typically enjoyed much more success in getting through German checkpoints than did men. They naturally seemed more innocent and they didn't have to explain why they hadn't been conscripted for labor.

Simone Le Göeffic, the attractive young schoolteacher who had given food to the Jeds that first night after the German raid on the SAS camp in the Duault forest, came to help out at the new command post. Her chores included preparing meals, and she cooked using the cottage's ancient fireplace. The Jeds soon found themselves eating well. Simone was assisted by a petite woman in her mid-twenties named Aimée Pouhaër. Although Aimée was quiet by nature, Bob Kehoe found her easy to talk to, and he enjoyed listening to her describe what life in Brittany was like before the Germans came.

A young man named Josef Forestier acted as the camp's supply officer and proved himself resourceful in quite unexpected ways. One day he arrived at camp with a supply of women's underwear that he had managed to find. The Jeds, still in the unwashed clothing they had left England in a month before, were not too proud to accept a pair each and wear them.

Kehoe found the Canihuel camp ideal for radio communications. By this time, Kehoe had grown confident that the reliable Jed set would never let him down. It had worked perfectly so far, even when making a scheduled contact while German troops were nearby—even in the next field—which often happened. He spent most nights sitting at a table in the small cottage, listening for broadcasts and encoding or decoding messages by the glow of a flashlight while the others, both men and women, slept in the single room.

A week had passed at the new camp when Wise and Kehoe were interrupted one morning during a scheduled radio contact with London. An excited maquisard arrived warning of "Boche and Russian cavalry" searching the woods nearby for maquis. (Some of the Wehrmacht—or German army—units in Brittany were composed of East European volunteers in German uniform, and among them was a squadron of Ukrainian horse cavalry.) There were also reports from nearby farmers of unusually heavy movement of Germans on the roads, including slow-moving vehicles—a sure indicator of radio direction-finding activity.

At this point, the Jeds should have been on the alert. Only a few days earlier, one of the young female couriers had arrived suddenly on bicycle as the Jeds were having dinner. The young woman was visibly shaken and told of a raid on a farmhouse to the east. A group of men had gathered there to prepare for the reception of an airdrop which team Frederick had arranged. While the men were sitting at dinner in the farmhouse, German soldiers kicked in the

door and came in shooting, killing everyone present and then burning the house down. Major Wise was concerned enough by the
woman's story to send Simone and Aimée elsewhere as a caution-
ary measure.

The Jeds should have thought out a procedure for hastily abandoning the command post in an emergency situation, but they had
been busy with other things. Wise and Kehoe had been working
hard to keep up with the radio messages required by the increasing
operational tempo. The demand for airdrops was growing daily, and
reports of impending danger had become somewhat commonplace,
so the men were not overly concerned with this morning's development. Still, they had posted a sentry as a precaution.

Shots rang out, and they weren't far off. Both rifle and machine
gun fire, and Bob Kehoe judged it to be no more than a few hundred
yards away. With only five or six men in the cottage, fighting it out
with a German raiding party was out of the question. There was
nothing to do but run, only taking time to grab weapons, hand
grenades, radio crystals, cipher books, and the already enciphered
messages. German bullets chipped at the stone walls of the cottage
as the men quickly gathered what they could and bolted out the
door and down the hill opposite the fast approaching enemy. The
radio was left behind, but the Jeds were more concerned with their
own survival, and got away from the building only seconds before
the Germans closed in.

Maquisards who had been in the command post had scattered to
nearby farms. But the Jeds were conspicuous in their uniforms.
They ran into a wooded area about a hundred and fifty yards downhill from the cottage and followed a small stream to a spot from
which they could observe the enemy soldiers. This was more than
a mere probe; it was later estimated that six hundred to eight hundred enemy troops were scouring the area. Most appeared to be
infantrymen, but there were also troops on horseback.

Then a German officer noticed the aerial strung between two
trees next to the cottage, and he sent troops to search the small
house. Soon they discovered the radio and they almost certainly
found a map, which had been inadvertently left behind, showing
dropping grounds throughout the department. It was a devastating

loss and one that had to be reported to England as soon as possible to enable cancellation of all planned air operations. But the urgent need was for the Jeds to get away.

The Germans, however, seemed in no hurry to leave. Enemy troops were spread far and wide, and the Jeds knew that the entire area would be thoroughly searched. Already, they could tell by the voices of men shouting directions and by the occasional gunfire that they were completely surrounded.

Major Wise decided to lead the team out of the trap that had closed around them. After luckily crossing three fairly open fields without being noticed, the team crawled into a thirty-yard-square patch of gorse next to a trail. Once the men had dug deep into the brush, they remained still, waiting for darkness before going any farther. And they prayed that the Germans would not bring search dogs.

Only thirty minutes passed before the first German patrol stalked by, just a few yards away, on the trail. The Jeds froze. Again and again people walked by. The Jeds could tell which ones were German soldiers by their boots, and while the Germans sometimes fired shots they never thought to shoot into the brush. The three Jeds remained motionless all afternoon, only moving onto their sides when necessary to relieve themselves.

One group of perhaps a dozen soldiers came strolling down the trail and stopped right next to the gorse. Only a few feet separated the Jeds from the men in the hobnailed boots. By this time, the Jeds had agreed that they would not be taken alive. Their weapons were charged and ready, and if they were discovered they would come out shooting and make a break for it, knowing that they would probably be cut down before getting far. Lying on the ground under the gorse, First Sergeant Kehoe kept his .45-caliber pistol held at arm's length, aimed toward the trail a few feet away. Curiously, he noticed that his hands, which moments before had been trembling uncontrollably, were now still.

The enemy soldiers were carrying on a lively conversation and the Jeds feared that if the talking stopped the Germans might hear them breathing. None knew enough German to understand what the conversation was about. After a while the soldiers left, firing a few random shots as they continued down the trail.

When dusk came, the Jeds sensed that the immediate danger was passing. Gunfire had become intermittent and it eventually stopped altogether. The men crawled backward out of their hiding place and looked around. They saw no Germans, but they did spot a farm boy tending to some cows. The men questioned the boy and learned that the Germans had been patrolling nearby all day but had left shortly before dusk, apparently not wanting to remain in the area after dark.

Wise, Aguirec, and Kehoe moved out to the east, keeping under the cover of the woods as much as possible, and crossed the road which ran into Canihuel. It had been down this road that the German troops had come. Darkness had settled in by the time the men reached a farm owned by a resistance sympathizer. The farmer fed the men, and the team then continued on for a few miles before finding a spot in a wooded area where they might get some sleep.

In the days to follow, word passed quickly throughout the resistance to avoid the small cottage which had been team Frederick's command post. The Jeds heard that people in the area feared reprisals from the Germans if they made any contact with the Jeds or with the maquis. They also learned that several members of nearby maquis groups had been killed during the attack or as a result of the subsequent searches. Most of the maquisards, however, had been able to melt away into the surrounding forests and farms.

The Jeds had learned a hard lesson about the risks involved in operating from a farmhouse, abandoned or otherwise. From here on, the men decided, they would stick to the woods and the fields and ditches of the countryside, avoiding villages and hard-surfaced roads. And, for the time being, they would have to be extra careful. The Gestapo by now had learned much about team Frederick's operations and would be redoubling efforts to track the men down.

Sergeant Kehoe even thought that the team should change into civilian clothes. One reason the Jedburghs operated in uniform was to be accepted by the resistance as representatives of Eisenhower's command. That, Kehoe felt, had already been accomplished. The Gestapo probably had descriptions of the three men and was hunting them—their uniforms only made them easier to spot. But the Jeds remained in uniform, and in the days that followed, the team would, from time to time, encounter a German patrol and come under fire. The Germans would always break contact, however, as soon as the Jeds retreated into the woods. That was where they were safest.

Reestablishing radio communication with London was Major Wise's first concern. With the loss of the radio, the Jeds, for the time being, would have to relay messages through another team's radio operator. They had been able to get word of their situation to Jedburgh team Giles in the Finistère almost immediately, for Giles reported the attack and the loss of Frederick's radio to Special Force Headquarters on July 18. Thus alerted, SFHQ avoided using any drop zones already identified by team Frederick, because the Germans undoubtedly now were aware of them.

On the nineteenth, Jedburgh team Felix, located about forty miles east of Canihuel, also reported team Frederick's situation to London and asked that a new radio for Frederick be dropped as soon as possible to one of team Felix's drop zones. SFHQ complied, but when the new radio was dropped a couple of nights later, its parachute failed to open and the package crashed to the ground, destroying its contents.[9]

Another set was dropped and this time the precious cargo survived. For delivery to team Frederick, the radio set was broken down into three parts, each to be carried by a separate bicycle courier. Carrying such cargo was highly risky for the couriers; discovery of the radio parts at a German checkpoint would almost certainly result in death for the carrier. All went well, though, and less than ten days after abandoning their Canihuel command post, the Jeds had their new radio and were back in business.

They quickly went about rebuilding their network of contacts. Marceau soon rejoined them, arriving on bicycle one day after passing through a German checkpoint on the main road and sweating out a close inspection of his false papers. The schoolteacher couriers courageously continued to deliver food to the men, and someone provided small pieces of canvas that the men could use as makeshift tents under the thick cover of gorse the Jeds had found and were using as their base.

Once again, the Jeds had been lucky. It had been a close call, but they had kept their wits about them and they had survived. Life in the brush, with the damp nights and the occasional rain, was not comfortable, but the men were still alive. Because of this their morale remained high. Bob Kehoe couldn't help but think, "We beat them again."[10]

By late July, the Jeds were on the move once again, first to a spot about six miles to the north, then on to another area even farther north. Near this site they were pleased to find a maquis force of three well-disciplined guerrilla units, which the Jeds inspected on Sunday, July 30. The maquisards were all in uniform, looked sharp, and were armed. They also had been active enough in the area to become targeted by the Germans. Commanding the best of them was Sergeant Kehoe's comrade Robert, the French SAS sergeant who had saved the wounded SAS men after the raid on the Forêt de Duault, and who later had helped Kehoe recover the Jeds' radio. But Robert was now a lieutenant.

Early Monday morning, while most of the partisans were engaged in physical training, a German force numbering several hundred attacked the maquis camp. At first, only the gate sentry, armed with a Bren light machine gun, was able to put up a fight, and he killed thirty Germans before they could dismount from their trucks. Although the sentry was killed shortly thereafter, the rest of the maquis rallied and put up a stiff fight. Major Wise estimated that German casualties (killed and wounded) numbered about five hundred, while twenty-seven patriots had been killed. Wise also learned that the Germans had paid dearly for attacking another maquis camp farther to the east just two days earlier. That assault had kicked off a fifteen-hour firefight which resulted in a withdrawal by the Germans—after suffering high losses. Only two maquisards were reported killed in that engagement.

But the Germans were not finished yet; that afternoon, they attacked team Frederick's camp. Once again, the Jeds gathered up their gear and got away in the nick of time. When the men thought that they'd moved far enough away so as to be out of immediate danger they established a new camp, well concealed in a gorse thicket on top of a hill. Once again, the Jeds had avoided capture or worse. Major Wise and his teammates had not only been sticking to the woods and the gorse but also had limited the size of their immediate group to include just the Jeds and a few others. The men could only hope that the increased efforts of the Germans to hunt them down were not the result of betrayal by an informant.

The large-scale raids such as those that team Frederick had survived through June and July, however, were not likely to continue—for the Germans had a greater threat to confront. The Allied ground forces in Normandy had been continually building up since the first landings on June 6 and, by the middle of July, the force in the lodgment area had grown to thirty divisions, seven of those armored. The Germans had feared that Eisenhower's forces would soon be strong enough to break out, and that time had come. Although the Jedburghs in Brittany did not know it, help was on the way.

6

THE MAQUIS DE SAFFRÉ

IKE Jedburgh team Frederick in the north, team George, operating from the Dingson SAS base in southern Brittany, would experience a harrowing survival ordeal in the weeks to come. But the team's immediate difficulty upon landing was in communicating with London.

Part of team George's problem was the result of damage their radios had received on the parachute jump. To make matters worse, the Germans were jamming the team's assigned frequency and the Jeds had been unsuccessful in getting London to assign them an alternate. As a result, team George was forced to use a frequency that was reserved for emergency use by all Jed teams. Team George also faced an increasing threat from German radio-locating cars.

After four years of tracking down underground intelligence and sabotage agents, the Germans had become skilled at locating clandestine radio transmitters. Intercept stations, usually located in the larger cities, would pick up a signal originating from within occupied territory and would take bearings on the direction of the source. The intersection of bearings taken from two or more intercept stations identified the general area from which a radio was transmitting. Radio direction-finding cars, stationed throughout the country, were then quickly dispatched to the area. Such cars or vans were equipped with circular, rotating antennae mounted on top, and they would circle the area until they had determined the site of the transmitter. The work of these radio direction-finders was not a problem easily overcome, and it was one which endangered not only Jed team George, but the Dingson SAS base as well.

The early success enjoyed by the Dingson base near the commune of St-Marcel in southern Brittany was due to the energetic and efficient men of the 4th (French) SAS Battalion. Their commander, Pierre-Louis Bourgoin, perhaps by then a lieutenant colonel, had jumped in to take control by the middle of June.[1] Under his aggressive and capable leadership, the battalion's railroad sabotage campaign had virtually shut down all rail traffic between Brittany and Normandy. German units were forced to use road transport as they tried to reach the Normandy battlefield. Scarce gasoline supplies were further depleted as a result, and many units had to resort to horse-drawn vehicles and foot movement. This also slowed the Germans' progress and increased their vulnerability to ambush by the maquis and to merciless strafing and bombing by Allied planes. By June 15, the only functioning rail line in Brittany was a single north-south track running between Rennes and Nantes, on the Loire River to the south—and the SAS planned to attack it that night.[2]

The French SAS operating out of the Dingson base had been tremendously successful in arranging airdrops of arms for the resistance. Five thousand patriots had been armed and newly arrived weapons for another five thousand were stockpiled at the camp, awaiting distribution. The coordination of so many drops, however, meant many radio transmissions and a huge amount of air time. Radio locating cars were often seen within a mile of the farm called La Nouée; and often, when Lieutenant Lejeune, the radio operator on Jedburgh team George, tried to send a message, the cars would arrive in the area within ten minutes.[3]

Radio traffic wasn't the only threat to the Dingson base, though. Flagrant disregard for security had reached the point that members of the St-Marcel maquis, after meetings at their headquarters in the barn at the Pondard farm, had been seen walking back to their homes in Malestroit (a mile and a half to the east) with their

weapons in full view. German police had many sources for information. Everyone in small St-Marcel and in nearby Malestroit
knew about the maquis and the camp at La Nouée, and too many
people had been talking. There also had been some recent arrests.
On June 17, team George radioed London with news that the Germans had captured a French parachutist and taken him away in
handcuffs.[4] Would the Germans get any information out of him?

Bourgoin's SAS base had been successful, but that success came
at a price and the bill was coming due.

Aside from the radio problem, Jed team George soon began to feel
like a fifth wheel at La Nouée, suspecting that they might be more
useful elsewhere. They had heard from a resistance leader familiar
with the region that maquis groups in the department of Loire-
Inférieure, just to the southeast, were badly in need of help.
According to him, the maquis of the Loire-Inférieure were the
worst in the region in terms of organization, training, and leadership; and arms were in very short supply. The resistance leader was
especially familiar with a large group near the village of Saffré.

So Captains Cyr and Erard of team George met with Colonel
Bourgoin and resistance leaders and proposed that their Jedburgh
team, because it did not appear to be needed at the SAS base, move
to the Loire-Inférieure and see what it could do to help the situation there. Bourgoin approved and the Jeds made preparations for
the move. They planned to depart the following morning, Sunday,
June 18, in civilian clothes.

At about eight-thirty the next morning, the men were awakened
by an explosion. Then they heard machine gun and rifle fire, and
realized that the base was under attack. They scrambled to burn
sensitive papers, and hid their radios and code books. Plans for a
rendezvous point, in case the men became separated, were quickly
made. But then the shooting stopped, almost as suddenly as it had
begun.

As they learned later, two carloads of German feldgendarmes
(military police) had come down the narrow road toward the farm
that morning, stopping from time to time as if searching for something. When the cars reached the point where the SAS had posted

sentries a maquisard had fired a Piat anti-tank weapon at the lead car. It was a direct hit and the car had blown up, killing everyone inside. The sentries had then fired up the second car with a machine gun and put another Piat round into the engine of that car. When the shooting stopped they found three Germans unconscious and one badly wounded in the second car. One German had gotten away.

The SAS had brought the Germans who had been knocked unconscious back to the command post for questioning once they came around. The wounded German had been taken to a farm building where a maquis doctor treated him.

As soon as the prisoners regained consciousness they were interrogated. A large airdrop, some thirty planes in all, had been received at the farm the previous night, and one of the prisoners told the SAS that they had been sent out to investigate.

About an hour later, a force of at least a hundred Germans approached the camp behind a screen of about two dozen civilians from nearby St-Marcel. The civilians had been rounded up at random and forced to walk in front of the Germans. The enemy came quite close to the camp before being spotted; and then a fierce firefight erupted, and the civilians scattered. SAS machine guns ripped into the Germans, who quickly fell back to the outskirts of St-Marcel. More wounded, including Germans, were brought in for the maquis doctor and nurses to treat.[5]

Then German machine guns opened up with tracer rounds that ignited a fire in the woods next to the SAS camp. Thick smoke began rolling across the camp, making it difficult for the SAS and maquis to see their targets and, at the same time, masking the movement of the Germans. Four jeeps with mounted light machine guns had arrived for the SAS in the previous night's parachute drop, and they were now put into action. When the Germans saw these vehicles they were convinced that an Allied airborne division had landed—which is what they told their higher headquarters.

As a result, in the early afternoon German paratroopers arrived and launched an all-out assault on the camp—the SAS had a whole new fight on their hands. Making skilled use of machine guns and mortars, the enemy paratroopers advanced steadily on the camp—

even though they were taking heavy losses. German snipers, too, were taking their toll on the maquis and SAS defending the camp, who numbered between six hundred and a thousand.

Meanwhile, the Pondard sisters bravely remained at work in the farmhouse kitchen, preparing sandwiches for the men fighting outside. During the first lull in the battle, however, Bourgoin made sure that they were evacuated to another farm.

The only reason the SAS stubbornly fought to hold the farm was to avoid losing the five thousand weapons stockpiled there. The SAS shot off a radio message to London requesting air support, and by late afternoon a squadron of American P-47 Thunderbolts arrived overhead. The planes stayed as long as their fuel allowed, strafing and bombing those troops that could be identified positively as German.

Bourgoin and his officers had done a masterful job of leading the men in the defense of the farm, but the colonel realized that they could not hold out much longer. Many of the SAS men had been killed or wounded. Germans had approached to within five hundred yards of the camp on three sides by eight that evening. The camp was not quite surrounded; an opening remained to the northwest, through the drop zone. Bourgoin decided they would have to make a break for it. The remaining men were organized for the attempt, and Captain Erard and Captain Cyr were each assigned a company of maquisards to lead.

First, at nine that evening, Bourgoin ordered a counterattack which drove the Germans back about a thousand yards. But the fighting was fierce, and Cyr lost eighty-five of the two hundred men in his company. Bourgoin decided they would wait for dark and attempt to move through the German lines in small groups, and he gave leaders the location of a rendezvous point about fifteen miles away. Explosives were set to blow up the stockpile of arms and ammunition at the camp and men began to form into small teams. The Jeds of team George found each other and were determined to break out as a group.

Once darkness came, the Jeds carefully crept through the German perimeter and headed toward the established rendezvous point. Rifles and automatic weapons bickered with one another in every direction through most of the night. Sometimes the firing was very heavy, other times sporadic. The Jeds were slowed some-what by the weight of their rucksacks and radios. At times they had to lie still in tall grass next to a road while small German patrols—and even battalion-sized formations of enemy paratroop-ers—marched by not more than five yards from them. Late that night they lay down to sleep in the middle of a wheat field, only to awaken in the morning to the sound of German-uniformed Rus-sians on horseback searching for them. Eventually they made it to the rendezvous point.

The Jeds learned that Bourgoin had decided to move farther west and establish a new camp. Those maquis fighters who had been able to get away from the farm were scattered through the sur-rounding forests. Jedburgh team George was to continue on to the Loire-Inférieure accompanied by two resistance leaders. Working under the code names Hauteur and Fonction, these men were oper-ating jointly as General de Gaulle's military delegates for the Brit-tany region.[6] The group set out on foot with a long journey ahead of it.

André Hue, the SOE man at La Nouée, would later learn that the Germans had had two spies among the maquis at the farm. He also learned that the attack on the farm had been made by several para-chute and infantry battalions—in all, it had been a force estimated at four thousand to five thousand men. Nearly six hundred Ger-mans had been killed, as were some fifty SAS and as many as two hundred maquisards. The Pondard family and the wounded had been safely hidden at other farms.

In retaliation, and in an attempt to find members of the maquis or the SAS, Germans had questioned and beaten many people in the surrounding area, and had burned several farms and buildings in St-Marcel.[7]

Jedburgh team George, along with traveling companions Hauteur and Fonction, arrived at their destination in the Loire-Inférieure department at two o'clock on the afternoon of June 27, nine days after the attack on the Dingson SAS base. The men were now about a hundred and fifty miles southeast of team Frederick and about the same distance straight south of the nearest Allied ground forces back at the Normandy beachhead.

For the final leg of their journey through the undulating pastoral countryside of eastern Brittany, the men were able to ride in the back of a French farmer's pickup truck. But they had to share the space with a couple of hogs, and the driver covered the back of the truck with a tarp to conceal his cargo. Twice along the way the driver was stopped by Germans who wanted to see his papers. When the soldiers asked the driver what he was hauling the Frenchman lifted a corner of the tarp on the back of the truck just enough to reveal the pigs, and the Germans had opted not to make a more thorough search.

There were other close calls along the way, too, and the small group had narrowly avoided capture. One farm where the men had briefly taken shelter had been raided by the Germans shortly after the team got out, having been tipped off that danger was on the way. The farmer who had sheltered them was reportedly tortured and then killed by having his head pulled off, and his wife and children were then bayoneted to death. On another occasion, the team's guide found himself needing directions in an unfamiliar area. Although it was three in the morning and well past the ten o'clock curfew for civilians, the guide decided to wake the occupants of a house. When a German officer answered, the men had to run for it.

Lying at the mouth of the Loire River on France's Atlantic coast, the Loire-Inférieure department encompassed the port city of St-Nazaire, one of the ports the Allies hoped to capture and use. (Today the department is called the Loire-Atlantique.) The maquis group to which Hauteur took Jedburgh team George was located on a farm about forty miles northeast of St-Nazaire, north of the river town of Nantes. The group called itself the Maquis de Saffré, after the nearby village bearing the same name.

Right from the start, the Jeds could see that there was much work to be done. Of the two hundred or so men in the maquis, only about twenty-five were armed, and many of them carried .22-

caliber rifles and old shotguns. Some, though, had Stens which they had gotten from one of the drops at the Dingson SAS base. The Jeds learned that there were at least two thousand partisans scattered throughout the area who were awaiting weapons, so the first priority was to get arms sent from England. To their credit, the men of the Maquis de Saffré were enthusiastic, and the camp was thrilled at the arrival of the Jeds (who had changed back into uniform). What the Jeds didn't know was that a Gestapo agent lurked among the elated maquisards.

At supper that evening, plans were made to disperse the men in the morning for the sake of security. Later that night, the man who was secretly working for the Gestapo left camp with information to share about the important new arrivals. Because of him, the Germans had known about the maquis camp for some time. But they had not considered the group a threat and had decided just to keep an eye on it. The arrival of the Jedburghs and the two resistance leaders changed all that. The Gestapo was fully aware of the intent of these men—to arm and train the maquis—and they did not intend to let that happen.

At six in the morning the Jeds awoke to news that German trucks had been spotted closing in on the camp from all directions. Lieutenant Lejeune, team George's radio operator, was three hundred yards away in the middle of receiving a message from London. By the time he got his radio broken down and packed up, German troops were within a hundred yards of him.

The attack came suddenly, and German bullets tore into the camp before any kind of defense could be organized. The untrained maquis recruits had no idea what they should do. Automatic weapons fire raked the camp, and men were hit; some were killed. Hauteur and Fonction coolly gave orders for establishing a hasty defense, but it quickly became obvious that this would soon turn into something like a seal clubbing if they didn't make a break for it. Again, small groups were formed for a breakout. The Jeds took a group of forty to fifty men, along with the farmer and his family, and ran for a position just outside the farm. A maquisard with an automatic rifle was shot dead and Captain Cyr grabbed his weapon. Just as the men reached the position some German trucks pulled up, not more than fifteen yards away, and Cyr and the others emptied their magazines into the trucks before the enemy troops could dismount. They continued on but soon met a maquisard coming from the opposite direction who told Cyr that the group was heading toward some Germans that were approaching the farm.

Cyr's group needed to move fast. While the man they had just met fired at the approaching Germans to keep them at bay, Cyr and the others took off. But they were slowed by the farmer's wife, who could not keep up. So they hid her in a thicket and hurried on.

Suddenly, a German machine gun opened up on them, killing three or four of the men in Cyr's group. The rest took cover in some brush, and the leaders quickly gathered and decided that they should break up into even smaller units of no more than two or three people each. Among the group were five pilots, three Americans and two Brits, who had been shot down over France and had been under the care of the maquis. Before they split up, the pilots and the Jeds quickly exchanged names and addresses so that anyone who made it out could provide information about what had happened to the others.

The Jeds took off to the east. They didn't get more than twenty-five yards when the German machine gun opened up again, but it apparently was firing at the group of pilots, who had gone in a different direction. The Jeds stopped and threw a grenade in the direction of the machine gun and then ducked into some bushes. German soldiers were shouting to each other all around them. Hauteur was still with the Jeds, but Fonction had become separated from the group and was nowhere to be seen.

An odd sort of standoff began. There were others besides the Jeds and Hauteur hidden in the stand of thick brush, which extended over a wide area. The Germans knew they were in there somewhere; they just didn't know exactly where. For the next seventeen hours the men remained as still as they could. The bushes were about five feet tall, and German soldiers climbed trees in an attempt to spot the hidden men. And from time to time they threw hand grenades into the brush at randomly chosen locations. Dogs were even brought in to help pinpoint the hidden maquisards, but they proved useless because too many people had been moving about the area.

Hours seemed like days as the men lay motionless, wondering

how they would get out of the fix they were in. At times, softly and among themselves, the Jeds and the unflappable Hauteur even laughed at their predicament.

After dark, the four men decided it was time to get out. Not far away they found two of the pilots hiding in the brush. The Jeds told the airmen that they were going to attempt to sneak out and head east, and that the pilots should follow in an hour's time if they didn't hear any shots fired. Before leaving, and just in case they were unable to link up with them again, the Jeds gave the pilots eight thousand francs.

Shortly before midnight, the Jeds moved out, slowly and quietly. The only German they saw was a sentry on a road, and they were able to sneak past him. Soon they approached a farm, but when a dog began barking someone blindly fired shots in their general direction, so the men skirted the farm and ran across a field and into some woods. Then they came to another road guarded by another sentry. As the German paced back and forth the small group made it across the road, one man at a time.

Another five hundred yards into the woods they were suddenly startled by the sound of people jumping through some brush nearby. Assuming them to be a German patrol, the Jeds pulled out hand grenades and got ready to use them. But just then they heard members of the group speaking to one another in French. The Jeds whispered to them in French to get their attention, and when the two groups met the Jeds were happily surprised to find Fonction among the others. After spending the remainder of the night in the woods, the men continued walking until they felt they were well away from the area where the Germans continued to search.

Lejeune had gotten a message off to London on the day the Jeds had arrived at the camp of the Maquis de Saffré. The message had reported the team's arrival and expressed the urgent need for arms: "BEGIN TOMORROW 28 DROPPING FOR 2,000 IN SLICES OF 500. RECEPTION COMMITTEE STANDING BY EVERY NIGHT FROM 28TH."[8] It was three days before Lejeune could get off another message informing SFHQ of the attack on the morning of the twenty-eighth and advising that all air operations be suspended. In the meantime, on the night of June 29, four aircraft dropped forty-three containers and eight packages to a field near the abandoned Saffré camp.[9]

In a later message, Lieutenant Lejeune was able to give London an update: "SITUATION LOIRE INFERIEURE BOILING. PATRIOT IS ENEMY AGENT. ALL LOST EXCEPT LIFE AND SET. HUNTED BY GESTAPO. DESPITE STORM ATTEMPTED UNSUCCESSFULLY TO CONTACT YOU. EVERYTHING HAS TO BE DONE AGAIN. REMAINING AND DOING OUR BEST."[10]

Jedburgh team George moved about the area, staying briefly in a small town on the north bank of the Loire River, and then spent a few days in a large château as guests of the count and countess of Landemont, who were supporters of the resistance. The count set up quarters for the men in the library and, for the first time since their arrival in France, the Jeds slept in beds. But they had to be quiet and remain out of sight, because the château also housed many children who had been evacuated from Nantes.

Within a few days, however, the count received a phone call from the Germans, informing him that they were coming to inspect the house with an eye toward occupying it. The Jeds and the resistance leaders (Hauteur and Fonction) were forced to leave the château and hide in a wooded area nearby. When it was safe to move they continued to search for a place to set up camp and begin rounding up the scattered maquisards.

Hauteur and Fonction had been trying to persuade Captain Erard to accept the position of délégué militaire, or military representative for de Gaulle's provisional French government, for the Loire-Inférieure department. Erard had demurred because he felt that, by accepting the position, he would be unjustly expanding the mission of the Jedburgh team. But Hauteur and Fonction argued that there was no one else in the department qualified to fill the role, and so, after a meeting on the night of July 4, Erard agreed.

Hauteur and Fonction left the following morning, confident that they had found someone capable of organizing the resistance in the Loire-Inférieure. Resistance in the department had struggled to organize itself from the very beginning, with seemingly every group of patriots riddled with traitors and informers. Every new leader who appeared capable of creating a viable resistance in the department soon found himself in the hands of the Gestapo in their torture cells in Nantes. Periodic waves of arrests had stifled any further development and even the Jeds, as newcomers, were viewed with suspicion by some. Terror and deception and distrust and fear of one's own neighbor had become the dominating features of life in the Loire-Inférieure. Much work lay ahead of team George if the men were to turn all that around.

The Jeds at once drew up a plan and began work. Probably the most difficult step, but one which had to be taken first, was to identify leaders. Nearly every potential leader they talked to implicated the others as traitors. But, eventually, the right men were found and work proceeded. All leaders had to agree to put political differences aside and commit to the common task of ridding the area of Germans, and agree that all operations were to be conducted in accordance with orders issued by the Allied high command.

Maquis battalions were to be formed, each with its own dropping ground for the delivery of arms. A disciplined system of recruitment was established with security overriding all other concerns—every person recruited was to be vetted by at least two trusted maquisards before being accepted. Instructors were trained and set up to rotate from battalion to battalion to train recruits, and a roving reception committee cadre would likewise help prepare for parachute drops.

Strict adherence to the plan was demanded of all. Maquis groups that failed to comply with orders would receive no pay, no arms, no ammunition, and no supplies. Leaders who were found to be working for the Germans or for individual gain would be dealt with harshly—killed, if necessary.

Shelter for team George continued to be a problem, and the men moved frequently from one safe house to the next. Then a place was found for them, an unoccupied two-room house in a dusty, deadpan one-story village about five miles north of the Loire. The men remained there for eight days. But after a few close calls, including a Gestapo car parking just outside the front door on one occasion, the Jeds packed up and moved on. After hiding out in a ruined chapel for a couple of days, the men were taken by a member of the resistance to another abandoned house. This house was near a village on the north bank of the Loire River, about thirty miles northeast of Nantes. Jed team George rented the house and began to set up a command post.

General Eisenhower got the time that he'd said was needed to prepare for a breakout from the lodgment area in Normandy. The Transportation Plan had been brilliantly executed by the air force; key bridges and some major rail centers had been destroyed. And the French resistance fighters, aided by ever increasing numbers of Jedburghs and other special forces, had done much damage and continued to do more. By the end of June, they had made nearly five hundred more railway cuts, ambushed untold numbers of German convoys, and rendered the enemy's telecommunications almost completely ineffective.[11]

The combined efforts of the air forces and the resistance had succeeded in delaying the movement of several German divisions to Normandy. Eisenhower would later be able to report to the Combined Chiefs of Staff that the enemy had committed some of its nearest divisions—four panzer and six infantry—by June 19, but that "it was not until the beginning of July, when the scale of the Allied effort was no longer in any doubt, that reinforcements began to arrive from more distant locations."[12]

Later estimates would conclude that the actions of the FFI resulted in an average delay of two days for all German units moving toward Normandy, although some units fared much worse. One of the first units ordered to Normandy in response to the landings was the 2nd "Das Reich" SS Panzer Division, which at the time was near Toulouse in southern France. Expected to arrive at the invasion area by June 9, it was two weeks after that date before the demoralized remnants of the division staggered into Normandy.[13] The 1st SS Panzer Division had taken seven days to travel one hundred and eighty-six miles by rail from Louvain, Belgium, to Paris— normally a one-day journey. Even then, the division was still ninety miles from the fighting, and it had to make the remainder of the journey by road.[14] After reaching the Rhine from the Eastern Front in one week, the 11th Panzer Division had needed another three weeks to reach Caen.[15] And it had taken the 276th Infantry Division nineteen days to get from Nice to Normandy.[16]

Two panzer divisions of the II SS Panzer Corps had been sent by rail to Normandy on June 12, each division requiring more than one hundred trains for the movement. Attacks by the resistance had caused their trip to take five days rather than the planned two and a half. And in the end, damaged locomotives and railways had forced the divisions' tracked vehicles to drive under their own power for the final leg of the journey, nearly two hundred punishing miles which reduced vehicle service life by half at a critical time.[17]

Even units much closer to Normandy had found just getting there to be difficult. Germany's 275th Division had been less than a hundred and thirty miles southwest of the battlefield, in Redon, when it was ordered to Normandy. Six rail cuts, a number of maquis ambushes, and strikes by the air force combined to delay the division's arrival at St-Lô until June 11.[18]

All of this bought precious time for the Allies at a stage in the operation when thousands of troops and tons of material were being brought ashore every twenty-four hours. In addition to the delays in troop movements, the enemy's ability to resupply its divisions fighting in Normandy was devastated by the destruction of the transportation network—and maquis and air force attacks on fuel and ammunition supply dumps only compounded the problem.

But just as important were the FFI's attacks on German communications. By destroying landline communications facilities—telephone exchanges, switchboards, junction boxes—and cutting telephone lines and underground cables, the maquis forced the Germans to make greater use of radio, which was much easier for the Allies to intercept. And Allied success in breaking the German Enigma code made such interceptions invaluable in learning of enemy movements and intentions.

Eisenhower took action to reinforce success. On June 15 he wrote to General Sir Henry Maitland Wilson, the British supreme commander of the Mediterranean Theater, and informed him that he was ordering significant increases in air-dropped supplies to the resistance, "which at the moment is giving unexpected results."

Eisenhower's plans included massive daylight supply drops by Eighth Air Force bombers as far into France as they could reach. He asked Wilson if he could do likewise in southern France. Wilson responded two days later that he was "delighted by Eisenhower's proposal" and that he had already made preparations for such drops into the Rhône Valley of southern France.[19] On June 25, 180 bombers dropped 300 tons of supplies to the resistance in four locations, and another major drop would come on July 14, Bastille Day.[20]

The resistance and the special forces had done their parts in helping Eisenhower build up an Allied force on the Continent, and the time had come for that force to go on the offensive.

7

BRITTANY LIBERATED

BRITTANY was all about the ports. Normandy had attracted Overlord planners as an invasion site for a number of reasons, not the least of them its proximity to the port at Cherbourg and those on the Brittany peninsula—mainly Brest, Lorient and nearby Quiberon Bay, and St-Nazaire. Although the Allies planned to rely heavily on an artificial harbor called Mulberry in the initial stage of the invasion, fixed ports soon would be needed for supplying the growing armies in France. They would also be needed for unloading troops that would be arriving from the United States at the rate of three to five divisions per month.

Opening the ports of Brittany, it was hoped, could be accomplished before rough weather had a chance to knock out the temporary facilities at the Normandy beaches. Plans, therefore, called for the rapid capture of Brest, Lorient, Quiberon Bay, and St-Nazaire. To help Allied ground forces rapidly reach these objectives, Supreme Headquarters Allied Expeditionary Force (SHAEF) intended to develop a resistance force of more than thirty thousand armed men throughout Brittany by August 1.[1]

In the six weeks since D-Day, fifteen U.S. divisions and fifteen British and Canadian divisions had come ashore in Normandy. On July 18, U.S. forces captured the key crossroads town of St-Lô in

Normandy, allowing final preparations for a breakout from the lodgment area west of that town. Facing the Americans in the immediate area were twenty-seven German divisions. But, of the 540,000 men that the enemy had committed to the Normandy battle, at least 160,000 already had been lost, along with 30 percent of the 1200 German tanks which had taken part in the fighting.[2] And, thanks to the air force and the French resistance, the Germans were not receiving sufficient reinforcements. Following a heavy air bombardment of enemy positions on the morning of July 25, the First U.S. Army launched operation Cobra with an attack from the Allies' extreme right flank. By the thirtieth, American forces had reached Avranches, near the base of the Brittany peninsula.

On the first day of August, General Eisenhower launched the newly operational Third U.S. Army, commanded by Lieutenant General George S. Patton, Jr., to force the breakout from the Allied lines at Avranches and drive south and west into Brittany. This gave the Americans two armies in the field—the First and the Third. On that same day, Twelfth Army Group headquarters was activated under the command of Lieutenant General Omar N. Bradley to direct the operations of the two armies. Bradley turned over command of his First Army to Lieutenant General Courtney H. Hodges.

After clearing Avranches, Third Army forces were to enter the northeast corner of the Brittany peninsula. From there, Patton planned to have an armored division strike out for Brest, one hundred and fifty miles to the west. He would send another armored division straight south to isolate the peninsula and capture ports on the south coast.

As an added measure, Third Army was given power to direct the activity of resistance forces throughout Brittany.[3] In exercising this authority General Patton set a precedent which would later be followed by other army commanders. According to early SHAEF plans, when Allied ground forces overran FFI elements the guerrillas were to be relieved of their arms and their mission was to be considered as ended. Patton, however, soon ordered that some of the maquis be allowed to keep their arms and remain with the advancing Allied forces, fighting alongside while serving as guides and carrying out reconnaissance patrols. Others would remain armed to continue mopping up by-passed German pockets and to guard roads, bridges, pipelines, and supply dumps.[4]

With the breakout about to begin, Special Force Headquarters radioed new orders to the field, alerting all Jedburghs and other special forces in Brittany that Allied ground forces would soon be approaching their region. It was imperative, the message said, that everything be done to help speed the advance of the ground troops. Jedburgh teams throughout Brittany should take action to prevent the demolition of bridges and installations by the Germans. Team Frederick was assigned responsibility for the main east-west highway which ran along the north coast of Brittany. They were specifically responsible for the central portion of that highway, a stretch running westward from Lamballe through St-Brieuc and Guingamp and on to Morlaix, although the brief message from London did not explain to the Jeds the importance of the road to the Allies.[5]

Route Nationale 12 was the main highway connecting the port city of Brest, at the western tip of Brittany, with Rennes, the Breton capital located at the base of the peninsula, some one hundred and fifty miles to the east. Running parallel to the highway—sometimes north of the road, sometimes south of it—ran the main rail line inland from Brest, a double-track railway extending all the way to Paris. General Patton's staff realized that, if the Allies ever hoped to supply their armies in France from the port at Brest, this rail line would be needed to rapidly move cargo inland.

Patton's chief of staff, Major General Hugh Gaffey, directed his special forces advisor to coordinate with Special Force Headquarters for the FFI to protect the rail line from demolition by the Germans.[6] Special Force Headquarters sent messages to Jedburgh teams in Brittany to arrange this. Cuts which the FFI had made in the railway to impede the movement of German reinforcements to Normandy could easily be repaired by Allied engineers. Some large railway bridges along the route, however, if destroyed by the Germans could not be repaired so easily or quickly. Some of the largest were at St-Brieuc, Guingamp, and Morlaix. The Germans had to be prevented from destroying these bridges, and the immediate task of protecting them and the highway which provided rapid access to them went to Jedburgh team Frederick and the FFI. Their job was to guard the bridges and hold the road until American forces arrived.

The job of capturing the bridges went to Task Force A, a Third Army provisional unit made up of armored cavalry, tank destroyers, and combat engineers. This unit was to race westward on the highway which team Frederick would be protecting and, if all went well, seize the railway bridges intact. Leading the task force was Brigadier General Herbert L. Earnest, commander of a tank destroyer brigade. Earnest planned to move fast, bypassing any pockets of German resistance and securing the railroad bridges as quickly as possible.[7]

To support team Frederick, the FFI called two thousand armed patriots into action to guard the road, and the Jeds increased the number of airdrops to be able to arm the expanding guerrilla force.

Patton wasted no time. He launched a corps with two armored divisions south from Avranches on Tuesday, August 1, and by evening the 6th Armored Division had turned west and had taken the first town on the road toward Brest. Next day, the division tore off in two columns through the center of the peninsula, straight for Brest, without accompanying infantry support. Plans had called for an infantry division to follow each of the armored divisions, but the infantry which was to follow the 6th Armored Division had been committed to defending the Avranches area. Villagers waved as their liberators passed through in a cloud of dust. No forces were left to even guard rear areas and supply routes. Whenever the division ran into German resistance, it relied on the local FFI for infantry support, and when it moved on the FFI guarded the roads and bridges and ensured that supply lines remained open.[8]

By this time, eleven Jedburgh teams were active throughout Brittany and three more would arrive by week's end. As the 6th Armored Division closed in on Brest, Jed teams in western Brittany linked up with forward elements, attaching themselves to the headquarters of American combat units. They provided up-to-date information on the enemy situation, organized FFI support to the armored units, and served as guides and interpreters. By the end of the first week in August, Third Army was even supplying jeeps to some Jedburghs and FFI chiefs.

*   *   *

Meanwhile, tanks of the 4th Armored Division struck out from Avranches on Tuesday and, by evening, had reached the outskirts of the Breton capital of Rennes, a city of about a hundred thousand some fifty miles to the south. But the division ran into strong German resistance at Rennes, and the division commander decided to bypass the city the next day and continue on southward, leaving the follow-on 8th Infantry Division to clean the Germans out of Rennes. Late that night, a series of explosions shook the area. Colonel Bruce Clarke, commander of one of 4th Armored's combat commands, called around on the radio to determine the source of the mysterious explosions. He eventually learned that the midnight eruptions had resulted from the FFI blowing up an enormous German ammunition dump. After skirting around Rennes to the west, the division continued its dash toward Brittany's south coast.

By the time the 4th Armored Division reached Vannes, on Brittany's south coast, the American tankers were working hand in hand with the FFI. One division officer, who characterized the maquis as "bloodthirsty," later recalled having as many as two hundred of the FFI fighters riding on his tanks.[9] The division captured the town of Vannes on Brittany's south coast on August 5; and six thousand maquisards helped by taking the high ground north of the town, a mission which again had been assigned to the FFI by Patton's chief of staff, General Gaffey. This attack by the FFI, judged one Third Army historian, prevented the Germans from making a fortress stand in the Quiberon Bay area as they would do at Brittany's other ports.[10]

On Sunday night, August 6, an armored cavalry patrol from General Ernest's Task Force A entered Lamballe. When no Germans were met, the patrol continued west on Route Nationale 12 until it reached St-Brieuc. There, the soldiers found all three railroad bridges in the town safely in the hands of the FFI. When the main body of the American task force arrived, an engineer company was assigned to help guard the St-Brieuc bridges while the rest of the task force moved on.

On Monday the task force approached Guingamp, where the Ger-

mans had a large supply base. After fighting through some weak
roadblocks, the Americans pushed into the town and, with supporting attacks conducted by the FFI, captured it by midnight.
About four hundred German prisoners were bagged in the process.

General Earnest then dispatched a small force to race ahead to
Morlaix, where the largest railroad bridge in all of France stood. A
thousand feet in length, the monumental granite structure
spanned the Dossen valley, a deep ravine at the head of an estuary. Built eighty-three years earlier to support the Paris-Brest railway, the massive two-story viaduct (the lower level a pedestrian
bridge) featured more than a dozen arches and, at two hundred
feet tall, towered over the medieval town below. Standing atop
the bridge, one could look down over the old town, once an
important Channel port, which rose narrow street by narrow
street up the steep slopes. To help the FFI secure the bridge until
the American forces arrived, an SAS party had jumped in on the
night of August 5.[11]

At about this time, a new development required the attention of
Major Wise's Jed team and General Earnest's task force. As American tanks swept across Brittany, kicking up clouds of hot August
dust, many German units retreated to towns and cities along the
coast, hoping to dig in and hold out. A group of nearly three thousand heavily armed Germans had taken shelter on a peninsula on
the coast due north of Guingamp. The Germans had started causing trouble for the inhabitants of some small fishing villages on the
peninsula and, because they were in position to threaten the flank
of Task Force A, Major Wise was able to persuade General Earnest
to send help. With tanks provided by Earnest, a little air support,
and the FFI fighting as infantry, the threat was eliminated.

General Earnest's task force finally reached the Morlaix viaduct
and secured the bridge in force. The Americans had found fairly
clear sailing all along Route Nationale 12, and all the railroad
bridges had been captured intact—most of them already in the
hands of the FFI when the Americans arrived. Aside from the skir-
mish in Guingamp, the only fighting took place when lead elements of the task force ran up on the tail end of a large German
convoy near Morlaix. A brief firefight resulted in the capture of many
more enemy soldiers. Task Force A's mission was successfully

completed and, by August 9, it was ready to move on to help the armored division which by then was closing in on Brest.

With much of the region under Allied control and the Germans only putting up sporadic resistance, Major Wise began to feel that team Frederick's work in Brittany was finished. Ambushes of any German columns venturing out on the roads had long since become routine. Task Force A had passed down its road clear to Morlaix and had not found a single bridge destroyed.

The ease with which Jed team Frederick had secured this route might give a false impression of both the criticality of the task and the difficulty of organizing and executing a mission over such extended ranges with nothing more than resistance forces. It was accomplished so painlessly only because Jed team Frederick had been on the ground long enough to have properly prepared the maquis groups throughout the department. The men had had weeks to develop effective working relationships with resistance leaders and to earn their trust. They had learned the strengths and weaknesses of the various FFI leaders, and about their dependability and leadership capabilities. The team also had facilitated the arming and training of a considerable number of maquis fighters.

But much more had been accomplished than securing Route Nationale 12. By one historian's later estimate, the maquis groups of the Côtes-du-Nord, during the last month of Jedburgh team Frederick's mission, had put twenty-five hundred Germans out of action, cut three hundred telephone and high-tension power lines, sabotaged many railroads and derailed at least forty trains, captured two hundred vehicles in the process of ambushing some fifty German convoys, burned ten thousand gallons of fuel stockpiled by the enemy, and freed thirty-two condemned Frenchmen from prison.[12]

On Saturday, August 19, the men of team Frederick attended a party at a St-Brieuc hotel, where Marceau, decked out in his uniform as a major in the French army reserves, served as master of ceremonies.

Almost immediately, Captain Aguirec departed for Paris. Once American forces had broken out from the lodgment area in Normandy on August 1 their advance had been fairly rapid. While one corps of Patton's Third Army had been liberating Brittany, the rest of his army had wheeled eastward and, by August 19, some elements had advanced to within fifteen miles of Paris. The Paris FFI rose up that same day and began battling the city's German garrison. The City of Light would be liberated within a week. Bob Kehoe thought their French officer was making the trip just to be there for the liberation and the celebrating which was sure to follow. But Paul Aguirec had a far better reason for going to Paris. His father had lived in the city through the entire war, all the while successfully hiding from the Germans the fact that he was a Jew. Captain Aguirec was anxious to see how his father had come through the occupation and the war. He would join his teammates in England a few weeks later.

Major Wise and First Sergeant Kehoe drove to an airfield north of St-Lô on Sunday and boarded a plane to England. Back in London, the two men underwent debriefings before returning to Milton Hall.

At a two-story flat on Devonshire Mews, Major Wise sat down to write his report of the mission. By his estimation, through airdrops of arms from England and the distribution of captured German weapons, the Jed team had armed forty-two hundred men in its sector of the Côtes-du-Nord. They had done much damage to the Germans through sabotage and ambush, and they had arranged for maquis forces to protect Route Nationale 12 and the railway bridges along the way until the American ground forces had arrived. The team had every right to be proud of its contribution. As for the admiration and respect Wise's team held for the FFI, he wrote, "We have found real pleasure in assisting the French patriots in the liberation of their country, and their splendid spirit of defiance to the Boche has repaid our work a hundredfold."[13]

Jedburgh team George had transplanted itself from southern Brittany to the north bank of the Loire—a wide, shallow, and sluggish river. It was the longest river in France, and its six-hundred-mile course reached its estuary on the Atlantic at St-Nazaire, not far downstream to the west. The area was one of lakes and woodlands to the north, with occasional cultivated flatlands and, more to the south, gently rolling terrain with vineyards where the Muscadet grape thrived.

Jed team Frederick's final mission had involved enabling Allied forces to speed westward, but team George was now in a position to aid the eastward advance of Patton's army. But team George's operation in the Loire-Inférieure would largely be one of frustration, as the men struggled to accomplish the mission with no support from London until the final days. Team Frederick, at least, had received fairly good service from London as far as response to the Jeds' requests for airdrops.

Team George's earlier radio difficulties would prove to be minor compared with the communications problem they were soon to have with London, and which nearly caused the mission to be a complete failure. That the team succeeded, in the end, in overcoming the handicap and completing its mission was a direct result of two things that the Allied special operations enterprise had done right. One was ensuring, through a demanding assessment and selection process, that Jedburgh teams were composed of men who were innovative and persevering—men who would tenaciously seek some alternative way to accomplish their missions rather than accept failure. The other thing that special operations planners did right was the providing of a special forces detachment at each field army headquarters, a team which advised the army commander and his staff, and which also was there to help elements—such as Jedburgh team George—to overcome difficulties and continue the mission.

In their cottage on the Loire River, Jedburgh team George lived in constant danger. German soldiers often bathed in the river right in front of the house. And people continually walked along the river, making radio transmissions risky because of the low whine usually made by the hand-cranked generator.

A girl named Paulette Peltier delivered food to the Jeds by boat each day, but the men had to do their own cooking. Lejeune prepared most of the meals. The team's main worry was a bothersome man, a refugee from Nantes—the historic port city nineteen miles down river—whose job it was to watch some cows nearby. He often came by to talk with the Jeds and he was very inquisitive, which naturally made the men nervous. Captain Cyr stammered as he spoke French in order to hide his accent, but the nosy man from Nantes was a natural stammerer, and the Jeds found conversations between the two amusing, even though they were troubled by the man's many questions.

Some days Paulette was unable to bring food, and then the men would have to cross to the south bank of the river to get something to eat in the village there. They went to the same little restaurant in the village many times, and it was usually crowded with German soldiers. But the Germans usually didn't bother the Jeds, who wore civilian clothes and appeared to be harmless. After a while, people became accustomed to seeing the men in the area.

One day, however, Captain Cyr got into an argument with a Luftwaffe lieutenant, and the men again worried about the American's accent. After that, Cyr wore a bandage over his mouth and the two French Jeds told everyone that he had been wounded. This kept people from trying to get Cyr to talk, but it also made it difficult for him to eat.

One person who often showed up at the restaurant when the Jeds were there always seemed to get a table right next to them. He was a Gestapo man, and the Jeds thought he had a Chinese look to him. Every time he came in and sat next to them he would smile and greet them, and to Captain Erard the Oriental-looking man seemed to be thinking, "Just wait a moment and I'll get you and all your gang."[14]

Erard, Cyr, and Lejeune had made great progress in putting their plan for the Loire-Inférieure into practice. The maquis battalions were shaping up nicely, and the Jeds traveled constantly to meet with the various leaders. Sometimes they bicycled thirty or forty miles in a day, and they had held as many as nine meetings at various camps in a single day.

The Jeds had also begun a sabotage campaign, although it was limited because they were short of explosives. The team had been sending messages continually asking London to drop arms and ammunition and explosives, but nothing ever came. They had to make do with some old French demolition materials which the locals had hidden away, and with explosives stolen from the Germans. Some demolition jobs were carried out by the Jeds themselves, but others were done by sabotage teams which the Jeds had organized and trained.

Targets for sabotage were found mostly in the area's extensive network of canals, which were an important form of commercial transportation in France. In late July, team George sabotaged the narrow Nantes-to-Brest Canal by blowing up two locks, stranding twenty boatloads of German munitions which were caught between the locks. The team lost two maquisards during the attack. The sabotage work was not confined to canals; the Jeds also cut rail lines and burned a key bridge, ambushed German convoys, and destroyed an enemy fuel dump.

But soon the men of team George agreed that it was time for them to leave their cottage on the Loire. They had been in the village long enough—there had been some close calls and too many people were trying to learn what the team was up to. So they packed up and moved to a farm about eight miles to the northeast.

The maquis battalions were growing and the Jeds liked the way they were progressing, but ammunition supplies were limited and thousands of men still needed weapons. Still the Jeds could not get London to send planes. Five more drop zones were found, and their locations were radioed to Special Force Headquarters along with the continued pleas for air drops. Captains Erard and Cyr were growing increasingly frustrated and angry, and knew that if this continued they would lose the confidence of the resistance leaders and their men.

Weapons and explosives were not the only things needed—the Jeds had long since run out of money to pay the maquis. Brave Frenchmen were leaving their jobs and families to join the maquis, but they and their families still had to eat. There was no money to pay them, and some maquisards had taken to stealing food.

Back in London, Special Force Headquarters had been receiving team George's messages. But after the message reporting the attack on the maquis camp at Saffré, at the end of June, they had heard nothing from the team for more than two weeks. And such gaps in radio contact always raised suspicions at the London headquarters.

They could not be certain that the Jeds had not been captured. The Germans had proved themselves quite capable of making Allied radio operators transmit while in captivity, requesting that arms and agents be dropped, only to have them fall into the hands of the Gestapo. The staff in London suspected that this might be the case with Jedburgh team George. Erard and Cyr did not know it, but no more parachute drops would come their way until the team's safety was verified.

Then, in late July, the Jeds obtained some important documents which the resistance had stolen from the Germans. They were copies of the German defense plans for the coast of the Loire-Inférieure, including the port and U-boat base at St-Nazaire. French engineers working for Todt, the German construction organization responsible for building military fortifications in France, were also working for the resistance. They had been working on the plans with the Germans, and had been able to take a copy from the Todt offices and bring it to the Jeds.

So far, the Allies had not captured one Breton port. St-Nazaire had always been one of the key targets. If an operation was to be launched to capture it, the detailed German defense plans which the Jeds now had in their hands would be priceless. But they would only be helpful if they were delivered to Allied ground forces soon. On July 29 the Jeds sent a message to London reporting the windfall and suggesting that a Lysander, a small single-engine plane, be sent to pick Captain Cyr up. Cyr would then deliver the plans to Special Force Headquarters. Of course, no Lysander came.

Then, at one o'clock on the afternoon of August 5, word reached the Jeds that American ground forces were rapidly approaching their area. In fact, they were told, the Americans could arrive within hours. The men decided Cyr should take the plans and head toward the approaching American force and hand them over to the first intelligence officer he could find. But first, Erard had to retrieve the plans from a château where the men had hidden them. He was able to do so, but on his way to rendezvous with Cyr at an agreed-upon spot, Erard was captured by a German tank crew. After being disarmed by the Germans, Erard boldly began yelling at the tank commander. The Frenchman claimed to be with the Milice, working for the Germans, and he warned that the tank commander would surely make trouble for himself by interfering with him. The German went back to his tank and spoke with his men, and soon they all climbed back into their tank and drove off, leaving Erard with the plans but without his weapon.

Erard made it to the rendezvous point and gave the plans to Paul Cyr. Soon, more German tanks rolled by after coming under fire by American armored cars. Captain Cyr took a man from the resistance named Colonel Felix with him, and they stopped the first Americans they could find. Cyr explained to the GIs, who were from a mechanized cavalry squadron, who he was and that he had important documents to get to the division or corps intelligence officer. The soldiers took Cyr and Felix to their squadron commander, who agreed to get them back to VIII Corps headquarters. Cyr and Felix were put in an armored car for the journey, and they were accompanied by a tank and a half-track.

Along the way back to the corps command post, the three vehicles were shot at a few times by scattered German forces, but at eight the next morning they arrived at corps headquarters. Cyr briefed the corps intelligence officer on the enemy situation ahead while the staff made photostat copies of the St-Nazaire defense plans. Then the intelligence officer sent Cyr and Felix on to deliver the plans to Third Army headquarters, located in a woods near Beauchamps, a dozen miles north of Avranches in Normandy.[15]

Upon arrival at Third Army headquarters, the two men were directed toward the war room, the nerve center of the command post and the place where they were most likely to find the intelligence officer and the operations officer. Before they could find either of those two men, however, Cyr and Felix were approached by a fit-looking man in his mid-forties, with receding hair and a conservatively clipped mustache, who introduced himself as Lieutenant Colonel Bob Powell.

Robert Powell, a Princeton-educated Manhattan architect with a pre-war commission in the National Guard, spent most of his time around the war room at the Third Army command post, where large situation maps showed the location of every division, Allied and German, on both the Eastern and Western Fronts. Another map displayed only Third Army's area of operations, with the position of all units down to battalion level depicted. Here, the staff brought General Patton up to date on the strategic and tactical situation twice daily, in twenty-minute briefings at nine in the morning and at five in the afternoon.[16]

But Powell wasn't so concerned with the locations of battalions or the combat strength of divisions. He tried to keep track of small teams of men who were trying to stay alive deep in enemy territory, out in front of Third Army. He also looked for ways that the French resistance might be able to help the regiments and the divisions and the corps which came under Patton's command. Lieutenant Colonel Powell was the special forces representative on Patton's staff, the link to Special Force Headquarters, and when the Third Army commander or his operations or intelligence officer wanted something done by the FFI, they came to Powell.

When the Allies began working on the Jedburgh plan back in 1942, they had foreseen the need for special forces staff representatives to be assigned to each field army headquarters to advise the army commander and his operations staff on special forces and resistance matters. Personnel for this purpose were recruited at the same time as for the Jedburghs, and they were put through a training program. Small groups, called special force detachments, were provided to each army and army group headquarters in the spring of 1944. Special Force Detachment 11 was attached to Third Army headquarters, while Special Force Detachment 12 served General Bradley at Twelfth Army Group headquarters. Even at SHAEF, General Eisenhower had an attached special forces team headed by Colonel Robin Brook of Special Operations Executive, who advised the general on special forces and FFI capabilities and helped to coordinate special operations.[17]

Powell was the commander of Special Force Detachment 11, which was composed of thirteen officers and twenty enlisted soldiers working under the direction of the Third Army operations officer. Some of Powell's men were further detached to forward corps and division headquarters.[18]

Paul Cyr had never met Powell before, but Powell recognized Cyr for what he was as soon as he arrived. Cyr was in civilian clothes, but he was wearing an army field jacket and the patch on the jacket's sleeve told Powell that this man was a Jed. Powell introduced himself and Cyr explained the purpose of his visit. Cyr turned the German plans over to Powell, who took them in and showed them to General Patton, Patton's operations officer, Colonel Maddox, and the intelligence officer, Colonel Koch.

Maddox told Powell that he wanted the FFI to help protect the army's right flank, generally along the Loire River, as the army advanced toward Paris and the Seine. He also wanted the FFI to protect certain bridges that Third Army planned to use in its advance, and if they found that those bridges already were blown then they were to locate alternate routes. Maddox also wanted the FFI to protect the army's resupply routes and to mop up pockets of German troops which were bypassed along the way. Colonel Felix left at once to begin making all the arrangements, but Captain Cyr was asked to remain with Powell.

Colonel Powell now would take action that would enable Jedburgh team George to complete its mission and contribute to Third Army's operations along the Loire. Paul Cyr explained to Powell the trouble team George had been having in getting arms and supplies and money from London. Powell immediately radioed Special Force Headquarters and, with Third Army's backing, was able to arrange an airdrop large enough to allow Team George to arm the thousands of maquisards that were still awaiting weapons. Special Force Headquarters was only too glad to hear that team George had not been captured after all, and they promised to send twenty-four plane-loads of arms within the next few days. Cyr then arranged for FFI guides to be attached to one of Third Army's corps headquarters as it prepared to attack toward the Seine. The FFI men knew the Germans' positions and where the enemy had laid minefields.

Captain Cyr then returned to the Loire-Inférieure to help get the FFI started on the tasks which Third Army had assigned it. The maquis battalions still were meagerly armed, mostly with weapons stolen from the Germans, but they established defensive positions along the north bank of the Loire. On some days the Germans hit them hard with mortars and artillery, and the maquis responded with nighttime forays across the river to attack the German positions.

On Friday night, August 11, the parachute drop from London came. Twenty-five bombers arrived over the Loire Inférieure and dropped nearly six hundred containers filled with seventy-one tons of arms and supplies.[19] Overnight, the maquis battalions organized by Jedburgh team George became much stronger. By the third week in August twenty-five hundred men had been armed and four thousand were standing by to receive weapons as soon as more arrived. Captured arms continued to come in as well. As the fighting continued, the maquis would capture German prisoners almost every day and send them back to the American units, but they would keep the German weapons for FFI units. Third Army also helped by sending the FFI German mortars and heavy machine guns captured in Normandy.[20]

Third Army units continued to ply the FFI every day for up-to-date information on the enemy—where the Germans were, in what strength, and what they were doing. Jed team George responded by organizing teams of men to collect the information and dispatched couriers to get it back to the Americans.

When it came time for the 4th Armored Division to attack the Loire River town of Nantes, the maquis groups working for team George played a big role. Nantes lies about thirty miles upriver from St-Nazaire and had itself once been a busy port. The maquis provided the Americans with information on all German positions in the Nantes area and then, when the division began its assault, the FFI attacked the enemy positions from the rear. The division captured the town easily.

General Patton had declared as early as the first week in August that the maquis were proving to be an important factor in the Brittany campaign.[21] General Bradley agreed, calling them a "valuable ally." Bradley also recognized the contributions of the Jedburghs and the SAS, however, when he later wrote, "With the aid of specially trained Allied detachments that had been parachuted into their hide-outs, the French underground blocked the Brittany roads and drove the Germans into their fortified forts."[22]

Eisenhower, too, had recognized how the maquis had helped the Allied effort by cutting communications, delaying the movement of German reinforcements to Normandy, and serving as infantry and guides to the American divisions liberating Brittany. But he also saw that they did much more than that. "Not least in importance," the supreme commander later wrote, "they had, by their ceaseless harassing activities, surrounded the Germans with a terrible atmosphere of danger and hatred which ate into the confidence of the leaders and the courage of the soldiers."[23]

The besieged ports of Brittany, however, were becoming less important to the Allied high command. The 6th Armored Division had reached Brest by August 10, and the city and its immense natural harbor and seventeenth-century port were encircled by American troops, the FFI, and a handful of Jedburgh teams. The Germans held Brest with a thirty-thousand-man garrison which included the remnants of an infantry division and the elite 2nd Parachute Division, which just had arrived from the fighting in Normandy.[24] German garrisons at St-Malo, Lorient, and St-Nazaire also held out. Hitler, understanding their importance to the Allies, had ordered the ports to be held to the last man. It would be forty-six days before Brest fell, and by then it was no longer needed.[25]

Cherbourg had been captured and its port facilities repaired, and supplies had begun unloading there on July 19. There was hope that the ports of Le Havre and Antwerp could be reached before too long. The Allied invasion of southern France, planned for the middle of August, also offered the prospect of opening the port of Marseilles.

This led Eisenhower to decide that the priority should be pushing eastward rather than spending time and forces capturing the ports of Brittany. Instead of devoting additional forces to that purpose, especially when the Germans were sure to leave the ports heavily damaged, Eisenhower decided they could best be used elsewhere. He saw an opportunity to strike eastward with the bulk of Patton's army, leaving only a corps to hold the Breton port cities under siege. With any luck, the Allies might be able to encircle much of the German army in Normandy.

Bradley had approved Patton's plan to attack eastward from Brittany on August 6, and Third Army had begun to move. Then, the next day, two German panzer divisions spearheaded a German counterattack toward Avranches in an attempt to slice through Third Army's rear. Fierce fighting took place around Mortain until the Germans began withdrawing on the twelfth. Over the next eight days the Allies fought to trap some nineteen German divisions in the pocket which had formed as a result of the German attacks and Patton's breakout from Brittany. By the time the Falaise-Argentan gap, as the jaws of the trap came to be known, was closed, however, much of the German force had escaped to the east.

Farther to the south, Patton also was driving to the east with two corps, and by August 19 Third Army had captured Chartres and Orléans and was reaching for the Seine River.

Meanwhile, other Jedburgh teams had been jumping into the French countryside ahead of Third Army. One team, which had dropped directly in the path of Patton's army, was headed by a skinny American captain who, twenty-nine years later, would become head of the Central Intelligence Agency.

8

"JUST IGNORE 'EM!"

NOTHING about Bill Colby suggested that the bespectacled twenty-four-year-old was a member of an elite special forces outfit. He was as thin as a teenager, about five foot eight, and had a studious look. People would more likely take him for the man who handles new accounts down at the bank. Although he qualified as an army brat—his father was a colonel—he didn't seem to fit that mold either. There was much more to Bill Colby, though, than met the eye.*

His father, Elbridge Colby, taught English literature at Columbia and then at the University of Minnesota. He met and married an Irish Catholic girl from St. Paul named Margaret Mary Egan, and in 1920 their first child was born, a boy named William Egan Colby. Elbridge Colby had served in Panama during the First World War and, by the time his son was born, he'd decided to make a career of the army. He would retire as a colonel in 1948.

Like all army brats, Bill Colby grew up on the move—Panama, China, Minnesota, Georgia. He was just sixteen when he graduated from Burlington High School in Vermont, and he went on to Princeton, where he was elected to membership in Phi Beta Kappa. After his junior year, he traveled to France and spent the summer

---

* William E. Colby would serve as head of the Central Intelligence Agency during the Nixon and Ford administrations, from 1973 to 1976.

with a French family in the Loire valley. When war broke out late that summer of 1939, Colby returned to the United States on an armed British ship. He graduated the following year; and when France fell shortly thereafter, he hoped to immediately enter the army. At Princeton, he had excelled as a member of ROTC, the Reserve Officer Training Corps. He had made cadet captain and had attended the Citizens Military Training Camp at Fort Devens, Massachusetts. He then awaited the commission which should come with his graduation. But there was a catch.

To be commissioned as an officer in the United States Army you had to be twenty-one years old, and Colby's twenty-first birthday wasn't until January 1941. He had thought about one day becoming a labor lawyer, and so, to make the best use of his time while he waited for his commission, Colby applied at Columbia Law School, was accepted, and entered in the fall of 1940.

By the following summer, America's involvement in the war seemed more likely with every passing month. Colby was by then old enough to accept his commission, and he entered the army in August and was sent to Fort Bragg, North Carolina. He was there when the Japanese attacked Pearl Harbor and when Hitler declared war on the United States.

Soon afterward, Colby moved on to the Field Artillery School at Fort Sill, Oklahoma. After completion of his training as an artillery officer, Colby was held at Fort Sill to teach tactics at the artillery Officer Candidate School. This was a disappointment to him, as he was anxious to get to a combat outfit. Six months later, when a notice appeared on the unit bulletin board calling for volunteers for the new parachute battalions, he signed up at once.

Back when Colby had graduated from high school he at first wanted to go to West Point, but his nearsightedness had kept him from competing for an opening. As he prepared to undergo the physical exam for jump school, he was determined not to let his eyesight get in the way again. He made a point of standing near the eye chart while he undressed for the physical, and memorized the 20/40 line. When time came for the eye exam, his performance was less than convincing, but an understanding doctor passed him anyway. Parachute training at Fort Benning, Georgia, began for him in the fall of 1942, but he broke an ankle on his second jump and it would be the following March before he got his silver jump wings and proceeded to an airborne unit.

Soon Colby was in an officer replacement unit at Camp Mackall, just outside Fort Bragg, where he watched with envy as hundreds of men left the replacement unit, all having been assigned to one of the new airborne divisions. Then, in September 1943, a major from Washington, D.C., arrived at Camp Mackall. Although he didn't announce it at the briefing he gave, the officer was from the Office of Strategic Services and he was looking for officers for the Jedburgh project. He asked for volunteers to jump into enemy-occupied territory, and to Bill Colby this sounded like a good opportunity to get into the war. So he volunteered.[1]

By December Colby had made it through the demanding selection process at the Congressional Country Club and the training in the hills of northern Maryland, and was sharing a cabin with twelve other men aboard the *Queen Elizabeth*, bound for Britain. During the voyage, he had even had the opportunity to dine with an old friend whom he had run into on the ship, an officer who was then serving as an aide to Major General Matthew Ridgway, commander of the 82nd Airborne Division.

When the Jeds began forming into teams at Milton Hall in the spring, Colby linked up with two likable French lieutenants named Jacques Favel and Louis Giry.*

Favel was a particularly lively and fun-loving sort, and already had earned a reputation among the Jeds as a skirt chaser. He was about Colby's height and of medium build, had brown hair, thick and untamed, and had rascally brown eyes. Favel also had a mustache which had been with him since he was a corporal, when he had grown it out of necessity because, without it, he appeared to be no more than fifteen years old.

Favel and Colby got along well despite some differences in how they liked to spend their free time. Favel enjoyed sitting in on the poker games which always seemed to be in progress at Milton Hall when training was done for the day, but Colby would never play. Colby was more likely to be found with his nose in a book, and one in which he was particularly absorbed was T. E. Lawrence's *Seven*

---

* Jacques Favel's real name was Camille Lelong; that of Louis Giry was Roger Villebois.

Pillars of Wisdom, which he had picked up in a London bookstore and was reading for anything it might offer a novice guerrilla leader. But often, on free weekends, Colby would join his two French teammates on a pass to London, where they would chase girls, visit the nightclubs, and go to the dog races, which Colby particularly enjoyed.[2]

It was Saturday, August 12, when Colby, Favel, and Giry were alerted for a mission. At their briefing in London the men learned that their team would be known as Bruce. Their work would involve helping a man named Henri Frager train and equip maquis groups in the Yonne department of central France. The broad valley of the Yonne, roughly sixty miles southeast of Paris, consisted mostly of rolling farmlands and pastures and vineyards. It was a landscape of gentle hills crowned in groves of pine, birch, and oak, where the old provinces of Orléanais, Burgundy, and Champagne converge.

The Jedburgh teams which had been sent to Brittany had worked at a disadvantage, having to start from scratch because F Section had never been successful in establishing a strong circuit there. Team Bruce, however, would be joining one of the largest circuits in France, one which had been active in the Yonne Valley since early 1943. The circuit was called Donkeyman.

Henri Frager was the organizer of the F Section circuit called Donkeyman.* The soft-spoken Alsatian with the hazel eyes and the prematurely gray hair and the slight limp had first gone to war against the Germans in 1914 at the age of seventeen. After that war he had become a successful architect. He had re-entered the army as a captain in 1939 and had joined the resistance when France fell a year later. By 1942 he had begun cooperating with Britain's Special Operations Executive and, by the summer of 1944, Frager

---

* Frager's case can be used to illustrate the security measures taken in referring to F Section agents. Henri Frager was his real name, but SOE and Special Force Headquarters would refer to him in message traffic by his code name Louba. In France, he was known by other agents and by special forces personnel by his field name Jean-Marie, yet if the Germans checked his false identification documents, they would see the name Henri Dupré. What name you knew him by depended on what your relationship to him was.

would head a circuit with nearly five thousand maquis fighters. But, from the very start, the Donkeyman circuit had experienced bad luck.

In May 1943, Frager had been joined by a radio operator named Marcel Clech, a forty-year-old courier named Vera Leigh, who had been a dress designer before the war, and a British captain named Sidney Jones. Special Operations Executive had hoped that these three eventually would be able to re-form a circuit next to Donkeyman which had been destroyed through arrests by the Germans.[3] Then, at the end of October 1943, Vera Leigh was arrested in Paris; she would later be executed at Natzweiler concentration camp.[4] Three weeks later Captain Jones was arrested. More bad luck followed on December 19, when radio direction-finders tracked down a transmission signal from Marcel Clech's set. Agents from the Sicherheitsdienst (SD)—the German Security Service—burst into Clech's room and captured him while he was in the middle of tapping out a message.[5]

But it was more than simple bad luck that had been at work in Henri Frager's circuit. He had been working under a serious handicap of which he was not yet aware. Frager's adjutant, a man named Roger Bardet, was a traitor and had been feeding information about the circuit to an agent of the Abwehr, Germany's military intelligence service, for more than a year. Bardet's Abwehr contact was a sergeant named Hugo Bleicher. Bardet and Bleicher had been responsible for the arrests of Vera Leigh and Captain Sidney Jones (with Bleicher making the actual arrests), and almost certainly had been involved in the arrest of Marcel Clech, with whom the two men had met on two occasions.

Forty-four-year-old Hugo Bleicher was one of Germany's most effective agents in France, and his work in 1943 and 1944 had been devastating to some F Section circuits. The former clerk from Hamburg had the appearance and demeanor of a schoolteacher. He had a gift for languages and an even greater gift for manipulating and betraying those who so easily trusted him. The Abwehr had recruited him early in the war.

Bleicher's history with Henri Frager and Roger Bardet dated back to the beginning of 1943. Bardet had become Frager's right-hand man during their early resistance work in the south of France in late 1942. While Frager had been absent on a visit to SOE in London in March 1943, Bardet had fallen into a trap set by the wily Sergeant Bleicher and found himself behind bars. When Bleicher first visited him in his cell to question him, Bardet offered to work for the German and immediately gave the Abwehr man many names of key resistance and SOE people. Bardet had then been released in such a way that it appeared to his fellow resistance members that he had escaped. Frager, of course, was unaware of Bardet's treachery, and when he returned from England to establish the Donkeyman circuit southeast of Paris, he kept Bardet with him.

Many resistance and SOE operatives in southern France were arrested as a result of the information Bardet had given Bleicher. By early 1944, probably as a result of information which interrogators had gained from Leigh, Jones, and Clech, the Germans had caught many more Donkeyman members and had seized a number of the circuit's arms dumps. Frager himself had survived that wave of arrests only because he had been absent on another trip to London at the time.[6]

Unfortunately, the staff at Special Force Headquarters in London knew none of this.

The Donkeyman circuit had survived nonetheless, and had actually grown in spite of Bardet and Bleicher, mostly due to the work of talented people such as Lieutenant Colonel Jacques Adam, Frager's deputy, and Ensign Peggy Knight, a courier. By the summer of 1944, the circuit was operating over an area reaching from Normandy to the Ardennes on the Belgian border. And, in the course of their work, Jacques Adam and Peggy Knight had grown leery of Roger Bardet. Knight, an attractive English girl who had been recruited by SOE after being overheard speaking fluent French in a London restaurant, had arrived by parachute in early May with an OSS radio operator, an American civilian named Henry Bouchard. Frager had warned the two newcomers to be alert because of the recent arrests, and he had put them to work organizing maquis groups in the valley of the Yonne River.

The twenty-one-year-old Knight excelled in the role of courier. She routinely passed through German checkpoints to deliver information to other FFI camps and several times, after the D-Day landings in June, to Allied army commanders. She also carried her weight in tactical operations, though, taking an active part in ambushes of German convoys as the FFI worked to delay the movement of enemy divisions to the Normandy battlefield.

When Frager had returned to France in February 1944, Roger Bardet had boldly arranged a series of meetings between Frager and the German agent Bleicher, whom he introduced as an anti-Nazi Luftwaffe officer interested in working for the British. Frager, taken in by the genial Bleicher, had come to trust the German so much that he had told him of his plans to build up the maquis of the Yonne department. So when Bleicher arrested Frager on the second day of July, as the Frenchman stepped off a train at the Montparnasse station in Paris, Frager was stunned. Three months later he was hanged at Buchenwald concentration camp.[7]

In London, as the briefer gave the men of Jedburgh team Bruce the final details of their mission, he told them that they were to meet Henri Frager in the drop zone, unaware that the circuit leader had already been arrested.

"What should we do if we fail to make contact with Frager or his men?" asked Colby. Any number of things could go wrong, Colby reasoned, and having an alternate plan just seemed prudent. For one thing, the contact plan the team had just heard was based completely on the premise that the team would be dropped precisely where it was supposed to be dropped. The briefer was speechless, however, and it was clear that no one had asked the question before and no one on the staff had apparently bothered to plan for such a contingency. At the last minute, the team was given the address of a safe house to which the Jeds should make their way if they had any problems finding their contacts.[8]

The men were then told that they would be departing for France that night. But bad weather moved in and the mission was scrapped for the night. The next day there was another development. Special Force Headquarters had just received word of Frager's arrest, but still was unaware of how he had been betrayed by his own adjutant. Consequently, a last-minute change was made to Jedburgh team

Bruce's mission: The team's contact would now be the man named Roger Bardet.

Bill Colby had been promoted to major five days before D-Day. But, according to Colby's autobiographical *Honorable Men*, Lieutenant Favel was designated team leader for the mission. Jacques Favel had been born in southern France, in the listless Catalan town of Perpignan—a coastal palm-tree town at the foothills of the Pyrénées, not far from the Spanish frontier. His mother had died when he was five years old, and his father emigrated to the United States in 1919 to join relatives who had been in the New Orleans area since the late nineteenth century. Favel had remained in France but had gone to the States as a teenager in 1931 to live with his father, who by then was the owner of an eight-thousand-acre plantation, raising corn, cotton, and cattle. Favel attended high school in New Orleans, but in 1934 returned to France, and in September of that year he joined the army, serving until 1937.

As the war approached, Favel was drafted back into the army in 1939, and he fought the German invaders in 1940 as a member of a reconnaissance platoon. He was discharged at the time of the armistice and lived for a time in unoccupied France. He then went to French North Africa and, on the day after the Allies landed there, he re-joined the French Army. Because he spoke English so well he had been sent to work in the intelligence section of a French army headquarters near the Kasserine Pass. It was there that the Jedburgh recruiters had found him in late 1943.[9]

As they drifted earthward in their parachute harnesses shortly after midnight on August 15, the men of Jedburgh team Bruce heard the Liberator from which they had jumped trail off into the night. But they soon realized that something was wrong. Hundreds of feet below them they saw a long fire, definitely not the drop zone bonfires they expected. Favel thought it looked like a village that had been torched by the Germans. It turned out to be the burning remains of a train which had been destroyed by an Allied air raid.

The three men came down in a large town, landing roughly among gardens and houses along the main street. Major Colby landed in someone's backyard. "In a burst of feathers," he later wrote, "chickens scattered hysterically; dogs began to bark; people, startled from their sleep, flung open their shutters and excitedly asked each other about the sudden racket."[10]

Indeed, the clamor caused by the metal containers falling on tiled rooftops and cobblestone streets aroused many of the local civilians, and a small crowd soon gathered around the Jeds. The townspeople informed the men that they had dropped into the town of Montargis in the Loiret department, east of Orléans, and had landed near the headquarters of the town's German garrison. Favel estimated that their intended drop zone was about twenty-five miles to the east. Sure that the growing crowd of townspeople would soon arouse the Germans, the men judged it too risky to take the time to retrieve their ten containers with radios and other equipment. They immediately set out to put some distance between them and the town, following a railroad track for a time and then crossing some wooded fields to the southeast.

Colby, Favel, and Giry walked until the first hint of daylight made further movement too dangerous, then found a ditch near a wooded area and crawled in. Only fifty to a hundred yards from the road into Montargis, the team watched all that day as German soldiers and armored cars converged on the town in an effort to locate the parachutists. Troops searched not only every house in Montargis, but surrounding villages and farms as well. As he lay in the grass throughout that long, hot August day, Bill Colby couldn't help wondering how he had gotten himself into such a fix.

When the lazy heat of summer had passed and darkness had returned, the men moved out again, this time following a compass azimuth calculated to deliver them to the safe house where they were to make their alternate contact. Then a thunderstorm hit, making their movement considerably more difficult. Rain beat down on the men, and the ground quickly became a slippery mire. A dreadful darkness made compass navigation nearly impossible. The men tied their pistol lanyards to one another to keep from being separated and struggled on through the pitch-black night, through the rain and the mud, until they heard voices directly ahead. It was nearly two in the morning, much too late for farmers to be up and about. Was it the resistance, or was it the enemy?

Lightning flashed and the men could see a single farmhouse in a clearing ahead of them. The team decided to take a chance and make contact with the occupants. While Colby and Giry covered him with their pistols, Favel approached the house and knocked on the door. At once the voices inside became silent, then one of them called out, "Qui est là?" ("Who is there?") Favel answered, "Un français."[11] Again there was silence from within. Then the door opened and Favel was admitted, and he soon opened the door and told Colby and Giry to come in; everything was all right. By a stroke of luck, the house was being used as a radio station by the resistance, and the men met a radio operator who had only arrived from London eight days earlier. The man quickly sent a message to London reporting Jed team Bruce's status.

Other maquis men arrived the next day and took the Jeds in a battered Citroën to the safe house which the briefer back in London had told them to use in just such a situation as this. The old car in which the Jeds were transported was gasogene-powered, which meant it was rigged with a wood- or charcoal-burning engine. Gasogenes had been around since the nineteenth century, but had come into widespread use among civilians in occupied France, where nearly all gasoline was reserved for military use. Rather than burning gasoline, they used a combustible gas generated by a charcoal- or wood-burning boiler mounted on the rear of the vehicle. Many maquis groups, of course, still used gasoline-powered cars, but these cars were either stolen from the Germans or had been hidden by civilians at the beginning of the war and now were operated on stolen gasoline.

From the safe house, Favel sent word through the local maquis to arrange for a meeting with someone from Roger Bardet's circuit. Within a few days the Jeds were taken to meet Bardet himself at a café in a village farther to the southeast, in the department of the Yonne. When they entered the café, they were met by the silent stares of a roomful of armed resistance men, and a man in his early thirties with coal-black hair, sitting at a table with food and wine, studied them with dark, deep-set eyes. After a moment, the man, tall and thin, stood and introduced himself as Roger Bardet, and he shook hands with each of the Jeds.

The resistance leader invited the men to sit down, and called for food to be brought. He asked the Jeds what had happened to them and where they had been, explaining that he and his men had waited at the drop zone with the fires lit, but no one had come. So Favel and Colby related the events of the past few days and Bardet seemed satisfied. Then he gave the Jeds a rundown on the local situation, and said that his scattered FFI groups currently totaled about five hundred armed men. But he could tell the Jeds nothing about the number of Germans in the area or where they were.

Colby described the meeting with Bardet in his 1978 autobiography *Honorable Men*, and wrote of the uneasy feeling he had about Roger Bardet from the very start. He did not yet know—or even suspect—that the Frenchman sitting before him was a traitor. Clearly, none of the maquisards in the café knew either, or Bardet would not still be alive. Something about the man, though, just didn't measure up to Colby's expectations of a guerrilla chief. In his book, Colby wrote that the uninspiring Bardet "had the look of a minor civil servant, a petty functionary, going through the motions instead of leading." He found Bardet, as head of a five-hundred-man resistance group, to be "anything but energetic, let alone daring."[12]

Luckily, Lieutenant Giry had kept his radio crystals with him on the jump, so, for the next few days, he was able to send team Bruce's messages to London on Bardet's radio. Giry had been a laborer in the city of Nancy before the war, and had been a sergeant in the Free French forces when he joined the Jedburghs. Like the other French radio operators, Giry also had received a lieutenant's commission prior to deploying. Now he was without a radio, however, as team Bruce's two Jed sets had been lost on the jump when the canisters came down in Montargis and been abandoned, and by then they were surely in German hands. But having to rely on Bardet's radio was tying the Jeds down. The cumbersome set could not be moved far, and its batteries continually required recharging.

As Giry busied himself with communications, Colby and Favel set about their work. They began by organizing Bardet's men into companies. Then they set up a training program, concentrating initially on the use of the weapons the maquis groups had already received from air drops. As the fighters began to show mastery of their individual weapons, the instruction advanced to small unit tactics. Before long, patrols were going on limited combat operations against the Germans, with the Jeds continually coaching, advising, and assisting the guerrilla leaders.

One day they attacked a German plane which had been grounded for lack of fuel, and there was a sizable enemy security force which put up a good fight. But in the end, the Germans had to burn the badly shot-up plane after the maquis force withdrew.

There were German garrisons of about five hundred men each in the larger towns of the Yonne, and many enemy convoys were passing through the area as German units retreated eastward. All of them appeared to be lightly guarded. These were tempting targets, but Bardet would not allow the maquis to attack them. He told the Jeds that he had received orders from London not to take any offensive action for the time being. London, he said, would send orders calling for direct action whenever it best supported Allied operations. To the Jeds, however, it simply seemed that Bardet, for whatever reason, wanted to avoid antagonizing the Germans. If they had at first believed Bardet to simply be incompetent, they now grew increasingly suspicious of his loyalties.

Favel and Colby began to look elsewhere for an effective resistance leader and, as soon as they could, they made contact with other groups. And in doing so, the men found that they could rely on Peggy Knight, the competent and energetic young courier of the Donkeyman circuit.

Soon the Jeds met a sixty-year-old resistance chief called Colonel Chevrier, a peacetime lawyer and reserve army officer whose real name was Adrien Sadoul. Chevrier challenged Bardet's authority over the FFI of the Yonne and told the Jeds that he had been appointed as their commander. The old man's immediate group only numbered about twenty men, but Major Colby judged him to be much more of a leader than the enigmatic Bardet. "He was flamboyant, charismatic, constantly on the move,"[13] Colby would later recall, and he was on good terms with other chiefs throughout the Yonne who commanded some two thousand fighters in all, perhaps more. This was the sort of man the Jeds were seeking.

Chevrier told the Jeds what he knew of the Yonne resistance. He told of another maquis chief named Georges, who had about four hundred armed men operating in the area southeast of Auxerre. And of a popular young leader named Vernouil, who commanded another six hundred. Additionally, communist FTP groups totaling about three hundred men, under the overall command of a man named Yvon, were scattered throughout the area. But all of these groups had one thing in common—their size was limited by the number of weapons they had available. If more arms were sent from England, Chevrier explained, they all could expand.

The Jeds immediately began making arrangements for parachute drops. They asked Chevrier for drop zone locations, and the old chief gathered information from all the groups in the department on fields which could be used and gave the information to the Jeds. Lieutenant Giry radioed the information to London along with a request for thousands of rifles, carbines, machine guns, bazookas, and mortars.

By this time, American forces were closing in on the Seine, and one of General Patton's corps began crossing the river south of Paris on Saturday, August 19. With Allied forces so close to Paris, the city's resistance groups began an uprising that same day, seizing newspaper offices, government buildings, and the city hall. Although the resistance in Paris was estimated to number as many as twenty thousand, few of them were armed. They were just strong enough to be a real threat to the German occupation force in the city, but not strong enough to take control of the city by themselves. So a truce was soon called between the resistance and the Germans, with Swedish consul general Raoul Nordling acting as intermediary.

Commanding the German garrison was the bulky Prussian Lieutenant General Deitrich von Choltitz. Hitler had given von Choltitz orders to leave Paris in rubble by way of pre-planted demolitions if the Allies tried to take it, and the city's landmarks had already been primed with tons of explosives. Choltitz, however, did not relish the thought of being remembered in history as the man who destroyed the City of Light, so he decided to put up only a limited fight for the city. The Parisian resistance leaders were unaware of this, though, and they were sure that the city would be destroyed if Allied forces didn't move in soon.

On Monday, an emissary from the Paris resistance, named Lefevre, drove to the Yonne, found Jedburgh team Bruce, and appealed to Lieutenant Favel and Major Colby for help. Lefevre, a city police official, explained the situation in the capital and asked the Jeds to help by arranging for arms and supplies, including anti-tank weapons, to be dropped to the Ile-de-la-Cité, the island in the middle of the Seine where the Palace of Justice and Notre Dame cathedral stood. Favel and Colby agreed to see what they could do and immediately sent off the request to London.

What neither the Paris resistance nor the Jeds knew, though, was that the Allies had planned to bypass Paris. Anxious to maintain the momentum of their drive toward the German border, they wanted to avoid having to commit a large number of troops to costly and time-consuming street fighting in the capital. The German garrison in the city, it was thought, would be compelled to capitulate, at any rate, once their supply lines were cut. Eisenhower, however, had another reason for wanting to defer the liberation of Paris. As the Allied armies advanced farther from the Normandy coast, maintaining an adequate flow of supplies to the front lines was becoming a real challenge. And the supreme commander was in no hurry to add to this burden the responsibility for supplying food and coal to the entire population of the city.

On August 21, Special Force Headquarters received Jedburgh team Bruce's message requesting a parachute drop of arms and ammunition to the Paris resistance, and began at once to prepare to make the drop. But on the twenty-second, General Pierre Joseph Koenig, de Gaulle's London-based commander of the FFI, postponed the operation for a day in hopes that the arrival of Allied forces in the city would preclude the need to further arm the Paris resistance. Koenig, like de Gaulle, was in no rush to provide more weapons to the Paris resistance, because it was predominantly communist. Both men were anxious to install a provisional non-communist government in the city as soon as it was freed.[14]

While the Paris policeman was meeting with the Jeds of team Bruce, another emissary named Roger Gallois drove to General Patton's forward command post. Gallois pleaded with Patton to send a force at once to liberate the city. But Patton refused, citing General Eisenhower's plan to bypass the city, and so Lieutenant Colonel Powell, Patton's special forces advisor, drove Gallois to General Bradley's command post. They met with Bradley and with the commander of the French 2nd Armored Division, which was under Bradley's command. Paris, Gallois assured the army group commander, could easily be taken if the Allies moved at once. The truce with General Choltitz, he feared, might end at any time. Bradley quickly phoned General Eisenhower.[15]

By this time, General de Gaulle was also pressuring Eisenhower to reconsider and to send forces to liberate the city at once rather than bypass it. Eager to see the capital freed of its German occupiers, de Gaulle was equally intent on preventing the communists from taking over the city. Finally, Eisenhower relented—partly, he was to say later, as a reward to the resistance for their contribution in the French campaign. He told Bradley to order First Army to move in.

An FFI group of eight hundred men in Chartres made plans to enter the city with the Allied divisions, but an officer from Colonel Powell's special forces detachment was able to dissuade them, explaining that the group would only get in the way.[16]

Eisenhower wanted French forces to be the first to enter the city, so the French 2nd Armored Division drove on Paris from the west while an American infantry division made a supporting attack from the south. The attacks began in gloomy weather on the morning of the twenty-third and soon ran into stiff resistance by Germans on the city's outskirts. French tanks were also slowed by crowds of Parisians swarming around the vehicles. But, by the morning of the twenty-fifth, the sun was out and the city was liberated, and de Gaulle and his supporters wasted no time in occupying government buildings and establishing political control.

London soon began responding to Jed team Bruce's calls for arms drops to the Yonne, and the maquis throughout the department flourished. Within the first two weeks the Jeds arranged at least a dozen drops, and almost overnight maquis groups grew as farmers and townspeople alike joined the fight. Thousands of weapons ranging from rifles, carbines, and Stens, to bazookas and mortars and machine guns fell from Allied planes onto fields throughout the Yonne. Anticipation of victory and liberation caused many fence-sitters to join the side of the resistance. And with the arms and explosives which London provided, the maquis of the Yonne also began ambushing German columns, attacking German garrisons, and blowing up enemy supply depots.

The Germans were reeling from the onslaught of Patton's Third Army. And as difficult as it was for them to deal with Patton's tanks and with punishing Allied air strikes, they also had to contend with countless hit-and-run attacks by the maquis.

But while Third Army was advancing toward Germany north of the Loire River, tens of thousands of German troops from southwestern France were trying to withdraw to the homeland south of the Loire. Some of Patton's staff officers were becoming concerned about the security of the army's right flank, and because Third Army was the southernmost of Twelfth Army Group's forces, General Bradley had charged it with protecting the army group's flank. Only a shallow river lay between the Americans and as many as a hundred thousand Wehrmacht troops. Patton's own intelligence officer, on August 22, had become so concerned about heavy German traffic south of Orléans that he feared a counterattack by the enemy into Third Army's flank.[17]

On that same day, a U.S. infantry division attacked the Germans holding Montargis, the town where Jedburgh team Bruce had landed just a week earlier. The town fell to the Americans late the next day after a difficult fight. Then the Jeds heard that an American armored unit had reached a town fifteen miles east of Montargis and just north of team Bruce's camp. Colby and Favel decided that they should try to make contact, and they would take with them an American fighter pilot whose P-38 had been shot down some time earlier. The pilot had been taken in by the FFI, outfitted with civilian clothes and false papers, and kept hidden until just such an opportunity arrived.

The U.S. forces east of Montargis turned out to be from the 4th Armored Division. Making it through the Allied lines, the Jeds found their way to the division headquarters and were able to talk with the intelligence officer and the operations officer. They provided the division staff with all the information they had about what lay ahead.

Then, at the request of the division, team Bruce sent maquisards on information-gathering missions to towns throughout the area immediately ahead of the Americans. Primarily, they were to look for German concentrations and report back. The maquis did so, and some of the best information came back from Peggy Knight and from a French woman, each of whom moved alone through some of the most heavily occupied towns.

The Allies did not pause, even briefly, after the capture of Paris, but pushed on, taking full advantage of their momentum. The 4th Armored Division, spearheading Patton's army, swept through the northern part of the Yonne and pressed on for Troyes, in the department of the Aube, where the Seine passed through the old provincial capital of Champagne. And the division made good use of the FFI. On August 24, as the division's leading combat command prepared for its assault on Troyes, the operations officer ordered the FFI to protect all roads leading into the city. They were also to block all side roads that could be used by the Germans in launching counterattacks against the Americans. While the division was making final preparations for the attack scheduled for the following morning, an FFI commander arrived to report that his men had all roads blocked as ordered and that he had several more companies standing by in reserve.

Shortly after the attack kicked off, a jeep carrying a lieutenant from Colonel Powell's Third Army special forces detachment caught up with the commander of the 4th Armored Division's lead element, Colonel Bruce Clarke. The lieutenant, who was accompanied by a French major, asked if there was anything else the FFI could do for him. Clarke said that he wanted the FFI to help secure another bridge downriver from Troyes. The lieutenant and the Frenchman set off at once to make it happen, and Clarke sent a reconnaissance platoon along with them.

Upon arriving at the bridge the FFI found that it had been damaged, but the men secured the area while division engineers brought up a temporary Bailey bridge and installed it. Meanwhile, another maquis group secured a bridge site within the city of

Troyes, and the lead tank battalion from the 4th Armored Division, led by Lieutenant Colonel Creighton Abrams, crossed the Seine there on the twenty-fifth.* The maquis then assisted an infantry division in securing the bridgehead on the far side.

On Saturday, August 26, Chevrier's FFI group occupied Auxerre, the old capital city of the Yonne, with its timbered houses and cobbled streets, and the old resistance leader established his command post there. Jacques Favel and Bill Colby had been keeping an eye out for an airstrip capable of handling C-47 transport planes to bring in more supplies. On Sunday they inspected the airfield at Auxerre, measured the runway, and signaled London that it was suitable.

Meanwhile, back at his command post northeast of Orléans, General Patton continued to be pressured by General Bradley's headquarters to commit forces to the flank protection mission. Grudgingly, the Third Army commander complied by committing an infantry division to the task in the area immediately east of Orléans. But, for the most part, Patton purposely left his right flank essentially open from St-Nazaire on the Atlantic to Troyes, a distance of more than three hundred miles. In his postwar memoir, Patton wrote that he felt confident that the tactical air force unit supporting his army could warn him of any impending attack from the Germans south of the Loire.[18]

Patton couldn't assuage the worriers on Bradley's staff, but to his own staff he was blunt: "Forget this goddamned business of worrying about our flanks. . . . Some goddamned fool once said that flanks must be secured, and since then sons-of-bitches all over the world have been going crazy guarding their flanks."[19] And when his southernmost corps commander, whose flank it was to be left open, expressed concern about the tens of thousands of Germans south of the Loire, Patton replied, "Just ignore 'em!"[20]

But there was more to Patton's cavalier attitude toward flank

* Bruce Clarke and Creighton Abrams would both later rise to the rank of four-star general. General Clarke would retire as the commander in chief of United States Army Europe in 1962. General Abrams would command all U.S. forces in Vietnam from 1968 to 1972 and would serve as army chief of staff from 1972 until his death in 1974.

security than faith in the air force. As a recipient of top secret "Ultra" message traffic, Patton had a fairly accurate picture not only of what German forces lay ahead of him, but also of the intentions of the German forces south of the Loire. The Allies had been intercepting and reading German messages sent by means of the Enigma cipher machine ever since they had broken the code early in the war, and Ultra was the designation applied to intelligence gained as a result of this work. Through Ultra message traffic, Patton knew he could afford to commit only a token guard force on his right flank because the German forces south of the river were under orders to withdraw to the east. They had little interest in crossing the Loire to attack his flank. The FFI, of course, already occupied the entire flank area clear to the German border, including the southern bank of the Loire. Thus, flank protection had become, de facto, a mission perfectly suited to the resistance on the ground while the air force kept watch over the area from above. As an officer on Bradley's staff later quipped, "Patton, as usual, trusted his flank to God, the air force and the maquis."[21]

That was the situation at the Third Army command post on Sunday, August 27, when Major Colby and Lieutenant Favel drove there in search of a new mission for the FFI of the Yonne department. Upon arrival at Patton's headquarters, the Jeds met with Colonel Powell and his special forces staff. One of the first things the men learned was that Chevrier had been officially named chief of the FFI of the entire Yonne department. London had notified Powell's staff of this but had failed to inform Jedburgh team Bruce. Then Powell told the Jeds that General Patton wanted the FFI to guard Third Army's right flank during its advance eastward. To help the Jeds in executing the new mission, Powell requested London to place top priority on arms drops to team Bruce's area. Powell's men also gave Favel and Colby a radio to replace the two they had lost on their jump.

Third Army published a written order to the FFI on Monday. It was addressed to both Chevrier and Roger Bardet in the Yonne, as well as to the FFI leaders of two adjacent departments, and it directed them to ensure the protection of the army's right flank.[22]

As soon as Favel and Colby returned to Chevrier's command post, they began helping the chief and his men draw up a plan for the new mission. To better organize the FFI for the task they divided Chevrier's department into area commands, and they distributed the communist Francs-Tireurs et Partisans (FTP) groups throughout the department so that they were interspersed with Chevrier's units. By the last day of August, Chevrier's guerrillas were occupying positions along a line which ran straight through the center of the Yonne department. Each town along the line was occupied by an FFI company whose commander reported to his parent resistance organization which, in turn, reported to Chevrier.

Jed team Bruce returned to the northern Yonne on Thursday and went over the details of the plan with Colonel Powell and his staff. As an added measure, Powell directed that the FFI blow as many of the Loire bridges as possible. The river approaches the town of Briare from the south before gently curving toward the west and then running in a westerly direction to St-Nazaire on the Atlantic coast, and Powell gave Chevrier's FFI the responsibility for blowing all bridges south of Briare. As soon as the Jeds returned to Chevrier's command post, Major Colby accompanied the maquis chief on a reconnaissance of all the bridges in their assigned stretch of the river, and they found that some had already been destroyed. They issued orders for the demolition of those that remained.

More and more Germans withdrew eastward through the department, their goal simply to reach the German border. Seldom did they halt long enough to engage Chevrier's FFI in any pitched battles, but the FFI attacked enemy columns at every opportunity. Small, isolated German elements became easy targets for the maquis and were quickly found and destroyed. To better protect themselves, the Germans began moving only in large formations along main routes, with security patrols guarding the columns. Such large convoys were easy targets for the air force, however, and soon the Germans learned that they could only move that way at night.

Since crossing the Seine, Patton's army had been in relentless pursuit of the retreating Germans. Caution was thrown largely to the wind in the interest of moving as far and as fast as possible, keeping the enemy off balance and unable to establish a defense.

Small pockets of enemy resistance were bypassed. Infantry kept up with armor the only way possible—by riding along. Tanks often had eight to ten infantrymen riding on top. Tank destroyers could carry a dozen or more foot soldiers and jeeps carried four or five. Other men found every means of transport available—artillery prime movers, quartermaster trucks, and engineer and medical vehicles. Men rested their heads on an arm as they rolled along, trying to grab a few minutes of sleep whenever possible. More infantry followed in two-and-a-half-ton trucks, dismounting to move on foot only when necessary.

Units moved so fast that they ran off their maps almost daily, through grassy plains and wooded hills, through crowds of cheering men, women, and children in every village and town. Church bells rang as the red, white, and blue French tricolor was raised for the first time in four years. And people showered the troops with flowers and fruit and kisses, and rewarded the liberators with bottles of wine, cognac, and calvados. In return, the Americans shared chocolate and gum with the French kids to shouts of "Vive l'Amérique." But, always, the troops kept on rolling.[23]

At this time the FFI was given an additional job. As the Germans departed French towns and cities, FFI units were to immediately occupy them. Roadblocks were built and strongpoints established, forcing any following German units to circumvent the town, further slowing their movement and making them vulnerable to harassing attacks in the surrounding countryside. Hasty occupation would also, it was hoped, prevent demolition by the retreating Germans.

When German forces vacated the town of Monéteau, three miles north of Auxerre, in late August, an FFI company of about a hundred and fifty men occupied the town to protect a large supply of gasoline located there. Later that day, a German force numbering more than two hundred returned to either retrieve or destroy the gasoline, and attacked the FFI with small arms, mortars, and machine guns. Even though they had nothing larger than Bren light machine guns, the FFI fighters held off the enemy and saved the gasoline, which supplied the FFI throughout the Yonne for the next month.[24]

* * *

At the end of August, General Eisenhower sent a message to his senior commanders outlining the next phase of operations. Montgomery's army group was to continue attacking to the northeast to seize the Pas de Calais area, capture airfields in Belgium, and take the port of Antwerp. Bradley's army group was to continue attacking in a northeasterly direction in support of Montgomery's assault, but it was also to prepare to attack to the east towards the Saar Valley. The FFI, the message added, "will continue to provide direct support to the operations of the Army Groups by harassing, sabotage, counter-scorching (and mopping-up action), and by protecting important installations of value to Allied lines of communication."[25]

The next day, in a cable to his superiors, the Combined Chiefs of Staff, Eisenhower provided an update on the progress of the campaign in Europe, noting that the FFI had "done much valuable work."[26] He echoed these sentiments when talking to the British press the next day, when he proclaimed that the maquis "had been far more effective than many doubting Thomases thought before D-Day."[27]

By September 15, Third Army had advanced to the Moselle, the last river obstacle before the Rhine. Patton's forces had now advanced beyond Jed team Bruce's area of operation, and other maquis groups and other Jedburgh teams would pick up the work team Bruce had been doing. Team Bruce's work was finished, and Special Force Headquarters signaled for the men to return to London.

The Jeds made their way to Paris, where OSS had established a headquarters soon after the city's liberation and taken over a hotel for the use of agents returning from the field. There Colby, Giry, and Favel met and celebrated with other Jeds, OSS Operational Groups, and circuit personnel also en route to England.

Among those who came to Paris at about that time to catch a plane back to London was an American woman named Virginia Hall. Under the code name Diana, she had just completed her second mission to France. She had conducted her first as an SOE agent, before OSS had become established in Europe, then had switched to the American organization and was deployed to run a circuit named Wrestler with the assistance of a Jedburgh team. Despite having lost a leg in a pre-war hunting accident, Hall had proved herself a most capable circuit organizer and had caused so much trouble for the Germans that they had put a price on her head. But she had been out of contact with SFHQ for several days. Upon her arrival in Paris, she apologized for her tardiness, explaining that she had been hiding from a Gestapo search party. As one OSS officer who was there observed, "One might have thought she was apologizing for having missed a train connection and deplored the inconvenience it might have caused those waiting for her."[28]

One Jedburgh team arrived in a black Cadillac which had reportedly belonged to Vichy Premier Pierre Laval, and when the team boarded a plane for England they relinquished the car to Bill Colby for his temporary use. In late September, the three men of Jedburgh team Bruce returned to London for their debriefing. Both Favel and Giry later returned to the French Army, Favel becoming a liaison officer with an American unit.

Roger Bardet, the man who had betrayed so many in the resistance and had been an unknown threat to Jedburgh team Bruce, successfully kept a low profile for many months. Once he saw that Allied victory was imminent he essentially became a bench-sitter, doing nothing to aggravate either side or to draw attention to himself. In the end, though, he was found out and was arrested, tried, and convicted of treason after the war.

Meanwhile, as Third Army was making its dash across central France in August 1944, the First U.S. Army was doing the same, though with much less fanfare, just to the north. And Jedburgh teams, dropped much later than they should have been, struggled to work in an area increasingly crowded with retreating Germans.

9

A RAINY NIGHT IN PICARDY

U NDER the terms of the 1940 armistice with conquered France, Germany had allowed the collaborationist Vichy regime to retain a small army. Permitted to carry only small arms, this Armistice Army had been limited in size to one hundred thousand in metropolitan France and an army in North Africa which eventually numbered more than twice that.[1] Among the officers assigned to that Armée d'Afrique was a former sergeant by the name of Jean Delviche and, like most Frenchmen, he had seen his world turned upside down when France capitulated to the German invaders. The handsome native of the Picardy region of northern France had gone through officer training and earned a commission in the artillery. When the German invasion came that summer, he fought with distinction, commanding a battery of guns. But then France fell.

The young lieutenant had remained in uniform as part of the Armistice Army and been sent to a small garrison in Morocco. He had gotten married and he and his new wife had been able to obtain military family housing at the garrison. There was great camaraderie among the soldiers and their families at the small post and they had many friends, and Lieutenant Delviche had grown content with the military life in sunny French North Africa.

All that changed when U.S. and British forces stormed ashore in

Morocco and Algeria in November 1942. The Vichy French forces at first offered token resistance but were quickly persuaded to lay down their arms and throw in with the Allies as Free French. Germany had responded by occupying what had been the unoccupied southern portion of France. For the French military community in North Africa, all ties with France had been severed and they soon found it impossible to get many items from their homeland, including badly needed medical supplies.

Lieutenant Delviche's wife had been carrying their first child and there were difficulties with the birth. Because the medical care was not what it should have been, both mother and baby died. Grief-stricken, Delviche sought any opportunity to leave the land where he had once been so happy. He applied to his commander to be sent anywhere, as long as it would get him away from that place. When recruiters came looking for French volunteers for a secret mission involving parachuting behind enemy lines, Jean Delviche was one of the first to step forward.[2]

Delviche was a little older than most of the French Jeds, and while most of the men at Milton Hall had taken advantage of every opportunity to visit a pub in the evening or to get a pass to London, Delviche had seldom joined them. He was a captain by the time the Jedburgh trainees had begun forming teams in the spring of 1944, and he had hooked up with a likable American, Major John Bonsall.

Like Delviche, Bonsall was an artillery officer. He hailed from Morristown, New Jersey, where he had been raised by his mother and her parents. He had been named for a father he never knew. John Bonsall's mother had been carrying him when his father left for France in the First World War. A lawyer in civilian life, his father had died in France, a victim of the great influenza epidemic which swept through Europe in 1918, killing more American soldiers than German guns did. News of his death had hit John's mother hard, and it was then that his grandparents moved in to help raise John and his older sister, Katherine.[3]

John had attended The Haverford School, a prominent school for boys in Pennsylvania, had been a top student there, and graduated with honors. In other ways, as well, he had shown himself to be an unusually bright and talented young man. He learned French at an early age, and proved himself to be mechanically clever. As a teenager, he would find old cars, have them towed home, tear them apart, and rebuild them to running condition. And he demonstrated that he had inherited his family's love of music by learning to play the piano—and play it well.

From Haverford Bonsall had gone on to Princeton. Outgoing and sociable, he had joined the University Cottage Club—which had been whimsically characterized by F. Scott Fitzgerald in *This Side of Paradise* as "an impressive mélange of brilliant adventurers and well-dressed philanderers." John Bonsall at least qualified as the brilliant adventurer. He stood around six feet tall with an athletic build; he made friends easily and was known to have a mischievous sense of humor. He had talked of a future in law following the war, but law school would have to wait. For among his many activities at Princeton, Bonsall had been in the ROTC program, and when graduation came in 1941 he received an army commission in the artillery. His call to active duty came in August of that year. Two years later he volunteered for the Jedburghs, made it through the selection and training process, and was standing by with all the others at Milton Hall, awaiting his call to London. His twenty-fifth birthday came just five days after the Allied landings in Normandy.

Joining Major Bonsall and Captain Delviche as the team's radio operator was a twenty-one-year-old sergeant from Manchester, New Hampshire, named Roger Côté.

Finally, two weeks into August, Bonsall's team was summoned to London for its mission briefing. There the men learned that they were bound for the department of the Aisne in the northern region of Picardy, where Captain Delviche had his roots. It was an area surrounded by battlefields of the last war: Soissons, Arras, Cambrai, the Somme, Verdun, and Château-Thierry. When the briefing concluded, the three men were driven to an airfield. It was not a particularly good night for jumping; the weather was nice, but there was no moon at all. The next full moon would not come until the beginning of September, but London had many teams to get into the field soon if they were to be of any use. The plane carrying team Augustus took off late on Tuesday night, August 15, just twenty-four hours after Bill Colby's team had left for the Yonne.

★   ★   ★

First thing Thursday morning, Sergeant Côté broke out his radio gear and got his first message off to London. The message simply read, "AUGUSTUS ALL WELL. RECEPTION PERFECT."[4] It was succinct, but it told those at SFHQ all they needed to know at that time. Team Augustus's jump had gone well; the men landed in flat farmland about a hundred miles northeast of Paris. Once all of their gear had been collected from the drop zone, the Jeds had been driven to the departmental FFI headquarters for a brief rest and then on to a farm in a more remote area. There, the men were briefed by FFI leaders on the status of maquis groups throughout the area.

Roger Côté was well-suited for the job of Jedburgh radio operator. His father, Elzear Côté, had been a radio operator in World War I and had shared some of his knowledge of radios with Roger, even teaching him some Morse code. Like Major Bonsall, Roger Côté was a French speaker, but to Côté the language came naturally, a result of his family's French Canadian roots. He had been born in Manchester in southern New Hampshire, where his parents had been married, and had grown up in the area.

Elzear Côté had, for a time, sold Singer sewing machines door to door. Then he had worked in a bakery, but the flour-saturated air caused some health problem and, on a doctor's advice, the family moved to a farm. Because of his poor health, Roger's father had often been out of work, and the family never had much money. Roger had a younger brother, Roland, an older sister, Zita, and two younger sisters, Violette and Jeannine, and they were a close and devout Catholic family.

Roger was of slight build and no more than about five feet, two inches tall, with hazel eyes; people around Manchester sometimes commented that he looked like a little Frenchman. He had been a good student at St. Anthony's High School in Manchester and had harbored a desire to go to college, but it was out of the question because there was no money. Halfway through his senior year, he quit high school and, in early November 1942, joined the army along with two of his friends. Roger's family had thrown a farewell party for the three young men, complete with a large American flag and a cake decorated with many smaller flags. Elzear Côté wore his World War I uniform—which still fit him perfectly—for the occasion.

Roger had asked for a Signal Corps assignment at the time of his enlistment because of his early interest in radio. The army had sent him to the radio school at Fort Monmouth, New Jersey, and it was there that he had heard the Jedburgh recruiter's briefing and volunteered.

Because of the secret nature of his assignment, the Côté family knew nothing of what Roger's role in the war would be when he shipped out in December 1943. But, with his son off to do his part, Elzear Côté decided that the whole family should get involved in the war effort. And so they had packed up and moved to Newton, Massachusetts, where Violette, Zita, and Elzear took jobs with the Raytheon Company in Waltham, making radio tubes for the army.

The family missed Roger, and was always glad to get his letters and hear how he was doing—even if he couldn't say what he was doing. Roger always wrote to his family in French, and in his last letter home he had asked the family to pray for him.[5]

At the farm in northern France, Major Bonsall, Captain Delviche, and Sergeant Côté were enjoying true château living, with good French cooking and plenty of wine. But there was work to be done, and the Jeds soon got started. Resistance leaders from throughout the area gathered to meet with the Jeds on Saturday, August 19. The group decided that the Jeds should begin their work in the southern part of the Aisne department, in the area around Soissons. The Germans had built some fairly extensive fortifications in that area which might be of interest to the Allies. Besides, there were many Germans in the Soissons area and a move southward would allow the Jeds to quickly arrange the delivery of weapons so badly needed by the resistance there.[6]

In a message to London on the twentieth, the Jeds told of their conference with the resistance leaders. They reported that there were some eleven hundred men armed and trained throughout the Aisne department and nearly five thousand more in need of arms. The message conveyed the Jeds' confidence in the FFI leaders and the team's readiness to get to work. But because the area was saturated with Germans, and perhaps at the suggestion of the FFI leaders, the Jeds had decided that the only way they could move about the area would be in civilian clothes. Already the FFI was at work preparing false papers for the men to carry during their journey southward.[7]

About an hour before noon on Monday, a man called Seigneur arrived in a gasogene-powered truck to pick up the Jeds and take them south. Driving the truck was a man named Gaston Costeaux; and another FFI man named Fontaine, who was the operations officer for the department, was with them. Seigneur and Fontaine went into the house while Costeaux prepared a hiding place in the back of the truck for the team's radios and rucksacks. When everything had been loaded aboard the truck, the Jeds thanked their hosts and said their good-byes and climbed aboard for the sixty-mile journey to Soissons. Captain Delviche and Sergeant Côté climbed into the cab of the truck with Costeaux, while Major Bonsall got into the back and found a place to sit on a pile of rabbit skins. Seigneur and Fontaine joined the American in the back and by eleven-thirty they were on the road.

The resistance people had produced false identity papers for the Jedburghs and the team had received them that morning. As the truck rolled along the men studied the papers. Every detail about their new identities had to be quickly committed to memory in case the truck was stopped along the way and they were questioned. In the cabin, Sergeant Côté learned from his papers that he was a student named René Chabaud. He had been born in 1928 at a place called Motteville in the Seine-Inférieure department, and he was currently living in St-Quentin. When he had studied this for awhile, Captain Delviche tested him.

"What's your name?"

"René Chabaud," said the sergeant. Gaston Costeaux noticed that the American rolled his R's slightly.

"Where were you born?"

"In the USA," responded Côté.

"No! If you fall into the hands of the Gestapo you'll be a goner. Come on. Again, where were you born?"

"In Motteville, in the Basse-Seine."

"Not *Basse*-Seine, it's Seine-*Inférieure*. You're a student in St-Quentin, but you are on vacation and staying with us. I am your uncle."[8]

Delviche's assumed identity was that of a thirty-three-year-old wood merchant from Coucy-le-Château named Jean Derval. "As for you," he said to Costeaux, "you picked us up hitchhiking on the road."[9]

In the back of the truck, with Seigneur, Major Bonsall studied his own identity. His papers described him as Joseph Porteval, a forester from Anizy-le-Château.

As the old truck plugged along southward, the men saw many convoys of German army vehicles. For many weeks, Hitler had refused to listen to all proposals from his commanders in France for a withdrawal in the event of an Allied breakthrough. He had refused, that is, until it was too late for any sort of organized withdrawal.

Although a considerable number of Germans, including some panzer units, had succeeded in escaping encirclement by withdrawing through the narrow Falaise-Argentan gap before the Allies could close it, they had paid a heavy price. Of an estimated one hundred thousand German troops caught in the pocket, only half had been able to escape. Some forty thousand troops from fifteen German divisions had been captured and another ten thousand killed.[10] Those lucky enough to have escaped were making a mass exodus eastward to man the defense works on the Siegfried Line.

Passing through one village, the FFI truck suddenly met an oncoming German truck convoy. The German driver in the lead truck was taking too much of the road as they met on a curve, and the truck carrying the Jeds, which had built up a respectable speed for a gasogene, was forced off the street and onto the sidewalk. But Costeaux was familiar with the road, and he remained calm and kept the truck under control.

Just outside a village on the Oise-Aisne canal north of Soissons, Costeaux stopped the truck when he recognized a man standing with his bicycle as a friend named Jean Nöel. Nöel told Costeaux that a German tank had broken down about a half-mile from the village and was blocking the road. He added that Costeaux should be able to get around it with the truck, so Costeaux drove on toward the village.

As the truck came around a curve in the road Costeaux saw the tank, a model known as the Panther, and he slowed as they approached it. The gray forty-four-ton behemoth was eleven feet wide, nearly ten feet tall, and almost thirty feet long—and it was indeed blocking the road. Then, just when the Jeds feared the worst, a German soldier walked out and calmly guided the truck around the tank and they were once again on their way. The Panther was obviously flotsam from one of the many columns of retreating Germans.

At last, at two-thirty in the afternoon the truck pulled into Braine, a town about eleven miles east of Soissons, and drove directly to the Costeaux home, where Madame Costeaux was waiting for the men with lunch prepared. The men climbed out of the truck and went into the house; and when they entered the dining room, they were surprised to find it all done up in red, white, and blue—the colors of the Allies. Jean Delviche also noticed that the dishes were decorated with the Cross of Lorraine. They sat down and enjoyed the fine lunch and good wine and topped it off with champagne.

At eight that evening, the men climbed back into the truck to go to the farm where they were to stay. Seigneur, Costeaux, and another FFI man named Jean Plantier got into the truck with the Jeds and they got underway. When they'd left Braine they found their route blocked by a train, which was stopped at a road crossing, obstructing traffic. After waiting for about ten minutes, the men decided to try a different route. They drove around the train station and made what they considered a long enough detour before heading back to the main road. But then a column of German army trucks cluttered the road and, as if that weren't enough, it began to rain.

Eventually, the road cleared and the men drove on to the farm, near the hamlet of Rugny, where the Jeds would be staying with a family named Mathieu. The team was cautioned to remain as inconspicuous as possible, for there were an estimated three thousand Germans in the immediate area.

In the week that followed, the Jeds of team Augustus helped the FFI get organized for guerrilla operations and sent messages urging Special Force Headquarters to drop weapons. German convoys continuously passed through the area and would have made lucrative targets, but the FFI lacked enough weapons and explosives to carry out anything more than harassing attacks. If only the Jeds had arrived back in June.

While they waited for London to come through with the parachute drops, the men gathered information about enemy activity in the area and radioed it back to SFHQ. During their first three days at Rugny, they reported on German train and convoy movements and on the general disorganized state of the enemy units withdrawing through the area to the northeast. They also informed London that they had gotten their hands on German demolition plans for the channel port of Le Havre. The port was a hundred and forty miles west of the Jeds' location, and the plans apparently had been smuggled out to an area where the resistance could hand them off to the Allies. Of more immediate interest to team Augustus, though, were details they were given on some extensive fortifications located just north of Soissons.

Four and a half miles northeast of Soissons, the Margival fortification had been constructed early in the war to serve as Hitler's headquarters during the planned invasion of England. It was an expansive steel-reinforced concrete bunker system, complete with shelters and pillboxes, underground and above-ground command posts, and a network of connecting trenches. Ingeniously well-camouflaged in a sheltered and heavily wooded valley, the complex was difficult to see at ground level, and had been built away from cities to protect it from Allied bombing. Anti-aircraft batteries had been placed in surrounding villages. Comfortable accommodations lay inside the thick concrete walls and the bunkers had armored roofing. There were well furnished and decorated quarters for the theater commander and his staff, conference rooms, and an operations room complete with map cases. Outside the buildings, concrete streets and winding, paved walkways were lined with lampposts and large camouflage netting covered the entire works.[11] There was even a swimming pool.

But the Margival complex had gone largely unused since its construction, although Hitler had met there with Field Marshals Gerd von Rundstedt and Erwin Rommel on June 17 to discuss operations in Normandy.[12] Major Bonsall, probably unaware that the complex might be unoccupied, was determined to get details of the Margival fortifications, as well as the Le Havre demolition plans, to London.

Bonsall and Côté didn't leave the Mathieu farm very often, but occasionally would walk to Seigneur's command post located in a village about a mile up the road. Otherwise, contact between team Augustus and the command post was maintained twice each day through a young female courier. Captain Delviche often accompanied Seigneur to meetings with FFI leaders in the surrounding area. On Wednesday, August 23, all three Jeds met with the departmental FFI chief and the chief of the Soissons FFI at Rugny to discuss planned guerrilla operations. Still, though, little could be done without the delivery of arms and other supplies from London.

Every night, remnants of the German armies from Normandy continued to shuffle through the area to the northeast. Most didn't remain in the Soissons area for long. The Panzer Lehr Division, for example, had been ordered to an assembly area just north of Soissons on August 17 but, by the twenty-fourth, most of the division had moved on to the east.[13] The Panther tank which the Jeds had seen stalled on the road as they neared Soissons from the north on the twenty-first might have belonged to the Panzer Lehr.

Special Force Headquarters in London heard from team Augustus again on the twenty-fifth, and the message was one of frustration. "IMPOSSIBLE TO FORM MAQUIS NOW DUE TO ONE, TOO MANY BOCHE; TWO, LACK OF GOOD HIDING AREAS; THREE, VERY FEW ARMS."[14] The remainder of the message reiterated the Jeds' assessment of the quality and potential of the guerrilla forces in the Aisne. Many small maquis groups had been trained and they all had good leaders, but they were ineffective because of the shortage of arms. The Jed team repeated its urgent need for an immediate arms drop and asked for a second load to be dropped two days after the first.

The Allies had gotten most of their lead divisions across the Seine by August 26, and were pushing eastward on the heels of the retreating Germans. At the northern extent of the Allied lines, General Montgomery's army group drove northeastward toward Belgium and Holland, following the coastline. To his right was General Bradley's army group, whose First Army was attacking to the northeast, along Montgomery's right flank, while Patton's Third Army attacked due east toward Metz.

Brigadier General Maurice Rose's 3rd Armored Division—spear-heading First Army's attack—set out on a northeasterly track from its starting point near Paris, a course which would take it straight through Soissons and Laon and on into Belgium. Following close on its heels were two infantry divisions, one on each flank.

After pushing off from the Seine, the 3rd Armored Division fought through a German infantry division which had been deployed as a covering force for the withdrawing enemy. Rose's division initially followed a broad corps reconnaissance screen but, as the division picked up speed, the cavalry group split to the north and south to provide flank security and Rose's tanks rolled forward in the lead.

The pursuit by Bradley's armies quickly became a rout, a war of attrition, the Allies intent on destroying as much of the German army in France as possible before it reached the frontier. For once the Germans reached the Rhine and the Siegfried Line—their string of fortifications along the border—they surely would throw up a stiff defense. Breaking through such a fortified line could be costly for the Allies; the more Germans that could be knocked out of the war—before they reached the Rhine—the better.

The 3rd Armored Division approached Soissons from the west and southwest, and its first objective—much more important than capturing the city—was the seizure of crossings over the Aisne River, which runs on an east-west course through Soissons. From there, plans called for the division to continue moving toward Laon, capital of the Aisne department, which lay about nineteen miles to the northeast.

Eager to contribute to the Allied advance, just as it had done in Brittany and the Loire Valley, Special Force Headquarters proceed-ed to drop Jedburgh teams ahead of the divisions driving eastward. Divisions of the First and Third Armies began advancing much more rapidly than expected, however, overpowering everything in their path, and they overran some of these Jed teams shortly after the teams jumped in.

Jeds operating ahead of General Bradley's army group found life behind enemy lines to be even more hazardous than usual as areas became congested with retreating German formations. Movement by Jeds became so risky that some teams, like Augustus, found it necessary to operate in civilian clothes, forfeiting whatever protection of combatant status the uniform might have provided in the event of capture. The provisions of the Geneva Conventions offered no protection to soldiers operating in civilian clothes and carrying false identification papers.

News soon reached team Augustus that U.S. ground troops were approaching Soissons, and the Jeds decided to attempt to get through to them. They discussed how to go about it with Seigneur and Costeaux and made plans to leave on Monday morning, August 28.

German forces withdrawing through French towns and villages often grabbed everything they could carry—and it wasn't just a matter of soldiers filling their pockets. In one case, an Allied unit captured a thirty-four-car train headed for Germany, loaded to the hilt with wine and cognac, liver paste and sardines, canned foods and margarine.[15] On Sunday morning, Seigneur and Costeaux went out to get tobacco, but a German convoy had pulled out at five that morning and enemy troops had beaten them to it—there was none to be had. Some SS troops broke the lock to the courtyard where Costeaux kept the truck and looked it over, seeming tempted to take it. Costeaux and the others felt very lucky, for they had just removed some munitions from the vehicle and hidden them nearby. The truck didn't prove enough of a temptation, though, and the Germans left it alone. Luckily, it would still be available to haul the Jeds the next day.

The Jeds planned to head out to the west of Soissons on Monday, because that was where they expected to find U.S. troops approaching the town. But the Americans weren't the only ones heading for the Soissons area. Germans, too, would soon be approaching, from the northwest.

By late August, Germany's Fifth Panzer Army was an army in name only. On the twenty-eighth, the army reported that it had only twenty-four tanks, thirteen hundred men, and sixty artillery pieces remaining. In all, only about one hundred and twenty German tanks had made it back across the Seine to join in the withdrawal toward Germany.[16] The Allies estimated that, since D-Day, the enemy had lost the equivalent of about thirty divisions.[17] What remained of the enemy marched eastward, occasionally making a stand to fight for time to create a more orderly withdrawal. Rear guard formations tried to slow the advancing Allies, tried to provide some protection for the dusty columns of tired tanks and half-tracks, trucks and staff cars, horse-drawn artillery, and even troops on bicycle. The rear guards were often overrun or cut off by Allied units, however, or were simply brushed aside to be mopped up by follow-on units or by the FFI.

Overwhelmed by the speed of the Allied advance, German troops often were taken completely by surprise. On one occasion, the 3rd Armored Division caught a group of Germans resting under a stand of trees, drinking wine. The Wehrmacht was fleeing France like a street gang being run out of a rival's turf. It was as if the great blitzkrieg machine had been thrown into reverse.

Hauptmann (Captain) Helmut Ritgen, a tank battalion commander in the Panzer Lehr Division, later wrote that, for stragglers and small groups of Germans, the retreat was "like running the gauntlet through a hate-filled enemy country in an uprising." Which, of course, is exactly what it was. Going on to assess the effectiveness of the Jedburghs and the FFI, Ritgen (who would retire from Germany's NATO contingent as a colonel in 1976) wrote, "As time went by and they gained experience, they developed into a real threat for the German withdrawal."[18]

Seigneur and Jean Plantier were in the Soissons area on Monday morning, and they needed to return to Rugny to pick up the Jeds. But Germans were on the roads in such numbers that the men could not risk making the trip with their weapons, so they hid the guns in Vaux, a hamlet just west of Soissons. Then they drove back to Seigneur's command post, arriving at noon, and began preparations for driving the Jeds toward the American lines. More Germans had arrived in the village and, when it came time for the men to leave, they had to be careful.

The Jeds had heard that American forces were only seven or eight miles away, and they had heard right. The 3rd Armored Division had crossed the Marne on Sunday and was approaching Soissons and Braine, fighting through elements of two German divisions to get there.

At one o'clock the truck arrived at the Mathieu farm. The FFI men helped the Jeds load their equipment in the back and hide it under a pile of rags. An FFI man named Émile Fortier joined them as they all climbed aboard and got under way. They headed for a town on the Oise River about nineteen miles west of Laon, where they thought they could make contact with an American unit, but they first intended to stop at Vaux and retrieve the weapons Seigneur and Plantier had hidden there that morning. Suddenly, about a half mile before reaching Vaux, the men saw a column of tanks on the horizon.

"What's that?" asked Fortier.

"They're American tanks," answered Major Bonsall.

"Hell, they're shooting. Maybe they'll shoot at us."

"Maybe," Bonsall said, "and they aim well."[19]

The men in the truck had made it this far without incident, so they took a chance and drove straight for the lead tank. Bonsall and Delviche were determined to get the information they had gathered on German defenses north of the Aisne to the American commander. After delivering the information, the Jed officers hoped to be able to make their way back behind German lines again to continue their work. Perhaps, they thought, they would be able to break back through the lines tomorrow with the help of a patrol of three or four Sherman tanks.

When the truck reached the tank column, the Jeds got out and approached the lead tank. The men identified themselves and Major Bonsall asked to see the commander of the column. When they met the commander, Bonsall said he needed to be taken to the commanding general of the division, and arrangements were quickly made. Captain Delviche then told the FFI men to take the truck and return to Rugny and wait for the Jeds there.

The tanks were from the 3rd Armored Division, and by day's end they would seize two crossings over the Aisne, one at Soissons and another nearby. But they quickly ran into increased resistance from

Germans dug in north of the river. The Americans were probably unaware that they were running Hitler's senior commander in the west out of his headquarters. Field Marshal Walther Model, commander of Army Group B and acting commander in chief of Germany's Western Front, had temporarily occupied the Margival complex north of Soissons. After less than two weeks in the place, however, he was now forced to scurry sixty miles to the north to relocate his headquarters west of Cambrai.[20]

It was a thin defense which the Germans had thrown up along the Aisne; and by the morning of the twenty-ninth, in bleak weather, Americans were pouring across the river. Near Soissons and Braine tanks and anti-aircraft guns of the 3rd Armored Division shot up three German trains.

Late that day, Jedburgh team Augustus briefed officers of the 3rd Armored Division's tactical command post, which was setting up in a village about six miles east of Soissons. The division staff was very interested in any information the Jeds had on the Margival fortifications. Division units were already crossing the Aisne and earlier FFI reports had indicated the existence of expansive concrete fortifications in the area.[21] The Jeds gave them everything they had.

That evening, team Augustus was driven by jeep back to the village where Seigneur had his command post. The village was by then in American hands, and Gaston Costeaux decided to drive the three Jeds to Soissons, where they took a room at the Hotel de la Croix d'Or and remained there until five the next afternoon.

Sherman tanks and self-propelled artillery, tank destroyers and anti-aircraft guns, trucks and half-tracks continued to pour across the Aisne throughout Tuesday and Wednesday as the 3rd Armored Division expanded its bridgehead, seizing the high ground north of the river and then pushing out to the northeast. Troops soon found the extensive concrete fortifications at Margival and, to their great relief, they found the complex vacant. The enemy had fallen back to the north. And the Allied troops had no idea of the prize they had just missed—Field Marshal Model, senior German commander in the west.

A dozen miles ahead, atop a long narrow ridge, with its thirteenth-century Gothic cathedral rising above all else like an over-sized cake decoration, lay the town of Laon, capital of the Aisne department. A thousand years earlier it had been a royal city and capital of all of France. From its ridge-top perch, Laon looked out over the broad flat plains of the Aisne more than three hundred feet below, a panorama of pasturelands and rivers and gray villages huddled around church steeples.

Wednesday, August 30, began as another day of dreary weather with an overcast sky. Troops of the 1st Infantry Division, on the 3rd Armored's left flank, had been marching through the same wheat fields south of Soissons, up the same chalky-white farm roads, through the same homely villages, that the division's dough-boys had known twenty-six years earlier during the great Aisne-Marne counteroffensive of World War I. Now they entered Soissons and took over security of the crossing sites while the 3rd Armored Division pushed on, moving into Laon in force, catching up with lead elements which had entered the town the night before. There the division shot up three more German troop trains, and reconnaissance elements moved out about three miles to the north and east of the town. That afternoon the Germans began forming another thin defense, this time north of Laon.

Fifth Panzer Army had ordered its 116th Panzer Division, after crossing the Seine, to pull back to an area east of Laon, where it was to be refurbished. By the twenty-ninth, the division was still about seventy miles west of Laon, but another German tank division was much closer.

With the British pushing them from the west, officers of the Fifth Panzer Army began to see a new threat from the U.S. forces advancing along their right flank. Swift action was needed to avoid encirclement by the American First Army's drive to the northeast across the Germans' path of retreat. The 9th SS Panzer Division had been ordered to pull back eastward to the Somme, and while the division's rear guard was still engaged by British armor west of Amiens, its lead units were sent southward to establish blocking positions in the area between Laon and Soissons. In fact, the regimental-size combat group, or kampfgruppe, which attacked toward Soissons to establish the blocking positions constituted virtually all the division's remaining effective combat power. The group probably had no more than five to ten tanks left, however, and it was stopped cold when it ran into the 3rd Armored Division at the Oise-Aisne Canal north of Soissons.[22]

That same day, lead elements of the 116th Panzer Division began arriving in the area northwest of Laon. At around noon on Wednesday, Generalleutnant (Major General) Gerhard Graf von Schwerin, commander of the 116th, learned that the Americans had already taken Laon. He immediately decided to establish an east-west defense line along the Serre River, about nine miles north of Laon. Units of the 116th began moving into position along the north bank of the Serre immediately and continued to do so throughout the night.[23]

By late in the day of August 30, units of the 9th SS Panzer Division were falling back from their fight with 3rd Armored Division on the canal north of Soissons. Moving northward, they skirted around to the west of American-occupied Laon. Then they turned back to the northeast and pulled into the area north of Laon and south of the Serre River.

By nightfall, American forces of the 3rd Armored Division had begun probing to the north of Laon.

Stormy weather had moved into the Aisne, and it had been cloudy and rainy all day on the thirtieth, although the sun briefly peeked through the clouds in the evening. Major Bonsall's team did not consider its mission complete, even though it no longer was needed in the southern Aisne because the area was in American hands. So the Jeds were determined to get back behind German lines and continue their work farther north. And they were certain that this was the time to cross back over the lines, while the stormy weather could help conceal their movement.

Because the Jeds had been operating in civilian clothes and had obtained false French identity papers, they decided that their best means of getting through would be to travel in one of the horse-drawn peasant carts so common to the area. Among the maquis-ards that team Augustus had been training was a somewhat older local farmer by the name of Magniez. The Jeds decided to go to his farm and seek help.

At about five in the afternoon the men left the hotel in Soissons. They had arranged for a 3rd Armored Division jeep to take them to Laon, and from there got a lift on a tank to their starting point, Magniez's farm, a few miles northwest of Laon. Captain Delviche was familiar with the area, and the team soon arrived at the home of Monsieur Magniez, whose farm was scarcely more than a mile from the village where Delviche had been born. The Jeds dined at the Magniez home and then prepared for their journey.

The three men still all wore civilian clothing: Bonsall in gray pants with a white shirt with black stripes; Delviche in black pants, a white shirt and a black tie with white polka dots, a gray hat, and a black leather jacket; and Côté in a gray woolen sweater over a blue shirt, and a Basque beret on his head.

Magniez arranged for the men to use a horse-drawn cart that the Germans had abandoned earlier that day. He hitched one of his horses to it and the Jeds loaded their gear on the cart and hid it as best they could. By about nine-thirty they were ready to leave.

According to the latest information the Jeds had, they judged that the German lines should be just south of Froidmont, a town about nine miles, by the main road, north of Laon. Magniez gave the men directions to the home of his brother-in-law in Froidmont and told them to go straight there. Captain Delviche was anxious to avoid any main roads, such as Route Nationale 2, which ran north from Laon to Froidmont. They would be less likely to run into German convoys, strongpoints, or roadblocks if they stuck to back roads.

Magniez explained that there was another route, a road which passed through a few villages before reaching Froidmont. It was a longer way—about fourteen or fifteen miles long—but it should be safer. The farmer then decided to ride with the Jeds part of the way, until he was sure they were on the right road. As the Jeds and Magniez set out in the cart, others from the local maquis, mostly armed farmers, waited in the barn next to the old man's farmhouse.

At around ten o'clock, confident that the Jeds knew the way, Magniez left them and returned to his farm. The road took the Jeds past one village, then along a stretch of about five miles before they reached the next. A mile or two after that, the road curved to the right, crossed a railroad track, then curved back to the left and through another village. The men still were about five miles from Froidmont and had one more village, Barenton-sur-Serre, which was a couple of miles short of their destination, to pass through.

Barenton-sur-Serre was a quiet commune of about a hundred people. The roar of guns and the bedlam of battle had been almost continuous in this area during the First World War, and the village had been partly destroyed by shelling. The place had been mostly spared devastation during this war, although it had been in this very area, back when the Germans invaded in May 1940, that a young brigadier named Charles de Gaulle had led his tank division in a briefly successful counterattack. All told, in two world wars the good people of Barenton had lived through eight years of German occupation.

By the evening of August 30, the Germans were attempting to stabilize their retreat somewhat by establishing, as much as their reduced capabilities allowed, a line of defense north of Laon, running east-to-west generally along the Serre River. Any delay of the Americans along this line would aid in the retreat of the German armies to the northeast. Barenton-sur-Serre lies just south of the Serre, in an area where there now were scattered elements of the 9th SS Panzer Division. The 116th Panzer Division occupied positions along the river's north bank. Small strongpoints or roadblocks—often consisting of a few tanks and some infantry—were hastily thrown up at key road intersections throughout the area.[24] And it was into this area that Jed team Augustus now drove the horse-drawn cart.

A light rain had begun falling earlier that night and at about 10:15 it became a downpour. Lightning and thunder added to the miserable wetness of the driving rain, making visibility and hearing hopeless for the Jeds in the horse cart.

Two and a half miles short of Froidmont the cart approached Barenton-sur-Serre from the southwest. They crossed over a railway bridge and came to an intersection just inside the village, near the station, and the men possibly did not even see the three German tanks which were posted at the crossroads.

Although no one in the village witnessed what happened next, the Jeds were apparently stopped by German troops who then searched the cart and found the team's American weapons, British radios, and other gear hidden in the back. At ten forty-five that night, the people of Barenton heard seven shots. First there were two, followed a short while later by five more in rapid succession. About thirty minutes later the German tanks pulled out and left Barenton-sur-Serre.

Sixteen-year-old Armand Rot was at his home—about a hundred and fifty yards from the intersection—when he heard the shots. Just as he looked outside he saw a frightened horse pass by pulling an empty cart.

Back at the Magniez farm, the small group of farmers gathered in the barn wondered if the Jedburghs had been successful in crossing the lines. Outside, the storm continued to rage. Suddenly, the barn door blew open and the men saw a huge shape silhouetted against the night. They watched as the huge figure slowly entered and approached Magniez. Then the men recognized the outline of the horse, which had come home.

When morning came, young Armand Rot and others from the village discovered three bodies lying in the mud near the intersection. None of the villagers recognized the dead men. But among the items found on the bodies were military identification cards. The bodies of John Bonsall and Jean Delviche were found side by side. That of Roger Côté was about a dozen yards away, on the other side of the road. He lay face down, his arms twisted, looking as if he had tried to make a run for it. Around his neck the villagers found a silver chain with a tiny cross and a medal inscribed: "I am a Catholic; please call a priest."

All three men had large head wounds. Nearby lay a seat from the cart and it looked as if it had been ripped out during a search. The cart would later be found in a village just north of Barenton.

The mayor and people of Barenton-sur-Serre buried the three men in unmarked graves in the cemetery next to the village's small St. Martin church. Armand Rot went home and made a French flag from pieces of cloth he found in his mother's chiffonier, then lay the tricolor on the graves. Members of a nearby maquis arrived and, despite the fact that Germans were still in the area, formed a guard of honor and performed a military funeral ceremony.

Later, Armand Rot recovered the flag he had made and gave it to some American soldiers who mounted it on their jeep.

The meager defense line which the Germans had established along the Serre quickly dissipated when the 3rd Armored Division began its attack northeast from Laon later that morning. From Laon, the division pushed on to the northeast for about twenty miles and then straight north toward Mons, Belgium, crossing the border on September 2, just eighteen days after crossing the Seine.

In a final attempt to reach Jedburgh team Augustus, which had gone silent, Special Force Headquarters transmitted a message on September 16, informing the team that its mission was ended and that the men should return to London at once.

Jedburgh team Augustus was one of many teams dropped into eastern France in late August and September that found it nearly impossible to do its job. Major Bonsall's team had been able to provide some information to the 3rd Armored Division, but even that was of no great importance by then. The team simply had not had enough time to properly organize, arm, and train the maquis of the Aisne to take advantage of the lucrative targets provided by the German convoys withdrawing through the area. And it might have been this which caused the men to believe that their mission was not accomplished, and compelled them to attempt to re-cross to enemy territory and continue on, when they could just as easily have considered their work finished once they had briefed the staff of 3rd Armored Division.

In the end, more than anything else, the Jeds of team Augustus fell victim to simple bad luck. They had really not done anything unsound, and they had been correct in reasoning that the storm would help to conceal their movement. Of the many times Jedburgh teams would pass through German checkpoints, they were the one team unlucky enough to be caught.

Only one other complete Jedburgh team was lost in France. Team Jacob, dropped into the Vosges Mountains of eastern France on the night of August 12–13, lost its French officer when he was killed in action and lost both British members when they were captured. The radio operator spent the rest of the war in a prison camp and was liberated at war's end, but the British officer was executed.

*　*　*

Just one month after Patton's Third Army had broken out at Avranches and swept into Brittany, the Allies were on the frontiers of Belgium and Luxembourg and were about to enter the regions of Alsace and Lorraine in eastern France. But they were soon to be joined by another American army and a Free French army, which were driving northward from the Mediterranean coast. For, on August 15, the same day that Jedburgh team Augustus had departed England for the Aisne, Allied forces had made amphibious and airborne landings on the south coast of France. And roughly two dozen Jedburgh teams would be dropped into southern France to organize FFI support for those ground forces.

10

WAR COMES TO THE RIVIERA

O NE danger that the Jedburghs, and the circuit organizers before them, always warned resistance groups about was that of attempting a full-scale uprising before the time was right. Guerrillas were most effective against modern mechanized armies when those armies were simultaneously fighting conventional forces, or were at least under the threat of imminent engagement by such forces. Any attempt by guerrillas to engage large conventional combat forces in a toe-to-toe fight could be disastrous for the guerrillas. But the Allies were not always successful in persuading the FFI to wait for a signal that the time was right to begin full-scale guerrilla attacks against the Germans.

The fact that Grenoble, in the Alps of southeastern France, is known today as a former site of the Winter Olympics says much about the terrain of the region. Southwest of Grenoble lies a high mountain plateau, twenty-five miles long and ten miles wide, called the Vercors Massif. It is a natural citadel, a spectacular mountaintop wilderness of dense pine and beech forests with intermittent rolling grasslands, and in 1944 it could be reached only by discreet trails up steep, craggy mountain walls. There were deep gorges and mountain outcroppings, with one peak reaching nearly seven thousand feet.

Shortly after the Allied landings in Normandy, a large resistance force, which had been gathering on the Vercors Massif for the past year, had prematurely risen so boldly and in such numbers that the Germans could not ignore it. By the middle of June, some four thousand guerrilla fighters had rallied on the plateau and a German division based in Grenoble had begun probing the Vercors defenses. American bombers dropped more than four hundred containers of arms on June 25 and on Bastille Day, July 14, seventy-two B-17 Flying Fortresses from England dropped another 862 containers.

These drops were made in daylight, however, and as the maquis tried to gather up the containers from the open fields, German planes arrived and strafed them. Then, on July 19, German forces numbering nearly fourteen thousand, with tanks, armored cars, and artillery, attacked the resistance stronghold. After fighting for two days, and losing more than six hundred men, the overmatched maquis were forced to disperse. And then the Germans began taking their revenge, pillaging and burning villages on the plateau and killing innocent civilians.[1]

The FFI had learned a tough lesson, but the survivors of the Vercors debacle would be ready to work with Jedburgh teams and other special forces to rebuild, rearm, and re-engage the Germans. An American OSS Operational Group had fought on the Vercors plateau and a few Jedburgh teams had been in southern France at the time, but soon the region would receive many more.

When Henry McIntosh left his West Palm Beach, Florida, home in the fall of 1939 his goal was to become a physician. He entered the pre-med program at Davidson College in North Carolina just about the time Hitler's armies were pulverizing Poland to begin the European war. By the end of 1942, McIntosh had completed all requirements for his BS degree and had been accepted to the medical schools of the University of Pennsylvania, Johns Hopkins, and Thomas Jefferson University in Philadelphia. He was to begin medical school in January.

But that winter McIntosh enlisted in the army and because he had been in the ROTC program at Davidson (though he hadn't completed it) he was inducted as a corporal at Camp Blanding, Florida, in February 1943. Almost immediately, the army sent him to Officer Candidate School at Fort Benning, and he graduated with a commission in the infantry in late May. He stayed on at Benning for further training, completing the parachute jump course and the parachute demolition course, and then he was assigned to the post's 542nd Parachute Infantry, an airborne replacement training unit, in July.

That fall, the Jedburgh recruiter came to Fort Benning, and when he reviewed the qualification records of the regiment's officers he noticed that Second Lieutenant Henry McIntosh had taken two years of French in college. The twenty-two-year-old platoon leader was summoned to a large gym to hear the recruiter's pitch along with a few dozen other officers. McIntosh volunteered and reported to Washington in early November.

By the spring of 1944, McIntosh was going through the Jedburgh training program at Milton Hall. But in late April his team and fourteen others were told to pack up their gear; they were being shipped out to North Africa. Earlier that month, British and American special operations planners had proposed sending fifteen Jedburgh teams to North Africa to prepare for insertion from there into the south of France. Eisenhower's operations officer approved the transfer and, on May 2, the fifteen teams boarded a ship called the *Capetown Castle* bound for Oran. They would be joined by another ten teams in June.

To administer the insertion and resupply of special forces teams into southern France, and to maintain radio communications with them, an organization similar to Special Force Headquarters was created in North Africa. The British had established an SOE mission near Algiers in 1942. Code-named Massingham, it was located at a former seaside beach resort called the Club de Pins, at Cap Matifou, fifteen miles west of Algiers. OSS had set up its own office in Algiers the following year, and in May 1944 the two were combined to form the Special Project Operations Center, or SPOC.[2] Although SPOC was administratively subordinate to Allied Force Headquarters (AFHQ), the Mediterranean Theater command, it was to be under the operational direction of SHAEF headquarters in London. It was to be, in effect, a satellite office of Special Force

Headquarters. All operational orders and guidance would pass directly from SFHQ in London to SPOC, although close coordination was maintained with the operations section at AFHQ. A compound of tents and Quonset huts was built to house the Jedburghs as well as OSS Operational Groups. Most missions would be flown from an airfield near the town of Blida, about thirty miles southwest of Algiers.[3]

Lieutenant Henry McIntosh, the lanky six-foot-two future physician, liked the medical significance of the code name given his Jed team during their mission briefing.[4] The team of McIntosh and two Frenchmen would be known as Jed team Chloroform. Leading it was Captain Jacques Martino, a personable man in his early twenties—about the same age as McIntosh—athletically thin, and dark-haired. Martino had been recruited in North Africa, and he knew that his parents' home in France had been taken over by the Germans. Corporal Jean Nicole would be team Chloroform's radio operator.* The team had first been alerted soon after the Allied landings in Normandy, but bad weather had postponed its deployment until the end of June. This team would be the sixth Jedburgh team to deploy to southern France from North Africa.

Team Chloroform's mission would take the men to the beautiful Rhône Alps of southeastern France, between the valley of the mighty south-flowing Rhône River and the mountainous Italian border. There, they were to organize guerrilla operations in the departments of the Drôme and the Hautes-Alpes (High Alps), a land of breathtaking mountain scenery.

A few days after Jedburgh team Chloroform's jump to a drop zone in the Drôme on the night of June 29, the men were taken to a meeting of resistance leaders and special forces men. They were to meet some of the officers with whom they would be working.

One of the men they met was a handsome British officer who went by the field name Roger. A six-footer in his late twenties with

* Jacques Martino's real name was Jacques Martin; that of Jean Nicole was Jean Sassi.

a manicured mustache, he was actually Lieutenant Colonel Francis Cammaerts, and he had been the head of one of SOE's most successful circuits since March of the previous year.

Cammaerts' Jockey circuit was one of the largest and one of the longest-surviving because of his strict security practices. He never spent more than two or three nights in the same place and almost no one in the circuit knew exactly where he was at any given moment.[5] In fact, Cammaerts seemingly had something of a sixth sense when it came to security. When SOE sent him to the field in the spring of 1943, they had intended for him to become Henri Frager's lieutenant, before Frager had gone north to set up the Donkeyman circuit. But Cammaerts had backed out of that relationship largely because he mistrusted Frager's sidekick Roger Bardet.[6]

Cammaerts was a former schoolmaster, and he might have seemed an unusual choice for a circuit organizer. He had come from a distinguished family, his father a well-known Belgian poet, his mother a Shakespearean actress, and his grandmother a former Bayreuth opera singer. Early in the war, he had registered as a conscientious objector, but the death of a brother in the RAF had helped to change his outlook on the war.

By the summer of 1944, Cammaerts controlled a circuit with some ten thousand maquisards, about half of them armed, spread over an area that essentially included all of France south of Lyon and east of the Rhône River. He had so much territory to cover that he often used a motorcycle to travel about.

One man who was at the gathering of resistance leaders needed no introduction to the Jeds of team Chloroform. He was Major Neil Marten, the British officer and only surviving member of Jedburgh team Veganin, which had been dropped into the Drôme on the second night after D-Day. Marten's team had run into trouble that very first night when his radio operator was killed on the jump because his static line had not been hooked up securely. He and the French officer on his team had just received reinforcements, though, in the form of a two-man Jed team—an American officer and a French-Canadian radio operator—sent in four days ago to join them. (Six weeks later, the American officer was captured and spent the remainder of the war in a prison camp in Germany.)

The Jeds also met an FFI leader who was introduced as General

Joseph. He was actually General Henri Zeller, FFI commander for the entire southeastern part of France.[7] Zeller was a career army officer who, after the fall of France, had served as a colonel on the general staff of the Armistice Army at Vichy until it was disbanded in late 1942. As with many of the army's officers, he had then joined the resistance, and worked hard to maintain a military command structure within the FFI of the southeast.

The men of team Chloroform also met a subordinate of Zeller's, an FFI major called Hermine, who was military chief for the Drôme department. Hermine was a former sergeant who had been mobilized in 1939 and later had entered the French air academy. He, too, served in the Vichy government's Armistice Army after the French defeat in 1940, then later joined the resistance and made a name for himself as a flamboyant leader in the Lyon area. Hermine was the type of person who is often described as "colorful"; his fulsome personality made him popular with some but antagonized others.

In early 1944, the Drôme was estimated to hold slightly fewer than five hundred active maquisards, backed up by as many as fifteen hundred sédentaires, as the sedentary reserve—those ready to leave home and join the active maquis as soon as more arms were available—were called.[8] About 70 percent of the Drôme maquisards belonged to the communist FTP, however, and they had grown tired of Hermine's pompousness. The group was demanding his removal from command of the department, and General Zeller had finally agreed to move him. But Zeller thought highly of Hermine and he decided to move the young officer by promoting him to lieutenant colonel and giving him command of the entire "Central Alps" region. Jedburgh team Chloroform had arrived just as Hermine was moving his command post to an area north of Gap, the principal town of the Hautes-Alpes department farther to the east.[9]

One of the sabotage tasks which had been assigned to team Chloroform during its mission briefing was the destruction of a railway line between Gap and Valence. But the men learned from Zeller and Hermine that the FFI had already blown the line three times since D-Day, removing the rails from the scene each time to make repair by the Germans more difficult. In fact, the men were told, the line had not been put back into full operation since the Normandy invasion had begun. The Jeds were taken to inspect some of the maquis troops in the area and to verify the destruction of the Valence-Gap rail line.

Then Hermine and General Zeller asked the Jeds to go with Hermine and to work with him in the Hautes-Alpes, where there were an estimated three thousand Germans. To the Jeds, Hermine appeared to be a strong leader, and they seemed to get on well with him. They also thought that they would be more useful in the Hautes-Alpes, where there weren't as many Allied special forces already operating as there were in the Drôme, and so they agreed to move east into the mountains.

The Jeds set out with a small group of maquisards in a car and a truck on the fourth of July and soon found themselves in the beautiful terrain of the High Alps. They crossed rugged mountain ridges and passed through green meadows, where intermittent scrublands and wheat fields surrounded quaint gray villages with tile roofs the color of old pennies. Towering abruptly in the background were impressive, sometimes snow-capped mountains, with sparse stands of fir and pine clinging to the lower slopes.

After a journey which included a three-day gun battle with Germans in a mountain pass, team Chloroform arrived at a village in a valley northeast of Gap on the night of July 9. But the men soon realized that the villagers here were unaccustomed to resistance activity. Mistaking the Jeds for the hated Milice, the civilians ran for their homes. Then, as Henry McIntosh later reported, "One youngster rushed at us with a Sten and demanded our surrender." The Jeds, however, soon convinced the boy that they were friends, and he ran off to inform the rest of the town.

The Jeds set up a command post nearby and immediately radioed Algiers for a supply drop. They were now about twenty miles northeast of Gap. In addition to arming maquis groups throughout the area, the team needed replenishment of their own supplies, having left theirs cached back in the Drôme.

Then the men met a priest from a nearby village who told them of a drop which had been made in the area about a year earlier. The priest had helped to hide the weapons at the time, and he led the Jeds to the storage site. Luckily, they were also able to find some old French rifles and, at last, the team got down to the business of training guerrilla fighters.

For the next month Martino, McIntosh, and Nicole armed and trained maquis groups throughout the wild, roller-coaster alpine country around Gap, from the rugged Dévoluy Massif in the west to Barcelonnette and the rugged Queyras region in the east, and from Sisteron in the south to Briançon in the north.[10] The men joined the maquis in skirmishes with Germans along Route Nationale 85, the major north-south highway through the mountains which was lined with terraced villages. The highway entered Gap from the south and continued on northward from there to Grenoble. Since 1932, the road had been known as the Route Napoléon because it was up this road that Napoleon Bonaparte and his supporters had journeyed in March 1815 after his escape from exile on the island of Elba.

Team Chloroform also tried to bring in more arms and supplies for the survivors of the Vercors maquis. They began receiving air drops on July 24 on a plateau in the mountains northwest of Gap. Weasel was the code name given to the drop zone atop the plateau—some fifteen hundred to eighteen hundred meters above sea level—and by month's end the Jeds had received more than sixty tons of weapons and ammunition there. They tried in vain to get some of the material to the Vercors. But in the end they distributed all of it among their own maquis.[11]

By early August the Jeds estimated that they had armed and trained approximately fifteen hundred men in the area around Gap, and Hermine thought that his FFI was strong enough to force the town's German garrison to surrender.

The southern Alpine town of Gap sat in a glacier-carved valley where agriculture benefited from a richly fertile soil. It had been a staging post on the north-south route since Roman times and was still a key town on the Route Napoléon. And it would be an important route northward to Grenoble for Allied armies when the invasion of southern France came. From Gap, roads led eastward up to the mountain passes into Italy—roads which could be an avenue of approach if the Germans chose to send armored units across the border and into France.

But before he tried to gain the surrender of the German garrison in Gap, Hermine first wanted to further isolate the garrison by closing off the escape route to the east, a route which might also be used to reinforce the enemy in Gap. To cut this route, a key bridge over the Durance River in the mountains east of Gap, at a village called Savines, would have to be blown. On the afternoon of the fourteenth, the Jeds took forty men and the necessary explosives and set out. The steep approach to Savines was murderous to any-one unaccustomed to walking over such mountainous terrain. The maquis of the region had grown up hiking these mountains, but Lieutenant McIntosh—although in peak condition from months of Jed training—strained to keep up. Leg muscles screamed for relief as lungs labored in the thin mountain air. Eventually the men reached the long bridge and placed their charges. Then, on the afternoon of the fifteenth, a tremendous blast dropped the bridge into the Durance. Every escape route out of Gap had been cut with the exception of the road heading south toward the coast.[12]

An invasion of southern France had been envisioned by the Allies since the fall of 1943. Early plans for Operation Anvil, as it was called, envisioned landings on the beaches of the French Riviera at about the same time as the Overlord landings in Normandy. Such an assault in the south, it was hoped, would hold German forces in southern France that might otherwise be sent to Normandy. The British had argued instead for an operation in the Balkans, with Allied forces striking northward toward Austria. But in the end, and despite British objections, the coast of southern France was chosen as the landing site as much for logistical as for operational reasons; the capture of Marseilles would provide the Allies anoth-er badly needed port.

The timing of the invasion, however, came to be driven not by strategy but by landing craft production. To ensure availability of the required number of landing craft for Overlord, the Anvil opera-tion had to be postponed for more than two months.

Commanding the invasion force was a veteran of the fighting on Guadalcanal, Lieutenant General Alexander M. Patch. Troops of his Seventh U.S. Army began coming ashore in the St-Tropez area on the morning of Tuesday, August 15. Patch's invasion force included an American corps of three infantry divisions pulled fresh from the fighting in Italy, Free French forces eventually amounting to an army of two corps, a division-size provisional airborne unit which included both British and American paratroopers, and an independent American-Canadian special forces unit. Air support was provided by a tactical air command operating from Corsica. Because it was feared that the operation's code name, Anvil, had been compromised, the name was changed to Dragoon two weeks before the landings.

German forces defending the Mediterranean coast of France belonged to the Nineteenth Army, and in the middle of August it consisted of five infantry divisions and two reserve divisions. Then, virtually on the eve of the invasion, the Germans had sent the 11th Panzer Division, then at nearly full strength, from the Atlantic coast to the southeast to reinforce the Nineteenth Army.

Seventh Army commanders were relying on strong support from the French resistance, and planners estimated that there were as many as fifteen thousand to twenty thousand trained and armed maquis fighters in southeastern France. Another thirty thousand to forty thousand were estimated to be standing by, waiting for additional arms to be dropped. In fact, the expectation of strong support from the resistance had been a factor in the Allies' decision to launch the invasion.[13] General Eisenhower had reported on how FFI support for the Overlord operation had "exceeded his most optimistic anticipations," and the Allies hoped to build an FFI force as large as eighty-four thousand in southern France.[14] General Wilson, the theater commander in the Mediterranean, planned to drop as many supplies as he could, but he had a limited number of aircraft in North Africa for such missions. Eisenhower offered to help from his end by arming fifty-three thousand guerrillas through air drops from England-based American bombers, two hundred to three hundred sorties in all.[15]

Wilson's staff had coordinated with the Special Project Operations Center to provide the FFI with a list of targets to be attacked in support of the invasion. The staff had been kept abreast of German movements and activity throughout the planning period by reports from the maquis. And, as with the Overlord operation, execution orders signaling the FFI to hit their designated targets had been broadcast by the BBC on August 14 in the form of pre-arranged messages.[16]

At General Patch's Seventh Army headquarters, special operations planning and coordination was the responsibility of a sixty-four-man British-American attachment called No. 4 Special Forces Unit.

By this time, it had become obvious to the German high command, and even to Hitler, that France was all but lost, and that Germany's only hope lay in saving the greatest number of tanks, artillery pieces, and troops as possible to defend the homeland at its western border. On August 17, two days after the Dragoon landings, Hitler sent a message to his army group commander in southern France ordering him to begin withdrawing all of his forces back toward the Rhine. The only exception was to be a small force remaining at the ports of Marseilles and Toulon, and they were to be ordered to fight to the last man to keep these ports out of the hands of the Allies. Because the message went out by radio on an Enigma cipher machine, however, its contents were quickly provided to General Patch in the top secret Ultra message traffic. So Patch was reading the withdrawal order at about the same time as the German commander.[17]

Major General Lucien Truscott, the American corps commander under Patch, had planned, once his force was firmly ashore, to create a small, rapidly mobile strike force. While the main thrust of Seventh Army would be up the valley of the Rhône River, this force would strike northward farther to the east, up the historic highway known as the Route Napoléon, with the objective of reaching Grenoble as quickly as possible. Information about the planned withdrawal of the German Nineteenth Army added the opportunity of an envelopment by such a rapidly moving Allied force, hoping to drive northward fast enough to cut off the retreating Germans.

On August 18, the provisional unit was quickly formed—a battalion of motorized infantry, two companies of Sherman tanks, a company of tank destroyers, a battalion of self-propelled artillery, a cavalry reconnaissance squadron, and engineers and other support units. Command of the unit went to the deputy corps commander, Brigadier General Frederick B. Butler, and the unit became known as Task Force Butler.

Throughout the planning for Operation Anvil (Dragoon), and during the two-week period immediately following the landings, Seventh Army had some concern about the possibility of German reinforcements arriving from northern Italy. Along the mountainous border with France, there were five Alpine passes through which such a threat could emerge. On August 18, the Jeds of team Chloroform received word that a Panzer division was approaching Gap from Italy and would be coming south and west on the hairpin mountain road from Guillestre. It had to be stopped. The Jeds saw three possible routes which might be used by the tanks to cross the wide Durance River. They could use a bridge on the main route or they could take either of two secondary routes. Knowing that the Allies might need to use the bridges later, the Jeds decided to block all three routes without destroying them.

In the early morning hours of the nineteenth, trucks were put in place to block the main bridge. But when the Jeds went to the two smaller bridges they found that an FFI group from another district had already blown both of them.

If the Route Napoléon was to be used by the Americans as a speedy road to Grenoble to outflank the Germans, some key towns along the route had to be secured as soon as possible. One of these key towns, Gap, was in Jedburgh team Chloroform's area. Hermine had sent a message to the thousand-man German garrison in Gap on August 17 demanding its surrender, and two days later the Germans gave their answer. They understood the hopelessness of their situation but preferred to wait and surrender to an American unit, which they understood was already in Sisteron, thirty miles to the south.

So on the morning of Saturday, August 19, Captain Martino, Lieutenant McIntosh, and two FFI officers headed south to make contact with the American unit. They soon met vehicles of the 117th Cavalry Reconnaissance Squadron, the vanguard of Task Force Butler. It was the highly mobile recon squadron's job to probe ahead of the main part of the advancing task force with its half-tracks, light tanks, jeeps, and command cars, and locate the enemy. The main body of Task Force Butler had advanced roughly ninety miles inland, a third of the way to Grenoble, and was at Sisteron.[18]

The Jeds and the FFI officers proceeded to General Butler's command post, descending from the limestone mountains around Gap into the valley of the broad Durance River. They headed southward until the valley closed in at the confluence of the Durance and another river and where the Durance then cut between two mountains. At that spot lay the town of Sisteron, stretched out along the west bank of the Durance. It was an ochre town—pale yellow buildings with old rust-colored tile roofs—and it had a Mediterranean look and feel about it, unlike the more alpine character of Gap and the country to the north. At the point where the mountains on either side of the Durance pinched right up to the river's banks, the town was squeezed tight and narrow between the river along one side and the base of a nearly vertical wall of rock on the other.

Perched on a mountaintop high above were the remains of an impressive eleventh-century stone citadel, indicating that the strategic importance of the town's location, sitting as it does at a natural choke point, had been recognized for a very long time. Sadly, American bombers had largely destroyed the medieval citadel only four days earlier, at the time of the landings on the Riviera coast, because it had been occupied by German troops. Only the fortress's keep and sentry walk remained undamaged.

The Jeds found General Butler's command post just south of town. Martino and McIntosh met the white-haired Butler and explained the situation in Gap, and told of the German desire to surrender only to American forces. Could the general send an element of his task force ahead with the Jeds to accept it?

Butler agreed and sent a platoon of tanks and a reconnaissance element back with the Jeds at five that afternoon. The Jeds arranged for maquis groups to approach Gap from the direction of the three blocked roads while the tank platoon approached the town from the south. But it soon became clear that the Germans had changed their minds about surrendering, and a fierce battle raged for two hours. When the fighting was over, some twelve hundred Germans surrendered to the maquis and were turned over to the American recon force. According to General Truscott, the American corps commander, similar action occurred not far away five days later, when some four thousand Germans surrendered to the U.S. 36th Infantry Division rather than to the maquisards who had them surrounded.[19]

Intelligence reports indicating that the German Nineteenth Army had been ordered to withdraw northward up the eastern bank of the Rhône had now reached General Truscott, commander of the American VI Corps. Late on the night of the twentieth, he sent a message to General Butler ordering him to move his task force west to Montelimar, on the Rhône River, to block the enemy's withdrawal. The 36th Infantry Division, which had been following Butler, would continue north on the Route Napoléon, through Gap and on toward Grenoble.

Seventh Army, in what came to be called the Champagne Campaign, pushed northward at a pace the troops had never known during the months of fighting in Italy. Division command posts moved many times a day, and signalmen laid as much as a hundred and sixty miles of wire every twenty-four hours.[20] Quartermaster drivers stayed at the wheel twenty to twenty-four hours a day to keep up, as supply lines from the beaches grew steadily longer. One driver, returning to the beaches with a truckload of German prisoners, reported to those in the rear that the maquis was "going wild" and that the Germans were "surrendering by the thousands."[21]

All along the Rhône Valley the maquis were taking a terrible toll on the enemy. Sergeant Audie Murphy of the 3rd Infantry Division—later to earn the Congressional Medal of Honor, a battlefield commission, and the distinction by war's end of being America's most decorated soldier—later recalled how the infantry would sometimes "find whole towns liberated by the FFI and waiting our entrance."[22] When a *Stars and Stripes* correspondent asked a staff sergeant in the 45th Infantry Division about the maquis, the noncom remarked, "They've been terrific. Boy have they saved us trouble."[23]

With help from the FFI, the 36th Infantry Division took the

mountain resort city of Grenoble on August 23, and the bells of the city's university echoed throughout the valley. Back on the coast, Marseilles and Toulon, with their valuable ports, were in Allied hands by the twenty-eighth.

Tough battles were fought by American and Free French forces at blocking positions north of Montélimar, on the Rhône, through the end of August. But, in the end, the better part of five German divisions broke through and continued up the valley toward Lyon, France's second city, eighty miles to the north.

On August 30, just as the Americans were approaching Lyon, General Truscott learned that the FFI wanted to take the city, which had been a hotbed of resistance since early in the war. And, for political reasons, the Allied high command preferred that French forces enter the city first. So when an American division reached Lyon in the first days of September, it was ordered to stay to the east of the city. The maquis, aided by two Jedburgh teams and four OSS Operational Groups, were already fighting within the city. When the commander of the 36th Infantry Division finally sent a patrol of officers into Lyon on September 2, the men found that the maquis had cleared the city of Germans. The next day a Free French infantry division entered Lyon from the west.

Team Chloroform continued to work with the maquis of the Hautes-Alpes on into September, providing protection to Seventh Army's right flank and blocking German forces on the roads leading from the mountain passes along the Italian border. By September 20, however, its work was finished. Nearly three months after jumping into the Drôme, team Chloroform went to Grenoble, then on to Paris, and on the twenty-fifth they flew to London.

Seventh Army continued the chase, advancing twenty-five to forty miles a day in an attempt to keep up with the Germans as the enemy raced toward the Belfort Gap. The Germans would next try to delay them at Besançon, a fortified city of about eighty thousand on the Doubs River southwest of Belfort.

11

UKRAINIANS IN THE FFI

B Y late August, General Bradley's and General Montgomery's army groups were pursuing the Germans eastward from Normandy while American and French forces were driving northward after landing on the Mediterranean coast. The east-bound and north-bound Allied armies were on a course to converge near the town of Dijon in eastern France.

What remained of Germany's army in southern France was racing to reach an area in the mountainous eastern part of France near the borders of Germany and Switzerland. Known throughout history as the Gate of Burgundy, the Belfort Gap is a natural fifteen-mile-wide pass between the Jura Mountains, girdling the Swiss Alps to the south, and the much older and heavily forested Vosges Mountains to the north, in Alsace, just across the Rhine from Germany's Black Forest. It had been a strategic corridor since Roman times, and in August 1944 it provided the surest route for German forces trying to withdraw into southern Germany to establish a defense along the Rhine. And the primary route for the Germans to use through this picturesque region called the Franche-Comté was the road leading up the valley of the Doubs River, running northeastward from Besançon to Belfort.

Special Force Headquarters hoped to make the most of the guerrilla warfare opportunities provided by such a concentration of enemy movement through such a narrow corridor. On Friday, August 11, SFHQ called three more Jedburgh teams down to London from Milton Hall to be briefed for deployment to the region. One of those teams was assigned the code name Cedric, and it was led by probably the most flamboyant of the American Jedburgh officers.

Captain Douglas DeWitt Bazata was a modern-day swashbuckler. In a unit full of colorful personalities, he was in a class by himself, unabashedly contemptuous of military rank and never fully submissive to uniformed authority. Fellow Jedburgh Captain Bernard Knox would later write that Bazata "was famous among us for a brazen audacity, both physical and verbal, that took people's breath away and enabled him to get away with actions and remarks that were, in a military milieu, outrageous. He used to address full colonels, for example, as 'Sugar.'"[1] The rusty-haired thirty-three-year-old former Marine from Pennsylvania had proved himself as a boxer and as a marksman by the time he accepted an army commission in 1942, and he had joined OSS a year later.

Bazata's French counterpart on team Cedric was Captain Chapel,* a dark-haired man of medium height with a quick, handsome face. Like most of the French Jeds, he had been a soldier in the regular army before the war. The two officers had settled on a tall, quiet young American as their radio operator. He was Technical Sergeant Dick Floyd, a handsome nineteen year old from Brooklyn who had entered the army in April 1943 after having graduated from high school in January of that year.[2]

Bazata's team was to jump into the department of the Haute-Saône, in the upland region of eastern France known as the Franche-Comté, bordering the northwest corner of Switzerland. The quiet Franche-Comté, with its heavily forested hills laced with winding roads, had been largely overlooked by pre-war tourists, and had slumbered through much of the war. Captain Chapel had originally come from the area but had not been there since his youth, though he retained the distinct Franc-Comtois accent.

* Chapel's real name was Louis Lesne.

This had been an active, but perilous, territory for SOE's F Section circuits since April 1943. Jed team Cedric's mission, the briefer explained, would be to work in support of one of those circuits known as Treasurer. Specifically, the team would be working for a British agent whose code name was Émile.

When the briefer had finished providing the Jeds with details of their mission, he introduced a British army captain named Harry Rée, who was to provide the team with some additional background on the area they were going to, and it was information based on first-hand experience. It had been Harry Rée who had steered Francis Cammaerts, organizer of the Jockey circuit in southeastern France and an old friend, to SOE. Like Cammaerts, Rée had been a schoolmaster before the war and had been a conscientious objector for a time after the war began. And, like Cammaerts, he eventually saw reason to change his views and to volunteer to fight the Germans. What made Harry Rée of interest to Jedburgh team Cedric was that he had worked with the resistance in the very area to which the team was headed.

After joining Special Operations Executive and completing training, Rée and another lieutenant had been dropped into France in April 1943. Not long afterward, he had been sent to help an SOE captain establish a circuit known as Acrobat in the area of the Doubs encompassing Besançon and Belfort, and he eventually broke off and created a sub-circuit of his own called Stockbroker.

Rée soon showed an aptitude for sabotage work, and he pulled off one of the more innovative industrial sabotage schemes of the war. A Peugeot factory in the town of Sochaux was making gun carriers and tank turrets for the German army. Factory owner Rudolphe Peugeot carried on such work in compliance with the orders of the German occupation authorities, but he was no collaborator. In fact, Peugeot was secretly a patron of the resistance.

Rée met the industrialist and got him to agree to allow saboteurs to make a surgical strike in his factory, one which would not greatly damage the plant but would halt production of the war material for the Germans for some time. The Royal Air Force had already tried bombing the factory and had only caused minor damage. If the saboteurs were unsuccessful, Rée convinced Peugeot, the air force bombers would return, and his factory could face total destruction and innocent townspeople could be killed. Peugeot not only agreed to cooperate, he also provided plans of the factory and arranged for the help of workers inside the plant. The operation was a complete success, not only halting production but also destroying a large stock of finished tank components.[3]

Then, over the span of a few months in the latter half of 1943, the F Section organizer and many other members of the Acrobat circuit were arrested by the Gestapo. When, at last, a Gestapo man came for Lieutenant Rée, he fought with the German and was able to get away, although he was shot twice during the struggle. Friends were able to get him across the border into Switzerland, where he recovered in a hospital. Rée then made his way across France and over the Pyrénées to Spain, and by early July 1944 he was back in London. Since his return to England he'd made himself useful by talking to Jedburgh teams bound for the Jura and the Doubs, telling them of the country and its people, and warning them of the dangers.[4]

And the area did indeed remain treacherous. An American civilian sent there in April 1944 to rebuild Captain Rée's Stockbroker circuit had been killed just two days after his arrival. When two American OSS lieutenants had then jumped in to establish a new circuit to replace Stockbroker they, too, met with trouble and had to escape.

But one portion of the Stockbroker circuit had survived, the subcircuit called Treasurer, and since D-Day it had been very active in attacking telecommunications and railway targets. Then, in the middle of July, the circuit's organizer had sent his lieutenant, Émile, to take control of some small maquis groups near Besançon. This was the man that Jedburgh team Cedric was being sent to support.

Based on reports from the field, it was known that Émile was working in the area north of the road that connected Besançon and Belfort and that he had two maquis groups—one outside a village called Vieilley and another one nearby. Both camps were fairly well hidden deep in the forested hills. Small as these groups were, Émile had been successful in training the men in the use of weapons and explosives, and in carrying out some sixty-four attacks on local road and railway targets—bringing traffic to a virtual standstill on three major routes.

Émile was actually Captain George Millar, a British army officer in the SOE whose war had already included enough excitement for most men. He was the thirty-four-year-old son of a prosperous Glasgow architect, and had studied architecture while at Cambridge. After leaving the university, he had learned to fly, had worked for a time as an ordinary seaman on a freighter, and then, in 1936, had taken a job with the *Daily Telegraph*. Millar later moved to the *Daily Express* and soon was working out of its Paris office, having proved himself a talented journalist. When war came, he had returned to Britain and enlisted in the army.

Millar had received his commission through an officer cadet training unit, becoming a second lieutenant at the age of thirty-one. He soon was off to fight Rommel's Afrika Korps in North Africa but was captured by the Germans while leading a scout platoon on reconnaissance. Millar escaped from a prisoner of war camp in Italy, made his way through southern France, across the Pyrénées, and returned to England in January 1944.

By April, he was interviewed by Special Operations Executive and, largely because of his fluent and almost accent-free French, was accepted. The organization's French Section had then rushed Millar through training so that he could be dropped during the upcoming June moon period. And just a few days before D-Day, he had jumped from a Liberator in civilian clothes into eastern France to serve as assistant to the organizer of the Treasurer circuit. He had been promoted to captain just before leaving England.[5]

The maquis leader whom Captain Millar had been sent to assist near Besançon was an FFI chief named Joseph Bartholet. An intelligent man in his thirties, he was tall and thin and carelessly dressed, and the men of the maquis called him Boulaya. He and his family had lived for a time in England, but he was a native of Besançon and he knew the area well. Boulaya had brought his family back to France in 1938 and opened a business school for women in Metz. Early in the war he served as a captain in the army, was captured, and escaped. He made his way to Besançon and when his family got word of his whereabouts, they joined him. There was no question of returning to Metz, for the Germans had occupied their house and carted off all their furniture and other belongings.

In Besançon, Boulaya had again opened a school, but his hatred for the German occupiers continued to grow, and he had soon begun working with the resistance, eventually becoming chief of all the FFI in the Besançon area.

Millar had also come to rely on another exceptional resistance man in the area by the name of Georges Molle. Boulaya and Molle and Millar liked each other, and they worked well together. The Briton learned much from the Frenchmen about the region, about the people, and about the meager maquis forces and their needs. As they bicycled throughout the area Boulaya showed Millar hideouts, told him whom he could trust in each town and village, and explained where Millar could get a meal or seek medical care.

As the weeks passed, Millar saw the maquis force in his area grow, and new young leaders took their places in key positions. But he also saw the desperate shortages that existed—in arms and explosives, in clothing and blankets, in boots and bicycle tires, in food and money and all the other things necessary for a guerrilla force to survive and be effective when called on to perform. He looked forward to the day when these things would begin to arrive from London.[6]

Team Cedric's destination, the Franche-Comté, had, like Brittany, always existed on the periphery of France proper. It had always been considered somewhat remote, even when Caesar's legions settled in the area. Politically, it had more recently been an appendage of Germany, only permanently becoming part of the French nation in the eighteenth century. But, unlike the predominantly Catholic Brittany, the Franche-Comté was strongly Protestant. And while Bretons lived off the sea and the soil, the Franc-Comtois were more likely to build clocks, watches, and music boxes; to tan hides; or to work in foundries or cotton mills. There was some agriculture, of course—dairy cows, fields of corn and hay, vineyards, and rolling meadows and pastureland in the lower lying valleys. In general, the people of the region were well-educated, healthy, courteous, and amiable.

The Jeds were to be dropped near the border between the departments of the Haute-Saône to the north and the Doubs to the south, an area characterized by long forested ridges running from southwest to northeast. Along the valleys between these ridges ran southwesterly flowing rivers such as the wide, swiftly flowing Doubs and the smaller and somewhat slower Ognon. Along their banks lay rich flatlands with fields of wheat and corn.

George Millar had learned soon after his arrival in the Franche-Comté that arranging for parachute drops in this part of France would be a challenge. His area of operations lay in the farthest eastern part of the country, midway between London and Algiers. This meant, first of all, that he was the farthest of all organizers from the front lines and, therefore, that many circuits which were closer to the fighting would have priority for arms and supplies. Secondly, he knew that he was located at the farthest extent of the range of the aircraft flying such missions from either England or North Africa. As the war drew closer in the last half of August 1944, however, with the British and American armies approaching from the west and American and French forces approaching from the south, the majority of supply drops began to focus on Eastern France.

Millar had done everything he could to prepare for the day when London would turn its attention to his remote corner of France. He had selected and trained people for the reception committees, found a safe house for operators who jumped in and places where arms and supplies could be taken and stored, and arranged for the use of draft horses and wagons to haul containers from the dropping grounds. He also had gotten the maquis in the habit of listening to the BBC twice each day for the personal messages —impatiently awaiting the one which would signal the impending arrival of the group's first air drop. And then it came.

A girl in the village of Vieilley had been tasked with listening for the message, "La langoureuse Asie et la brûlante Afrique" ("The languishing Asia and the burning Africa"). She jumped with excitement when she finally heard it on August 27. She ran off at once to find George Millar and Georges Molle, for this was the signal that they were to receive a parachute drop that night from two planes on the drop zone code-named Onion, a field not far from the village, next to the brown Ognon River.[7]

Millar and Molle made the final arrangements on the drop zone, which was about eight miles north of Besançon. Unlike the FFI in Brittany, though, they ran a textbook reception operation with a minimal number of people involved.

Captain Chapel was the first to arrive at the assembly point on drop zone Onion, led by a maquisard carrying his parachute. Captain Millar greeted him and introduced himself as Émile. Chapel asked for some wine and was given some in a tin cup. Next, Millar's driver came in leading a tall American, and Millar noticed a procession of maquisards following closely as the American officer laughed and cheerfully handed out chewing gum and chocolate. Millar met Captain Bazata and wondered what sort of rascal was joining him. Again introductions were made and Bazata explained that they had been trying for three weeks to get to France. As soon as the plane dropping the parachutists had passed overhead, Georges Molle had yelled to the maquisards to put the bonfires out, and they had all been extinguished by the time the third jumper arrived. Millar watched as a thin, six-footer with dark hair was brought in. Without the glow from the fires, Millar had to use his flashlight to get a look at the young man who was introduced as Sergeant Floyd, the radio operator.

Soon the men heard the drone of aircraft engines again, and Millar and Molle ordered the maquisards to re-light the fires for the second Liberator.

Bazata was impressed with the efficiency of the reception committee; it was clear that the resistance here had been well trained. Millar, the "Émile" whom Bazata's team had been sent to assist, turned the three Jeds over to his driver and returned to his spot in the center of the drop area to prepare for the arrival of the second plane.

The driver was René Berger, the tall, strong-looking man who had led Captain Bazata in from the drop zone. Berger had a swarthy complexion and wore an absurd-looking leather helmet when carrying out his driving duties. He had been a house painter before the war.

Twelve more canisters and some packages fell from the second plane. But unseen—because they were dropped wide of the drop zone—were two more parachutists, and they walked up just as Millar and Berger were guiding the Jeds to their car hidden in a wooded area. The two unexpected arrivals introduced themselves as Colonel Relativite and Captain Masure. Captain Millar greeted the two men and led all five jumpers to his car. The vehicle was a large and fairly new black Citroën "familiale" with red wheels and, being the family model, a roomy interior. It had been given to Millar by a small man named Jacques Painchaux, a garage owner and leader of a nearby maquis band.

Millar grew restless as the parachutists all began asking for the containers that carried their equipment. The circuit leader wanted to get the new men clear of the area as quickly as possible in case a German patrol arrived. He assured them that their luggage would be brought to them later. With some coaxing, he got four of the jumpers to crowd into the back seat of the Citroën. Then Sergeant Floyd crawled into the front seat next to Berger, who was behind the wheel and had fired up the engine. Millar took the window seat next to Floyd and they were off, down rough back roads along the south bank of the river.

"Shall I use lights, mon capitaine?" asked Berger.

"Only dipped," replied Captain Millar. "Full speed through Venise, Moncey, Rigney. No lights after the hairpin two kilometers beforc la Barre, and then avoid making tracks." Glancing at their five passengers, he asked, "Are you armed, gentlemen? The roads in this part are still unsafe for people like us, I regret to say."[8] Millar carried a .45-caliber pistol in the pocket of his denim jacket and kept a Sten on his lap pointed out the window.

Soon they turned off the road, pulled into an orchard, and got out. The men followed the British officer as he walked through the orchard and across a garden to a house called the Château de la Barre. They were taken inside the old house, where a woman and her daughter lived, and the parachutists stripped off their jump smocks and all their gear and piled it on the floor of the living room. In their haste to leave the drop zone, they now realized, not all of the leg bags and other gear which had been strapped to the jumpers had been picked up, and the team's radio was among the missing items. But the men were assured that the equipment would be recovered and brought to them. Captain Bazata then asked the woman if they might have some coffee.

Millar and Berger left to check that the drop zone had been thoroughly cleared and to look for the missing items. The Jeds and the other two jumpers remained in the care of the very capable woman of the house, who was a war widow and mayor of the hamlet of La Barre. She saw that they were given a place to sleep.

Back at the drop zone, Millar found the work of clearing the field to be capably overseen by Georges Molle, and almost finished. All the canisters had been loaded aboard horse-drawn hay wagons and driven off to the designated arms storage location. The priceless cargo of weapons, ammunition, and explosives would be hidden in a place unlikely to attract German interest—the Vieilley garbage dump—there to be neatly stacked and covered with rubbish.

Millar and Berger helped the others as they swept through the entire area, up to a mile from the drop zone, to make sure that nothing was left for the Germans to find. Millar eventually found the package containing the Jed radio as well as a leg bag containing twenty-four million francs in cash. He thought that the Jeds had been careless in not maintaining more control over these items, but he was even more disturbed by his discovery of a parachute left in the field by one of the two men who had jumped from the second plane. (The other man's chute would be found and hidden by an alert farm boy the next day.)

Millar was furious at such blatant disregard for security. German planes overflew the area every day and the discovery of parachutes would have resulted in widespread searches and reprisals. He and Berger gathered up the remaining Jed gear, including the radio, and drove back to the château and dropped it off. Then, after one more trip back to Vieilley to check on the storage of the supplies, the two tired men drove back to the château at La Barre and fell asleep in the garden.

Early the next morning, Millar and Berger entered the house for breakfast. The two men who had jumped from the second Liberator, Colonel Relativite and Captain Masure, came into the room dressed in civilian clothes. They told Millar that they had orders to report to a man called Ligne, who was General de Gaulle's appointed military delegate for the region, so Millar had them load their gear aboard the Citroën and Berger drove them to Boulaya's command post at Vieilley.

Then, to Millar's dismay, the three Jedburghs of team Cedric appeared for breakfast in full uniform. Millar explained to the newcomers that the Germans were very active in the area and that the Jeds would certainly not survive long in uniform. They would have to operate in civilian clothes, and he asked that they change as soon as they had finished their breakfast. While they ate, the Jeds had their first relaxed conversation with the man they knew as Émile. They saw that he was in his mid-thirties, with boyish good looks, reddish fair hair, and blue eyes.

Captain Millar was interested to know more about the Jeds. What sort of team was this? Why had the men come here? What was their mission? Who were they supposed to work for?

Captain Bazata spoke up and explained the Jedburgh concept, and made it clear that the team was there to serve Millar (Émile).

As Millar listened, he quickly came to realize that his private guerrilla war, small and fairly easily controlled, would never be the same. These Jeds, and especially the man named Bazata—clearly the dominant personality of the trio—seemed eager to make a much more active war of it. But Millar didn't think the time had yet come for that. He was clearly uneasy about doing anything to further agitate the enemy in this region and possibly bring vicious reprisals down on the villagers. Millar brought the Jeds up to date on the local situation. Many Germans, he explained, were moving through the area to the northeast, seizing all available means of transportation and severely punishing the people for any interference.

Most of the work Millar had done with his maquis thus far had been in the area around Besançon, the old clock- and watch-making city and departmental capital of the Doubs. He told the Jeds that he had been organizing a small maquis band in an area along Route Nationale 83, the highway running northeast from Besançon to Belfort. The department of the Haute-Saône, lying north of the

Ognon River, Millar explained, was largely devoid of any organized maquis.

To Bazata, the Besançon-Belfort road appeared to be the main German artery for withdrawal through the area, and he agreed that the valley of the Doubs should be the focus of their work. Millar added, though, that he still hoped to eventually expand northward into the Haute-Saône.

Geographically, the Doubs is an area of transition, where the great river valleys and gently rolling plateaus of eastern France and the Saône River basin give way to forested ridges, where the foothills of the Doubs rise to the Jura mountain range which, in turn, hugs the Swiss Alps to the east. As the hills of the Doubs push closer to the Swiss border, they grow steadily steeper, rising like stadium seating, wrinkling into deep, narrow gorges lined by craggy ridges. Forests of oak and beech give way to pine and fir— many of which reach heights of more than a hundred feet. Some of the ridges slope to lush mountain valleys, with winding roads and turbulent streams alive with pike and trout, and placid lakes nestled among the hills.

Such terrain as that of the eastern Doubs might be picturesque, but it was hardly conducive to the speedy movement of large columns of vehicles. The German Nineteenth Army's shortest and fastest route back to the Rhine clearly followed the gentle valley of the Doubs River in the western part of the department. Up Route Nationale 83, through the orchards and vineyards and poplar groves that skirted the north bank of the river. The valley was also a busy air corridor, and every day lumbering German Junkers 53 transport planes passed overhead toward Belfort and on to Germany. Millar thought they probably carried German soldiers wounded in the fighting in southern France.[9]

The men decided that they first needed to arm some two thousand guerrillas, and they planned to prepare four fields to receive air drops.[10] Sergeant Floyd set up his radio in his bedroom at the Château and, with Captain Chapel turning the hand-cranked generator, he got a message off to London reporting the team's safe arrival and requesting another delivery of arms and supplies. Captain Millar couldn't help noticing how Floyd tapped out his message while lying on the floor, unlike his own radio operator, who preferred sitting at a desk or table while working. Floyd had grown accustomed to his method after lengthy training in the transmission of messages from remote outdoor locations. But Millar also noted that the thick walls of the old house were unable to completely muffle the piercing whine of the set's generator, and he worried for the safety of the old woman and her daughter. He would have to find another place for these Jeds to stay.

Jacques Painchaux, the little garage owner who doubled as a maquis leader, suggested moving the Jeds to a convent outside a village not far away. He knew the Mother Superior there and was sure that she would be glad to help. Millar found the thought of housing Bazata in a nunnery appealing, and he agreed at once to meet with the Mother Superior. She turned out to be as charming and hospitable as Painchaux had described her, and the men were shown five rooms which the three-man Jedburgh team, plus Millar and Berger, could occupy. Millar happily accepted.[11]

When Millar returned to the château at la Barre, he and the Jeds dined together with the old woman and her daughter, and he revealed the new billeting arrangements. Bazata again dominated the conversation, speculating on the value of various items of antique furniture in the château.

Next morning, Millar and the Jeds were just about to leave in the Citroën for the convent when a messenger from Jacques Painchaux arrived on motorcycle and stopped them. Painchaux himself soon arrived on a moped and explained that the nunnery was out—they would have to find another safe house. The old gardener at the convent, it seems, had gone into a café in town and announced that the supreme Allied command was coming to set up a radio station in the convent. If the Germans had not already heard the news they soon would, and would be keeping an eye on the place. So Millar again began looking for a new hideout.

In the meantime, Millar and Painchaux decided to put the Jeds up for one night in a mill near the village where Painchaux lived. When they arrived at the mill, sentries, arranged for by Painchaux, were posted on the approaching roads and Berger hid the car nearby. Inside, the miller made the men comfortable and provided a supper of roast duckling.

By evening a terrific storm rolled into the area, with wind and driving rain. While the men were eating and enjoying the miller's champagne, a maquis leader by the name of Menigoz arrived with news of a revolt by Ukrainian troops from one of the East European units which had been integrated into the German army. According to Menigoz, an entire six-hundred-man battalion had overthrown their German officers and wanted to fight on the side of the Allies. They came armed with German weapons, including mortars and anti-tank guns, and they had horse-drawn transport. Menigoz had taken charge of them and had put them in the Cherlieu Forest, about thirty miles north of Besançon.

There were actually two battalions of Ukrainian mutineers, double the number that Menigoz was aware of at the time. The bizarre revolt was all a result of Germany's ill-conceived practice of putting East Europeans into uniform to fight for the Third Reich.

Desperate for manpower on the Western Front, in early August the German high command had formed a Waffen SS grenadier division in East Prussia from battalions of anti-Soviet Russians, Belorussians, Ukrainians, and Cossacks. The Waffen SS was the armed branch of the SS. It was composed of army-like regiments and divisions, such as the 9th SS Panzer Division which Jedburgh team Augustus had run into farther north, but they were not part of the army. In addition to the pure German Waffen SS units, the German high command organized such divisions from volunteers from occupied countries.

In the middle of August, the SS grenadier division composed of East European troops had been shipped to the German Nineteenth Army in eastern France to fight the maquis of the Franche-Comté. German officers held all key leadership positions within the division, and German military police units were added to help enforce their commands. Some units within the division, however, clearly were not inclined to fight anything other than Soviets for the Fuhrer.

On the night of August 26—just twenty-four hours before team Cedric jumped into France—a battalion of Ukrainians billeted at a camp twenty miles southeast of Besançon attacked the barracks of their German officers and noncommissioned officers and killed them all. The following morning, another Ukrainian battalion from the same division, deployed to an area north of Besançon, likewise killed their German leaders—all twenty-five officers and seventy noncoms. The two battalions then openly defected to the FFI.

In addition to nearly thirteen hundred trained combat troops, the two Ukrainian battalions brought anti-tank guns, dozens of mortars and machine guns, and hundreds of small arms. They also came with a considerable stock of ammunition, thousands of grenades, a cavalry unit complete with ninety mounts, and a transportation unit which included more than two hundred wagons and five hundred draft horses.[12]

Menigoz asked Captains Bazata and Chapel if a message could be sent to London explaining the situation and requesting an arms drop for the Ukrainians. The maquis leader was concerned that the defectors' supply of ammunition for their German weapons would not last long. A switch to Allied weapons would make it easier to keep them resupplied. Millar was glad to let the restless Bazata and his team handle the situation. Bazata, who hoped that such an act would encourage other groups of Russians nearby to turn against the Germans as well, drafted the message and Sergeant Floyd sent it. Captain Chapel agreed to accompany Menigoz on a visit to the Ukrainians first thing in the morning.

The Ukrainians, in the woods north of Besançon, were shelled by German artillery on the third and fourth of September, but they were able to hold out. Special Force Headquarters received team Cedric's request for an arms drop for the two battalions, but decided instead to send a small OSS team on the night of the seventh to make an assessment of the situation.

Meanwhile, accommodations had finally been found for Millar, Berger, and the Jedburghs.

12

ON THE REICH'S DOORSTEP

A WELL-TO-DO citizen by the name of Landel, who was mayor of a town called Loulans and a member of the local maquis, offered to provide room in his home for Jedburgh team Cedric and Captain Millar. Monsieur Landel was a small, nice-looking man with white hair, and he smoked continuously. He owned and managed a cheese factory and was the richest man around.

Landel lived in a roomy chalet on the outskirts of town with his wife, their ten children, a few grandchildren, and some children of friends. It was common during the war for large households in rural areas to keep the children of friends or relatives living in urban areas. It protected the children from bombings and usually meant better access to dairy products, which were all but unavailable in the cities. In Landel's case, because of the cheese factory the family had a steady supply of milk and butter and cheese—one of the reasons that there were so many children staying with them.

By sending eight of the younger children off to stay with Madame Landel's sister in the next village, the family could make room for the men. Of course, the entire family understood the risk inherent in housing a team which would be transmitting radio signals, but they accepted the risk without complaint.[1]

The arrangement worked out well. While staying at the Landel house, Sergeant Floyd would often go out into the woods nearby to transmit his messages. Landel's eldest son, Bernard, about twenty years old and also a maquisard, helped Floyd by turning the hand-cranked generator during radio transmissions. At times, one of the older daughters also performed this chore.

The house was spacious and warm and dry, and the men enjoyed generous meals with the family around a large table. Captain Millar contributed by providing the Landels with food which his maquisards had stolen from German stocks.

With a base of operations established, Jed team Cedric and Captain Millar began a campaign of sabotage on the road and railway running between Besançon and Belfort. Until they were able to bring in more air drops from London, the men would be limited to the small number of arms and the meager amount of explosives which Millar's maquis groups had been able to acquire and store. To this, of course, would be added the material which had been dropped with team Cedric.

With so many German units passing through the area, the Jeds wanted to keep the telephone lines constantly cut to make communications more difficult for the enemy. They found this particularly easy to do. They soon became adept at hitting larger targets as well—targets with a much higher payoff. On Sunday, September 3, the men blew a section of the Besançon-Belfort railroad, cutting the track and derailing a German troop train. On the same day, they also ambushed an artillery convoy north of Besançon.

But the village of Loulans lay north of the Ognon River in the Haute-Saône department. Working from their command post at the Landel house in Loulans, the men gradually began shifting their operations more to the north, away from the department of the Doubs south of the Ognon. Bazata soon found that what George Millar had said about the maquis north of the river, in the Haute-Saône, was true. Maquis bands were scattered about and poorly organized. They lacked arms, were largely untrained, and their security was weak.

Because of the danger involved in moving about with so many Germans in the area, Bazata decided to have Sergeant Floyd remain with the radio either at the Landel house or with the maquis of Loulans. Captain Chapel was spending most of his time with a maquis group north of Besançon, and Bazata decided that he would be most useful sticking by Millar's side. So he began accompanying the British officer everywhere he went—an arrangement which, at times, must have tried the patience of both men.

Doug Bazata and George Millar were clearly a contrast in personalities. Politically, militarily, and in seemingly every other way, they each saw the world through different eyes. Once, while the two were bathing on the south bank of the Ognon, Millar spoke of his admiration for President Roosevelt and his policies and programs. But Bazata, he quickly learned, was an ardent Republican. The two men also could not have been more divergent in their approaches to irregular warfare. Millar, whom Dick Floyd would later describe as quiet and aloof, was content to continue the small-scale sabotage that had worked so well for him in the past, waiting to be eventually overrun by Allied ground forces. He had seen many months of war, had been a prisoner of war, and had little stomach for killing. But Bazata was new to the war, had come in full of piss and vinegar, and clearly preferred a more aggressive approach. Millar later would write that, whenever he found a chance to rest, Bazata would spoil the moment by demanding, "For Pete's sake, Émile, let's get down to that road and bag us a couple of Krauts."[2]

Jedburgh team Cedric had yet to receive an air drop from London and, as supplies of ammunition and explosives dwindled, sabotage and guerrilla warfare opportunities were missed. It was the same old problem that had plagued Jed teams George and Augustus. For whatever reason, team Cedric was having trouble getting Special Force Headquarters to respond to its needs, and the team was quickly running out of time.

Americans of the Seventh Army were rapidly approaching from the southwest, with some forces only about fifty miles from Besançon, and more and more German convoys were moving through team Cedric's area. Captain Chapel had been organizing road blocks with the maquis on the major routes north of Besançon and, with the successful attacks on the Besançon-Belfort route by team Cedric and the maquis groups in the Doubs Valley, vehicle convoys of the German Nineteenth Army were being forced onto secondary roads. Some of these convoys chose to take the D15 route, a secondary road which would allow them to cut farther to the east in search of an open northbound road. And route D15 passed right through the village of Loulans.

On Monday, September 4, Millar and Bazata, trying to appear as just two more curious villagers, ambled to the center of town to watch the enemy retreat. A lengthy convoy of camouflaged cars, poking along at about thirty-five miles per hour, took an entire day to pass through town. Some of the soldiers even rode on bicycles.

Bazata was irritated that London had not come through with the air drops. The roads were rich with targets, if only the Jeds had the means of attacking them and had had more time to organize and train the maquis of the Haute-Saône. He noticed that most of the cars in the convoy were on the verge of breaking down—and he was certain that, had the maquis been sufficiently trained and armed, they could have inflicted a good deal of damage on the enemy. As it was, all they could do was radio messages to London asking for air strikes. At least the Jeds and the maquis, by forcing the Germans to use the slower secondary roads, were making such air strikes more effective.

Back at the Landel house, however, while Bazata and Millar were watching the German convoy and ruing their lack of means to attack it, Sergeant Floyd received a message from London which offered hope. The Jeds were to expect a drop the following night on field Onion, the same drop zone where team Cedric had arrived a week earlier. On Tuesday morning, excited at the prospect of receiving the air drop, Bazata and Millar departed to check out the field. But what they saw when they approached the field next to the river gave them a jolt. An estimated eight hundred Germans were camped on the drop zone known as Onion.

George Millar and Doug Bazata had to decide whether to radio London and warn headquarters of the danger—and risk losing the arms and equipment they so badly needed—or to let the mission continue in the hope that the Germans would pull out before nightfall.

Before heading back to Loulans, the two men decided to stop in Vieilley for a bite of lunch at the home of a family that Millar knew. While the men ate in a room at the back of the house, a few villagers came by to share the news that American forces were near. Rumor had it that they were just south of the Doubs, and indeed they were. Lead elements of the 3rd Infantry Division were just southwest of Besançon and were beginning their attack on the city.

But there was also bad news. German troops had begun arriving in nearby villages, one just a mile and a half to the west, and American shells were pounding another village about six miles away.

Suddenly, the woman of the house broke in with news that Germans had arrived in Vieilley, and she urged the men to leave at once. Millar and Bazata scrambled out the back and hurried to their car, which they had left behind the house, and sped out of town to the north and back to Loulans. Finding that village also full of Germans, they snuck to the Landel house by a back route and hid the car in the garage.

Later that day, Berger came to Millar and reported that he had seen two German soldiers in the garage eyeing their car. Millar feared that the soldiers might have gone to report the vehicle to their commander, and he was anxious to keep it out of enemy hands. The car had been essential in helping the men move among the scattered maquis elements. Berger had worked hard to keep the large black Citroën washed and shined. Such a car, rolling through the countryside and passing quickly through towns and villages, appeared to the casual observer to be a Gestapo vehicle, and it had allowed the men to enjoy a certain lack of scrutiny by German soldiers.

The German army, particularly during the hectic weeks of the withdrawal from France, often seized whatever means of transportation they needed, and especially such attractive vehicles as the big black Citroën. Millar knew that he had to get the car out of there before the Germans could return and commandeer it. So he, Berger, and the Jeds hastily gathered up their gear, loaded it in the car, and sped off down a back road.

Five miles southeast of Loulans they approached a village on the north bank of the Ognon. Suddenly, just outside the village, they drove upon a German roadblock. Berger braked the big car to a stop and quickly began to wheel it around for a hasty departure. But just as he had gotten the car turned halfway around it stalled, sitting crosswise in the middle of the road.

While Berger struggled to bring the Citroën back to life, the Germans sensed that this was not a Gestapo car, but rather one full of "terrorists." They opened fire with rifles and submachine guns. While dozens of rounds ripped the air around the car, Millar and Bazata fired back as best they could with pistols and somehow avoided being hit. Finally, the car came to life and Berger, who had been nicked in the ear by a bullet, sped back down the road, around a bend, and off into an adjacent woods. Amazingly, they had driven at least a hundred yards under fire and had gotten away, and Millar and Bazata laughed heartily, as if they had just pulled off a high school prank.

When Berger had driven up a rise and into the woods as far as he could, the men jumped out, hid the car in a thicket, and continued on foot until they thought it was safe to stop. They hid in the woods for the remainder of the night, high up on a hill and hidden by thick brush. Late in the night, a German cavalry unit left the road below and came up into the woods to rest before moving on. Soon Millar, Bazata, and Berger could hear German voices all around them, and they wondered what the morning would bring. Then it began to rain.

As they lay in the woods, sometime after midnight, the men could hear four-engine planes circling overhead. They were sure the planes were their bombers, looking for the lights marking drop zone Onion, and they agonized at the thought of losing the badly needed arms.

The German cavalry unit left at four in the morning. At first light, about two hours later, the men crawled out of the woods and made their way to the home of a man Berger knew. There they were fed breakfast. Then Millar gave his weapons to the others and set off on foot alone to learn what, if anything, had happened at drop zone Onion. Bazata and Berger headed in the opposite direction, toward Loulans, so that Bazata could check for any radio messages from London.

When George Millar neared the drop zone he discovered that Georges Molle had come through again. The imperturbable Frenchman had arrived at the field the night before just in time to hear the approaching planes and flash the recognition signal on his flashlight. Even though the area was still saturated with Germans, Molle and his maquisards were able to recover all forty-eight containers from the drop, including three which had landed in the river. That day, Millar saw that the weapons were distributed, including a number that were given to local villagers who needed them to protect their homes and families. The Germans had begun burning some villages in retaliation for maquis roadblocks.

General Wiese, commander of the German Nineteenth Army, had chosen the Doubs River as a place where he could fight a brief delaying action against the pursuing Allied Forces by blowing all bridges across the river and forming a hasty defense line along the valley. Wiese also sent an infantry division into Besançon with orders to hold the town at all cost for ten days to protect German units withdrawing through the area.

Much of the heart of Besançon is encircled by a large loop in the Doubs River, and the town is surrounded by hills and encircled by seven massive stone forts. The greatest fort among them had been designed by Vauban, Louis XIV's brilliant military engineer. German troops now occupied the forts, intent on stopping the Americans. But after just three days of fighting, the town fell to American infantry, and by September 8 it was cleared of all German troops.

Word soon reached Jedburgh team Cedric that American troops were in Besançon. Bazata convinced Millar that they should make their way through the German lines and link up with the nearest division. The Jeds had much information on German troop locations and activities that would be useful to the Americans.

Before sunup on Thursday, September 7, Millar and Bazata set out on foot, proceeding in a southwesterly direction along the river. They walked through two villages and had just reached a third when it began to rain. The two men ducked into a barn to take shelter from the downpour, but a villager soon came by and told them that German soldiers had surrounded the village and were rounding up all males aged sixteen to sixty. Millar and Bazata feared that the Germans might be organizing a mass slaughter in retribution for maquis attacks, and they chose not to wait around.

Slowly, the two men made their way to the edge of the village, where they stopped at a house and borrowed two blankets from the woman who lived there. Then, stooped over with the blankets draped over their backs and heads, hoping to appear as elderly peasants, they puttered across a neighboring field, picking the mushrooms which were abundant in the area as they proceeded. Once they had wandered far enough from the village and were certain that they had made it through the German cordon, they took off and made it back to an unoccupied village. There, Bazata insisted on having a mushroom stew prepared. It had been a very close call.

That afternoon, the men tried once again to cross the German lines and link up with the Americans. This time they would be accompanied by Georges Molle, whom they met outside Vieilley. Molle was reputed to be the best poacher in the region, and he knew the local hills as well as anyone. With him as their guide, Millar and Bazata set out across the hills to the south and up into the Chailluz Forest. They found the woods thick with Germans—thousands in Bazata's estimation. The men took careful note of the German defensive positions along the road and even talked to some of the German soldiers, hoping to gain information which they could pass on to the American forces. They had to be careful, however, for the slightest mistake would invite closer scrutiny by the Germans—and the men had some close calls.

Soon they could go no farther without arousing suspicion, and so the three men spent a wretched night in the forest. All night they suffered the cold and the rain—and Georges Molle quickly tired of hearing Bazata say, "If only it would *rain*."[3] It had become a favorite expression of Bazata's in such circumstances but, to Molle, on this night it was not funny, and he asked Millar to keep the American quiet. Doug Bazata was determined to get through to American units with the information they had gathered, but another way would have to be found.

The next day the men walked back to Vieilley and got a ride from there to Loulans, which by then was overrun with Germans. Captain Bazata checked with Sergeant Floyd for an update on message traffic from London, and learned that a message from Special Force Headquarters told of a thousand-man force of paratroopers which could be dropped to team Cedric's area if needed. The ever-cautious Millar was against it, sure that it would result in greater danger for the local people. Bazata, though, saw this as just one more piece of information requiring delivery to the approaching American forces. So he and Millar began planning another attempt at passing through the German lines.

General Wiese's weak defense along the Doubs had hardly caused the three infantry divisions belonging to Major General Lucien Truscott's VI Corps to break stride. They had jumped that river and were on the banks of the Ognon.

Late on the afternoon of the eighth, Bernard Landel arrived home on a bicycle with startling news. American forces had advanced beyond Besançon and were in Rigney, on the south bank of the Ognon, not far from the Château de la Barre where the Jeds had spent their first night. That put them just a few miles south of the Landel house. Millar and Bazata decided to head south to the village of Cenans, where they could cross the Ognon and go into Rigney. But Bernard then told them that German soldiers were preparing to blow all bridges across the Ognon. He had just seen ten Germans and two trucks on the Cenans bridge.

Millar and Bazata decided on a highly risky method of getting across the bridge before the Germans blew it. Some time earlier, Millar had gotten his hands on huge Terrot motorcycle—a popular pre-war French model. He had kept it well hidden among some thick shrubbery near the Landel house. With the motorcycle, Millar thought, they might be able to shoot across the bridge before the Germans could blow it, but they had to move at once. Millar instructed Bernard to go immediately and get his maquis to attack the Germans on the bridge. "But hold your fire when you see me coming on the Terrot. I'll have Captain Bazata up behind, if he's managed to stay on that far."[4]

With help from some of the Landel boys Captain Millar pushed the Terrot out and got it started. Bazata climbed on back, held Millar around the waist, and they tore off down the road toward

Cenans, armed only with pistols. It was only a mile to Cenans, and Millar raced down the road at nearly seventy miles per hour, almost losing Bazata, at times, when he couldn't avoid hitting pot-holes. When they reached the village, Millar slowed the big bike and cruised through the place at a steady pace. Then, upon hitting the downhill slope to the bridge southeast of town, he opened it up. They hit the bridge at full speed and a bump at the entry sent them briefly airborne. Bazata held on and they roared straight across—right through the startled Germans.

In his post-war memoir, George Millar would describe how, through tearing eyes, he only saw the German trucks and soldiers on the bridge as grey blurs. But the grey blurs quickly recovered from their initial shock and opened fire at the motorcycle as it disappeared up the rise on the opposite bank and around the bend. Once again, Millar and Bazata had made it through a tight spot. The Terrot roared down the road to Rigney and pulled up to a group of American soldiers in front of the Hôtel de la Gare. The stunt had worked.

Once the Americans (who turned out to be from the 3rd Infantry Division) saw Captain Bazata's papers, the two men were put in a jeep and driven back to the division command post in Besançon. There they met with the division commander, Major General John W. O'Daniel, a stout man with a hard face, who listened to Bazata's report and decided that the two men should be taken on back to VI Corps headquarters at Tarcenay, south of Besançon.

A jeep deposited the men at the VI Corps command post, and Major General Truscott, the corps commander, invited Bazata and Millar to dine with him in his tent. Staff officers served Bazata and Millar dry martinis while they visited with the general.

Captain Bazata briefed the general on German locations and activities ahead of the corps. Interestingly, in the mission report which Bazata filed upon his return to London, he indicates that Truscott, when told of SFHQ's proposed dropping of paratroopers, asked Bazata to radio a request that they be dropped to a spot in the Vosges Mountains. In his book *Road to Resistance*, however, George Millar wrote that Truscott rejected the proposal outright, and he quotes Bazata's later description of the general's opinion of the idea: "He pissed on it from a great height."[5] The general then asked Millar how long he had been in the area and expressed admiration for the work of Special Operations Executive.

When their audience with General Truscott had ended, Bazata and Millar were taken by jeep back to Rigney, arriving there at about three in the morning. Millar had been very much impressed with what he saw of the American soldiers and their leaders. He knew that they must be as exhausted as the Germans were, but they showed no signs of it.

Bazata was eager to return to the Landel house to get a message off to London. When the American lieutenant in Rigney saw that the two men planned to re-cross the German lines on the motorcycle, he told them they were crazy. But, against the lieutenant's advice, the men tore off on the big bike for the return trip to Loulans. The motorcycle's headlight did not work, but there was sufficient moonlight for them to find their way. They were stopped by an American patrol at one point, but were eventually allowed to proceed. The men learned from the American troops that the Germans had blown the bridge they had crossed earlier at Cenans, so they had to make a detour to another village which still had a bridge up. There they were able to cross and they sped back to Loulans, killing the engine as they neared the Landel house and then coasting into the driveway. Bazata ran into the house to get a message off while Millar hid the Terrot under a weeping willow.

Loulans was full of Germans, many of them searching for food or temporary billeting; it was inevitable that some would find their way to the large Landel house. One day two German officers, one of them a colonel, came to the house and knocked on the front door. When Monsieur Landel answered, the colonel politely asked if he could use the house for his headquarters. But Landel explained to the Germans that he had a large family and that many of his daughters and grandchildren were living with them. The house was full. Millar, Bazata, Chapel, and Floyd listened to the conversation from the other side of the wall in the next room. Fortunately, the German said that he understood and then left—although the Germans did take the liberty of billeting some troops in the Landels' farm buildings.[6]

Millar grew increasingly concerned about the high concentration of Germans in Loulans. Loud singing by German soldiers, seemingly inspired by alcohol, drifted to the Landel house from nearby buildings. Apparently fearing the possibility of a search, Millar saw that all of Sergeant Floyd's radio gear was gathered up and stored in a cupboard in an upstairs bedroom. He then persuaded the Landels to place their baby's bed closely against the cupboard to discourage any inspection.

In the second week of September, acting on a request from Special Force Headquarters, Millar, Berger, and Bazata attempted to get through to the OSS mission which had jumped in to join the Ukrainians in the forest north of Besançon. London had asked Bazata to provide the OSS team whatever assistance he could. But the 3rd Infantry Division was attacking the nearby town of Vesoul that day, and the three men were unable to get through to the Ukrainians' position. Suddenly the men found themselves caught in the middle of an artillery duel. The Americans were attacking Vesoul from the south and, for a time, the men were on the receiving end of both German and American artillery fire. But they came through all right, except for a small shrapnel wound which Bazata received on one hand. Then, after the men made it back to the Landel house, the Germans began shelling Loulans.

At this same time, farther to the west, Allied forces from the Dragoon landings in southern France were linking up with the Overlord forces driving eastward from the Normandy breakout. On September 11, Third Army patrols made contact with a French element of Seventh Army west of Dijon. The two converging armies linked up in force shortly thereafter. In doing so, the Allies effectively cut off the escape route of the remaining German forces in southwest France. Most of the German First Army had long since been pulled from southwest France to reinforce the armies in the north. What remained of Germany's Atlantic defenses, not much more than a corps, had been repeatedly and mercilessly harassed and ambushed by maquis and Allied special forces. For a month the Germans had been struggling to get back to the Rhine while at the same time trying to avoid being slaughtered by the maquis.

The maquis had been urging General Elster, senior commander of the remaining German forces in the southwest, to surrender. But

Elster demurred. With his personal honor—as well as that of his army—at stake, the general said that he would only discuss surrender with American ground forces. The maquis relayed this message to the U.S. 83rd Infantry Division north of the Loire. And at three-thirty on the afternoon of September 17, Major General Robert C. Macon, commander of the 83rd, accepted the surrender of the German general and nearly twenty thousand troops at a bridge southwest of Orléans.[7]

According to the Overlord invasion plan, Field Marshal Montgomery was to be in overall control of the ground campaign in northern France until the Allies had broken out of the lodgment area and advanced far enough for General Eisenhower to fully relocate his headquarters to the Continent. At that time, the supreme commander would assume control of all ground forces. This Eisenhower did on the first day of September. Two weeks later he also assumed command of the Dragoon invasion forces from southern France as they linked up with the Allied armies in northern France to form one continuous front from the channel coast to the Swiss border. Furthermore, the Seventh U.S. Army and French Army B (to be renamed the French First Army) now would be controlled by a newly activated headquarters, Sixth Army Group, commanded by General Devers. Soon after the fall of Vesoul, the new army group changed direction, attacking directly eastward toward the Vosges mountains and the Rhine River beyond.

One afternoon, not long after Doug Bazata, George Millar, and René Berger had escaped the artillery duel, the three men were in the woods just outside Loulans. Artillery rounds exploded not far from the Landel house. The men were trying to determine whether the shells were coming from German guns or American guns when suddenly they saw American army vehicles coming down the road from the west. An armored car was in the lead, and right behind it were three Sherman tanks with infantrymen riding on top. They were from the 3rd Infantry Division, and they drove on into the center of Loulans, where the armored car shot a German engineer truck loaded with explosives, causing a tremendous explosion.

When Dick Floyd heard that American troops had arrived, he ran out to the road and stopped the first jeep full of GIs he saw. Floyd approached them and said, "You guys aren't going to believe this, but I'm a first sergeant in the United States Army. If you could direct me to your S–2 [intelligence] section, I'd appreciate it."[8]

The Landel property became host to the 3rd Infantry Division's vehicle maintenance facility. In thirty days the division had come four hundred miles. Tracks were falling off tanks and other vehicles were likewise in need of work, so the maintenance shop was a busy place.

George Millar and the Jedburghs of team Cedric would never get over the way the Landels had taken them in—risking arrest or worse by the Germans—and made them feel at home. One morning, near the end of their stay, Millar counted seventeen at the breakfast table, children included.

Bazata, Chapel, and Floyd spent their remaining days in France serving the 3rd Infantry Division as liaison to the maquis, helping units clear out bypassed pockets of Germans and sending maquisards through the lines to gather intelligence. One day, a message came from General de Gaulle's military deputy for the region—ordering Captain Millar back to London. Millar was puzzled and sent a message through Sergeant Floyd to F Section asking for confirmation of the order. London confirmed the order and informed Millar that a plane would be sent to pick him up. As Millar would later learn, General de Gaulle, in one of his smallest acts, had ordered all British agents of SOE out of France that day. The general had always been at odds with F Section's work, and now that he was firmly in power he declared F Section's circuit organizers to be nothing more than British mercenaries.[9]

That night, Captain Millar went into Besançon to attend a dinner party, found an old friend in town—CBS war correspondent Eric Sevareid, one of (Edward R.) "Murrow's Boys"—and took him along. Sevareid had been with the Dragoon forces since they came ashore and would stay with them all the way to Germany.

The next day, Bazata and Berger went to the airfield to see George Millar off to London; Boulaya was going with him. The four of them, and Georges Molle, who was absent, had been through a lot together. Now that peace had returned to the valley of the Ognon, however, Molle was on the river with his skiff, relaxing and getting reacquainted with the fish. So Bazata and Berger and Millar said their good-byes. "If only it would *rain*," added Bazata.[10]

In the end, some of the German Nineteenth Army succeeded in making it all the way back to Germany, but there were at least as many Germans who were stopped along the way—never making it to the Belfort Pass or the Rhine. Roughly half of the two hundred and fifty thousand troops of Hitler's army group in southern France had been lost. Allied losses had been a fraction of that. Dozens of Jedburgh teams throughout the south and the eastern portion of France had participated in the campaign and had contributed to the victory.

In the south and in the east, however, just as had happened in the north of France as the Allied forces grew nearer to the German frontier, many Jedburgh teams—like Cedric—were sent in too late and were poorly supported from London once they were in. It is hard to imagine how much more they could have contributed had they been given the time and the support to organize, arm, and train a resistance force to the level that should have been possible.

But team Cedric, and the Jeds of many other teams who ended up in that situation, had managed to find ways to help the Allied cause. In team Cedric's case, the men were successful enough in their sabotage of the highway and railway in the Doubs valley to force the Germans to use the secondary road network, further slowing and complicating their withdrawal and making them more vulnerable to air attack. Captain Bazata's team also provided much valuable information to the Americans as they prepared to advance northward toward Vesoul, and continued to assist them as guides afterward.

Team Cedric also had alerted London to the status of the turn-coat Ukrainian battalions. No sober-minded military man would ever consider such units dependable as a fighting force. The Ukrainians had betrayed their own Soviet government and army and then had betrayed the Germans. They certainly gave little reason for anyone to trust them. By sending in an OSS team to stay with the Ukrainians for the short time until they were overrun by Allied forces, however, those in London were at least able to keep tabs on them. And, at the very least, it removed two combat battalions and much equipment from the German order of battle.

Other Allied successes came farther to the north, with Montgomery's forces capturing Brussels on September 3, and Bradley's armies taking Luxembourg on the tenth and Nancy on the fifteenth.

By October 1944, nearly all of France had been liberated. But as Eisenhower's armies approached the threshold of Hitler's Germany, the enemy which they had chased across France from Brittany in the west and from the shores of the Mediterranean in the south began to fight with a new fierceness. More Jedburgh teams were dropped into eastern France and took part in the fighting in the Vosges Mountains and Alsace and Lorraine, areas which would not be completely liberated until early February 1945.

The sons of the Reich, determined to protect home and family, would give the western Allies some of the war's bloodiest fighting along Germany's western border, in places such as Arnhem in Holland, and Aachen and the Hürtgen Forest in Germany. "By this time," a member of an American division later noted, "we had lost a colorful and gallant team that had been fighting with us." He was referring to the men the division's chief of staff called the "dashing soldiers" of the FFI.[11]

Punishing German offensives in the Ardennes Forest of Belgium and in the Colmar area of France still lay ahead. Once those battles were won, though, the armies of the Third Reich were beaten. Allied forces swept through Germany without the support of active resistance elements. In Germany such irregulars—and the special forces to fit them and train them and guide them—were not needed. For the Reich had been scraping the bottom of the manpower barrel for a year, and the barrel was dry.

EPILOGUE

Most provisional military enterprises, like summer help, sooner or later reach the point where their missions have been accomplished, their purposes fulfilled. That time came for the Jedburgh project—indeed for virtually all of the special operations work shepherded by Special Force Headquarters—in the late fall of 1944. Nowhere in the German homeland were there resistance movements—indigenous or otherwise—strong enough to be worthy of exploitation. The work of the Jedburghs and other special forces in France was finished.

A half dozen Dutch Jedburgh teams deployed in September during Operation Market-Garden, the bold and ambitious plan conceived by British Field Marshal Bernard L. Montgomery to seize three bridges in Holland and the road corridor connecting them, as a means of gaining a bridgehead across the Lower Rhine. Unfortunately, the operation fell short of its objective and cost many casualties.

By October, much of the FFI had been incorporated into the French Army by General de Gaulle and would march into Germany alongside the Anglo-American armies.

On October 13, Special Force Headquarters ordered all American and British Jedburghs still in France to return to England. Upon completion of their Jedburgh missions in France, team members were asked to volunteer for missions in other countries or other theaters. Most Jeds did so, with a considerable number going on to fight the Japanese in the China-Burma-India (CBI) Theater. For the most part, the British who went this route were reassigned to Special Operations Executive's Force 136, operating out of India and Ceylon (now known as Sri Lanka). Americans mostly went to an Office of Strategic Services detachment in China. The French Jeds who went to the Far East usually ended up in French Indochina (the area today known as Vietnam, Laos, and Cambodia), which had been a French colony before the war.

Some Jeds found other work in Europe, such as those who volunteered for a provisional unit called the Special Allied Airborne Reconnaissance Force, which prepared teams to parachute into areas by German POW camps. Near war's end, these soldiers were to make contact with German camp administrators and coordinate the medical treatment and evacuation of Allied prisoners.

Major Bill Colby led a Norwegian special operations team on a sabotage and guerrilla warfare mission in Norway. Captain Aaron Bank prepared for a mission, in German uniform and leading a makeshift unit of German POW volunteers, which was to have dropped into the Austrian Alps where it was believed the Nazi leaders were establishing a redoubt. The team's mission was to capture as many of the top leaders as possible. For a number of reasons, however, the mission was aborted.

Special Force Headquarters was, quite simply, going out of business.

The swiftness with which the end came can be seen in the personnel strength figures of the American contingent of SFHQ. As of the end of September 1944, the OSS Special Operations Branch had 1,114 personnel in the European Theater of Operations. More than seven hundred Americans had received special operations training in SOE schools between July 1943 and November 1944. By the end of November, all American personnel had returned from France, and by December 30 the roster numbered only 437.[1]

SFHQ's Mediterranean alter ego, the Special Project Operations Center in Algiers, was shut down on September 12, 1944. On the day after Christmas, General Gubbins, the head of Britain's Special

Operations Executive, recommended to General Donovan, director of the U.S. Office of Strategic Services, that Special Force Headquarters be officially dissolved.

On May 7, 1945, Eisenhower's headquarters announced the surrender of all German air, sea, and land forces.

Bernie Knox, the U.S. Army captain on Jedburgh team Giles, whose jump into France is described in the prologue to this book, completed a very successful mission with his team in western Brittany, including leading maquis attacks on elements of the hard-core German 2nd Parachute Division. OSS later sent him to Italy, where he led Italian partisans in the mountains until the Germans surrendered. He was back in the States on leave, en route to the Pacific to fight the Japanese, when the war ended. Discharged in September 1945, Knox began graduate work in the classics at Yale, under the GI Bill, in the spring of 1946. Two years later, he received his doctorate and a teaching position in the Yale classics department. He later served as director emeritus of the Harvard Center for Hellenic Studies in Washington, D.C. He was awarded the Croix de Guerre from France for his service with the Jedburghs. Dr. Knox has written a number of books, and the introduction to his *Essays Ancient and Modern* (Johns Hopkins, 1989) includes an account of his wartime Jedburgh experiences. He lives with his wife, Bianca, in a Maryland suburb of Washington, D.C.

Adrian Wise, the British major and team leader of Jedburgh team Frederick, went on to serve as a career officer in the British Army. He retired as a brigadier in the early 1970s and died in 1980.

Paul Bloch-Auroch, who, under the pseudonym Paul Aguirec, served as the French officer on team Frederick, played a big part in the effort to prepare leaders of the FFI and the FTP to serve in the regular French army. Once France had been liberated, the French established a number of schools for this purpose and Bloch-Auroch headed one in the Aisne department, where he had six former Jeds on his staff of instructors.

In late 1944, several of the French Jeds volunteered to go to Southeast Asia to carry on Jedburgh-like missions against the Japanese. But in fighting to regain their pre-war colony of French Indochina they also found themselves battling anti-French Vietminh insurgents. This conflict would continue beyond the end of World War II. Paul Bloch-Auroch (Aguirec) was among those who volunteered, and in late August 1945 he parachuted into Indochina with four other French Jeds on a mission to make contact with Bao Dai, the former figurehead emperor of Vietnam, in Hue. The team was headed by Captain Paul Grall, who had been the French officer on Bernie Knox's Jedburgh team Giles in France. Bloch-Auroch was second in command. The team was captured by Vietminh guerrillas, however, shortly after its arrival. The men were able to escape at the end of October, but were re-captured almost immediately. They escaped again on March 8, 1946. Late in March, as the Jeds were being pursued through the jungle, Bloch-Auroch became separated from the others and was never seen again.[2]

Bob Kehoe, team Frederick's radioman, received the Distinguished Service Cross, the French Croix de Guerre, and a Mention in Despatches from Britain for his service in Brittany. Kehoe had completed two years of college before entering the army. After the war, he went to Rutgers for two years to finish his undergraduate degree, then on to Columbia where he earned a master's degree in international relations. In 1970, he was granted a Ph.D. in Far Eastern studies from American University. Dr. Kehoe began work as an analyst for the Central Intelligence Agency in 1949 and spent thirty-five years with the agency, including work in the training division and in management. He has kept in touch with many of the men and women of the resistance who worked with Jed team Frederick in 1944, and he has visited many of them in France over the years since the war. Dr. Kehoe now lives in retirement with his wife, Ann, in Boulder, Colorado. They have a daughter, two sons, and four grandchildren.

★   ★   ★

Marceau, the resistance leader who had worked so closely with Jedburgh team Frederick in the Côtes-du-Nord, abandoned his career as an educator, as well as his political ambitions, to serve as a regular officer in the post-war French Army.

Jedburgh team George returned to France on a second mission in early September 1944. Working in support of a special inter-Allied mission called Shinoile, the team, reinforced by four additional Jedburgh teams, organized the FFI investment of the German fortresses at La Rochelle and St-Nazaire. The mission concluded in November of that year.

Philippe Ragueneau, the French captain who led Jedburgh team George under the assumed name of Erard, began a lengthy and distinguished career in journalism and broadcasting following the war. Beginning in 1947, he took a leading role in Charles de Gaulle's new political party, becoming a member of the party's executive commission in 1951. He later served de Gaulle—upon his return to power in 1958—as a member of his private cabinet, charged with handling press relations. In 1959 he began a career as an administrator in French television and went on to become a successful television writer and producer, as well as the author of more than twenty books.

Mr. Ragueneau was made a commander of the Legion of Honor and a companion of the Order of Liberation. Among the military decorations he received for his service in the war were three awards of the Croix de Guerre and the Medal of French Resistance. From Great Britain he received the 1939–45 War Medal with the emblem signifying a Mention in Despatches, and from the United States he received the Silver Star. He was married to Catherine Anglade, who died in 1994. Mr. Ragueneau died at Gordes, in the Vaucluse, on October 22, 2003, at the age of eighty-five.

Paul Cyr, the American captain on Jedburgh team George, received the Distinguished Service Cross for actions during his first Jedburgh mission in France. After his second mission in France, he was transferred to the OSS detachment in China. There, he led team Jackal—made up of OSS men and Chinese guerrillas—on a demolition job to destroy a mile-long railway bridge over the Yellow River in August 1945. The bridge was blown just as a Japanese troop train was crossing it, dropping the train and its cargo of two thousand Japanese soldiers into the Yellow River. Cyr's account of the mission was published in *The Saturday Evening Post* ("We Blew the Yellow River Bridge," March 23, 1946).

Mr. Cyr made an unsuccessful bid for a congressional seat from Indiana in 1950, and later went to Washington as aide to Indiana Republican Senator Homer E. Capehart. He subsequently served as a government civilian employee of the Army Materiel Command and with the Federal Energy Administration. He lived in retirement with his wife, Donna, in Mt. Pleasant, South Carolina, until his death on September 5, 1994.

Pierre Gay (pseudonym Christien Lejeune), the French lieutenant and radio operator on Jedburgh team George, joined Bloch-Auroch and the others who volunteered to go to Southeast Asia to fight the Japanese and the Vietminh. He parachuted into Indochina with Bloch-Auroch's team in late August 1945, and escaped with the others in early March 1946 after they had been captured and imprisoned by the Vietminh. Lieutenant Gay, like Bloch-Auroch, became separated from the others while being pursued through the jungle in late March and was never seen again.[3]

Today, the Museum of Breton Resistance is located in a wooded park on the outskirts of St-Marcel, not far from a monument to the resistance which stands on the grounds of the farm called La Nouée, where Jedburgh team George fought in the battle to defend the Dingson SAS base. The farmhouse at La Nouée, destroyed during the battle, has been restored.

★   ★   ★

Bill Colby, the American major on Jedburgh team Bruce, followed his Jedburgh mission by leading a Norwegian special operations (Norso) group on a daring mission to occupied Norway in the spring of 1945. He received the Bronze Star Medal and the French Croix de Guerre for his service in France, and the Silver Star and Norway's St. Olaf's Medal for the Norso operation.

Colby returned to New York at the end of the war, left the army, and entered Columbia Law School. He married Barbara Heinzen in September 1945, and the couple had five children—three boys and two girls. Upon his graduation from Columbia in 1947, Colby joined the law firm of Donovan, Leisure, Newton, Lumbard and Irvine.

He began work for the National Labor Relations Board in Washington in 1949, and joined the Central Intelligence Agency in November 1950. Mr. Colby served in various CIA positions in Stockholm, Rome, Saigon, and Washington. President Richard Nixon appointed him director of central intelligence in September 1973 and he served in that capacity until January 1976. At his departure, President Gerald Ford awarded Colby the National Security Medal. Mr. Colby then returned to the practice of law and later worked as a consultant in Washington. He and Barbara were divorced in 1984, and he later married Sally Shelton, a former ambassador and a top official at the U.S. Agency for International Development. Mr. Colby authored two books, *Honorable Men: My Life in the CIA* (Simon and Schuster, 1978) and *Lost Victory* (Contemporary Books, 1989), the latter covering his service in Vietnam. He died in a canoeing accident, at the age of seventy-six, on April 27, 1996, and was buried at Arlington National Cemetery.

Roger Bardet, the Frenchman—and traitor—who was Bill Colby's contact in the Yonne resistance, survived the war. He was arrested at war's end, tried for treason in a French court, and sentenced to death in December 1949. The sentence, however, soon was commuted to a term of imprisonment and, in 1955, he received a reprieve and was released from prison. Mr. Colby told me in 1989 that Bardet subsequently disappeared and had not been seen nor heard from since that time. According to one source, Bardet changed his name and became a prosperous businessman.

Upon completion of team Bruce's mission, Lieutenant Camille Lelong (pseudonym Jacques Favel) served as French Army liaison officer to an American unit. After the war, he returned to Louisiana to look after his family's eight-thousand-acre plantation there, raising cotton, corn, and cattle. He now lives in retirement with his wife in the town of Coushatta, Louisiana. They have three daughters and a son, and several grandchildren and great-grandchildren.

Roger Villebois, the French lieutenant who, under the name Louis Giry, served as radio operator on Jedburgh team Bruce, joined those French Jeds who transferred to the Far East. He and two other French Jeds parachuted into the Tonkin area of northern Vietnam on the first day of March 1945. Shortly thereafter, they joined a French unit which was garrisoned in the imperial city of Hue, near the coast of central Vietnam. Lieutenant Villebois was killed in action during a Japanese assault on the garrison on March 9, 1945.[4]

The three members of Jedburgh team Augustus who were killed on that rainy night of August 30, 1944—Major John Bonsall, Captain Jean Delviche, and First Sergeant Roger Côté—have not been forgotten. Every year since 1944, in late August or early September, a small ceremony is held in Barenton-sur-Serre at the spot where the men were killed. On September 9, 1984, in commemoration of the fortieth anniversary of their liberation, the people of Barenton-sur-Serre named the village's main street after Captain Jean Delviche, the French member of the team. A bronze plaque bearing the names of all three men was mounted on a stone wall at the cemetery to mark the site where they had initially been buried by the villagers. Jean Delviche remains interred there.

The remains of John Bonsall and Roger Côté were later moved to the Épinal American Military Cemetery located in the Vosges foothills. Both men were posthumously awarded the Distinguished

Service Cross and the Purple Heart. John Bonsall's sister, Mrs. Katharine B. Strong, established a music scholarship in his memory at Princeton University in 1950. The John Halsey Bonsall Fellowship in Music is still awarded each year to an outstanding graduate student in the university's music department.

Jacques Martin (pseudonym Martino), the French captain who led Jedburgh team Chloroform, served as one of the instructors at the school in the Aisne run by Paul Bloch-Auroch to retrain resistance fighters for service in the French army. After the war, he went on to a distinguished career in the diplomatic service. He was France's ambassador to Yugoslavia during the 1970s and was serving as deputy head of the Direction Politique in the French Foreign Ministry at the time of the Jedburgh reunion in Paris in 1984.

Henry McIntosh, the American lieutenant on Jedburgh team Chloroform, returned to the United States for a month-long leave before shipping out to the China-Burma-India Theater. There, he served with OSS behind the lines in China, much as he had in occupied France. At war's end, he returned home and married Harriet Lee Owens—the sister of a close friend and fraternity brother—on November 6, 1945. He was discharged from the army as a captain the following month. McIntosh's war decorations include the Silver Star, the French Croix de Guerre with Silver Star, and a Mention in Despatches from Britain.

He resumed the study of medicine which had been interrupted by the war, and graduated from the University of Pennsylvania Medical School in 1950. Dr. McIntosh taught medicine at Duke University, Baylor University, the University of Florida, and the University of South Florida, and joined the Watson Clinic in Lakeland, Florida, as a cardiologist in 1975. He served as president of the American College of Cardiology (1974–75) and chairman of the Council of Clinical Cardiology of the American Heart Association (1975–76). In 1984, Dr. McIntosh founded and served as Chairman of the Board of Heartbeat International, an organization committed to making cardiac-related medical devices (cardiac pacemakers) available to needy patients worldwide. President Ronald Reagan recognized his work by presenting him The Presidential Citation in the Rose Garden of the White House in June 1986. Dr. McIntosh is retired and lives with his wife, Harriet, in Lakeland, Florida.

Lieutenant Jean Sassi, who served as radio operator on team Chloroform under the name of Jean Nicole, was another who made the journey to the Far East to fight the Japanese. He jumped with two other Jeds as team Vega into northern Laos in June 1945 to gather intelligence and organize guerrilla strikes against Japanese lines of communication. Sassi survived the war and was among a number of French Jeds who were instrumental in creating the French special forces in the immediate post-war years. He later became an executive with the Citroën automobile manufacturing company.[5]

Doug Bazata, the American captain on Jedburgh team Cedric, earned the Distinguished Service Cross, four Purple Hearts, and the French Croix de Guerre with two palms during the war. After leaving the army as a major in 1947, he studied wine making in Paris and spent a number of years working in the wine industry in Europe. In the fifties he became an artist, painting in the abstract expressionist style so popular at the time, and held one-man shows in France, England, Germany, and the United States. In Maryland, in the early 1970s, he ran a pheasant preserve and hunting club. Government work followed with service in the Veterans Administration and at the Navy Department, where, in the 1980s, he served as a special assistant to Navy Secretary John Lehman. Mr. Bazata lived with his wife, Marie-Pierre, in Chevy Chase, Maryland, until his death at the age of eighty-eight on July 14, 1999. He is buried in Arlington National Cemetery.

Doug Bazata had a well-earned reputation among the Jeds as a great storyteller, and I never tired of listening to him during the few opportunities I had to spend time with him. My last visit with him, in 1988, resulted in an unforgettable incident. I was in a roomful of Jeds and their families at the French Embassy in Washington for an award ceremony. There were perhaps three hundred people in the crowd. I was standing next to Mr. Bazata, with whom I had been chatting before the ceremony began, about three-fourths of the way back in the crowd. The French ambassador began speaking and a hush fell over the crowd. Suddenly, Bazata leaned over to me and asked, "Hey Will, did I ever tell you about the time I slept with Bill Colby's daughter?" And he said it loud enough for everyone within a radius of about six feet to hear him. What's more, Bill Colby was standing immediately in front of me!

I responded negatively and hoped that he would drop it at that, but Bazata went on to say that it was true, even though she always denied it. Just then, Mr. Colby turned around with a grin on his face and said, "I think I need to tell you the rest of that story." As it turned out, Colby had been a major when the war ended in 1945 and had received orders to Fort Leavenworth to attend the Army's Command and General Staff College. But he had decided to get out of the army and resume his studies at Columbia Law School. So he and Barbara had taken a small apartment on Manhattan's upper west side. One day, a year or two later, Bazata showed up at their door, having just returned from Europe and needing a place to stay for the night. So the Colbys let him sleep on the floor in the nursery, where their baby girl, only weeks old, was asleep in her crib. When Colby finished explaining this, everyone within earshot began laughing and the French ambassador had to stop the ceremony and ask us to keep quiet.

Bazata was just an unforgettable character, plain and simple. Eric Pace of *The New York Times*, in his August 16, 1999, obituary of Mr. Bazata, wrote that Salvador Dali, whom Bazata had known, once painted a likeness of Doug "done up as Don Quixote," and called the painting "Homage to Bazata."

Louis Lesne (pseudonym Chapel), the French captain on team Cedric, is deceased.

Dick Floyd, team Cedric's radio operator, was discharged from the army in October 1945 and started school under the GI Bill at St. John's University in February 1946. He finished his degree and then stayed at St. John's to complete law school. He married Sheila Charles—whom he met on a blind date shortly after leaving the army—on March 26, 1951. Following graduation from law school three months later, Mr. Floyd went to Europe as an employee of the Central Intelligence Agency. He crossed the Atlantic traveling First Class on the *Queen Elizabeth*, and found it to be a decidedly better voyage than his crossing on the *Queen Mary* in December 1944. He remained with the CIA from 1951 to 1953, then began a career in sales and marketing in the paper business, working for Owens-Illinois, Inc. The Floyds now live in Berkeley Heights, New Jersey. They have five sons (a sixth died shortly after birth) and twenty-two grandchildren—fourteen girls and eight boys.

George Millar, the British captain who, as a Special Operations Executive agent in the Doubs, worked so closely with Jedburgh team Cedric, returned to England immediately upon the completion of his mission. He received the Distinguished Service Order and the Military Cross for his service in France.

In the years following the war, he authored nine books and edited a tenth. Among his books are three in which he relates his war experiences: *Maquis* (William Heinemann Ltd., 1945; published in the United States by Doubleday & Company, Inc., in 1946, as *Waiting in the Night*), *The Horned Pigeon* (Doubleday & Company, Inc., 1946), and *Road to Resistance* (Little, Brown and Company, 1979). Despite being ordered out of France by General de Gaulle, along with all the other SOE circuit leaders, in September 1944, Millar was later invited to visit President de Gaulle in his office in Paris, and de Gaulle told Millar that he had read his book *Maquis* and had enjoyed it immensely. He told Millar that, on a recent trip to eastern France, he had even gone out of his way to visit the village of Vieilley.

Sir Peter Wilkinson, KCMG, DSO, OBE, who, as a Special Operations Executive staff officer in 1942 was the principal author of the Jedburgh concept, commanded No. 6 Special Force (SOE) from 1943 to 1945. He entered the Diplomatic Service in 1947 and subsequently served in the British Embassies in Vienna, Washington, and Bonn. In 1955, he served as secretary general of the Geneva Summit. He was later under secretary at the Cabinet Office and a senior civilian instructor at the Imperial Defence College. He served as British ambassador in Saigon and Vienna, retired from the Diplomatic Service in 1972, and became coordinator of intelligence at the Cabinet Office that same year. Mr. Wilkinson published his war memoir in 1997 under the title *Foreign Fields: The Story of an SOE Operative* (I. B. Tauris Publishers, 1997).

The Jedburghs held their first reunion, a four-day affair, in Paris in late May 1984, marking the passage of forty years since their wartime exploits. An American Jedburgh reunion was held at Fayetteville and nearby Fort Bragg, North Carolina, in 1985. In May 1988, the second international Jedburgh reunion took place in Washington, D.C., drawing fifty-one American, eighteen British, and twenty-six French Jedburgh veterans, as well as their families.[6] The next such gathering was held in England in May 1991. At the earliest of these reunions, Jeds often found themselves greeting old friends whom they had not seen since Milton Hall, before departing for missions in France or Holland. Some first learned the real names of their French colleagues, whom they had only known until then by their noms-de-guerre. Most recently, twenty-two surviving Jedburgh veterans were among the attendees at a reunion held in Peterborough, England, near Milton Hall, in June 2004.

The Jedburgh project was a bold experiment. We should remember that as late as 1943 the outcome of the Second World War was, at the very least, uncertain. Allied success in the invasion of France was by no means guaranteed and, because of that, military leaders were reluctant to turn their backs on any option which might contribute to final victory.

How successful was the project? The value of any special operation, particularly within the context of total war, is difficult to assess, and people often minimize the contributions made because there is a tendency to overestimate the expected results of such operations. Maurice Buckmaster, who headed Special Operations Executive's French section, later wrote of early unfriendly attitudes of the high command toward SOE. "They demanded miracles and when we failed to work them they became disillusioned and sarcastic."[7] The Jedburghs and other special forces did not win the war in Western Europe—far from it. Nor were they designed to or expected to. Like the signal corps or the artillery or the air force, they simply did their part to *help* win the war.

The answer to the question of how successful the Jedburgh project was, I think, is in the effectiveness of resistance activities in support of the Allied campaign in France. Resistance folklore aside, operations carried out by the FFI in the summer of 1944 would have been far less effective if they had not been tied to the Allied ground campaign. And they would have been of little consequence at all without the tons of material and the training and advice provided them by the British and Americans. Special forces such as the Jedburghs played such a key role in making all of that happen, and in effecting such close coordination between the conventional and the unconventional war efforts, that no other measurement of their success seems appropriate. What is certain is that the activities of these special forces and the resistance groups they worked with helped to shorten the Allied campaign in France.

The most important task assigned to the resistance was that of disrupting the movement of German reinforcements to the Normandy beachhead or to oppose the Allied landings in southern France. And this they did remarkably well, delaying many divisions and completely stopping others. According to British historian M. R. D. Foot, the resistance kept eight German divisions from ever reaching the Overlord and Dragoon battlefields.[8]

An often unrecognized contribution of the Jedburghs was their ability to keep maquis groups of wide-ranging political and ideological backgrounds focused on working together to defeat the common enemy—the Germans. More than a few Jedburgh veterans have told me that they expended as much effort in preventing clashes between rival maquis groups as they did in fighting the Germans.

General Bradley referred to the maquis as a valuable ally in the Brittany campaign, and he often paid tribute to their work in his messages to SHAEF. Ralph Ingersoll, a planning officer on Bradley's staff, shortly after the war wrote about how he and others, while still in England, had not been impressed with the romantic tales they had heard of the resistance. After entering France, though, they were able to witness firsthand the FFI's "solid efficiency and hard accomplishments." Ingersoll went on to explain that, "what cut ice with us was the fact that when we came to France the resistance was so effective that it took half a dozen real live German divisions to contend with it, divisions which might otherwise have been on our backs in the Bocage."[9]

Colonel Robert S. Allen, a staff officer at General Patton's Third Army headquarters, also wrote of the FFI's contribution. During Third Army's sweep through Brittany, Allen later wrote, "over 30,000 armed FFI rendered invaluable fighting and intelligence aid to the spearheads. These unknown and humble resistance combatants, fighting heroically and effectively, deserve undying tribute for their great contribution to this crucial victory."[10] Allen's praise continued when writing of how the resistance later helped protect Third Army's right flank during its race across France, including the capture of an entire German corps approaching from southwest France. "To these unknown resistance fighters and the XIX [Tactical Air Command] pilots," wrote Allen, "belongs the real credit for the capture of [German Major General Eric] Elster's command."[11]

General Patton received laudatory comments about the work of special forces in a letter from one of his corps commanders, who wrote: "SF operations, including the employment of FFI personnel in support of this corps, have been particularly effective. . . . It is believed that a very definite role has been created for SF personnel in support of this corps and that continuing support will definitely be gained from their activities."[12]

Patton himself was so pleased with the work of Special Force Detachment 11, which was attached to his army staff, that in September, when operations in France were all but over, he requested to keep the detachment when Third Army moved on into Germany.[13]

Praise also came from the officers and men of the Seventh Army who came ashore in southern France, where the FFI was credited with the capture of an estimated forty-two thousand German prisoners. Brigadier General Frederick B. Butler, the commander of Task Force Butler, acknowledged that "without the Maquis our mission would have been far more difficult."[14]

Butler is also supposed to have judged that the FFI who supported Operation Dragoon were equivalent to four or five divisions.[15] Echoing that sentiment, the 3rd Infantry Division's official history of the campaign states: "A major factor aiding the speed and success of our movement was the activity of the French resistance groups." All along their northward march, the division's history records,

> whole towns were seized and held to await our coming. In addition to this sabotage activities were coordinated with our movements. If the Air Force failed to destroy a bridge, that bridge might be demolished anyway—from the ground and with hand-laid demolitions. Speeding convoys of enemy reserves ran into mysteriously laid roadblocks, and ambush.[16]

In the war report of the U.S. 180th Infantry Regiment we read of how the "continual harassing by the Maquis cost the Germans heavily and rendered them unable to put up an organized resistance."[17] The regiment's history, however, also recognizes how the maquis helped in so many other ways. When, for example, a regimental reconnaissance element was surrounded by Germans northeast of Lyon, the maquis rescued all but two of the Americans and saw them safely back to friendly lines.

The 179th Infantry Regiment's official history explains how the FFI initially helped by ambushing German columns and blowing up enemy munitions dumps, and how they would then seize towns and bridges and await the arrival of the tanks and infantry. "Then, when the doughboys did arrive, the local FFI served as informants and guides. After four years of spying, these men knew everything there was to know about the enemy. And they knew the terrain."[18]

Knowledge of the terrain was particularly valuable to American armored and motorized units that were moving too fast for map supplies to keep up with them. Tactical elements typically operated from Michelin road maps rather than from detailed military topographical maps. Seventh Army's official war report elaborates on the importance of this information, explaining how "the FFI had made careful note of German gun positions and their fields of fire, the location of pillboxes, minefields, and antitank obstacles, they were of invaluable service in guiding patrols to objectives with least loss of time and lives."[19]

Lieutenant General Lucien K. Truscott, Jr., the U.S. corps commander in southern France, later expressed his admiration for the work of the resistance and the Jedburghs when he wrote,

> So effective were the Maquis that the Germans moved only in large numbers. The Maquis were well provided with arms and explosives by the Allies, and Allied officers with communications had parachuted in to assist them in coordinating their operations. We had expected a good deal of assistance from them, and we were not disappointed. Their knowledge of the country, of enemy dispositions and movements, was invaluable, and their fighting ability was extraordinary.[20]

British General Sir Henry Maitland Wilson, supreme Allied commander in the Mediterranean Theater and responsible for the launching of Operation Dragoon in southern France, was equally generous with his praise when he estimated that the FFI "reduced the fighting efficiency of the Wehrmacht in southern France to forty per cent at the moment of the Dragoon landing operations."[21]

Not all Allied units shared these views of the FFI, though. Sadly, a few units saw only those "eleventh-hour" resistance fighters—bands of men who appeared only after the fighting was over and then boasted of their role in capturing a town. Others witnessed small groups, often claiming to be of the leftist FTP, whose members were little better than gangsters and seemed only interested in exacting revenge on alleged collaborators. Such groups as these were small in number, however, and were equally despised by the true resistance fighters.

Much was learned about the effectiveness of the resistance from captured German officers. "And it made the most cynical sit up and take notice," observed Ralph Ingersoll, "when we learned from German field officers that the Germans in central France were truly terrified, had to live under arms, could not move freely, had lost all control in sizable sectors even before we came."

Attempts by the Germans to deal with the threat had only made the guerrillas more effective. "Caught between the devil and the resistance, the German High Command had finally to draw on its police divisions in central France to reinforce its army in Normandy." But as they thinned out such police forces in the interior, "the effectiveness of the maquis increased in geometrical proportion."

Ingersoll's final assessment of the contribution made by the resistance was that:

> [i]t would be an empty history of the campaign in France and Belgium that tried to credit the success of the Allied arms in those countries to the Allied weight of guns and aircraft alone. It was a military fact that the French were worth at least a score of divisions to us, maybe more.[22]

He concluded by comparing the way the Allies sliced through France to the bloody fighting at the German border, when they no longer had "any friends beyond our own lines."[23]

One German officer referred to the Jedburghs in a post-war memoir when he wrote of how they helped in increasing the effectiveness of the FFI by August 1944. "As time went by," he wrote, "and they gained experience, they developed into a real threat for the German withdrawal."[24]

Field Marshal von Rundstedt, German commander on the Western Front, had recognized as early as 1943 that "a serious turning point in the interior situation of France" had been reached when the "organized supply of arms from England to France became greater every month." By the end of that year, he observed, "It was already impossible to dispatch single members of the Wehrmacht, ambulances, couriers or supply columns without armed protection to the First or Nineteenth Army in the south of France."[25]

By 1944, according to von Rundstedt, the situation in southern France had become

> so dangerous that all commanders reported a general revolt. ... Cases became numerous where whole formations of

troops, and escorting troops of the military commanders were surrounded by bands for many days and, in isolated locations, simply killed off. . . . The life of the German troops in southern France was seriously menaced and became a doubtful proposition.[26]

In a telephone conversation with a general on Hitler's staff, just five days after the Normandy landings, the German commander-in-chief in the west explained how the morale of his troops was suffering as the FFI, "feeling the end approaching, grow steadily bolder."[27]

But probably no one was in a better position to offer an informed opinion on how well those resistance activities directly supported the Allied ground campaign—which was the whole purpose of the Jedburghs—than the supreme commander himself. And General Eisenhower never hesitated to express his admiration and appreciation for the work of the irregular warriors. He did so to his superiors in Washington and to others on many occasions during the war. In his 1948 war memoir, *Crusade in Europe*, Eisenhower judged that, "[w]ithout their great assistance the liberation of France and the defeat of the enemy in western Europe would have consumed a much longer time and meant greater losses to ourselves."[28]

At the close of the war in Europe, General Eisenhower wrote to Major General Colin Gubbins, SOE director, and Colonel David Bruce, head of OSS in the European Theater, to express his thanks and admiration for the work of SFHQ and the many special forces missions it directed.

"In no previous war," wrote Eisenhower,

and in no other theater during this war, have resistance forces been so closely harnessed to the main military effort. While no final assessment of the operational value of resistance action has yet been completed, I consider that the disruption of enemy rail communications, the harassing of German road moves and the continual and increasing strain placed on the

German war economy and internal security services throughout occupied Europe by the organized forces of resistance,
played a very considerable part in our complete and final victory.[29]

It also was recognized at the highest levels that the French resistance would have been much less effective without the assistance
of Allied special forces. In a secret assessment of resistance and
special forces contributions provided to the Combined Chiefs of
Staff in July 1945, U.S. Lieutenant General Walter Bedell Smith and
British Lieutenant General Sir Frederick E. Morgan, Eisenhower's
chief of staff and deputy chief of staff, respectively, wrote that
"without the organization, communications, material, training and
leadership which SOE supplied, . . . 'resistance' would have been of
no military value."[30]

Lastly, author Blake Ehrlich quotes former United States Army
chief of staff, General of the Army George C. Marshall, as stating
in 1946 that, "[t]he resistance surpassed all our expectations, and it
was they who, in delaying the arrival of German reinforcements
and in preventing the regrouping of enemy divisions in the interi-
or, assured the success of our landings."[31] As this book hopefully
has shown, the Jedburghs contributed to that success.

As successful as they were, however, the Jedburghs perhaps could
have made even greater contributions, as the teams were not
always used as effectively as they might have been. The complaint
most often heard from the Jeds themselves is that they were sent
in too late. Sir James R. H. Hutchison, a Jedburgh officer who
would later serve as Britain's under-secretary of state for war, probably best articulated this sentiment and hinted at lost opportunities in his mission's after-action report.

Jedburgh teams were more than justified. The pity is that more
were not sent sooner as requested. The maquis wanted them
and asked for them. Their help in carrying out a common
training and a coordinated tactical policy was invaluable; their

example in action and their acceptance of a military discipline and hierarchy would have borne unconscious fruit in the minds of maquisards now relapsing into unrestrained and violent action reminiscent of the middle ages. The arrival of Allied officers in uniform was, not only to the men of the maquis but also to the civil population, an earnest that the Allies took resistance seriously; a pledge that the people's gallant and tragic resistance throughout the years had not gone unnoticed or uncounted. Allied officers were recognized immediately as having and offering views unbiased by French internal questions; they could have no axe to grind. The Jedburgh conception was truly founded. It was, alas, not used to the full.[32]

The work of the Jedburghs, it should be added, would never have been possible without the facilities, the expertise, and the indoctrination so magnanimously provided by Britain's Special Operations Executive. And it certainly could not have been done without the support of the British and American air force special operations squadrons responsible for delivering the teams to the field and responding to their requests for air resupply drops. A generation before FedEx and UPS, these British Special Duty Squadrons and American "Carpetbaggers" were providing next-day (actually next-night) delivery from England and Algiers to points throughout Western Europe and the Balkans. Approximately four thousand supply drop sorties, delivering more than six thousand tons of arms and other supplies, were flown to the French resistance from July through September, when the Jedburghs were most active.[33] The Jeds in Brittany alone armed more than twenty thousand men of the maquis with weapons from such drops.[34]

For the men who served in the Jedburghs, it was the defining experience of their young lives; it changed these men, forever bonding them and setting them apart from all others. In some ways, the Jeds were a reflection of their time—a time of segregated armies and of limited opportunities for women. As with most front-line units of the Allied armies in Western Europe during the war, there were no blacks in the Jedburghs. Nor were there any women, even though many brave women had performed superbly in the field as members of SOE circuits and were decorated for their actions. The men who served with the Jeds, however, laid the foundation for the special forces of the future—special forces which grew even stronger and more capable by becoming more ethnically diverse in their makeup.

In 1989, William E. Colby sent me a photocopy of a memorandum he had written in May 1945. Colby had carried out guerrilla warfare with the French resistance as a member of a Jedburgh team and had led a special forces team into German-occupied Norway on a railway sabotage mission. In the memorandum, addressed to the chief of the Special Operations Branch of the Office of Strategic Services in Washington, Colby offered suggestions on how special forces teams should be organized and how they should function in the future. The team he proposed would be organized similarly to the American Operational Groups employed in France, Italy, and Norway, but its methods would be closer to those used by the Jedburghs. It was a concept, in fact, not far from that of the Green Beret "A-detachments" of the future.

America's special operations capability was lost when President Harry S. Truman ordered the Office of Strategic Services disbanded at the end of WWII. Five years later war erupted in Korea, however, and the need for an unconventional warfare force once again became apparent. So, in 1952, the United States Army Special Forces officially was established, and the first group activated was commanded by Colonel Aaron Bank—a former Jedburgh.

Many French Jedburgh veterans carried their experiences with them in the development of that country's modern special force, the 1er (Premier) Regiment Parachutiste d'Infanterie de Marine (1st Marine Parachute Infantry Regiment)—not a naval marine force, as the name implies, but more a descendent of the French SAS of World War II. And in the United Kingdom, the legendary Special Air Service remains the premier special force.

Today, these units carry on the Jedburgh tradition, and the same high-caliber young people continue to come forward to aid those living under the yoke of oppression—especially those who decide to stand up and fight for the freedoms which we, ourselves, too often take for granted.

APPENDIX
THE FRENCH JEDBURGH TEAMS

The following is as accurate a roster of Jedburgh teams and personnel deployed to France as I could put together from the sources at hand. I have relied most heavily on the information provided in the OSS Special Operations (London) Branch *War Diary*, as well as similar documentation prepared by the Special Project Operations Center in Algiers. While these sources contain most Jedburgh team after-action reports, they do not contain them all. I have been able to locate other reports as separate documents in the National Archives. Jedburgh veterans have helped with corrections to some name spellings which are incorrect in *War Diary* or other documents. Especially helpful in this respect were Arthur Brown, Général Paul Aussaresses, Joe de Francesco, Lou Lajeunesse, and Camille Lelong.

In the interest of standardization, I have chosen to cite the rank of personnel—as accurately as official documents and other sources allowed me to—as the rank held when the team deployed to the field—even though many of the men subsequently were promoted. Ranks that may be unfamiliar to some readers are explained in the notes following the roster. The initials "W/T" following a name identify the wireless telegraph, or radio, operator.

Lastly, casualties shown in the remarks column refer only to those casualties suffered on that specific mission or as a direct result of that mission. Some of these men later were killed or wounded elsewhere during World War II or in later conflicts. Gaston Vuchot, for example, was killed in action while fighting in a conventional French army regiment during the battle for Colmar in February 1945.

French Jeds killed in action in Indochina in 1945 and 1946 include: Paul Bloch-Auroch, Pierre Gay, Jean-Pierre Herenguel, Alexandre Martelli, Lucien Paris, Pierre Rousset, Maurice Stasse, and Roger Villebois. Pierre Bloch, Roger Crétin, and Paul Scherrer were killed in action in Algeria during the 1950s insurgency there. British Jeds Godfrey Marchant, Peter Vickery, and Peter Colvin were killed in 1945 in India, when they were leaving for a mission in Burma and their plane crashed during takeoff.

Mission
Rank,* Name & (*Nom-de-guerre*)

ALAN
Deployed from Tempsford, England, to the Sôane-et-Loire department of Central France on the night of 12–13 August 1944.
Capt. Robert Toussaint (*André Gairaud*)
Capt. Stanley M. Cannicott
S/Lt. Robert Clause, W/T (*François de Heysen*)

ALASTAIR
Deployed from Harrington, England, to the Vosges department of Northeast France on the night of 24–25 August 1944.
Maj. Oliver H. Brown
Lt. René Karrière (*René Maître*)
Sgt. G. N. "Smithy" Smith, W/T

ALEC
Deployed from Harrington, England, to the Loire-et-Cher department of Central France on the night of 9–10 August 1944.
1st Lt. George C. Thomson
Lt. Alain Bordes (*Bernard Allet*)
S/Sgt. John Augustine White, W/T

ALEXANDER
Deployed from Tempsford, England, to the Creuse department of Central France on the night of 12–13 August 1944.
Lt. René de la Tousche (*Richard Thouville*)
1st Lt. Stewart J. O. Alsop
1st Sgt. Norman R. "Dick" Franklin, W/T

ALFRED
Deployed from England to the Oise department of Northern France on the night of 24–25 August 1944.
Capt. Lewis D. MacDonald (*Leslie MacDougall*)
Lt. Jean-Pierre Herenguel (*G. de Wavrant*)
Sgt. Albert W. Key, W/T

---

* All ranks are as of the date of deployment and do not reflect later promotions. Most of the American radio operators were promoted to the rank of first sergeant by the time their missions were completed. Many officers also were promoted while in the field.

American ranks in the table above include: **Lt. Col.** (lieutenant colonel), **Maj.** (major), **Capt.** (captain), **1st Lt.** (first lieutenant), **2d Lt.** (second lieutenant), **1st Sgt.** (first sergeant), **M/Sgt.** (master sergeant), **T/Sgt.** (technical sergeant), **S/Sgt.** (staff sergeant), **T/3** (technician, 3d grade), **Sgt.** (sergeant), **S3Cl.** (seaman third class [U.S. Navy]).

Code Name	Nationality	Remarks
Ariège	French	
Pembroke	British	Wounded in action
Kroner	French	
Kent	British	
Donegall	French	
Lincoln	British	
Cromarty	American	
Oxford	French	Died of wounds
Colorado	American	
Leix	French	
Rona	American	
Cork	American	
Argyll	British	
Aude	French	
Wampum	British	

British ranks include: **Lt. Col.** (lieutenant colonel), **Maj.** (major), **Capt.** (captain), **1st Lt.** (first lieutenant), **2d Lt.** (second lieutenant), **CQMS** (quartermaster sergeant), **Sgt.** (sergeant), **LAC** (leading aircraftman [Royal Air Force]).

French ranks include: **Col.** (colonel), **Cmdt.** (commandant [major]), **Capt.** (capitaine [captain]), **Lt.** (lieutenant [first lieutenant]), **S/Lt.** (sous-lieutenant [second lieutenant]), **Asp.** (aspirant [officer cadet]).

Mission
Rank, Name & (*Nom-de-guerre*)

AMMONIA
Deployed from Blida, Algeria, to the Lot department of Southwest
France on the night of 9–10 June 1944.
Capt. Benton McDonald "Mac" Austin
Capt. Raymond Lecompte (*R. Conte*)
Sgt. Jacob B. "Jack" Berlin, W/T

ANDREW
Deployed from England to the Ardennes department of Northeast
France on the night of 15–16 August 1944.
Maj. A. H. S. "Henry" Coombe-Tennant
Lt. Édouard C. Antoine, Comte d'Oultrement
Sgt. Frank Harrison, W/T

ANDY
Deployed from Harrington, England, to the Haute-Vienne department
of South Central France on the night of 11–12 July 1944.
Maj. Ronald A. Parkinson
Cmdt. J. Verneuil (*J. Vermeulen*)
Sgt. Glyn R. Loosmore, W/T

ANTHONY
Deployed from Keevil, England, to the Saône-et-Loire department
of Central France on the night of 14–15 August 1944.
Capt. Maurice Stasse (*Claude Deprez*)
1st Lt. Mason B. "Buz" Starring
T/Sgt. John L. Bradner, W/T

ARCHIBALD
Deployed from Harrington, England, to the Meurthe-et-Moselle
department of Northeast France on the night of 25—26 August 1944.
Maj. Arthur du P. Denning
Lt. François Costes (*A. Montlac*)
M/Sgt. Roger L. Pierre, W/T

ARNOLD
Deployed from Tarrant Rushton, England, to the Marne department
of Northeast France on the night of 24–25 August 1944.
Capt. Michel de Carville (*Michel Coudray*)
Capt. James H. F. Monahan
Sgt. Alan de Ville, W/T

Code Name	Nationality	Remarks
Gaspard	American	
Ludovic	French	
Marcial	American	
Rupel	British	
Demer	Belgian	Wounded in action
Nethe	British	
Fife	British	Fractured leg on jump
Carlow	French	Fractured ankle on jump
Lundy	British	Joined Jed Hamish in the field
Perth	French	
Nebraska	American	
Pfennig	American	
Cumberland	British	Wounded in action
Montgomery	French	Wounded in action
Sen	American	
Sussex	French	
Londonderry	British	
Escudo	British	

Mission
Rank, Name & (*Nom-de-guerre*)

ARTHUR
Deployed from Tempsford, England, to the Côte-d'Or department
of Eastern France on the night of 18–19 August 1944.
Capt. Cecil F. "Skip" Mynatt, Jr.
S/Lt. Xavier Humblet (*Louis Hache*)
T/Sgt. Albert Victor Bacik, W/T

AUBREY
Deployed from Harrington, England, to the Seine-et-Marne
department of Northern France on the night of 11–12 August 1944.
Capt. Godfrey Marchant
Lt. Adrien Chaigneau (*J. Telmon*)
Sgt. Ivar Hooker, W/T

AUGUSTUS
Deployed from England to the Aisne department of Northern France
on the night of 15–16 August 1944.
Maj. John Halsey Bonsall
Capt. Jean Delviche (*Jean Dechville*)*
T/Sgt. Roger E. Côté, W/T

BASIL
Deployed from Harrington, England, to the Doubs department of
Eastern France on the night of 25–26 August 1944.
Capt. Robert Rivière (*R. Raincourt*)
Capt. Thomas A. "Tom" Carew
T/Sgt. John L. Stoyka, W/T

BENJAMIN
Deployed from Fairford, England, to the Meuse department of
Northeast France on the night of 20–21 August 1944.
Maj. Hubert "Terry" O'Bryan-Tear (*A. J. Forrest*)
Lt. Paul Moniez (*P. Marchand*)
S/Lt. Henri Kaminski, W/T (*J. Camouin*)

BERNARD
Deployed from Fairford, England, to the Meuse department of
Northeast France on the night of 20-21 August 1944.
Capt. Jocelyn de W. "Jock" Waller
Capt. Étienne Nasica (*E. Prato*)
Sgt. Cyril M. Bassett, W/T

* Although the Augustus mission report found in the Office of Strategic Services
War Diary shows this name spelled "Delwich," I have followed the spelling used
in French documents provided to me by General (Ret.) Paul Aussaresses.

Code Name	Nationality	Remarks
Connecticut	American	Fractured spine on jump
Smabrère	French	
Millième	American	
Rutland	British	
Kildare	French	Killed in action
Thaler	British	
Arizona	American	Captured and executed
Hérault	French	Captured and executed
Indiana	American	Captured and executed
Amblève	French	
Sutherland	British	
Ore	American	
Stirling	British	Wounded in action
Ulster	French	
Serre	French	Wounded in action
Tipperary	British	
Argens	French	Wounded in action
Lancashire	British	Wounded in action

Mission
Rank, Name & (*Nom-de-guerre*)

BRIAN
Deployed from Harrington, England, to the Doubs department of
Eastern France on the night of 27–28 August 1944.
Maj. Francis P. C. Johnstone
Capt. Roger Crétin (*R. Francomte*)
Sgt. Norman A. Smith, W/T

BRUCE
Deployed from Harrington, England, to the Yonne department of
Central France on the night of 14–15 August 1944.
Maj. William Egan "Bill" Colby
Lt. Camille M. Lelong (*Jacques P. Favel*)
S/Lt. Roger Villebois, W/T (*Louis Giry*)

BUGATTI
Deployed from Blida, Algeria, to the Hautes-Pyrénées department of
Southwest France on the night of 28–29 June 1944.
Maj. (USMCR) Horace W. "Hod" Fuller
Capt. Guy de la Roche du Rousset (*G. Rocher*)
S/Lt. Martial Sigaud, W/T (*J. Guillemot*)

BUNNY
Deployed from England to the Haute-Marne department of
Northeast France on the night of 17–18 August 1944.
Capt. J. F. D. Radice
Lt. Maurice Geminel (*M. Gerville*)
Sgt. James T. Chambers, W/T

CECIL
Deployed from Harrington, England, to the Aube department of
Central France on the night of 25–26 August 1944.
Maj. David J. Nielson
Capt. Alfred Keser (*A. Frayant*)
Sgt. Ronald "Boxer" Wilde, W/T

CEDRIC
Deployed from England to the Doubs department of Eastern
France on the night of 27–28 August 1944.
Capt. Douglas DeWitt "Doug" Bazata
Capt. Louis Lesne (*F. Chapel*)
T/Sgt. Richard C. "Dick" Floyd, W/T

Code Name	Nationality	Remarks
Illinois	British	
Orkney	French	Wounded in action
Lira	British	
Berkshire	American	
Galway	French	
Piastre	French	
Kansul	American	
Hopei	French	
Chekiang	French	Killed in action
Peso	British	Died of wounds
Yen	French	Wounded in action
Drachma	British	
Delaware	British	
Lys	French	
Centavo	British	
Vesdre	American	Wounded in action
Dendre	French	
Guilder	American	

Mission
Rank, Name & (*Nom-de-guerre*)

CHLOROFORM
Deployed from Algeria to the Drôme and Hautes-Alpes
departments of Southeast France on the night of 29–30 June 1944.
Capt. Jacques Martin (*Jacques Martino*)
1st Lt. Henry Deane McIntosh
S/Lt. Jean Sassi, W/T (*Jean H. Nicole*)

CHRYSLER
Deployed from Blida, Algeria, to the Ariège department of
Southwest France on the night of 16–17 August 1944.
Capt. Cyril H. Sell
Lt. Paul Louis Aussaresses (*Jean Soual*)
Sgt. Ronald E. "Ron" Chatten, W/T

CINNAMON
Deployed from Blida, Algeria, to the Var department of Southeast
France on the night of 13–14 August 1944.
Capt. Robert Harcourt
Capt. Henri Lespinasse-Fonsegrive (*F. L. Ferandon*)
S/Lt. Jacques Morineau, W/T (*J. G. Maurin*)

CITROËN
Deployed from Algeria to the Vaucluse department of Southeast
France on the night of 13–14 August 1944.
Capt. John E. Saint C. Smallwood
Capt. Pierre Bloch (*René-Clément Alcée*)
Sgt. Frederick A. "Fred" Bailey, W/T

COLLODION*
Deployed from Algeria to the Aveyron department of Southwest
France on the night of 6–7 August 1944.
Capt. Harold Hall
Lt. Henri Marsaudon (*P. Morgan*)
Sgt. Theodore "Theo" Baumgold, W/T

DANIEL
Deployed from Fairford, England, to the Côtes-du-Nord department
of Brittany in Western France on the night of 4–5 August 1944.
Capt. Kemys D. "Ed" Bennett
Lt. Albert P. de Schonen (*Pierre de Schonen*)
Sgt. Ron Brierley, W/T

* Team also known as **Loch**.

Code Name	Nationality	Remarks
Joshua	French	
Lionel	American	
Latimer	French	
Elie	British	
Bazin	French	
Artus	British	
Louis	British	Fractured both legs on jump
Orthon	French	
Luc	French	
Anne	British	
Laurent	French	
Rétif	British	
Augustine	British	
Benoît	French	Wounded in action
Jules	American	
Apôtre	British	
Argentier	French	
Florin	British	

Mission
Rank, Name & (*Nom-de-guerre*)

DESMOND
Deployed from Harrington, England, to the Côte-d'Or department
of Eastern France on the night of 3–4 September 1944.
Capt. William H. "Bill" Pietsch, Jr.
Capt. Gilles Maunoury (*Henri Bourriot*)
M/Sgt. Robert R. "Bob" Baird, W/T

DODGE
Deployed from Algeria to the Drôme department of Southeast
France on the night of 24–25 June 1944 (reinforced Jed Veganin).
Maj. Cyrus E. "Cy" Manierre, Jr.
Sgt. L. T. Durocher, W/T

DOUGLAS
Deployed from Keevil, England, to the Morbihan department of
Brittany in Western France on the night of 6–7 August 1944.
Capt. Richard A. "Dick" Rubinstein
Lt. Jean Roblot (*Jean Ronglou*)
Sgt. John D. Raven, W/T

DOUGLAS II
Deployed from Harrington, England, to the Doubs department of
Eastern France on the night of 15–16 September 1944.
Capt. Richard A. "Dick" Rubinstein
Capt. Jean Roblot (*Jean Ronglou*)
T/Sgt. John T. Van Hart, W/T

EPHEDRINE
Deployed from Blida, Algeria, to the Savoie department of Southeast
France on the night of 12–13 August 1944.
1st Lt. Lawrence E. "Larry" Swank
Lt. Louis Donnard (*Louis Rabeau*)
S/Lt. Robert Desplechin, W/T (*J. Bourgoin*)

FELIX
Deployed from Fairford, England, to the Côtes-du-Nord department
of Brittany in Western France on the night of 8–9 July 1944.
Capt. Jean-Paul Souquet (*J. Kernevel*)
Capt. John J. Marchant
Sgt. Peter M. Colvin, W/T

Code Name	Nationality	Remarks
Skerry	American	
Shetland	French	
Hampshire	American	
Rupert	American	Captured-POW, liberated 1945
Oswald	Canadian	
Augure	British	
Anachorere	French	
Half Crown	British	
Augure	British	
Anachorere	French	Killed in action
Half Crown	American	
Gantor	American	Killed in accidental shooting
Julien	French	
Léon	French	
Carnavon	French	
Somerset	British	
Middlesex	British	

Mission
Rank, Name & (*Nom-de-guerre*)

FRANCIS
Deployed from Harrington, England, to the Finistère department of
Brittany in Western France on the night of 9–10 July 1944.
Maj. Colin M. Ogden-Smith
Lt. Guy Le Borgne (*Guy Le Zachmeur*)
Sgt. Arthur J. Dallow, W/T

FRANK
Deployed by sea from Plymouth, England, to the Vendée department
of Western France on 27–28 September 1944.
Capt. Idris Isaac
Lt. Alexandre Martelli (*A. Massoni*)
Sgt. Thomas Henney, W/T

FREDERICK
Deployed from Fairford, England, to the Côtes-du-Nord department
of Brittany in Western France on the night of 9–10 June 1944.
Maj. Adrian W. Wise
S/Lt. Paul Bloch-Auroch (*Paul Aguirec*)
T/Sgt. Robert R. "Bob" Kehoe, W/T

GAVIN
Deployed from Harrington, England, to the Ille-et-Vilaine department
of Brittany in Western France on the night of 11–12 July 1944.
Cmdt. Joseph Jean Carbuccia (*Daniel Jean-Claude*)
Capt. William B. "Bill" Dreux
S/Lt. Paul Valentini, W/T (*G. Masson*)

GEORGE
Deployed from Fairford, England, to the Morbihan department of
Brittany in Western France on the night of 9–10 June 1944.
Capt. Philippe Ragueneau (*P. Erard*)
Capt. Paul Cyr
S/Lt. Pierre Gay, W/T (*Christien Lejeune*)

GEORGE II
Deployed from Harrington, England, to the Loire-Inférieure
department of Western France on the night of 7–8 Sept. 1944.
Capt. Philippe Ragueneau (*P. Erard*)
Capt. Paul Cyr
S/Lt. Pierre Gay, W/T (*Christien Lejeune*)

Code Name	Nationality	Remarks
Dorset	British	Killed in action
Durance	French	
Groat	British	
Westmoreland	British	
Dumbarton	French	
Cheshire	British	
Kinros	British	
Vire	French	
Peseta	American	
Shilling	French	
Sixpence	American	
Halfpenny	French	
Save	French	
Wigton	American	
Rupee	French	
Save	French	Fractured leg on jump
Wigton	American	
Rupee	French	

Mission
Rank, Name & (*Nom-de-guerre*)

GERALD

Deployed from Harwell, England, to the Morbihan department of Brittany in Western France on the night of 18–19 July 1944.
Capt. Stephen J. "Steve" Knerly
Lt. Claude l'Herbette (*Jean-Luc Beaumont*)
1st Sgt. Berent E. Friele, Jr., W/T

GILBERT

Deployed from Harrington, England, to the Finistère department of Brittany in Western France on the night of 9–10 July 1944.
Capt. Christopher Gillian W. Blathwayt
Lt. Paul Carron de la Carrière (*P. Charron*)
Sgt. Neville Wood, W/T

GILES

Deployed from Harrington, England, to the Finistère department of Brittany in Western France on the night of 8–9 July 1944.
Capt. Bernard M. W. "Bernie" Knox
Capt. Paul Grall (*Paul Lebel*)
Sgt. Gordon H. Tack, W/T

GODFREY

Deployed from Harrington, England, to the Haut-Rhin department of Northeast France on the night of 11–12 September 1944.
1st Lt. Ian Forbes
Lt. Pierre Laval (*Jacques Morhange*)
Sgt. Frank A. Hanson, W/T

GRAHAM

Deployed from Algeria, via Corsica and Italy, to the Basses-Alpes department of Southeast France on the night of 8–9 August 1944.
Maj. Michael C. M. "Bing" Crosby
Capt. Pierre "Papa" Gavet (*P. Gouvet*)
1st Sgt. William H. "Bill" Adams, W/T

GREGORY

Deployed from Harrington, England, to the Doubs department of Eastern France on the night of 4–5 September 1944.
Capt. Kemys D. "Ed" Bennett
Capt. Albert P. de Schonen (*Pierre de Schonen*)
Sgt. Ron Brierley, W/T

Code Name	Nationality	Remarks
Norfolk	American	
Suffolk	French	
Selkirk	American	
Surrey	British	
Ardèche	French	
Doubloon	British	
Kentucky	American	
Loire	French	
Tickie	British	
Rhode Island	American	
Roscommon	French	
Roxburgh	American	
Huge	British	
Crispin	French	
Desire	American	Did not deploy to the field with team
Apôtre	British	Wounded in action
Argentier	French	Wounded in action
Florin	British	

Mission
Rank, Name & (*Nom-de-guerre*)

GUY
Deployed from Harrington, England, to the Ille-et-Vilaine department
of Brittany in Western France on the night of 11–12 July 1944.
Capt. André Duron (*A. Dhomas*)
Capt. Aubrey A. E. "Troff" Trofimov
S/Lt. Roger Groult, W/T (*J. Deschamps*)

HAMISH
Deployed from Harrington, England, to the Indre department
of Central France on the night of 12–13 June 1944.
1st Lt. Robert M. "Bobby" Anstett
Lt. René Schmitt (*Lucien Blachère*)
Sgt. Lee J. Watters, W/T

HAROLD
Deployed from Fairford, England, to the Vendée department of
Western France on the night of 15–16 July 1944.
Maj. Valentine E. Whitty
Lt. Pierre Jolliet (*Pierre Rimbaut*)
Sgt. Harry Verlander, W/T

HARRY
Deployed from Tempsford, England, to the Nièvre department of
Central France on the night of 6–7 June 1944.
Capt. Duncan Dunbar Guthrie
Lt. Pierre E. Rousset (*Pierre Etienne Dupont*)
S/Lt. René Couture, W/T (*Roger Legrand*)

HENRY
Deployed from Harrington, England, to the Belfort department of
Eastern France on the night of 9–10 September 1944.
Capt. Stephane Jean-Moncler (*S. Montcler*)
1st Lt. Raymond E. "Ray" Moore
T/Sgt. Vincent M. Rocca, W/T

HILARY
Deployed from Tempsford, England, to the Finistère department of
Brittany in Western France on the night of 17–18 July 1944.
Lt. Edgar Mautaint (*E. Marchant*)
1st Lt. Philip H. "Phil" Chadbourne, Jr.
S/Lt. Roger Hervouet, W/T (*R. Pariselle*)

Code Name	Nationality	Remarks
Dronne	French	
Gironde	British	
Dordogne	French	
Alabama	American	
Louisiana	French	
Kansas	American	
Ross	British	
Tyrone	French	
Sligo	British	
Denby	British	
Gapeau	French	
Centime	French	
Anglesey	French	
New Mexico	American	
West Virginia	American	
Charente	French	
Nevada	American	
Kopek	French	

Mission
Rank, Name & (*Nom-de-guerre*)

HORACE
Deployed from Tempsford, England, to the Finistère department of Brittany in Western France on the night of 17–18 July 1944.
Maj. John W. Summers
Lt. Georges Leclercq (*C. Levalois*)
T/3 William F. Zielski, Jr., W/T

HUGH
Deployed from Tempsford, England, to the Indre department of Central France on the night of 5–6 June 1944.
Capt. William R. "Bill" Crawshay
Capt. Louis l'Helgouach (*Louis Legrand*)
S/Lt. René Meyer, W/T (*Robert Mersiol*)

IAN
Deployed from Harrington, England, to the Vienne department of Central France on the night of 20–21 June 1944.
Maj. John J. Gildee, Jr.
Capt. Alexandre Desfarges (*Yves Delorme*)
Sgt. Lucien J. Bourgoin, W/T

ISAAC*
Deployed from Fairford, England, to the Nièvre department of Central France on the night of 10–11 June 1944.
Col. F. G. Viat (*Dubac*)
Lt. Col. James R. H. Hutchison (*John L. Hastings*)
Sgt. John Sharpe, W/T

IVOR
Deployed from Harrington, England, to the Cher department of Central France on the night of 6–7 August 1944.
Capt. John H. Cox
Lt. Robert Colin (*Yves M. Dantec*)
1st Sgt. Lewis F. "Lew" Goddard, W/T

JACOB
Deployed from England to the Vosges department of Eastern France on the night of 12–13 August 1944.
Capt. Albert Victor Gough

Lt. Maurice Boissarie (*Guy Baraud*)
Sgt. Kenneth Roy "Ken" Seymour, W/T

* Team name changed to **Verveine** after deployment; team deployed as the core of a larger special inter-Allied mission. Col. Viat, not a Jedburgh, was the mission leader.

Code Name	Nationality	Remarks
Wyoming	American	
Somme	French	
Dime	American	
Crown	British	
Franc	French	
Yonne	French	
Oklahoma	American	
Maine	French	
Mayo	American	Killed in action
Diagramme	French	Joined team in the field on 22 July
Télémètre	British	
	Canadian	
Monmouth	British	Injured on jump
Selune	French	Injured, accidental gunshot wound
Oregon	American	Killed on jump (parachute failed)
Arran	British	Captured-POW, executed November 1944
Connaught	French	Killed in action
Skye	British	Captured-POW, liberated 1945

Mission
Rank, Name & (*Nom-de-guerre*)

JAMES
Deployed from Fairford, England, to the Corrèze department of Southwest France on the night of 10–11 August 1944.
1st Lt. John K. "Jack" Singlaub
Lt. Jacques Le Bel de Penguilly (*Dominique Leb*)
T/Sgt. Anthony J. "Tony" Denneau, W/T

JEREMY
Deployed from Blida, Algeria, to the Haute-Loire department of Southern France on the night of 24–25 August 1944.
Capt. George M. Hallowes
Capt. Henri-Charles Giese (*H. Fontcroise*)
Sgt. Roger A. Leney, W/T

JIM
Deployed from Harrington, England, to the Ain department of Eastern France on the night of 15–16 September 1944.
Capt. Philip W. "Phil" Donovan
Lt. Joseph A. "Joe" de Francesco (*Jean Lavige*)
T/Sgt. Michael F. "Mike" Henely, W/T

JOHN
Deployed from Blida, Algeria, to the Ariège department of Southwest France on the night of 16–17 August 1944.
Capt. David L. Stern
Lt. Maurice de Galbert (*J. Lerocher*)
Sgt. Donald Gibbs, W/T
S/Lt. Jean Verneuil

JUDE
Deployed from Fairford, England, to the Loire department of Southeast France on the night of 14–15 August 1944.
Capt. William L. O. Evans
Capt. Jean Larrieu (*J. Lavisme*)
Sgt. Alfred E. Holdham, W/T

JULIAN
Deployed from Harrington, England, to the Indre-et-Loire department of Central France on the night of 10–11 August 1944.
Maj. A. H. Clutton
Lt. Marcel Joseph Vermot (*Joseph Brouillard*)
CQMS James S. Menzies, W/T

Code Name	Nationality	Remarks
Mississippi	American	Wounded in action
Michigan	French	
Massachusetts	American	
Aimable	British	
Dur	French	
Ferne	British	
Pennsylvania	American	
Leitrim	French	
Wexford	American	
Beau	British	
Lucide	French	
Silencieux	British	
Marcellin	French	W/T replacement for Jed Ammonia
Glamorgan	British	
Rence	French	
Guinea	British	
Stafford	British	
Vermont	French	
Essex	British	

Mission
Rank, Name & (*Nom-de-guerre*)

JULIAN II
Deployed from Tarrant Rushton, England, to the Haut-Rhin
department of Northeast France on the night of 18–19
November 1944.
Capt. Jean-Paul Souquet (*J. Kernevel*)
S/Lt. Paul Scherrer (*Sauvage*)
S/Lt. René Meyer, W/T (*Robert Mersiol*)

LEE
Deployed from Keevil, England, to the Haute-Vienne
department of Southwest France on the night of 9–10 August 1944.
Capt. Charles E. Brown III
Lt. Pierre Angoulvent (*N. Viguier*)
S/Lt. Maurice Pirat, W/T (*André Chevalier*)

MARK
Deployed from Blida, Algeria, to the Tarn-et-Garonne department
of Southwest France on the night of 16–17 August 1944.
1st Lt. Lucien E. "Lou" Conein
Lt. Joannés Thévenet (*F. G. de Thévenet*)
Sgt. James J. Carpenter, W/T

MARTIN
Deployed from Blida, Algeria, to the Gers department of Southwest
France on the night of 16–17 August 1944.
Capt. Thomas Anthony "Tony" Mellows
Lt. Georges Redonnet (*G. Rémond*)
Sgt. Neville E. S. Carey, W/T

MASQUE
Deployed from Maison Blanche, Algeria, to the Isère department of
Southeast France on the night of 27–28 August 1944.
Capt. Nelson E. Guillot
Lt. Jacques Bouvery (*J. René Gramont*)
Sgt. Francis M. "Jack" Poché, Jr., W/T

MAURICE
Deployed from Tempsford, England, to the Jura department of
Eastern France on the night of 31 August–1 September 1944.
Capt. Charles MacArthur Carman, Jr.
Lt. Hubert Reveilhac (*Hubert Dumesnil*)
T/Sgt. Francis J. Cole, W/T

Code Name	Nationality	Remarks
Carnavon	French	
[none]	French	
Yonne	French	
Pice	American	
Sous	French	Killed in action
Reis	French	
Intrepide	American	
Sympathique	French	
Leste	American	
Blasé	British	Captured, died of wounds
Substantif	French	
Placide	British	
Harmonieux	American	
Succulent	French	
Idéal	American	
Utah	American	
Virginia	French	
Georgia	American	

Mission
Rank, Name & (*Nom-de-guerre*)

MILES
Deployed from Blida, Algeria, to the Gers department of Southwest
France on the night of 16–17 August 1944.
Capt. Everett T. "Ev" Allen
Lt. René Estève (*Pierre Fourcade*)
T/Sgt. Arthur "Art" Gruen, W/T

MINARET
Deployed from Blida, Algeria, to the Lozère department of Southern
France on the night of 13–14 August 1944.
Maj. Lancelot C. M. Hartley-Sharpe
Capt. Pierre Cros (*Pierre Mutin*)
Sgt. John W. Ellis, W/T

MONOCLE
Deployed from Blida, Algeria, to the Vaucluse department of Southeast
France on the night of 13–14 August 1944.
Capt. Jacques Fiardo (*J. Tozel*)
1st Lt. Ray H. Foster
T/Sgt. Robert J. Anderson, W/T

NICHOLAS
Deployed from England to the Vosges department of Northeast
France on the night of 10–11 September 1944.
Capt. John C. C. Maude
Lt. Henri Penin (*H. Puget*)
Sgt. Maurice A. Whittle, W/T

NORMAN
Deployed from Harrington, England, to the Jura department of
Eastern France on the night of 27–28 August 1944.
Lt. Konrad C. Dillow
Lt. Marc Lautier (*Frederic Bataille*)
1st Sgt. Lucien E. "Lou" Lajeunesse, W/T

NOVOCAINE
Deployed from Blida, Algeria, to the Hautes-Alpes department of
Southeast France on the night of 6–7 August 1944.
1st Lt. Charles J. Gennerich
Lt. Jean-Yves Pronost (*Jean-Yves Lelann*)
Sgt. William T. "Bill" Thompson, W/T

Code Name	Nationality	Remarks
Libre	American	
Lumineux	French	
Fidèle	American	
Edmond	British	
Hector	French	Did not deploy due to illness
Arsène	British	
Immense	French	
Solide	American	
Raieux	American	
Leicester	British	
Breaknock	French	
Northumberland	British	
Minnesota	American	
Washington	French	
Tennessee	American	
Mathieu	American	
Herve	French	
Gilles	American	

Mission
Rank, Name & (*Nom-de-guerre*)

PACKARD
Deployed from Blida, Algeria, to the Lozère department of
Southern France on the night of 31 July–1 August 1944.
Capt. Aaron Bank
Capt. Henri Denis (*C. Boineau*)
Lt. Marcel F. Montfort, W/T

PAUL
Deployed from Tempsford, England, to the Côte-d'Or department
of Eastern France on the night of 18–19 August 1944.
Maj. Ernest Hugo Migesson Hood
Lt. Michel Vallée (*François Cormier*)
Sgt. Kenneth John Wilde Brown, W/T

QUENTIN
Deployed by sea from Plymouth, England, to the Vendée
department of Western France on 27–28 September 1944.
Capt. Ronald S. "Ronnie" Fenton
Lt. Jean Raux (*J. Lasserre*)
Sgt. David Rawson, W/T

QUININE
Deployed from Blida, Algeria, to the Cantal department of
Southwest France on the night of 8–9 June 1944.
Maj. R. Thomas "Tommy" MacPherson
Asp. Michel de Bourbon-Parme (*Maurice Bourdon*)
Sgt. O. Arthur Brown, W/T

RAYMOND
Deployed by sea from Plymouth, England, to the Vendée
department of Western France on 27–28 September 1944.
Capt. R. Dehosses (*R. Waguet*)
Lt. Henri H. L. Cadilhac (*H. Chaulais*)
Sgt. Walter Adams, W/T

RODERICK
Deployed from England to the Doubs department of Eastern
France on the night of 31 August–1 September 1944.
Capt. Jean Preziosi (*Albert Paoli*)
Lt. William C. "Bill" Boggs
T/Sgt. Charles P. Mersereau, W/T

Code Name	Nationality	Remarks
Chechwan	American	
Fukien	French	
Formosa	British	
Shropshire	British	
Durthe	French	
Limerick	British	
Cornwall	British	
Wicklow	French	
Merioneth	British	
Anselme	British	
Aristide	French	
Felicien	British	
Waterford	French	
Gloucester	French	
Kincardine	British	
Nairn	French	
New Hampshire	American	
Stronsay	American	

Mission
Rank, Name & (*Nom-de-guerre*)

RONALD
Deployed from England to the Finistère department of Brittany in Western France on the night of 4–5 August 1944.
1st Lt. Shirly Ray Trumps
Lt. Georges Desseilligny (*J. Dartigues*)
T/Sgt. Elmer B. "El" Esch, W/T

RUPERT*
Deployed from Harrington, England, to the Vosges department of Northeast France on the night of 31 August–1 September 1944.
Capt. C. Jean Liberos (*J. G. de Rouen*)
1st Lt. Robert A. "Bob" Lucas
S3Cl. (USN) Joseph M. Gergat,†W/T

SCEPTRE
Deployed from Blida, Algeria, to the Var department of Southeast France on the night of 13–14 August 1944.
1st Lt. Walter C. "Walt" Hanna, Jr.
Lt. François G. Franceschi (*François Tévenac*)
T/Sgt. Thomas J. Tracy
M/Sgt. Howard V. Palmer, W/T

SCION
Deployed from Maison Blanche, Algeria, to the Isère department of Southeast France on the night of 29–30 August 1944.
Maj. Osborne P. Grenfell
Lt. Roger Gruppo (*G. Revard*)
Sgt. Thomas F. "Cobber" Cain, W/T

SIMON
Deployed by sea from Plymouth, England, to the Vendée department of Western France on 27–28 September 1944.
Capt. Anthony W. C. Coomber
Capt. Maurice Fouéré (*M. Fontaine*)
LAC (RAF) Claud Somers, W/T

---

* Name changed to **Philip** after deployment.

† U.S. Navy Seaman Third Class Joseph Gergat's name is spelled "Grgat" in official records. The family of Mr. Gergat, who is now deceased, provided this version to the author as the correct spelling.

Code Name	Nationality	Remarks
Boursier	American	Wounded in action
Boutton	French	
Pound	American	
Kintyre	French	
Caithness	American	
Leincester	American	Became separated from team
Vaillant	American	
Intense	French	
[none]	American	Did not deploy due to illness
Dévoux	American	Replacement for Sgt. Tracy
Scintillating	British	
Vif	French	
Vibrant	British	
Coustard	British	
Fernard	French	
Stephane	British	

Mission
Rank, Name & (*Nom-de-guerre*)

STANLEY
Deployed from Tempsford, England, to the Haute-Marne department of Northeast France on the night of 31 August–1 September 1944.
Capt. Oswin E. Craster
Lt. Robert Cantais (*Robert Carlière*)
Sgt. Eric J. "Jack" Grinham, W/T

TIMOTHY
Deployed from Harrington, England, to the Doubs department of Eastern France on the night of 10–11 September 1944.
Capt. Louis Moutte (*L. Ambel*)
1st Lt. Robert E. "Bob" Heyns
1st Lt. Robert G. Mundinger

1st Sgt. Donald A. Spears, W/T

TONY
Deployed from Harrington, England, to the Vendée department of Western France on the night of 17–18 August 1944.
Maj. Robert K. "Bob" Montgomery
Lt. Lucien Paris (*Mark Devailly*)
T/Sgt. John E. McGowan, W/T

VEGANIN
Deployed from Algeria to the Drôme department of Southeast France on the night of 8–9 June 1944.
Maj. H. Neil Marten
Capt. Gaston Vuchot (*Claude L. Noir*)
Sgt. Dennis "Jesse" Gardner, W/T

WILLYS
Deployed from Blida, Algeria, to the Ardèche department of Southeast France on the night of 28–29 June 1944.
Capt. Georges Marchal (*P. J. Granier*)
Capt. John C. C. Montague
Sgt. F. A. "Ted" Cornick, W/T

Code Name	Nationality	Remarks
Yorkshire	British	
Meath	French	
Worcestershire	British	
Nesque	French	
Dyle	American	Fractured both ankles on jump
Marcelin	American	Joined team on 13 September 1944
Escaut	American	
Dollar	American	
Écu	French	
Quarter	American	
Cuthbert	British	
Derek	French	
Ernest	British	Killed on jump (parachute failed)
Simon	French	
Honan	British	
Chansi	British	

NOTES

PROLOGUE

1. Gen. Dwight D. Eisenhower, letter to Maj. Gen. Colin Gubbins, executive director of SOE, 31 May 1945, in *SOE in France: An Account of the Work of the British Special Operations Executive in France, 1940–1944*, by M. R. D. Foot (London: Her Majesty's Stationery Office, 1966), pp. 441–42; and Eisenhower, letter to Col. David K. E. Bruce, chief of OSS, European Theater of Operations, 31 May 1945, in *The Overseas Targets: War Report of the OSS (Office of Strategic Services), Volume 2*, intro. by Kermit Roosevelt (Washington, DC: Carrollton Press; New York: Walker & Company, 1976), p. 222.
2. Harry C. Butcher, *My Three Years with Eisenhower: The Personal Diary of Captain Harry C. Butcher, USNR, Naval Aide to General Eisenhower, 1942 to 1945* (New York: Simon & Schuster, 1946), p. 654.
3. Office of Strategic Services (OSS), London Office, *OSS/London: Special Operations Branch and Secret Intelligence Branch War Diaries* (1945), ed. Paul Kesaris, (Frederick, MD: University Publications of America, 1985), vol. 13, pp. 1–6, gives the total number of Jedburgh operators deployed as 281 (103 French, 90 British, 83 Americans, 4 Dutch, and 1 Belgian).
4. OSS/London, *OSS/London: Special Operations Branch War Diary*, vol. 13, pp. 1–6; and Associated Press, "D-Day Chutists Rate as Heroes: South Bend Officer One of International Secret Unit," unidentified Indiana newspaper, September 27, [1945?].
5. Ernie Pyle, *Brave Men* (New York: Henry Holt, 1944), p. 416.

CHAPTER 1

1. OSS/London, *OSS/London: Special Operations Branch War Diary*, vol. 4, bk. 1, p. 13.
2. Robert Kehoe, telephone conversation with the author, January 19, 2004.
3. Robert R. Kehoe, "Jed Team Frederick, 1944: An Allied Team With the French Resistance" (1997), article on the Central Intelligence Agency's Center for the Study of Intelligence webpage, http://www.cia.gov/csi/ studies/winter98_99/art03.html (accessed January 13, 2005).
4. Walter Bedell Smith, *Eisenhower's Six Great Decisions* (New York: Longmans, Green, 1956), pp. 41–51.
5. Roy Berkeley, *A Spy's London* (London: Leo Cooper, 1994), pp. 164–76.
6. Paul McCue, *SAS Operation Bulbasket: Behind the Lines in Occupied France, 1944* (London: Leo Cooper, 1996), pp. 1–2; and M. R. D. Foot, *Resistance: European Resistance to Nazism, 1940–1945* (New York: McGraw-Hill, 1977), pp. 53–55.
7. Robert Kehoe, telephone conversation with the author, January 19, 2004.
8. OSS/London, *OSS/London: Special Operations Branch War Diary*, vol. 4, bk. 1, report on Team Frederick, pp. 33–35, 143; SO Branch War Diary, vol. 4, bk. 1, report on Team George, pp. 39–42, 157; and Kehoe, "Jed Team Frederick, 1944."
9. Smith, *Eisenhower's Six Great Decisions*, pp. 28–29; and Stephen E. Ambrose, *D-Day, June 6, 1944: The Climactic Battle of World War II* (New York: Simon & Schuster, 1994), p. 189.
10. Robert Kehoe, telephone conversation with the author, January 19, 2004.
11. Kehoe, "Jed Team Frederick, 1944."
12. OSS/London, *OSS/London: Special Operations Branch War Diary*, vol. 4, bk. 1, report on Team George, pp. 157–58; and Kehoe, "Jed Team Frederick, 1944."

CHAPTER 2

1. Squadron and flight details are taken from the Royal Air Force WWII 38 Group website, http://www.raf38group.org (accessed September 21, 2004).
2. Kehoe, "Jed Team Frederick, 1944."
3. OSS/London, *OSS/London: Special Operations Branch War Diary*, vol. 4, bk. 1, report on Team Frederick, p. 143; and Kehoe, "Jed Team Frederick, 1944."
4. Robert Kehoe, telephone conversation with the author, January 19, 2004.

5. Kehoe, "Jed Team Frederick, 1944."
6. Roger Ford, *Fire from the Forest: The SAS Brigade in France, 1944* (London: Cassell, 2003), p. 255.
7. OSS/London, *OSS/London: Special Operations Branch War Diary,* vol. 4, bk. 1, report on Team Frederick, p. 144.
8. Special Operations Executive, *Secret Agent's Handbook: The WWII Spy Manual of Devices, Disguises, Gadgets, and Concealed Weapons,* reproduction of two wartime volumes with intro. by Mark Seaman (Guilford, CT: The Lyons Press, 2001), pp. 163–65.
9. OSS/London, *OSS/London: Special Operations Branch War Diary,* vol. 4, bk. 1, report on Team Frederick, p. 36; and Kehoe, "Jed Team Frederick, 1944."
10. Kehoe, "Jed Team Frederick, 1944."
11. Ibid.
12. This account of the incident at the farm on the evening of June 11 is based on Major Wise's after-action report and Bob Kehoe's account. In his book *Fire from the Forest* (p. 256), author Roger Ford gives a slightly different account based on Captain Leblond's report. All three of these reports, of course, are second-hand as neither Wise, Kehoe, nor Leblond was present at the farmhouse during the attack.
13. OSS/London, *OSS/London: Special Operations Branch War Diary,* vol. 4, bk. 1, report on Team Frederick, p. 144.
14. Julian Thompson, *The Imperial War Museum Book of War Behind Enemy Lines* (Washington, DC: Brassey's, 2001), p. 307.
15. Robert Kehoe, telephone conversation with the author, January 19, 2004.
16. William Colby and Peter Forbath, *Honorable Men: My Life in the CIA* (New York: Simon & Schuster, 1978), p. 26.
17. OSS/London, *OSS/London: Special Operations Branch War Diary,* vol. 4, bk. 1, report on Team Frederick, pp. 145–46; and Kehoe, "Jed Team Frederick, 1944."

CHAPTER 3

1. William Manchester, *The Last Lion: Winston Spencer Churchill; Alone, 1932–1940* (Boston: Little, Brown, 1988), p. 13; and Winston S. Churchill, *The Second World War,* vol. 2, *Their Finest Hour* (Boston: Houghton Mifflin Company, 1949), p. 128.
2. Winston Churchill, quoted in *The Last Lion: Winston Spencer Churchill; Visions of Glory, 1874–1932,* by William Manchester (Boston: Little, Brown, 1983), p. 650.
3. Nigel West [Rupert Allason], *MI6: British Secret Intelligence Service Operations, 1909–45* (New York: Random House, 1983), p. 60.

4. Foot, *SOE in France*, p. 11.

5. The fact that Donovan was a prominent Republican was of little concern to Roosevelt. The previous summer he had appointed two Republicans to fill the key defense positions in his bipartisan cabinet—Frank Knox as secretary of the Navy and Henry L. Stimson as secretary of war, as the Army's civilian leadership was then called. Donovan had actually been considered for the War Department post.

6. The complete text of Churchill's December 1941 strategy documents are in *Churchill and Roosevelt, The Complete Correspondence*, ed. Warren F. Kimball (Princeton: Princeton University Press, 1984), vol. 1, pp. 294–309; also see Winston S. Churchill, *The Second World War*, vol. 3, *The Grand Alliance* (Boston: Houghton Mifflin, 1950), pp. 582, 588.

7. Peter Wilkinson, *Foreign Fields: The Story of an SOE Operative* (London: I. B. Tauris, 1997), p. 128.

8. OSS/London, *OSS/London: Special Operations Branch War Diary*, vol. 4, bk. 1, p. i.

9. Churchill, *The Second World War*, vol. 5, *Closing the Ring* (Boston: Houghton Mifflin, 1951), pp. 580, 583.

10. See M. R. D. Foot, *SOE: An outline history of the Special Operations Executive, 1940–46* (London: British Broadcasting Corp., 1984), p. 127, for more on how code names were assigned. Foot also explains how entire blocks of approved code names were allocated to Special Force Headquarters (SFHQ) for use with Jedburgh and other special forces teams. This accounts for the many Jed teams that were assigned men's first names as code names, while other teams were assigned code names from other blocks—names of automobiles or drugs, for example. OSS Operational Groups were mostly assigned code names from a block of women's first names.

11. Arthur Brown, "The Jedburghs: A Short History," April 1991, photocopy of unpublished manuscript provided to the author by Mr. Brown, p. 5.

12. Bruce Marshall, *The White Rabbit* (Boston: Houghton Mifflin, 1952), pp. 84–85.

13. Stanley Cannicott, *Journey of a Jed* (Cheddar, UK: Cheddar Valley Press, 1986), pp. 12–13.

14. Gen. Paul Aussaresses, letter to the author, September 19, 1989.

15. Bernard Knox, *Essays Ancient and Modern* (Baltimore: Johns Hopkins University Press, 1989), p. xxiii.

16. Ibid.

17. Roger Hall, *You're Stepping on My Cloak and Dagger* (New York: W. W. Norton, 1957), p. 32.

18. Ibid.

19. Edmund F. Wehrle, *Catoctin Mountain Park: A Historic Resource Study* (2000), on National Park Service website, http://www.nps.gov/cato/hrs/hrs.htm, chap. 6, "War and Politics Shape the Park" (accessed January 24, 2005).

20. William L. Cassidy, ed., *History of the Schools and Training Branch, Office of Strategic Services* (San Francisco: Kingfisher Press, 1983), p. 72.

21. Albert Hemingway, "The Great Parachute Drop," *Military History*, April 1990, p. 48.

22. John K. Singlaub and Malcolm McConnell, *Hazardous Duty: An American Soldier in the Twentieth Century* (New York: Summit Books, 1991), p. 32.

23. Kehoe, "Jed Team Frederick, 1944."

24. Ibid.

25. Steve Harding, *Gray Ghost: The R.M.S. Queen Mary at War* (Missoula, MT: Pictorial Histories, 1982), p. 78.

26. Gen. Paul Aussaresses, letters to the author, September 17, 18, and 19, 1989, and January 24, 1990; and Michel de Bourbon, letter to the author, January 3, 1990.

27. OSS/London, *OSS/London: Special Operations Branch War Diary*, vol. 4, bk. 1, p. xxii; vol. 9, p. 8; Office of Strategic Services Assessment Staff, *Assessment of Men: Selection of Personnel for the Office of Strategic Services* (New York: Rinehart & Company, Inc., 1948); and M. G. M. Crosby, *Irregular Soldier* (United Kingdom: XB Publications, 1993), pp. 88–91. Col. Crosby served as a member of the assessments board and later deployed as part of a Jedburgh team.

28. OSS/London, *OSS/London: Special Operations Branch War Diary*, vol. 4, bk. 1, p. xxii.

29. Brown, "The Jedburghs: A Short History," p. 6.

30. Norman Longmate, *The G.I.'s: The Americans in Britain, 1942–1945* (New York: Charles Scribner's Sons, 1975), pp. 36, 38.

31. OSS/London, *OSS/London: Special Operations Branch War Diary*, vol. 4, bk. 1, p. xxii; and Thompson, *The Imperial War Museum Book of War Behind Enemy Lines*, p. 301.

32. Knox, *Essays Ancient and Modern*, p. xxiii.

33. James Hutchison, *That Drug Danger* (Montrose, Scotland: Standard Press, 1977), p. 86.

34. Cannicott, *Journey of a Jed*, p. 22.

35. Gen. Paul Aussaresses, letter to the author, September 1989.

36. OSS/London, *OSS/London: Special Operations Branch War Diary*, vol. 4, bk. 1, pp. 1–3.

37. Cannicott, *Journey of a Jed*, p. 23.

38. Ibid., p. 25.

39. Butcher, *My Three Years with Eisenhower*, pp. 510, 538, 544.

40. Ibid., p. 538.
41. Frederick Morgan, *Overture to Overlord* (Garden City, NY: Doubleday, 1950), pp. 155–56; Churchill, *The Second World War*, vol. 5, pp. 69–70, 327; and Hastings Lionel Ismay, *The Memoirs of General Lord Ismay* (New York: Viking, 1960), p. 311.
42. Stephen E. Ambrose, *Ike's Spies: Eisenhower and the Espionage Establishment* (Jackson: University Press of Mississippi, 1999), pp. 88, 97.
43. Col. C. S. Vanderblue, commander, Office of Strategic Services Detachment Third Army, memorandum to Gen. William J. Donovan, subject: Report of C. S. Vanderblue on OSS Operations with the Third Army, November 15, 1944, p. 5 (National Archives, Washington History Office, Record Group (RG) 226, OP–23, entry 99, folder 50, box 12), photocopy in author's files.
44. Maj. Gen. Harold R. Bull, operations officer (G–3), Supreme Headquarters Allied Expeditionary Force (SHAEF), memorandum to Chief, Plans and Operations Section, subject: "SOE/SO Assistance to Overlord," April 6, 1944 (National Archives, Washington History Office, RG 331, entry 23, box 47), photocopy in author's files.
45. Chief of Staff to the Supreme Allied Commander, Designate (COSSAC), "Operation 'Overlord'," app. P, "Support of Military Operations by Resistance Groups in Europe," July 15, 1943 (National Archives, Washington History Office, RG 331, entry 23, box 47), photocopy in author's files; and Butcher, *My Three Years with Eisenhower*, p. 510.
46. Butcher, *My Three Years with Eisenhower*, pp. 515, 540.
47. Joint Psychological Warfare Committee, minutes of 24th meeting (August 24, 1942) with attached Jedburgh concept paper, minutes of 33rd meeting (September 2, 1942), and minutes of 35th meeting (September 16, 1942); Gen. Walter B. Smith, memorandum to Operations Div., War Dept., subject: "Jedburghs," September 3, 1942; Gen. Eisenhower, message to War Dept., subject: "Jedburghs," September 16, 1942 (National Archives, Washington History Office, RG 218, box 8), photocopies in author's files; Dwight D. Eisenhower, *The Papers of Dwight David Eisenhower: The War Years*, ed. Alfred D. Chandler, Jr. (Baltimore: The Johns Hopkins Press, 1970), vol. 5, p. 76.
48. SHAEF, Office of the G–3, directive, subject: "Open Title for Headquarters, SOE/SO," May 1, 1944, copy in OSS/London: Special Operations Branch War Diary, vol. 12, p. 85; vol. 1, pp. 1–2, 4, 11–12; vol. 4, bk. 1, p. 14; vol. 12, p. 33.

CHAPTER 4

1. OSS/London, *OSS/London: Special Operations Branch War Diary*, vol. 4, bk. 1, report on Team George, p. 43.

2. Ibid., pp. 158–60; Ford, *Fire from the Forest*, p. 252; André Hue and Ewen Southby-Tailyour, *The Next Moon: The remarkable true story of a British agent behind the lines in wartime France* (London: Viking, 2004), p. 19.

3. OSS/London, *OSS/London: Special Operations Branch War Diary*, vol. 11, p. 589; and "Keeping Posted," *Saturday Evening Post*, 23 March 1946, p. 4.

4. Hue, *The Next Moon*, pp. 47, 64.

5. Special Force Headquarters (SFHQ) G–3 Periodic Report no. 9 (June 13, 1944), p. 2 (National Archives, Washington History Office, RG 226, OP–23, entry 99, box 93), provides numbers which conflict with those taken from Jedburgh team George's report, citing 85 SAS troops and 250 containers.

6. SFHQ G–3 Periodic Report no. 12 (June 16, 1944), p. 1.

7. OSS/London, *OSS/London: Special Operations Branch War Diary*, vol. 4, bk. 1, report on Team George, pp. 160–63.

8. OSS/London, *OSS/London: Special Operations Branch War Diary*, vol. 3, bk. 3, p. 14.

9. Ibid., vol. 3, bk. 1, pp. 6–7.

10. Foot, *SOE in France*, p. 388; Foot, "Special Operations," in *The D-Day Encyclopedia*, ed. David G. Chandler and James Lawton Collins, Jr. (New York: Simon & Schuster, 1994), p. 524; Maurice J. Buckmaster, *They Fought Alone: The Story of British Agents in France* (New York: W. W. Norton, 1958), pp. 219–20; Max Hastings, *Das Reich: The March of the 2nd SS Panzer Division Through France* (New York: Holt, Rinehart and Winston, 1982), p. 5.

11. The Reader's Digest Association, *Secrets and Spies: Behind-the-Scenes Stories of World War II* (Pleasantville, NY: Reader's Digest Assn., 1964), p. 387.

12. David Eisenhower, *Eisenhower at War, 1943–1945* (New York: Vintage Books, 1987), p. 255; and Alfred Goldberg, "Air Campaign Overlord: To D-Day," in *D-Day: The Normandy Invasion in Retrospect* (Lawrence: The University Press of Kansas, 1971), pp. 66–68.

CHAPTER 5

1. Kehoe, "Jed Team Frederick, 1944."

2. OSS/London, *OSS/London: Special Operations Branch War Diary*, vol. 4, bk. 1, report on Team Frederick, p. 36; and Kehoe, "Jed Team Frederick, 1944."

3. Richard Floyd, telephone conversation with the author, September 13, 2004.

4. Kehoe, "Jed Team Frederick, 1944."

5. Kehoe, "Jed Team Frederick, 1944"; and SFHQ G–3 Periodic Report no. 20 (June 24, 1944), p. 4.
6. OSS/London, *OSS/London: Special Operations Branch War Diary,* vol. 4, bk. 1, report on Team Frederick, p. 152.
7. Ibid., p. 37.
8. Ibid., p. 139.
9. OSS/London, *OSS/London: Special Operations Branch War Diary,* vol. 4, bk. 1, report on Team Frederick, pp. 140, 147–48; vol. 4, bk. 2, report on Team Giles, p. 328; vol. 4, bk. 2, report on Team Felix, p. 365; and Kehoe, "Jed Team Frederick, 1944."
10. Kehoe, "Jed Team Frederick, 1944."

CHAPTER 6

1. André Hue, who was with Bourgoin throughout this period, refers to him by that rank in his book *The Next Moon.*
2. SFHQ G–3 Periodic Report no. 12 (June 16, 1944), p. 1.
3. OSS/London, *OSS/London: Special Operations Branch War Diary,* vol. 4, bk. 1, report on Team George, pp. 163, 169.
4. Ibid., p. 44; and Hue, *The Next Moon,* p. 82.
5. OSS/London, *OSS/London: Special Operations Branch War Diary,* vol. 4, bk. 1, report on Team George, pp. 167–68; Hue, *The Next Moon,* pp. 134–35; and Ford, *Fire from the Forest,* pp. 253–54. While team George's report states that this attack was made by 150 German feldgendarmes screened by civilians, Hue's account calls it 50 Germans and makes no mention of the civilians. Ford cites French sources which described the German force as 125 infantrymen and also mentions the civilian screen.
6. Roger Ford, *Steel from the Sky: The Jedburgh Raiders, France, 1944* (London: Weidenfeld & Nicolson, 2004), pp. 67–68.
7. SFHQ G–3 Periodic Report no. 20 (June 24, 1944), p. 4; and Hue, *The Next Moon,* p. 151.
8. OSS/London, *OSS/London: Special Operations Branch War Diary,* vol. 4, bk. 1, report on Team George, p. 45.
9. SFHQ G–3 Periodic Report no. 26 (June 30, 1944), p. 3.
10. OSS/London, *OSS/London: Special Operations Branch War Diary,* vol. 4, bk. 1, report on Team George, p. 45.
11. OSS/London, *OSS/London: Special Operations Branch War Diary,* vol. 3, bk. 2, p. 160; and vol. 3, bk. 3, pp. 268–79.
12. Dwight D. Eisenhower, *D Day to VE Day, 1944–45: General Eisenhower's Report on the Invasion of Europe* (London: The Stationery Office, 2000), p. 97.
13. Ambrose, *Ike's Spies,* p. 106.

14. Samuel W. Mitcham, Jr., *Retreat to the Reich: The German Defeat in France, 1944* (Westport, CT: Praeger, 2000), pp. 13–14.
15. Foot, *SOE in France*, p. 411.
16. Sidney C. Moody and the Associated Press, *War in Europe* (Novato, CA: Presidio Press, 1993), p. 135.
17. Wilhelm Tieke, *In the Firestorm of the Last Years of the War: II SS-Panzerkorps with the 9 and 10 SS-Divisions "Hohenstaufen" and "Frundsberg,"* trans. Frederick Steinhardt (Winnipeg: Fedorowicz, 1999), pp. 80–81.
18. Arthur L. Funk, "French Resistance," in *The D-Day Encyclopedia*, ed. Chandler and Collins, p. 264.
19. Eisenhower, *The Papers of Dwight David Eisenhower*, vol. 3, pp. 1926–27.
20. Ambrose, *Ike's Spies*, p. 107.

CHAPTER 7

1. Etat-major des Forces Francaises de l'Interieur (EMFFI) [General Head-quarters of the French Forces of the Interior], "A Short History of the Organization of the Command of Operations Undertaken by the French Forces of the Interior," (1945), p. 12 (National Archives, Washington History Office, RG 226), photocopy in author's files; and OSS/London, *OSS/London: Special Operations Branch War Diary*, vol. 3, bk. 2, p. 364.
2. Eisenhower, *D Day to VE Day, 1944–45*, p. 117.
3. Robert S. Allen, *Lucky Forward: The History of Patton's Third U.S. Army* (New York: Vanguard Press, 1947), p. 89; and OSS/London: Special Operations Branch War Diary, vol. 2, p. 64.
4. OSS/London, *OSS/London: Special Operations Branch War Diary*, vol. 3, bk. 2, p. 374.
5. OSS/London, *OSS/London: Special Operations Branch War Diary*, vol. 4, bk. 1, report on Team Frederick, p. 140; and Kehoe, "Jed Team Frederick, 1944."
6. Vanderblue, OSS Detachment Third Army, memorandum to Gen. Donovan, subject: "Report of C. S. Vanderblue on OSS operations with Third Army," November 15, 1944, p. 9.
7. Jonathan Gawne, *The Americans in Brittany, 1944: The Battle for Brest* (Paris: Histoire & Collections, 2002), p. 19.
8. Ralph Ingersoll, *Top Secret* (New York: Harcourt, Brace, 1946), pp. 184–85.
9. Edward Bautz, interview posted on the Rutgers Oral History Archives of World War II website, http://fas-history.rutgers.edu/oralhistory/Interviews/bautz_edward.html (accessed October 18, 2004).
10. Brenton G. Wallace, *Patton and his Third Army* (Mechanicsburg, PA:

Stackpole Books, 2000), pp. 16–20; Allen, *Lucky Forward*, p. 96; and Vanderblue, "memorandum to Gen. Donovan," November 15, 1944, p. 9.

11. Special Force Detachment 11, Headquarters, Third United States Army, G–3 Section, "Operations Report," p. 3 (National Archives, Washington History Office, RG 226, entry 115, box 50), photocopy in author's files; and Gawne, *The Americans in Brittany*, p. 26.

12. Robert B. Asprey, *War in the Shadows: The Guerrilla in History* (Garden City, NY: Doubleday, 1975), p. 319.

13. OSS/London, *OSS/London: Special Operations Branch War Diary*, vol. 4, bk. 1, report on Team Frederick, p. 154.

14. OSS/London, *OSS/London: Special Operations Branch War Diary*, vol. 4, bk. 1, report on Team George, p. 204.

15. Ibid., p. 216; Charles M. Province, *Patton's Third Army: A Daily Combat Diary* (New York: Hippocrene Books, 1992), p. 20; and 12th Army Group, *Report of Operations, G–3 Section, 12th Army Group (Final After Action Report)*, (1945), photocopy in author's files, p. 75.

16. Allen, *Lucky Forward*, p. 50.

17. Foot, "Special Operations," in *The D-Day Encyclopedia*, ed. Chandler and Collins, p. 525.

18. Robert LeBlanc papers, U.S. Army Military History Institute Archives, Carlisle Barracks, PA, WWII–7396, box OSS/LONDON, WWII survey; and Vanderblue, "memorandum to Gen. William J. Donovan," November 15, 1944, p. 28.

19. SFHQ G–3 Periodic Report no. 69 (August 12, 1944), app. A, p. 1.

20. OSS/London, *OSS/London: Special Operations Branch War Diary*, vol. 4, bk. 1, report on Team George, p. 233.

21. SFHQ G–3 Periodic Report no. 66 (August 9, 1944), app. B, p. 1.

22. Omar N. Bradley, *A Soldier's Story* (New York: Henry Holt, 1951), p. 365.

23. Eisenhower, *D Day to VE Day*, p. 138.

24. Ibid., p. 154.

25. Ingersoll, *Top Secret*, pp. 186–87.

CHAPTER 8

1. William E. Colby, letter to the author, March 27, 1989; Colby and Forbath, *Honorable Men*, pp. 26–35; and OSS/London, *OSS/London: Special Operations Branch War Diary*, vol. 11, p. 564.

2. Camille Lelong, telephone conversation with the author, August 13, 2004.

3. Foot, *SOE in France*, p. 292.

4. E. H. Cookridge, *Set Europe Ablaze* (New York: Crowell, 1967), pp. 181–5.

5. Ibid., p. 185.

6. Jean Overton Fuller, *The German Penetration of SOE: France, 1941–1944*, rev. ed. (Maidstone, UK: George Mann Books, 1996), pp. 33–35.

7. Hugo Bleicher, *Colonel Henri's Story: The War Memoirs of Hugo Bleicher: Former German Secret Agent*, ed. Ian Colvin (London: William Kimber, 1954), pp. 139–41; and Cookridge, *Set Europe Ablaze*, pp. 190–5.

8. William E. Colby, interview with the author, July 28, 1989, in Washington, DC.

9. Camille Lelong, telephone conversation with the author, August 13, 2004.

10. Colby and Forbath, *Honorable Men*, pp. 23–24.

11. Ibid., pp. 39–40.

12. Ibid., p. 41.

13. Ibid., p. 42.

14. Richard Harris Smith, *OSS: The Secret History of America's First Central Intelligence Agency* (Berkeley: University of California Press, 1972), p. 196.

15. Special Force Detachment 11, "Operations Report," p. 16.

16. Ibid.

17. Province, *Patton's Third Army*, p. 29.

18. George S. Patton, Jr., *War as I Knew It* (Boston: Houghton Mifflin, 1947), p. 361.

19. George S. Patton, Jr., quoted in Allen, *Lucky Forward*, p. 85.

20. Smith, *Eisenhower's Six Great Decisions*, pp. 81–82.

21. Ingersoll, *Top Secret*, p. 196.

22. OSS/London, *OSS/London: Special Operations Branch War Diary*, vol. 4, bk. 4, report on Team Bruce, app. 1, p. 860.

23. 5th Infantry Division, United States Army, *The 5th Division in France* (Metz: La Lorraine Press, 1944), pp. 9, 13–14; and James A. Huston, *Biography of a Battalion: The Life and Times of an Infantry Battalion in Europe in World War II* (Mechanicsburg, PA: Stackpole Books, 2003), p. 76.

24. OSS/London, *OSS/London: Special Operations Branch War Diary*, vol. 4, bk. 4, report on Team Bruce, pp. 853–54.

25. Eisenhower, *The Papers of Dwight David Eisenhower*, vol. 4, pp. 2100–01.

26. Ibid., vol. 4, pp. 2100–03.

27. Butcher, *My Three Years with Eisenhower*, p. 654.

28. Robert Hayden Alcorn, *No Bugles for Spies: Tales of the OSS* (New York: Popular Library, 1964), p. 95.

CHAPTER 9

1. Ford, *Steel from the Sky*, p. 257.

2. Gen. Paul Aussaresses, letter to the author, September 21, 1989.

3. Background material on John Bonsall was provided by Sarah Drake (John Bonsall's niece), during a telephone interview with the author on November 8, 2004, and by Katherine Strong (John Bonsall's sister) and Sarah Drake during a telephone interview with the author on November 14, 2004.

4. OSS/London, *OSS/London: Special Operations Branch War Diary*, vol. 4, bk. 6, report on Team Augustus, p. 2; and SFHQ G–3 Periodic Report no. 76 (August 19, 1944), p. 5.

5. Violette Desmarais (Roger Côté's sister), telephone interview with the author, November 13, 2004, and letter to the author, November 22, 2004.

6. Unless otherwise indicated in footnotes, the account of Jedburgh team Augustus in this chapter was constructed using the following sources: Gaston Costeaux and Émile Fortier, "Rapport sur l'activité de la mission Auguste," first-person account dated October 5, 1944 (a photocopy of the report, which is also on file at the National Archives, was provided to the author by Jedburgh veteran Charles Carman, then serving as Jedburgh archivist at the Hoover Institution, Stanford University); Gen. Paul Aussaresses, letter to the author, September 25, 1989, with an enclosed map annotated with a chronology of the movements and activities of team Augustus; Gen. Paul Aussaresses, letter to the author, October 25, 1989, relating details provided to him by resistance veterans and others who had first-hand knowledge of the team's final days, including Armand Rot; and Armand Rot, "Compte-Rendu," statement written in 1944.

7. OSS/London, *OSS/London: Special Operations Branch War Diary*, vol. 4, bk. 6, report on Team Augustus, pp. 2–3. While Jedburgh after-action reports found in the *OSS/London: Special Operations Branch War Diary* were normally written by the team members, principally the team leader, the Augustus report was written by someone on the SFHQ staff. The report includes the text of radio messages received from the team and a report by Maj. William T. Hornaday, dated October 23, 1944, on the results of an investigation into the team's fate.

8. Costeaux and Fortier, "Rapport sur l'activité de la mission Auguste," p. 3.

9. Ibid.

10. Hans von Luck, *Panzer Commander: The Memoirs of Colonel Hans von Luck* (New York: Praeger, 1989), p. 184.

11. H. R. Knickerbocker, et. al., *Danger Forward: The Story of the First Division in World War II* (Atlanta: Albert Love, 1947), p. 270.

12. Gordon A. Harrison, *Cross-Channel Attack*, United States Army in World War II series (Washington, DC: Center of Military History, 1993), p. 412.

13. Helmut Ritgen, *The Western Front 1944: Memoirs of a Panzer Lehr Officer*, trans. Joseph Welsh (Winnipeg: Fedorowicz, 1995), pp. 121, 198–99.

14. OSS/London, *OSS/London: Special Operations Branch War Diary*, vol. 4, bk. 6, report on Team Augustus, p. 4; and SFHQ G–3 Periodic Report no. 84 (August 27, 1944), p. 5. The SFHQ G–3 Periodic Report indicates that 15 containers were dropped to the Aisne department on the night of August 24–25, another 24 containers the following night, 48 more the night after that, and another 60 on the night of August 27–28. It is unclear whether any of these were intended for Jedburgh team Augustus.

15. Martin Blumenson, *Breakout and Pursuit*, United States Army in World War II (Washington, DC: Center of Military History, 1961, 1984), p. 668.

16. Vincent J. Esposito, ed., *The West Point Atlas of American Wars*, vol. 2, *1900–1953* (New York: Praeger, 1959), pp. 55–56.

17. Blumenson, *Breakout and Pursuit*, p. 661.

18. Ritgen, *The Western Front 1944*, p. 201.

19. Costeaux and Fortier, "Rapport sur l'activité de la mission Auguste," p. 6.

20. Ritgen, *The Western Front 1944*, p. 201; and Robert A. Miller, *August 1944: The Campaign for France* (Novato, CA: Presidio Press, 1988), p. 249.

21. 3rd Armored Division, United States Army, "Spearhead History G–3 Supplement," in *Spearhead in the West: The Third Armored Division, 1941–45* (Nashville: Battery Press, 1980), p. 205.

22. Tieke, *In the Firestorm*, pp. 209–10; Heinz Günther Guderian, *From Normandy to the Ruhr: With the 116th Panzer Division in World War II*, trans. Ulrich Abele, Esther Abele, and Keith E. Bonn; ed. Keith E. Bonn (Bedford, PA: Aberjona Press, 2001), pp. 97–103, 592; and Robert J. Kershaw, *"It Never Snows in September": The German View of Market-Garden and the Battle of Arnhem, September 1944* (New York: Sarpedon, 1999), p. 14.

23. Guderian, *From Normandy to the Ruhr*, pp. 97–103, 592.

24. 3rd Armored Division, *Spearhead in the West*, p. 86.

CHAPTER 10

1. Arthur Layton Funk, *Hidden Ally: The French Resistance, Special Operaions, and the Landings in Southern France, 1944* (Westport, CT: Greenwood Press, 1992), pp. 46–55.

2. OSS/London, *OSS/London: Special Operations Branch War Diary*, vol. 1, pp. 28–29; vol. 3, bk. 2, pp. 162–63; and Martin Thomas, "The Massingham Mission: SOE in French North Africa, 1941–1944," *Intelligence and National Security* 11, no. 4 (October 1996): 696–721.

3. OSS/London, *OSS/London: Special Operations Branch War Diary*, vol. 1, p. 31; vol. 2, pp. 31, 47–51; vol. 3, bk. 2, p. 164; vol. 4, bk. 1, pp. 3, 14.

4. Henry McIntosh, interview with the author, November 10, 2003, in Lakeland, FL.

5. Foot, *SOE in France*, pp. 253–56; and Patrick Howarth, *Undercover: The Men and Women of the SOE* (London: Phoenix Press, 2000), pp. 79–80.

6. Fuller, *The German Penetration of SOE*, p. 33.

7. Arthur Funk, telephone conversation and e-mail with the author, February 22, 2005.

8. Funk, *Hidden Ally*, p. 19.

9. Office of Strategic Services, "OSS Aid to the French Resistance in World War II," report no. 980, Jedburgh Team Chloroform (1945), p. 2, photocopy on file at the Marquat Memorial Library, U.S. Army John F. Kennedy Special Warfare Center and School, Fort Bragg, NC, and in the author's files.

10. Jacques Martin, letter to the author, March 1, 1989.

11. OSS/London, "OSS Aid to the French Resistance in World War II," report 980, Jedburgh Team Chloroform, pp. 3–4; and Jacques Martin, letter to the author, March 1, 1989.

12. OSS/London, "OSS Aid to the French Resistance in World War II," report 980, Jedburgh Team Chloroform, p. 4; and Funk, *Hidden Ally*, pp. 123–25.

13. Gen. Sir Henry Maitland Wilson, *Report by the Supreme Allied Commander Mediterranean to the Combined Chiefs of Staff on the Operations in Southern France, August 1944* (London: His Majesty's Stationery Office, 1946), pp. 14, 26.

14. OSS/London, *OSS/London: Special Operations Branch War Diary*, vol. 3, bk. 2, p. 365.

15. Wilson, *Report by SACMED to the CCS*, p. 26.

16. OSS/London, *OSS/London: Special Operations Branch War Diary*, vol. 3, bk. 13, p. 378.

17. F. W. Winterbotham, *The Ultra Secret* (New York: Dell Publishing, 1975), p. 227.

18. John A. Hyman, ed., *From the Riviera to the Rhine: 36th Division in World War II* (1945), unit history, Texas Military Museum website, http://www.kwanah.com/txmilmus/36division/hyman.htm (accessed April 12, 2000).

19. L. K. Truscott, Jr., *Command Missions: A Personal Story* (New York: Dutton, 1954), p. 426.

20. Leo V. Bishop, Frank J. Glasgow, and George A. Fisher, eds., *The Fighting Forty-Fifth: The Combat Report of an Infantry Division* (Baton Rouge: Army and Navy Publishing Company, 1946), p. 97.

21. Clifford H. Peek, Jr., ed., *Five Years, Five Countries, Five Campaigns . . . with the 141st Infantry Regiment* (Munich: 1945), unit history, Texas Military Museum website, http://www.kwanah.com/txmilmus/36division/141con.htm, chap. 7 (accessed 4 December 2000).

22. Audie Murphy, *To Hell and Back* (New York: Henry Holt, 2002), p. 183.

23. Stan Swinton, "Thunderbirds Soar Over South France," *The Stars and Stripes* (Mediterranean Edition), September 4, 1944, quoted in George A. Fisher, *The Story of the 180th Infantry Regiment* (San Angelo, TX: Newsfoto, 1947), chap. 8.

CHAPTER 11

1. Knox, *Essays Ancient and Modern*, p. xxiii.

2. Richard Floyd, telephone conversation with the author, September 13, 2004.

3. Foot, *SOE in France*, pp. 286–87; and E. H. Cookridge, *They Came from the Sky* (New York: Crowell, 1967), pp. 40–41.

4. Howarth, *Undercover*, p. 79; and Cookridge, *They Came from the Sky*, pp. 2–3, 11–69.

5. George Millar, *Maquis* (London: Heinemann, 1945), pp. 30–51.

6. Ibid, p. 264.

7. Ibid., pp. 301–02.

8. George Millar, *Road to Resistance: An Autobiography* (Boston: Little, Brown, 1979), p. 378; and *Maquis*, p. 312.

9. Millar, *Maquis*, pp. 314–15, 319–20.

10. Office of Strategic Services, "Report of Jedburgh Cedric," (1944), p. 3 (National Archives, Washington History Office, RG 226), photocopy in author's files.

11. Millar, *Road to Resistance*, pp. 383–84.

12. Ronald B. Sorobey, "Ukrainians' Fight for France," *World War II*, September 2004, pp. 44–46.

CHAPTER 12

1. Millar, *Road to Resistance*, p. 385; *Maquis*, pp. 322–23.

2. Millar, *Road to Resistance*, pp. 386–87.

3. Millar, *Maquis*, pp. 347, 349.

4. Millar, *Road to Resistance*, p. 391.

5. Ibid., p. 392.
6. Richard Floyd, telephone conversation with the author, September 13, 2004, and letter to the author, October 28, 2004.
7. "20,000 Nazis Surrender," *83rd Spearhead*, vol. 1, no. 7 (September 25, 1944), p. 1.
8. Richard Floyd, telephone conversation with the author, September 13, 2004.
9. Foot, *SOE in France*, p. 133.
10. Millar, *Maquis*, p. 362.
11. Staff of Trailblazers Weekly, *Trailblazer: The 70th Division in Action* (Nancy, France: Trailblazers Weekly, [1945?]), p. 8.

EPILOGUE

1. OSS/London, *OSS/London: Special Operations Branch War Diary*, vol. 1, p. 111; vol. 4, bk. 1, p. 63; vol. 9.
2. Captain Paul Grall, "Report of Mission Landa-Sar-Sin," July 4, 1946, copy provided to the author by OSS veteran Caesar Civitella.
3. Ibid.
4. Document on post-war careers of French Jedburghs, copy provided to the author by OSS veteran Caesar Civitella.
5. Col. Jean Sassi, "Report on Experiences in the Far East, 1945–46," April 6, 1996; and document on post-war careers of French Jedburghs, both provided to the author by OSS veteran Caesar Civitella.
6. Associated Press, "Soldiers Remember Life Behind Enemy Lines," *Times Herald-Record*, (Middletown, NY), May 12, 1988, p. 25.
7. Buckmaster, *They Fought Alone*, p. 52.
8. Foot, *SOE in France*, p. xxii.
9. Ingersoll, *Top Secret*, pp. 181–82.
10. Allen, *Lucky Forward*, p. 96.
11. Ibid., p. 134.
12. Maj. Melvin A. Hoherz, Headquarters, XX Corps, letter to commanding general, Third U.S. Army, subject: "Report of assistance of SF personnel," August 31, 1944 (enclosure to Special Force Detachment 11 "Operations Report").
13. Special Force Detachment 11, "Operations Report," p. 18.
14. Brig. Gen. Frederick B. Butler, quoted in Funk, *Hidden Ally*, p. 121, from Frederick Butler, "Task Force Butler," *Armored Cavalry Journal*, January-February 1948, p. 15.
15. OSS/London, *OSS/London: Special Operations Branch War Diary*, vol. 3, bk. 2, p. 380.
16. Donald G. Taggart, ed., *History of the Third Infantry Division in World War II* (Nashville: Battery Press, 1987), p. 217.

17. Fisher, *The Story of the 180th Infantry Regiment*, ch. 8.
18. Warren P. Munsell, Jr., *The Story of a Regiment: A History of the 179th Regimental Combat Team* (Germany, 1946), p. 73.
19. Seventh United States Army, *Report of Operations, The Seventh United States Army in France and Germany, 1944–1945* (Heidelberg: Aloys Gräf, 1946), vol. 1, p. 168.
20. Truscott, *Command Missions*, p. 420.
21. Gen. Sir Henry Maitland Wilson, quoted in Foot, *SOE in France*, p. 442.
22. Ingersoll, *Top Secret*, p. 182–83.
23. Ibid.
24. Ritgen, *The Western Front 1944*, p. 201.
25. Field Marshal Gerd von Rundstedt, quoted in Foot, *SOE in France*, p. 233.
26. Ibid, p. 356.
27. Field Marshal Walther Model to Gen. Warlimont, June 11, 1944, from a captured journal of enemy telephone conversations, quoted in Butcher, *My Three Years with Eisenhower*, p. 667.
28. Dwight D. Eisenhower, *Crusade in Europe* (Garden City, NY: Doubleday, 1948), p. 296.
29. Eisenhower, letters to the executive director of SOE and to the director of OSS London, May 31, 1945 (see Prologue Note 1).
30. Lt. Gen. Walter Bedell Smith and Lt. Gen. Sir Frederick E. Morgan to the Combined Chiefs of Staff, July 1945, quoted in Foot, *SOE in France*, p. 442.
31. Gen. George C. Marshall, 1946, quoted in Blake Ehrlich, *Resistance: France, 1940–1945* (Boston: Little, Brown, 1965), p. 194.
32. Lt. Col. James R. H. Hutchison, "Report on operations of Mission Verveine," October 6, 1944, p. 13 (National Archives, Washington History Office, RG 226), photocopy in author's files.
33. Robert J. Jakeman, "Air Special Operations," in *The D-Day Encyclopedia*, eds. Chandler and Collins, p. 29; and Paul Gaujac, *Special Forces in the Invasion of France*, trans. Janice Lert (Paris: Histoire & Collections, 1999), p. 93.
34. Kermit Roosevelt, ed., *The Overseas Targets, pp. xii, 199.*

SOURCES

I. DOCUMENTS AND UNPUBLISHED SOURCES

Bautz, Edward. Interview posted on the Rutgers Oral History Archives of World War II Website, http://fas-history.rutgers.edu/oralhistory/Interviews/bautz_edward.html (accessed October 18, 2004).

Brown, Arthur. "The Jedburghs: A Short History." April 1991, photocopy. Unpublished manuscript.

Bull, Harold R. Memorandum to Chief, Plans and Operations Section, subject: "SOE/SO Assistance to Overlord." April 6, 1944 National Archives, Washington History Office, record group 331, entry 23, box 47).

Chief of Staff to the Supreme Allied Commander, Designate (COSSAC). "Operation 'Overlord.'" Appendix P, "Support of Military Operations by Resistance Groups in Europe." July 15, 1943. National Archives, Washington History Office, record group 331, entry 23, box 47.

Colby, William E. Letter to Chief, Special Operations Branch, Office of Strategic Services. May 23, 1945. Photocopy provided to the author by Mr. Colby.

Costeaux, Gaston and Emile Fortier. "Rapport sur l'activite de la mission 'Auguste.'" October 5, 1944. Photocopy in author's files.

Etat-major des Forces Francaises de l'Interieur (EMFFI). "A Short History of the Organization of the Command of Operations Undertaken by the French Forces of the Interior." 1945. National Archives, Washington History Office, record group 226 (Office of Strategic Services records).

Hoherz, Melvin A. "Report of assistance of SF personnel." August 31,

1944 (enclosure to Special Forces Detachment 11, "Third Army G–3 Section, 11th Special Force Detachment Operations Report," December 18, 1944).

Hutchison, James R. H. "Report on operations of Mission Verveine." October 6, 1944. National Archives, Washington History Office, record group 226.

Joint Psychological Warfare Committee. Meeting minutes and associated documents. National Archives, Washington History Office, record group 218 (Joint Chiefs of Staff records), Central Decimal File 1942–45, box 8.

Kehoe, Robert R. "Jed Team Frederick, 1944: An Allied Team With the French Resistance." Article on the Central Intelligence Agency's Center for the Study of Intelligence website, 1997. http://www.cia.gov/csi/studies/winter98_99/art03.html (accessed January 13, 2005).

LeBlanc, Robert. World War II veteran survey and other papers. United States Army Military History Institute Archives, Carlisle Barracks, PA, WWII–7396, box OSS, WWII survey.

Office of Strategic Services. "OSS Aid to the French Resistance in World War II." Report 980, "Jedburgh Team Chloroform," 1945. Photocopy on file at Marquat Memorial Library, U.S. Army John F. Kennedy Special Warfare Center and School, Fort Bragg, NC.

———. OSS/London: Special Operations Branch and Secret Intelligence Branch War Diaries, 1945. 13 vols. on 8 reels of microfilm. Edited by Paul Kesaris. Frederick, MD: University Publications of America, 1985. Also found in National Archives Microfilm Publication M1623.

———. "Report of Jedburgh Cedric." 1944. National Archives, Washington History Office, record group 226.

Rot, Armand. "Compte-Rendu." Statement about Jedburgh team Augustus written in 1944, photocopy in author's files.

Special Force Detachment 11. "Plan for Resistance Movements in Brittany." With attached operations summary. August 10, 1944. National Archives, Washington History Office, record group 226, London SO, entry 115, box 50.

———. "Third Army G–3 Section, 11th Special Force Detachment Operations Report." December 18, 1944. National Archives, Washington History Office, record group 226, entry 115, box 50.

Special Force Headquarters. SFHQ G–3 Periodic Reports, published and submitted daily to Supreme Headquarters Allied Expeditionary Force G–3 from June 5, 1944, to May 7, 1945. National Archives, Washington History Office, record group 226, OP–23, entry 99, folders 116–118, box 93.

Twelfth Army Group. Report of Operations, G–3 Section, 12th Army Group (Final After Action Report). 1945. Photocopy in author's files.

Vanderblue, C. C. Memorandum to General William J. Donovan, subject:

Report of C. S. Vanderblue on OSS Operations with the Third Army. November 15, 1944. National Archives, Washington History Office, record group 226, OP–23, entry 99, folder 50, box 12.

II. Unit Histories

3rd Armored Division. *Spearhead in the West: The Third Armored Division, 1941–45*. Nashville: Battery Press, 1980.
5th Infantry Division. *The 5th Division in France*. Metz: La Lorraine Press, 1944.
Seventh United States Army. *Report of Operations: The Seventh United States Army in France and Germany, 1944–1945*. 2 vols. Heidelberg: Aloys Gräf, 1946.
Bishop, Leo V., Frank J. Glasgow, and George A. Fisher, eds. *The Fighting Forty-Fifth: The Combat Report of an Infantry Division*. Baton Rouge: Army and Navy Publishing, 1946.
Colby, Elbridge. *The First Army in Europe, 1943–1945*. Nashville: Battery Press, 1993.
Fisher, George A. *The Story of the 180th Infantry Regiment*. San Angelo, TX: Newsfoto, 1947.
Hyman, John A., ed. *From the Riviera to the Rhine: 36th Division in World War II*. 1945. Unit history online at the Texas Military Museum website, http://www.kwanah.com/txmilmus/36division/hyman.htm (accessed April 12, 2000).
Knickerbocker, H. R., et. al. *Danger Forward: The Story of the First Division in World War II*. Atlanta: Albert Love, 1947.
Munsell, Warren P., Jr. *The Story of a Regiment: A History of the 179th Regimental Combat Team*. Germany: 1946.
Peek, Clifford H., Jr., ed. *Five Years, Five Countries, Five Campaigns . . . with the 141st Infantry Regiment*. Munich: 141st Infantry Regiment Association, 1945. Online at Texas Military Museum website, http://www.kwanah.com/txmilmus/36division/141con.htm (accessed December 4, 2000).
Taggart, Donald G., ed. *History of the Third Infantry Division in World War II*. Nashville: Battery Press, 1987.
Trailblazers Weekly (Staff). *Trailblazers: The 70ᵗʰ Division in Action*. Trailblazers Weekly, [n.d.].

III. Books

Alcorn, Robert Hayden. *No Bugles for Spies: Tales of the OSS*. New York: Popular Library, 1964.
Allen, Robert S. *Lucky Forward: The History of Patton's Third U.S. Army*. New York: Vanguard Press, 1947.

Alsop, Stewart, and Thomas Braden. *Sub Rosa: The OSS and American Espionage*. New York: Harcourt, Brace & World, 1964.

Ambrose, Stephen E. *D-Day, June 6, 1944: The Climactic Battle of World War II*. New York: Simon & Schuster, 1994.

Ambrose, Stephen E., with Richard H. Immerman. *Ike's Spies: Eisenhower and the Espionage Establishment*. Jackson: University Press of Mississippi, 1999.

Asprey, Robert B. *War in the Shadows: The Guerrilla in History*. Garden City, NY: Doubleday, 1975.

Bank, Aaron. *From OSS to Green Berets*. Novato, CA: Presidio Press, 1986.

Berkeley, Roy. *A Spy's London*. London: Leo Cooper, 1994.

Bleicher, Hugo. *Colonel Henri's Story: The War Memoirs of Hugo Bleicher: Former German Secret Agent*. Edited by Ian Colvin. London: William Kimber, 1954.

Blumenson, Martin. *Breakout and Pursuit*. United States Army in World War II. Washington, DC: Center of Military History, 1984.

Bradley, Omar N. *A Soldier's Story*. New York: Henry Holt, 1951.

Bruce, David K. E. *OSS against the Reich: The World War II Diaries of Colonel David K. E. Bruce*. Edited by Nelson D. Lankford. Kent, Ohio: Kent State University Press, 1991.

Buckmaster, Maurice J. *They Fought Alone: The Story of British Agents in France*. New York: Norton, 1958.

Butcher, Harry C. *My Three Years with Eisenhower: The Personal Diary of Captain Harry C. Butcher, USNR, Naval Aide to General Eisenhower, 1942 to 1945*. New York: Simon & Schuster, 1946.

Butler, Daniel Allen. *Warrior Queens: The Queen Mary and Queen Elizabeth in World War II*. London: Leo Cooper, 2002.

Calvocoressi, Peter. *Top Secret Ultra*. New York: Pantheon Books, 1980.

Cannicott, Stanley M. *Journey of a Jed*. Cheddar, Somerset, UK: Cheddar Valley Press, 1986.

Cassidy, William L., ed. *History of the Schools and Training Branch, Office of Strategic Services*. San Francisco: Kingfisher Press, 1983.

Chandler, David G., and James Lawton Collins, Jr., eds. *The D-Day Encyclopedia*. New York: Simon & Schuster, 1994.

Churchill, Winston S. *The Second World War*. 6 vols. Boston: Houghton Mifflin, 1949–53.

Churchill, Winston S., and Franklin D. Roosevelt. *Churchill and Roosevelt, The Complete Correspondence*. Edited by Warren F. Kimball. Princeton: Princeton University Press, 1984.

Clarke, Jeffrey J., and Robert Ross Smith. *Riviera to the Rhine*. United States Army in World War II. Washington, DC: Center of Military History, 1993.

Colby, William, and Peter Forbath. *Honorable Men: My Life in the CIA*. New York: Simon & Schuster, 1978.

Cookridge, E. H. *Set Europe Ablaze*. New York: Crowell, 1967.

———. *They Came from the Sky*. New York: Crowell, 1967.

Crosby, M. G. M. *Irregular Soldier*. United Kingdom: XB Publications, 1993.

Dolan, Anne Reilly. *Congressional Country Club, 1924–1984*. Baltimore: MacLellan and Associates, [n.d.].

Dreux, William B. *No Bridges Blown*. Notre Dame: University of Notre Dame Press, 1971.

Ehrlich, Blake. *Resistance: France, 1940–1945*. Boston: Little, Brown, 1965.

Eisenhower, David. *Eisenhower at War 1943–1945*. New York: Vintage Books, 1987.

Eisenhower, Dwight D. *Crusade in Europe*. Garden City, NY: Doubleday, 1948.

———. *D Day to VE Day, 1944–45: General Eisenhower's Report on the Invasion of Europe*. London: The Stationery Office, 2000.

———. *The Papers of Dwight David Eisenhower, The War Years*. 5 vols. Edited by Alfred D. Chandler, Jr. Baltimore: Johns Hopkins Press, 1970.

Esposito, Vincent J., ed. *The West Point Atlas of American Wars*, vol. 2, *1900–1953*. New York: Praeger, 1959.

Foot, M. R. D. *Resistance: European Resistance to Nazism, 1940–1945*. New York: McGraw-Hill, 1977.

———. *SOE: An Outline History of the Special Operations Executive, 1940–46*. London: British Broadcasting Corp., 1984.

———. *SOE in France: An Account of the Work of the British Special Operations Executive in France, 1940–1944*. London: Her Majesty's Stationery Office, 1966.

Ford, Roger. *Fire From the Forest: The SAS Brigade in France, 1944*. London: Cassell, 2003.

———. *Steel From the Sky: The Jedburgh Raiders, France 1944*. London: Weidenfeld & Nicolson, 2004.

Fuller, Jean Overton. *The German Penetration of SOE: France, 1941–1944*. Revised edition. Maidstone, UK: George Mann Books, 1996.

Funk, Arthur Layton. *Hidden Ally: The French Resistance, Special Operaions, and the Landing in Southern France, 1944*. Westport, CT: Greenwood Press, 1992.

Gaujac, Paul. *Special Forces in the Invasion of France*. Trans. by Janice Lert. Paris: Histoire & Collections, 1999.

Gawne, Jonathan. *The Americans in Brittany, 1944: The Battle for Brest*. Paris: Histoire & Collections, 2002.

Guderian, Heinz Günther. *From Normandy to the Ruhr: With the 116th Panzer Division in World War II*. Translated by Ulrich Abele, Esther Abele, and Keith E. Bonn. Edited by Keith E. Bonn. Bedford, PA: Aberjona Press, 2001.

Hall, Roger. *You're Stepping on My Cloak and Dagger*. New York: Norton, 1957.

Harding, Steve. *Gray Ghost: The R.M.S. Queen Mary at War*. Missoula, MT: Pictorial Histories, 1982.

Harrison, Gordon A. *Cross-Channel Attack*. United States Army in World War II. Washington, DC: Center of Military History, 1993.

Hastings, Max. *Das Reich: The March of the 2nd SS Panzer Division Through France*. New York: Holt, Rinehart and Winston, 1982.

Howarth, Patrick. *Undercover: The Men and Women of the SOE*. London: Phoenix Press, 2000.

Hue, André, and Ewen Southby-Tailyour. *The Next Moon: The Remarkable True Story of a British Agent Behind the Lines in Wartime France*. London: Viking, 2004.

Huston, James A. *Biography of a Battalion: The Life and Times of an Infantry Battalion in Europe in World War II*. Mechanicsburg, PA: Stackpole Books, 2003.

Hutchison, James. *That Drug Danger*. Montrose, Scotland: Standard Press, 1977.

Ingersoll, Ralph. *Top Secret*. New York: Harcourt, Brace, 1946.

Ismay, Hastings Lionel. *The Memoirs of General Lord Ismay*. New York: The Viking Press, 1960.

Kershaw, Robert J. *"It Never Snows in September": The German View of Market-Garden and the Battle of Arnhem, September 1944*. New York: Sarpedon, 1999.

Knox, Bernard. *Essays Ancient and Modern*. Baltimore: The Johns Hopkins University Press, 1989.

Ladd, James, and Keith Melton. *Clandestine Warfare: Weapons and Equipment of the SOE and OSS*. London: Blandford Press, 1988.

Longmate, Norman. *The G.I.'s: The Americans in Britain, 1942–1945*. New York: Scribner, 1975.

Lorain, Pierre. *Clandestine Operations: The Arms and Techniques of the Resistance, 1941–1944*. New York: Macmillan, 1983.

Mackenzie, W. J. M. *The Secret History of SOE: The Special Operations Executive 1940–1945*. London: St. Ermin's Press, 2002.

Manchester, William. *The Last Lion: Winston Spencer Churchill; Alone, 1932–1940*. Boston: Little, Brown, 1988.

———. *The Last Lion: Winston Spencer Churchill; Visions of Glory, 1874–1932*. Boston: Little, Brown, 1983.

Marshall, Bruce. *The White Rabbit*. Boston: Houghton Mifflin, 1952.

McCue, Paul. *SAS Operation Bulbasket: Behind the Lines in Occupied France, 1944*. London: Leo Cooper, 1996.

Millar, George. *Maquis*. London: Heinemann. 1945.

———. *Road to Resistance: An Autobiography*. Boston: Little, Brown, 1979.

Miller, Robert A. *August 1944: The Campaign for France.* Novato, CA: Presidio Press, 1988).

Miller, William H., and David F. Hutchings. *Transatlantic Liners at War: The Story of the Queens.* New York: Arco, 1985.

Mitcham, Samuel W., Jr. *Retreat to the Reich: The German Defeat in France, 1944.* Westport, CT: Praeger, 2000.

Moody, Sidney C., and the Associated Press. *War in Europe.* Novato, CA: Presidio Press, 1993.

Morgan, Frederick. *Overture to Overlord.* Garden City, NY: Doubleday, 1950.

Murphy, Audie. *To Hell and Back.* New York: Henry Holt, 2002.

Obolensky, Serge. *One Man in His Time: The Memoirs of Serge Obolensky.* New York: McDowell, Obolensky, 1958.

Office of Strategic Services Assessment Staff. *Assessment of Men: Selection of Personnel for the Office of Strategic Services.* New York: Rinehart, 1948.

———. *The Overseas Targets: War Report of the OSS (Office of Strategic Services), Volume 2.* Introduction by Kermit Roosevelt. Washington, DC: Carrollton Press; New York: Walker, 1976.

Parnell, Ben. *Carpetbaggers: America's Secret War in Europe.* Austin: Eakin Press, 1987.

Patton, George S. *War as I Knew It.* Boston: Houghton Mifflin, 1947.

Province, Charles M. *Patton's Third Army: A Daily Combat Diary.* New York: Hippocrene Books, 1992.

Pyle, Ernie. *Brave Men.* New York: Henry Holt, 1944.

Reader's Digest Association, The. *Secrets and Spies: Behind-the-Scenes Stories of World War II.* Pleasantville, NY: Reader's Digest Assn., 1964.

Ritgen, Helmut. *The Western Front 1944: Memoirs of a Panzer Lehr Officer.* Translated by Joseph Welsh. Winnipeg: Fedorowicz, 1995.

Roosevelt, Kermit, ed. *War Report of the OSS.* New York: Walker, 1976.

Singlaub, John K., and Malcolm McConnell. *Hazardous Duty: An American Soldier in the Twentieth Century.* New York: Summit Books, 1991.

Smith, Richard Harris. *OSS: The Secret History of America's First Central Intelligence Agency.* Berkeley: University of California Press, 1972.

Smith, Walter Bedell. *Eisenhower's Six Great Decisions.* New York: Longmans, Green, 1956.

Special Operations Executive. *Secret Agent's Handbook: The WWII Spy Manual of Devices, Disguises, Gadgets, and Concealed Weapons.* Reproduction of SOE's 1944 *Descriptive Catalogue of Special Devices and Supplies*, with an introduction by Mark Seaman. Guilford, CT: The Lyons Press, 2001.

Thompson, Julian. *The Imperial War Museum Book of War Behind Enemy Lines*. Washington, DC: Brassey's, 2001.

Tickell, Jerrard. *Moon Squadron*. Garden City, N Y: Doubleday, 1958.

Tieke, Wilhelm. *In the Firestorm of the Last Years of the War: II SS-Panzerkorps with the 9 and 10 SS-Divisions "Hohenstaufen" and "Frundsberg"*. Translated by Frederick Steinhardt. Winnipeg: Fedorowicz, 1999.

Truscott, L. K., Jr. *Command Missions: A Personal Story*. New York: Dutton, 1954.

von Luck, Hans. *Panzer Commander: The Memoirs of Colonel Hans von Luck*. New York: Praeger, 1989.

Wallace, Brenton G. *Patton and his Third Army*. Mechanicsburg, PA: Stackpole Books, 2000.

Wehrle, Edmund F. *Catoctin Mountain Park: A Historic Resource Study*. March 2000. On National Park Service website, http://www.nps.gov/cato/hrs/hrs.htm (accessed January 24, 2005).

West, Nigel [Rupert Allason]. *MI6: British Secret Intelligence Service Operations, 1909–45*. New York: Random House, 1983.

———. *Secret War: The Story of SOE, Britain's Wartime Sabotage Organisation*. London: Hodder & Stoughton, 1992.

Wilkinson, Peter. *Foreign Fields: The Story of an SOE Operative*. London: I. B. Tauris, 1997.

Wilson, Henry Maitland. *Report by the Supreme Allied Commander Mediterranean to the Combined Chiefs of Staff on the Operations in Southern France, August 1944*. London: His Majesty's Stationery Office, 1946.

Winterbotham, F. W. *The Ultra Secret*. New York: Dell Publishing, 1975.

IV. ARTICLES

"20,000 Nazis Surrender." *83rd Spearhead* 1, no.7 (September 25, 1944).

Associated Press. "D-Day Chutists Rate as Heroes: South Bend Officer One of International Secret Unit." Unidentified Indiana newspaper, September 27, 1945.

Goldberg, Alfred. "Air Campaign Overlord: To D-Day." In *D-Day: The Normandy Invasion in Retrospect* (Lawrence: University Press of Kansas, 1971).

Hemingway, Albert. "The Great Parachute Drop." *Military History* 6, no. 5 (April 1990): 46–52.

"Keeping Posted." The *Saturday Evening Post*, March 23, 1946, p. 4.

Sorobey, Ronald B. "Ukrainians' Fight for France." *World War II*, September 2004, pp. 42–48.

Thomas, Martin. "The Massingham Mission: SOE in French North Africa, 1941–1944." *Intelligence and National Security* 11, no. 4 (October 1996): 696–721.

V. CORRESPONDENCE AND INTERVIEWS

Americans
Everett T. Allen
Col. (USA, Ret.) Aaron Bank
Rev. Jacob B. Berlin
John L. & Anne Bradner
Franklin O. Canfield
Charles M. Carman, Jr.
Philip H. Chadbourn, Jr.
William E. Colby
Lucien E. Conein
Paul & Donna J. Cyr
Violette A. (Côté) Desmarais
Sarah Drake
René A. Dussaq
Richard C. Floyd
Ray H. Foster
Dick Franklin
Brig. Gen. (USMCR, Ret.) Horace W. Fuller
Jean Gildee
Mary D. Hanson
Dr. Robert R. Kehoe
Dr. Bernard M. W. Knox
Lucien E. Lajeunesse
Robert A. Lucas
Dr. Henry D. & Harriet McIntosh
Robert K. Montgomery
Cecil F. Mynatt, Jr.
Gordon Nelson
John M. & Elisabeth Olmsted
William H. Pietsch, Jr.
Jack Shannon
Maj. Gen. (USA, Ret.) John K. Singlaub
Donald A. Spears
Katherine B. (Bonsall) Strong
William T. Thompson
Allan & Amanda Todd
Thomas & Norma Tracy
Col. (USA, Ret.) S. Ray Trumps
George M. Verhaeghe

British
Arthur Brown
Stanley Cannicott
John C. C. Montague
Richard A. Rubinstein
Cyril H. Sell

French
Gen. (Ret.) Paul Aussaresses
Col. (Ret.) Robert Cantais
Gen. (Ret.) Jean Joseph Carbuccia
Robert Clause
Prince Michel de Bourbon de Parme
Lt. Col. (Ret.) René de la Tousche
Gen. (Ret.) Roland de Mecquenem
Baron Albert de Schonen
Mme. Hubert Dumesnil
René Estève
François G. Franceschi
Joe de Francesco
Col. (Ret.) Maurice Geminel
Adrien Grafeville
Col. (Ret.) Paul Grall
Xavier Humblet
Lt. Col. (Ret.) Pierre Jolliet
Col. (Ret.) Marc Lautier
Gen. (Ret.) Guy Le Borgne
Camille Lelong
Col. (Ret.) Claude l'Herbette
Georges Marchal
Jacques Martin
Edgar Mautaint
René Meyer
Jacques Morineau
Étienne Nasica
Mme. Paule Perraud
Maurice Pirat
Philippe Ragueneau
Jacques Robert
Gen. (Ret.) Robert Toussaint
François C. Verger
Marcel Vermot

ACKNOWLEDGMENTS

I was a captain on the staff of the John F. Kennedy Special Warfare Center at Fort Bragg when I was asked to help host a reunion of Jedburgh veterans in 1985. I had known what the Jedburgh project was from classes I'd sat through during Special Forces training. But when I met the veterans and heard their stories, my interest in their experience grew, and I began what would turn out to be two decades of research.

In 1988, former CIA director and Jedburgh veteran William E. Colby wrote me suggesting that I come to Washington for a reunion of Jedburghs scheduled to take place there that summer. He thought it would be a good opportunity for me to get to know more of them. So when he called me a few days later to see if I was coming, I said yes and packed my bags. And I was thus able to enjoy a few more days with the Jeds and get to know some of their families as well. I hoped someday to be able to write about them, but I knew that it would have to wait until my retirement from the service, when I could devote all of my time and energy to the project. In the meantime, I began writing to many of the Jeds or interviewing them whenever an opportunity presented itself. Eventually, I spoke or corresponded with more than sixty Jedburgh veterans—American, British, and French.

I wish to thank the many people who have helped in some way to make this book possible. Dr. Samuel J. Lewis of the Combat Studies Institute at the U.S. Army Command and General Staff College was generous with his time and Jedburgh expertise when I was a student of his in 1990–91. His assistance was not limited to academic guidance; he also provided me with copies of many archival documents and photographs.

John Taylor and Will Mahoney at the Military History Branch of the U.S. National Archives (in downtown Washington, D.C., when I began this, and later at College Park, Maryland) helped immeasurably in locating documents and photographs. Fred Fuller, at the Marquat Memorial Library of the U.S. Army John F. Kennedy Special Warfare Center and School, was very helpful in sharing with me Jedburgh after-action reports and other documents during my time there in the 1980s.

Dr. John Sweets, my faculty advisor during my brief time at the University of Kansas, gave me guidance on research approaches and shared his expertise on the French resistance. Dr. Arthur Layton Funk, retired professor of history at the University of Florida, took time to answer my questions and share his knowledge of resistance and Allied special forces activities in France. And Colonel Brian McMillan, friend and former boss, generously provided me copies of OSS training manuals.

I also want to thank those who read portions of early versions of the manuscript and provided many valuable comments and suggestions: Colonel Gordon Atcheson, John Hunt, Rick Brown, Robert E. Kehoe, and Dr. Henry D. McIntosh.

Thanks also go to the staffs at the Combined Arms Research Library of the United States Army Command and General Staff College at Fort Leavenworth, Kansas; the Watson Library at the University of Kansas; the Hoover Institution at Stanford University; the United States Army Europe Library and Research Center in Heidelberg, Germany; the United States Army Military History Institute Archives at Carlisle Barracks, Pennsylvania; the RAND Library in Santa Monica, California; the United States Special Operations Command Library at MacDill Air Force Base, Florida; and the public libraries in Redondo Beach, California, and Tampa, Florida. The staff members of these institutions showed both commendable perseverance in helping me locate source materials and remarkable patience with my delinquent returns.

I am grateful for the photographs provided by Donna J. Cyr, Violette A. Desmarais, Richard C. Floyd, Robert E. Kehoe, Michael G. Leemhuis and the Congressional Country Club, Dr. Henry D. McIntosh, Katherine B. Strong and Sarah Drake, and the Time Warner Book Group.

Thanks to Jedburgh wife Joann Henely for putting me in touch with the families of John Bonsall and Roger Côté, to OSS veteran Caesar Civitella for information on the activities of the French Jedburghs following their missions in France, and to Kathleen Price for providing translations of many of the French documents I used.

My most profound debt of gratitude, of course, is owed to the many former Jeds and their families who have given so freely of their time for interviews and correspondence and who have provided so much in the way of source documents and photographs. Their names are included in the list of sources provided in this book.

Special thanks go to my agent, John A. Ware, and to my editor at Public-Affairs, Clive Priddle. Needless to say, this book never would have seen the light of day without them. They were constant sources of encouragement, and they taught me much about turning a truly rough draft into something readable.

Finally, thanks go to my wife, Angie, and my sons, Donovan, Thomas, and William, for their many sacrifices and unwavering support.

INDEX

PublicAffairs is a publishing house founded in 1997. It is a tribute to the standards, values, and flair of three persons who have served as mentors to countless reporters, writers, editors, and book people of all kinds, including me.

I. F. Stone, proprietor of *I. F. Stone's Weekly*, combined a commitment to the First Amendment with entrepreneurial zeal and reporting skill and became one of the great independent journalists in American history. At the age of eighty, Izzy published *The Trial of Socrates*, which was a national bestseller. He wrote the book after he taught himself ancient Greek.

Benjamin C. Bradlee was for nearly thirty years the charismatic editorial leader of *The Washington Post*. It was Ben who gave the *Post* the range and courage to pursue such historic issues as Watergate. He supported his reporters with a tenacity that made them fearless, and it is no accident that so many became authors of influential, best-selling books.

Robert L. Bernstein, the chief executive of Random House for more than a quarter century, guided one of the nation's premier publishing houses. Bob was personally responsible for many books of political dissent and argument that challenged tyranny around the globe. He is also the founder and was the longtime chair of Human Rights Watch, one of the most respected human rights organizations in the world.

. . .

For fifty years, the banner of Public Affairs Press was carried by its owner Morris B. Schnapper, who published Gandhi, Nasser, Toynbee, Truman, and about 1,500 other authors. In 1983 Schnapper was described by *The Washington Post* as "a redoubtable gadfly." His legacy will endure in the books to come.

Peter Osnos, Publisher

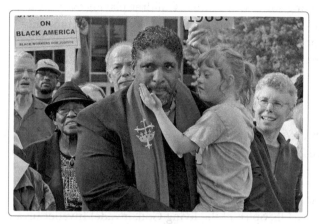

With Mary Evelyn Rider O'Neill *(Phil Fonville photo)*

What Is Life?

What is life? Is it to be lived for or dreamed about? Perhaps both.

Maybe our dreaming determines our living to some degree. Yet so much tries to kill our dreams, snatch our dreams, take away our dreams, defer our dreams, and keep our dreams from reality.

Maybe then, we must fight for, pray for, and ask God to grant us the gift of dreaming afresh and anew. Dreaming *God's Dreams!* Dreaming, hoping, and delighting in the things of God freshly poured out upon our hearts and minds like the morning dew. How we need it so! Then, perhaps if we dream right, we will live right, and then we shall know the answer to the inquirer's quest.

What is life? Is it to be lived or dreamed about, or both?

The Spirit brings the gift of dreaming into the now. What God has hoped, becomes, even if at first just in our thoughts, a new reality. We begin to see and dream in the now what God has always wanted since the beginning. *God's Dreams* become our desire when the Spirit is at work.

Men may never understand, but this is what happened deep in the soul place of Sojourner, Mary, Martin, Medgar, Malcolm, Harriet, Fannie Lou, and Mandela. What moved them and so many others?

God's Dreams! By the Spirit, come take a look.

The cow lying down with the bear. Children playing over the hole of a snake. Lion and lamb frolicking together. *God's Dreams!* Humanity redeemed. Grace imparted. Pain pushed away. Tears wiped. Death vanquished. The hungry fed. The hurting healed. Justice ruling. Righteousness prevailing. Deliverance complete. Satan snared.

God's Dreams! What a wonder! What a look!

Our lives are transformed when we dream *God's Dreams!* No longer mere mundane Movement. Away with despair and life without purpose! We now rise, captivated and controlled by *God's Dreams!*

And so, it seems our dreams determine our living, and we live because of our dreams. Oh, Spirit of the living God, invade! Invade! Invade! Invade once again the nightmarish corners of our minds. Loose the prophetic flow into the depths of our being with *God's Dreams*

...so that we might live anew and afresh!

– Rev. Dr. William J. Barber II

Dedicated to the genius of all the justice and freedom devotees since 2006 who embraced the vision, worked to design this movement and gave their souls and time to it. Worthy of note also is the huge collection of brilliant others—lawyers, scholars, clergy/theologians, organizers, administrators, interns, volunteers, allies—who keep this movement on course.

CONTENTS

WELCOME

PREACHING IN THE PUBLIC SQUARE

Moral March on Raleigh 2014 *(Eric Preston photo)*

Moral messages in the pulpit or the public square are designed not just to be spoken and heard, but to shape the prophetic consciousness of a Movement and of society. To paraphrase the Rev. Dr. James Forbes, longtime pastor of the historic Riverside Church in New York: *Prophets believe that what they proclaim on any day can be transformed into real action.*

Words can become flesh. The prophetic voice rises when government systems and sometimes even religious systems abdicate their responsibility to those whom scripture calls the *least of these.* When the forces of extremism become so overwhelming that they depress the hope of the people, the prophetic voice and mission is to connect words and actions in ways that build restorative hope, so a Movement for restorative justice can arise.

This book is an attempt to capture the practice of preaching in the public square, which is where prophetic inquiry must be at work.

Messages built from the perspective of authentic prophetic inquiry will insist that political decisions and public policies—which determine who will be the haves and the have-nots in the realms of wages; healthcare; public education; voting rights; workers'/ immigrants'/ LGBTQ/women's rights; and criminal and environmental justice–are all deeply moral concerns. The authentic call of the Spirit will not allow pastors and preachers to be satisfied with words quarantined within the walls of the sanctuary. The moment when misery abounds necessitates messages that can move the masses to engage in deeply moral actions that question mean and hurtful public policies.

Prophetic messages wake people up, not just emotionally but also to the possibility of change and their particular roles in moving **Forward Together** in the push for that change.

When I was a student at Duke Divinity School, Bishop Desmond Tutu of South Africa once raised a question at Duke Chapel: *Who will join God?* Progressive evangelical activist Rev. Jim Wallis has made the call for us to consider God's politics. Duke Divinity School professor of homiletics, Dr. William Turner, has suggested that any claim of spirituality is terribly suspect unless that claim is followed by a clear quarrel with the world and its systems of injustice. And my father, a preacher and teacher like Dr. Turner and me, taught me the following principle articulated by British statesman and philosopher Francis Bacon:

> *Knowledge is not a couch whereon to rest a searching and restless spirit; or a terrace for a wandering mind to walk up and down with a fair prospect; or a tower of state for a proud mind to raise itself upon; or a sort of commanding ground for strife and contention; or a shop for profit and sale; but a rich storehouse for the glory of the Creator, and the relief of man's estate.*[1]

The role of prophetic moral activity is to awaken people to deep consciousness first, and then to engage them to use this new consciousness as a guidance system for framing a Movement that shifts the center of gravity of political discourse and action away from its accommodation to domination, and back to the deepest moral values of our faith. In essence, the role of prophetic social consciousness is to say to both political systems and to the people:

> *"Woe to you, scribes and Pharisees, hypocrites! For you tithe mint and dill and cumin,*

and have neglected the weightier matters of the law: justice and mercy and faithfulness. "

MATTHEW 23:23 ESV

The messages necessary for building Moral Movements must constantly refocus and critique issues around "the weightier matters," or what matters most.

This book brings you messages spoken within a particular political context and climate—that of an extremist, regressive North Carolina legislation that disenfranchised and harmed multitudes of people in our state. However, the messages speak to universal needs, values, and hopes.

The proclamations recorded in this book employ our deepest prophetic moral framework to address the weightier matters before us all, in North Carolina and everywhere, as we must confront those who vow to act in our names but who act against the common good. Therefore the spirit of these messages is universal and useful to all of you who hope to enliven and strengthen your own efforts to achieve justice where you live.

There can be no Moral Movement or transformational politics without a decisive and deliberate attempt to use moral language and framing in a way that builds a new consciousness among the masses of people, which gives them the kind of critical analysis and charismatic hope to carry on and carry out the Movement.

Under the oppressive forces and pressures of extremism, people tend to *expire*, to give up. The role of prophetic moral messaging is to *inspire* people, to breathe life into the masses who hardly dare to hope for more. It is to give people permission to morally act up! Henry Thoreau in *Civil Disobedience* said: *The only thing I repent of is my good behavior in the face of injustice.* He did not write a book for mere academic purposes or give speeches for mere inspiration. His speeches were a form of his own repentance, as well as a call to action. In this spirit we offer the words you find here.

This book tracks our Forward Together Moral Movement in North Carolina during the key years of 2013 and 2014, as resistance to the hateful and regressive policies enacted by Tea Party extremists since 2010 gathered great force. This Movement did not spring up overnight after the 2010 election and redistricting to stack our state with right-wing leadership. Rather, it was built on the structural bones of long-lived North Carolina NAACP local chapters, and was forged on top of those with intentional alliances across many groups in our state and a vision that we could assert a united moral vision of political and ethical fusion against all odds. So in addition to the Historic Thousands on Jones Street and Moral Monday speeches, we include those that bound us with two key constituencies: our allies who have championed Lesbian, Gay, Bisexual, Transgender (LGBT) rights and labor rights. We hope you find our work of use for yours.

William J. Barber, II
Pastor, Greenleaf Christian Church (Disciples of Christ), Goldsboro, North Carolina
President, North Carolina Conference of the NAACP
Architect of the Forward Together Moral Movement

INTRODUCTION

TO THE FORWARD TOGETHER MORAL MOVEMENT
AND MORAL MONDAY RALLIES

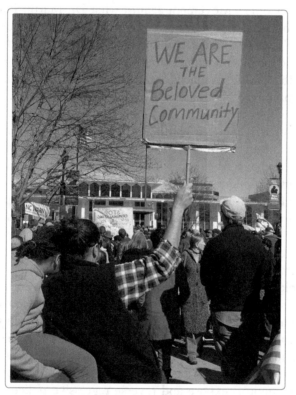

In the tradition of Dr. King *(Sue Sturgis photo)*

The speeches and scenes in this book focus on North Carolina and our NC NAACP-led Forward Together Moral Movement, which unexpectedly has ignited the interest of people across the nation and beyond. We hope that our experience informs and encourages yours, as you work for the common good in times of globalization and growing inequality everywhere. To

1

*understand the particular American Southern context from which our
Movement arose, the following words may be of use. They are adapted and
expanded from a narrative of 2013 Forward Together activities that was
written by Rob Stephens and attorney Al McSurely.*

The forces that profit from racial division and deprivation do not rest.
Since the mid-1960s, when the Southern freedom Movement was at
its peak, shaking the very structures of Jim Crow, opponents of equal
rights have been working on new tricks to divide and conquer the
multiracial people's Movement against what Dr. Martin Luther King
Jr. called the Evil Triplets in the United States: racism, poverty, and
militarism. They have set up a national network with their own hidden
funding and propaganda machines. They have directed billions of
dollars to the George Wallace-John Birch base in the South, believing
there are millions of whites who are open to racist appeals.

In November 2012, with the help of an unconstitutional racially
gerrymandered scheme in North Carolina, these forces hand-picked
extremist candidates, slipped them thousands of dollars for their
campaigns, and overwhelmed candidates who represented the interests
of poor and working people in North Carolina. In that 2012 election,
despite the highest turnout in history for black, Latino, and progressive
white voters, the extremists won a large majority of the seats in the
North Carolina General Assembly.

We were not just in the fight *of* our lives. For many of us, it was a
fight *for* our lives. We did not shrink from the challenge.

We took the struggle straight to our opponents' doors, armed with
the best research to wage a well-organized nonviolent policy debate
against their cruel policies. Tens of thousands of new friends joined the
Forward Together Moral Movement, grasping its principles of grace,
courage, and commitment. People all over the world are now looking
to us for guidance in building a moral anti-racism, anti-poverty, pro-
labor Movement to expose and reverse regressive policies wherever
they ascend.

One way to understand the current cultural context is through the
language of **Reconstruction**. We have talked with anti-racism forces
across the nation in dozens of speeches, internet videos, and private
conversations about a prophetic vision of a **Third Reconstruction** in
our land. It's a vision based on our faith in the good people of all races,
not just in North Carolina, but across the South. We sincerely believe
that millions of Southerners are prepared to join the effort to repair
the breaches caused by slavery and segregation within our Southern

human family. We have empirical evidence that tens of thousands of white sisters and brothers in North Carolina and beyond are prepared to join in this effort.

What are these three Reconstructions?

After most of our great-great-grandparents were liberated from slavery in 1865, there was a short period of the **First Reconstruction** in the South. A coalition of faith-based progressives and ordinary white tenant farmers and workers joined freed African Americans in a wildly hopeful effort known as the Fusion political movement in late 19th-century North Carolina. They succeeded in a hard-won push to build public schools, roads, and hospitals, and to move talented African American leaders into elected office and leadership positions of all kinds. A white backlash violently ended this period of political and social fusion, and white terrorists roamed freely in the South, enforcing a rigid apartheid system that lasted well past 1954.

The **Second Reconstruction** period began in 1954 with the NAACP's magnificent court victory over segregation in Brown versus Board of Education. In the next decade or so, Southern warriors in the NAACP and other organizations made great strides in dismantling the most blatant forms of segregation in schools, employment, and public life. Most people know this Second Reconstruction as the Civil Rights era of the 1960s. However, an insidious backlash developed in the mid-60s. Ironically, the vehicle for the backlash was the party of Lincoln. It now welcomed white extremists and politicians who appeared to have gained control over the once proud anti-slavery party.

We believe we are now in a period of the **Third Reconstruction**, our 21st-century wave of popular revolt against regressive extremism that has squelched economic human rights. The notion of individualism and social Darwinism and disinvestment in the common good has now reached a punitive extreme. People are suffering greatly in this era when jobs disappear to the lowest global bidder and the social safety net is seen as a crutch for the undeserving.

The Historic Thousands on Jones Street (HKonJ) movement, led by the NC NAACP in coalition with organizations across the state, took form in 2007. It was an annual protest gathering at our state legislative center to bring people together to stand against our then-Democratic leadership to demand the basic rights guaranteed by our state Constitution. Coalition members developed a 14-Point People's Agenda that articulated common goals.

Although thousands of people have been coming to our annual Historic Thousands on Jones Street People's Assemblies and other protests since 2005, it was not until April of 2013 that our prophetic vision materialized every Monday. Total attendance at the Raleigh Moral Mondays exceeded thirty-five thousand. People of all races, classes, sexual identities, and political persuasions drove hundreds of miles from the mountains and the coast to Raleigh for 13 Moral Mondays during the 2013 Raleigh legislative session to bear moral witness against the cruel policies of the extremists. Nearly 950 persons were arrested: some in wheelchairs, some with cancer, some unemployed and seeking work, some overwhelmed with college debt, some police officers who understood flaws in our criminal justice system, and regular people who simply knew things were stacked against their hard-working habits as they still suffered from lack of health insurance and other hurdles such as the North Carolina legislative cuts in unemployment insurance. Thousands more came to show solidarity with the witnesses whose conscience drove them to civil disobedience. For both rally participants and those engaging for the first time in civil disobedience, this was a brand new and scary experience. But the moment demanded action, and the Forward Together Moral Movement was a catalyst with an open door for ordinary people to speak their minds.

Beyond all this action in Raleigh in 2013, at least thirty thousand more attended Moral Monday rallies from Sylva in the western North Carolina mountains to the Outer Banks on the state's eastern coast. Many people who attended these rallies returned to Raleigh for later weekly protests, comparing the events to a personal spiritual revival of solidarity and hope. Many thousands of others enthusiastically joined in from afar through Livestream, videos, YouTube, and news media.

The media caught the spirit and spread the word nationally and internationally about our self-described Moral Monday Movement in North Carolina. Our critics also helped the Movement go viral. One North Carolina legislator, desperate to minimize our power and message, called our growing weekly protests Moron Mondays. Opponents also resorted to 1950s McCarthy-era fear tactics and called us *outside agitators*, *leftists*, and *radicals*, because they could not debate the foundations of our claims, the breadth of our coalition, or the faces and pain of the people who kept telling their stories and driving even deeper our moral critique.

Through this Forward Together Moral Movement during our **Third Reconstruction**, the NC NAACP has added many new black, white, and Latino members to our local NAACP branches, strengthening our position as the largest State Conference in the South and the second largest in the nation. We convened 38 separate Moral Monday

Forward Together direct actions (13 in Raleigh; 25 around the state) in 2013, and also led a 26-county Spring 2013 tour.

Through all this organized action against regressive legislation in our state, we have reinvigorated and continued the historically venerable Long Walk to Justice in North Carolina. This work is challenging and demands persistence, strategic action on multiple fronts (the streets, courts, media, and voting booths). It is undergirded with a keen sense of hope and possibility.

We are faced by forces extremely hostile to our purposes. Warriors from the 1960s Movement tell us they underestimated the viciousness and the power of their opponents. The right-wing extremists view the emerging new Southern electorate as destructive to their way of life. Their fear about the fundamental change that is happening in the South causes them to view us with suspicion. Our work is dangerous and daunting. We find strength in the words of Paul:

> *But we are not among those who shrink back and so are lost,*
> *but among those who have faith and so are saved.*
>
> HEBREWS 10:39 NRSV

By staying the course, we know:

> *...if you pour yourself out for the hungry and satisfy the desire of the afflicted, then shall your light rise in the darkness and your gloom be as noonday. And the LORD will guide you continually, and satisfy your desire with good things, and make your bones strong, and you shall be like a watered garden, like a spring of water, whose waters fail not. And your ancient ruins shall be rebuilt; you shall raise up the foundations of many generations; you shall be called the repairer of the breach, the restorer of streets to dwell in.*
>
> ISAIAH 58:10-12 ESV

My brothers and sisters, we must live into the moral standard for all—individuals and political systems as well—that was proclaimed by the prophet Micah:

> *He has told you, O mortal, what is good; and what does the LORD*
> *   require of you*
> *but to do justice, and to love kindness, and to walk humbly with your*
> *   God?*
>
> MICAH 6:8 NRSV

We must also stand on the principles embodied by moral leaders like the Rev. J.W. Hood and the Rev. Samuel Ashley, who insisted in 1868 that the following words be inscribed in our North Carolina Constitution:

> *Section 1. That we hold it to be self-evident that all men are created equal; that they are endowed by their Creator with certain unalienable rights; that among these are life, liberty, the enjoyment of the fruits of their own labor, and the pursuit of happiness.*
>
> *Section. 2. That all political power is vested in and derived from the people; all government of right originates from the people, is founded upon their will only, and is instituted solely for the good of the whole.*

I am comforted in the knowledge that we are gathering a mighty force of people of faith. I am aware there are many different names and beliefs about the nature of the faith we each hold. But I know if we take risks of faith, if we reach across old man-made breaches in our human family, steady in our march toward justice, we may be called repairers of the breach. As we say when groups of protesters leave the North Carolina Legislative Building in buses going to jail:

Thank you. We love you.

Forward Together. Not One Step Back!

Rev. Barber surrounded on stage at Mass Moral March on Raleigh, lifting the message of "Higher Ground."
(Eric Preston photo)

1

"THE NEED TO KNOW WHO WE ARE IN TIMES LIKE THESE"

HISTORIC THOUSANDS ON JONES STREET RALLY 7

February 15, 2013
[No civil disobedience]

The moral fusion across faiths, genders, generations, and ethnicities—Imam Adam Beyah, Rev. Nancy Petty, Rev. Nelson Johnson, Joyce Johnson *(Phil Fonville photo)*

We know who we are.
We know we are called to bear witness at this moment of history.

We have faith there is a better way for North Carolina.
There is a better way for America. There is a better way for our world.
We mobilize for a better way.

BACKGROUND

For the last six years on the Saturday nearest to the date the NAACP was founded (President Lincoln's birth date, February 12), the NC NAACP has organized thousands of diverse and equal people and organizations for an assembly known as "Historic Thousands on Jones Street" (HKonJ). Jones Street in Raleigh is where the North Carolina General Assembly meets and rules. This gathering's purpose has been to remind us and our representatives to whom we have temporarily ceded some of our powers that, as our state Constitution reminds us, *power must be based in the will of the people and used only for the good of the whole.*

Recognizing that the representatives sent by voters to the People's House on Jones Street have life-and-death powers over every man, woman, and child in North Carolina, the NC NAACP began in 2006 to build a diverse and inclusive People's Assembly. The convergence came after Rev. Dr. Barber and his team assumed leadership over the NC NAACP, the most powerful and oldest anti-racism organization in the nation. Starting with 16 partners and about five thousand delegates and individuals who attended the first People's Assembly in February 2007, each year more and more partners, delegates, and ordinary concerned people have joined the Movement.

At the seventh People's Assembly in February of 2013, individuals representing 145 coalition partners and others gathered at historic Shaw University, where the Student Nonviolent Coordinating Committee (SNCC) was founded in 1960, and walked the mile or so to the People's House on Jones Street. They came from diverse backgrounds, organizations, and regions of the state. They were old, young, middle-aged, gay, straight, black, white, Latino, Asian American, and Native American. They were pro-labor champions and people who had no idea what a labor union was. They were deeply religious people, and people who had given up on organized religion. But they all agreed with the essentials of the 14-Point anti-racist, anti-discrimination, anti-poverty, anti-militarism and pro-justice agenda of the Assembly.

The seventh HKonJ Assembly focused on ending poverty and economic injustice, following the highly successful Truth and Hope Tour of Poverty that the NC NAACP and some of its partners had conducted in 2012. Advocates, scholars, journalists, and students shared a big bus and drove across North Carolina to dozens of impoverished areas, putting a face on poverty.

The General Assembly—as opposed to the People's Assembly—had just arrived in Raleigh. It was dominated by politicians who were recruited and funded by national right-wing groups determined to consolidate the old conservative and discriminatory folkways of the South, in order to provide a Southern base for a national attack on civil rights advancement and progressive policies.

NORTH CAROLINA CONSTITUTION, ARTICLE I,
DECLARATION OF RIGHTS

That the great, general, and essential principles of liberty and free government may be recognized and established, and that the relations of this State to the Union and government of the United States and those of the people of this State to the rest of the American people may be defined and affirmed, we do declare that:

SECTION 1. THE EQUALITY AND RIGHTS OF PERSONS. We hold it to be self-evident that all persons are created equal; that they are endowed by their Creator with certain inalienable rights; that among these are life, liberty, the enjoyment of the fruits of their own labor, and the pursuit of happiness.

SECTION 2. SOVEREIGNTY OF THE PEOPLE. All political power is vested in and derived from the people; all government of right originates from the people, is founded upon their will only, and is instituted solely for the good of the whole.

SECTION 3. INTERNAL GOVERNMENT OF THE STATE. The people of this State have the inherent, sole, and exclusive right of regulating the internal government and police thereof, and of altering or abolishing their Constitution and form of government whenever it may be necessary to their safety and happiness; but every such right shall be exercised in pursuance of law and consistently with the Constitution of the United States.

Now the just shall live by faith: but if any man draw back, my soul shall have no pleasure in him.
But we are not of them who draw back unto destruction; but of them that believe to the saving of the soul.

HEBREWS 10:38-39 KJV

Properly defining oneself, one's nature, and one's calling is a critical philosophical discipline that has penetrating practical implications. This task is particularly compelling when one is in crisis or facing seasons of challenge or confronting threats that seek to take one's identity and/or redefine it. Knowing who you are is critical to your sanity and your ability to sustain yourself when facing what Paul Tillich called the very threat of non-being and non-existence. This is how the slaves made it through slavery. Yes, they were called everything but children of God by the oppressive slave masters and system of slavery, but somehow deep in their spiritual DNA they were able to yet sing: *Before I be a slave, I'll be buried in my grave, and go home to my Lord and be free.* They knew they were not slaves.

The civil rights and justice communities know this lesson well. For 104 years, the NAACP and other civil rights organizations have been dismissed, cussed, and feared by those who did not want to deal honestly with issues of racial and class disparities. When whites and blacks put out the call for forming the NAACP on what would have been Lincoln's one-hundredth birthday, February 12, 1909, they were called un-American and disturbers of the peace, even Communists.

Dr. King was called a troublemaker and even a race-baiter 45 years ago as he led the call for a civil rights and economic justice Movement. He called for a Poor People's Movement to address the glaring realities of poverty even as he loved America enough to say: *Let us be dissatisfied until America will no longer have a high blood pressure of creeds and an anemia of deeds.*[1] Dr. King loved the world enough to say that the Evil Triplets of poverty, racism, and war are forms of violence that exist in a vicious cycle, interrelated. They stand as barriers to our living in a Beloved Community. Few listened.

Nevertheless, this vision resonated with black and white students from the urban and rural communities of America, who started the sit-in Movement, and SNCC, the Southern Nonviolent Coordinating Committee that was born in Raleigh, North Carolina, under the tutelage of our own rural scholar and activist, Ella Baker. The young SNCC leaders were maligned and disrespected by those who wanted to maintain the status quo of inequality, but they kept on because they knew who they were.

From Moses to Jesus, the Bible tells us that those who fought for justice—those who spoke truth to power, those who refused to accept that injustice and inequality had to exist and that there was no better way—always found themselves hated, hounded, and heaped upon with false accusations simply because they believed in the necessity of speaking and working for the cause of righteousness and building a more just community. This lack of majority support is why the just must live by faith and must know exactly who we are.

As we gather here on February 9, 2013, some will try to define us in their own ways and will try to obstruct and obfuscate our message. Given that skewing, we must know ourselves. We must know where we stand.

The Historic Thousands on Jones Street (HKonJ) People's Coalition is made up of tens of thousands of ordinary North Carolinians: African Americans, Latinos, Americans of European ancestry, Native Americans, Asian Americans, old and young, gay and straight, all of us human beings who share a vision of enough for all.

We stand against systems and policies rooted in systemic classism and racism. The term classism can refer to personal prejudice against so-called lower classes as well as to institutional classism, just as the term racism can refer strictly to personal bigotry or to institutional racism that displays itself in areas of housing, jobs, education, banking, and every other area that shapes work life and opportunities for success in our land.

Our agenda is justice. We believe that when the economic, social, and spiritual life of our state moves toward justice, the circulation of the blood of politics improves, which is a healthy thing.

We mourn the grim realities of so many North Carolinians:

Today, roughly 8–10 percent of our workforce is officially unemployed; the real rate is much higher. Black unemployment is twice as bad. The gap between rich and poor is wider and deeper than during the Great Depression; 1 percent of Americans owns 40 percent of the nation's wealth.

There are 1.7 million North Carolina residents living in poverty, and more than seven hundred thousand of us live in deep poverty. Many of these are the working poor, and six hundred thousand of our suffering impoverished persons are children. More than one hundred thirty thousand of these children are Latino. Children of all races are crippled by poverty in our state: White children: 214,487; African American children: 207,421; Native American children: 11,239. These are real people with faces, hunger, and despair! And they represent well over 20 percent of our population!

Forty-four percent of African American children live in poverty. Ten of our 100 counties have had a poverty rate of over 20 percent for 30 years.[2]

Last year we visited 27 towns, cities, and counties on our Truth and Hope Poverty Tour, to put a face on these numbers. We cannot ignore this issue of dire poverty in our midst and the suffering of these individuals, our brothers and sisters. We cannot continue the attention-violence we commit against them in public policy and private activity. We are all tied together.

We know who we are. We know we are called to bear witness at this moment of history. We have faith there is a better way for North Carolina. There is a better way for America. There is a better way for our world. We mobilize for a better way.

We of the Forward Together Moral Movement in North Carolina have no partisan agenda. We do not care about Democrats or Republicans or regular politics. We stand together for five nonpartisan, human values:

1. **Economic sustainability and ending poverty.** We support this value by fighting for full employment, living wages, a green economy, labor rights, affordable housing, targeted empowerment zones, strong safety-net services for the poor, fair policies for immigrants, infrastructure development, and fair tax reform.

2. **Educational equality.** We support this value by pushing to ensure that every child receives a high-quality, well-funded, constitutional, racially diverse public education. We also support equitable funding for historically black colleges and universities (HBCUs), and funding so that every aspiring child has access to community college and university education that our state Constitution guarantees.

3. **Healthcare for all.** We seek to ensure access to the Affordable Care Act, Medicare and Medicaid, Social Security, and the forms of environmental protection that guarantee clean water, air, and lands—our ecological home must be clean.

4. **Fairness in the criminal justice system.** We will continue to challenge inequalities in our legal and court and prison systems, to gain our constitutionally granted equal protection under the law for black, brown, and poor white people.

5. **Voting rights.** We will defend the right to vote by standing against suppression tactics such as Voter ID mandates, restrictions of early voting, race-based redistricting plans, or any other effort that undermines equal protection under the law.

And yet instead of focusing on a progressive agenda, a unifying agenda, the new ultraconservative leadership unleashed a cruel and unusual quadruple attack on labor rights, unemployment benefits, Medicaid provision, and voting rights that will have devastating impact on all poor and working people in our state.

And beyond attacks on unemployment benefits, Medicaid, and voting rights, they are considering tax "reform" which would cut corporate income tax and force North Carolinians in these difficult economic times to pay higher sales tax on many everyday services like haircuts, so they can cut taxes on their corporate friends.

Seemingly insensitive to the lives of everyday people, these legislators speak in a strange tongue. Despite their constitutional charge to work for the good of the whole, they have suggested, for example, that the poor don't need healthcare, that every county's charities should take care of their own, that the federal government giving back billions of taxpayer dollars to help the poor is a violation of states' rights, and that lazy unemployed people will go out and find jobs if we take their unemployment insurance safety nets away.

They speak of the necessary evil of cutting benefits for the poor and the unemployed. But this is not necessary evil; it's unnecessary injustice! It is unnecessary meanness! It's wrong! It's hurtful! It's Robin Hood in reverse! It is morally unconscionable, constitutionally inconsistent, and economically insane public policy! It's sinful, and it's NOT a necessary evil.

The decisions being made in this legislative house may be a game for some, adhering to the partisan line for others, intoxication with power for a few, and payback to their wealthy donors. They say they won the election and that the state's people are on their side. But which people?

We are witnessing a revival and renewed commitment to implement policy rooted in the regressive policies of states' rights, classism, racial discrimination, and economic injustice. They may have the votes but we have the voice! And we must dramatize these shameful actions for all North Carolinians and even the nation to see, in hopes that they will change. And if they do not change, we must mobilize in hope that the people and voters will challenge them in their home districts and become educated for when they have to judge these elected leaders later at the ballot box.

We call on the leaders of North Carolina to reject efforts by extremists on the far right to govern for the good of a few. We call on you to remain moderate, to do what the North Carolina Constitution requires, and to govern for the good of the whole. We are here to call on elected leaders to remember who they are and why they were elected. You did not swear to be Democrats or Republicans, but to do what is best for the good of the whole. You swore to uphold our state Constitution and here is what it says in Article 1, the Declaration of Rights, Section 1. The equality and rights of persons:

We hold it to be self-evident that all persons are created equal; that they are endowed by their Creator with certain inalienable rights; that among these are life, liberty, the enjoyment of the fruits of their own labor, and the pursuit of happiness.

Section 2 of our state Constitution concerns the sovereignty of the people, and it says that:

All political power is vested in and derived from the people; all government of right originates from the people, is founded upon their will only, and is instituted solely for the good of the whole.

Section 12 of our state Constitution speaks to our right of assembly and petition:

The people have a right to assemble together to consult for their common good, to instruct their representatives, and to apply to the General Assembly for redress of grievances; but secret political societies are dangerous to the liberties of a free people and shall not be tolerated.

So governor and state legislators, let us instruct you!

We assemble here for hope.
We love this state and country and all people, even those we criticize.
We just want to see this state do God's will.
And don't mistake our gathering as just a moment!
We will bring the plight of the poor to the agenda again and again.
We will march in your community and educate voters and hold forums, and we will not rest!

Because we know there is a better way. You didn't just swear to uphold the Constitution; you put your hand on a Bible. That Bible says your private failings are, like for all of us, between you and God, but your public actions and your use of public power must be measured by the mandates of God's standard of justice. So if you are going to claim a commitment to morality and if you are going to keep having chaplains

open your legislative sessions with prayer, then be it known unto you
and all of us that the same Bible you swore on says:

> *Woe to those who make unjust laws,*
> > *to those who issue oppressive decrees*
> *to deprive the poor of their rights*
> > *and withhold justice from the oppressed of my people,*
> *making widows their prey*
> > *and robbing the fatherless.*
> *What will you do on the day of reckoning,*
> > *when disaster comes from afar?*
> *To whom will you run for help?*
> > *Where will you leave your riches?*
> *Nothing will remain but for you to cringe among the captives*
> > *or fall among the slain.*
>
> ISAIAH 10:1-4 NIV

It also declares in Isaiah 58:9-12 (NIV):

> *If you do away with the yoke of oppression,*
> > *with the pointing finger and malicious talk, and if you spend*
> > > *yourselves in behalf of the hungry*
> > *and satisfy the needs of the oppressed,*
> *then your light will rise in the darkness,*
> *and your night will become like the noonday.*
> *The LORD will guide you always;*
> > *he will satisfy your needs in a sun-scorched land*
> > *and will strengthen your frame.*
> *You will be like a well-watered garden,*
> > *like a spring whose waters never fail.*
> *Your people will rebuild the ancient ruins*
> > *and will raise up the age-old foundations;*
> *you will be called Repairer of Broken Walls,*
> > *Restorer of Streets with Dwellings.*

The prophet Jeremiah in chapter 5, verse 28 (NET) rebuked those
who win at the expense of the poor:

> [The wicked] *have grown fat and sleek.*
> *There is no limit to the evil things they do.*

*They do not plead the cause of the fatherless in such a way as to win it.
They do not defend the rights of the poor.*

And Jeremiah in chapter 22, verse 3 (NIV), interpreted the justice mandate of the divine:

This is what the LORD says: Do what is just and right. Rescue from the hand of the oppressor the one who has been robbed. Do no wrong or violence to the foreigner, the fatherless or the widow, and do not shed innocent blood in this place.

The prophet Micah in chapter 6, verse 8 (NKJV), gave three simple rules of the Lord for each of us to honor:

*And what does the LORD require of you
But to do justly,
To love mercy,
And to walk humbly with your God?*

Moving to the gospels, from Matthew 25:42-45 (NABRE) we learn how Jesus critiqued those who thought they were righteous in their adherence to the temple rules, even as they ignored real pain in the streets:

"'For I was hungry and you gave me no food; I was thirsty and you gave me no drink. I was a stranger and you gave me no welcome; naked and you gave me no clothing; ill and in prison, and you did not care for me.' Then they will answer and say, 'Lord, when did we see you hungry or thirsty or a stranger or naked or ill or in prison, and not minister to your needs?' He will answer them, 'Amen, I say to you, what you did not do for one of these least ones, you did not do for me.'"

Now some commentators have said: *Talk all you want, march all you want, organize all you want, even pray and say what the Bible says, but they have a supermajority in the General Assembly, so they can do all they want, and you cannot stop them.* And that's true, they do have a supermajority, due to the gerrymandering of our state House and Senate districts after the 2010 census. But the 170 legislators inside those buildings on Jones Street don't have the last word! They have some power, but not all power. And so we move with hope and with joy.

Now the just shall live by faith: but if any man draw back, my soul shall have no pleasure in him.
But we are not of them who draw back unto destruction; but of them that believe to the saving of the soul.

HEBREWS 10:38-39 KJV

By faith we warn those who pass policies that hurt the least of these and the sick:

Watch out; God might fix it!

And...you may one day need the very healthcare you try to take from others! Your money might get funny and you have to experience the poverty you ignore!

Wrong and evil have inbred the seeds of *can't*. Those who use their power *can't* stand, because God is not mocked! Remember there is a power higher than us all, and so by faith we will demand economic justice and address poverty. We will:

Stand courageously
Organize successfully
Mobilize consistently
Speak the truth relentlessly
Pray fervently
Preach prophetically
Sue legally
Vote massively

And we will not go away quietly or back down submissively. We will meet this challenge faithfully.

Even if we don't have political votes, by faith we know that wrong and meanness only have temporary victories. We serve a supernatural God who super-rules the world.

Why do we have hope? There was a time men had a supermajority over women, but the sisters didn't give up! They won the right to vote! A women named Myrlie Evers led women in the South, and my own mother helped her children to integrate schools, and a whole new group of young women are here today to lead the way.

At one time business had monopolies, and there were no labor laws, but workers organized! How do you think we got minimum wages, the

40-hour work week, and the right to express work grievances under Title 7 of the Civil Rights law? Somebody pushed against the odds and won!

In the 1960s the Dixiecrats thought they had a supermajority. Don't you remember that boastful line expressed by Alabama governor George Wallace: *Segregation now, segregation tomorrow, segregation forever!* But when people by faith pushed back, they made that governor out to be a liar.

Apartheid had a supermajority in South Africa, but it came down, and Nelson Mandela was elected up!

Meanness, money, hate, racism, and the deep dark vein of intolerance thought it had a supermajority, but on the MLK national holiday in 2013, for the second time the world heard:

> *I, Barack Hussein Obama, do solemnly swear that I will faithfully execute the Office of President of the United States, and will to the best of my ability, preserve, protect and defend the Constitution of the United States.*

If we do our part, God can still change hearts. And so we are not discouraged by one election. We are not dismantled or discombobulated. We stand on truth and justice and on the power of God and the power of the people. We the people still have a say.

Yes, these are tough times, but faith says there's still a God who can bless and keep us anyhow. Faith doesn't give in to evil. Faith stands up to Pharaoh. Faith speaks truth to power. Faith takes on Goliath. Faith refuses to accept sinister situations. Refuses to be a slave to other folks' oppression. Refuses to be chattel property of injustice.

Faith, and moving Forward Together, is the only way to save our souls and the soul of this nation. Faith is believing in spite of the obstacles. Faith is knowing that when God helps you, there is no challenge that can't be met, no mountain that can't be climbed, no valley that can't be crossed, no enemy that can't be defeated. No darkness that can't be overcome. No pressure that can't be pushed through. No political power that can't be overturned. No challenge that can't be survived. No war of the spirit that can't be subdued. Faith is believing despite the evidence. Believing despite the odds against us. The truth of the matter is we've come this far by faith.

We have got to hold on. Too many challenges abound. Too many injustices are real. Too much inequality still exists. Too much racism, too much meanness. But we are not those who fall back unto destruction.

We persevere. We must hold on to our faith and declare before God to this nation called America that when it comes to our rights ordained by God and guaranteed by the Constitution, we will never lose the faith, and we will never, ever, ever turn back!

Our faith might get bruised and battered. Our hope for this nation to live out its highest principles might get challenged. We might get discouraged. But we'll never lose our faith. Weeping may endure for a night, mean politicians may endure for a night, tea parties may endure for a night, but we still believe joy comes in the morning. Dry bones in the valley can come together. We will never lose our faith that the poor can be lifted, the sick can be healed, our children can be educated, and the falsely accused and imprisoned can be vindicated. We know and trust that our communities can come together. Our rights can be protected.

We will never lose our faith. We might have some dark Fridays. But we will not lose our faith, because we know that dark Fridays have to give way to bright Sunday morning resurrections. We shall overcome. We shall survive. Justice will win. Truth will live. We will never lose our faith!

2

"WITNESS AGAINST EXTREMISM"

MORAL MONDAY RALLY 1

April 29, 2013
Arrestees: 17

With Barbara Zelter, marching into the first witness
action on April 29, 2013 *(Phil Fonville photo)*

*We call on all people of goodwill to join us, that we might build
the bridges of understanding, not the walls of division.*

BACKGROUND

On April 29, 2013, 17 people and some of their friends and allies gathered
at Rev. Byron Wade's historic Davie Street Presbyterian Church in Raleigh

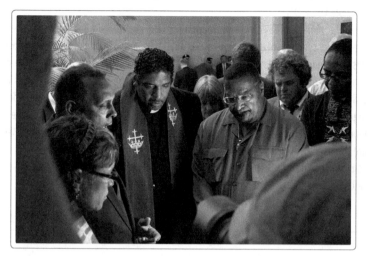

Clergy prayer on April 29, 2013, in the North Carolina Legislative
Building *(Phil Fonville photo)*

to prepare for the moral witness they had decided to make that evening
at the People's House on Jones Street.

The North Carolina General Assembly routinely held a short
session on Monday evenings, and we knew that 5:00 p.m., right
after work, would be the best time for working people to show their
support for the witness. Holding the witness action on Monday also
symbolized our belief that the moral call for justice goes hand-in-hand
with the constitutional call for the common good, on any day of the week.

That evening the 17 clergy, activists, and students walked up the
stairs of the People's House and began praying and singing outside the
golden doors of the North Carolina Senate and House. The message was
simple. They said they opposed the extremist policies coming out of
the People's House. They believed people had the right to instruct their
representatives in their House to pass laws for the good of the whole.
They had read the North Carolina Constitution.

After a short while, the 17 were arrested, handcuffed, and bused to
jail. In an impromptu rally, supporters outside tracked down the prison
transport bus in the back of the building and cheered the moral witnesses
as they were carried off in handcuffs and loaded onto the bus. They
repeated over and over again: *Thank you. We love you.*

ON APRIL 29, 2013, BEFORE THEIR WITNESS ACTION, THE
FORWARD TOGETHER MORAL MOVEMENT PUBLISHED AN OPEN

LETTER CALLED "WHY WE ARE HERE." THE LETTER INCLUDED
THESE WORDS:

From the moral framework of the Scriptures and our Constitution, we are calling
together a coalition of goodwill—a nonviolent volunteer army of love to oppose
this legislature's heartless, ideologically driven agenda. We call on all the people of
goodwill to join us, that we might build the bridges of understanding, not the walls of
division. We call on all residents of North Carolina who believe in the common good
to pray and partner with us as we use the tools of protest and the tactics of nonviolent
moral suasion to illuminate for the nation the shameful acts taking place here. We
are not alone. We shall speak and we shall act. We will become "the trumpet of
conscience" and "the beloved community" that the Rev. Dr. Martin Luther King Jr.
called upon us to be, echoing the God of our mothers and fathers in the faith.

Now is the time. Here is the place. We are the people. And we will be heard.

❝Today, in North Carolina's General Assembly, we will engage in an act of conscience—praying and protesting and violating with good conscience the rules of our legislature concerning our gathering. But we do it in love, and we do it in the spirit of justice. Forty-five years ago today, after Dr. King had been assassinated, the Rev. Ralph Abernathy and other ministers led our delegation to Washington, D.C., to meet with Cabinet members and congresspeople to challenge them regarding the ugly legacy of poverty and injustice. They continued the Movement then; we continue it now.

The greatest of all of the righteous principles in both the Hebrew and Christian scriptures have one common theme regarding matters of private failure: We are to go to our priests and be forgiven.

But in the public square, the constant refrain is: *Love the Lord, your God, with all your heart, mind, and soul, and then love your neighbor as yourself.* In the public square, the constant call is to *preach good news to the poor, to proclaim freedom to the prisoner, to heal the sick, and to set your prisoners free.* The constant refrain is: *Let justice roll down like water.* The constant refrain is: *Learn to do right. Care for the children. Lift up the widows and the vulnerable, and then you shall be called repairers of the breach.*

I could not help but think as we come here today that one of the signs in this Legislative Building includes the name of James Harris. Mr. Harris was a part of that early group of black and white Fusion politicians in 1868 who said we must move out of the past of slavery and racial division to a new land, and we must start with the writing of a fresh Constitution. James Harris, J.W. Hood, and ministers helped write the words that every legislator in North Carolina swears on a Bible to uphold, words that declare that everything legislators do must be done solely for the good of the whole of the people in our state. These North Carolina constitutional principles fit with the ethics of the federal Declaration of Independence when it declared that: We hold these truths to be self-evident, that all [persons] are created equal, that they are endowed by their Creator with certain unalienable Rights.

Our own North Carolina Constitution lists that our unalienable rights are *life, liberty, the enjoyment of the fruit of their own labor, the pursuit of happiness.* And listen—this is where we must hold them accountable. Section 2 of our state Constitution, regarding the sovereignty of the people, states that: *All political power is vested in and derived from the people; all government of right originates from the people, is founded upon their will only, and is instituted solely for the good of the whole.*

Love and justice for the good of the whole demands a witness. There must be a witness in the face of extremism and regressive public policy, when politicians in the 21st century decide they want to be like the George Wallaces of the 20th century. They are pushing a new Southern strategy here when they want to deny people fundamental rights.

It's one of the most well-known essentials of our federal Constitution that we have a right to bear witness. And so we here today are going to witness with love and justice because anything less would be an indictment upon our faith, an indictment upon whom we are called to be as human beings of conscience. Today we will read a document together. We want to make it clear why we are here today in this church. We are North Carolinians who today choose nonviolent civil disobedience in the face of an avalanche of extremist policies that threaten healthcare, that threaten education, that threaten the poor, that threaten creation of jobs, that threaten voting rights.

Micah 6:8 (NRSV) asks us our public policy question: *What does the Lord require of you but to do justice, and to love kindness, and to walk humbly with your God?* It is in the spirit of openness to the prophet's question that we gather here as people of faith and citizens of North Carolina.

We have written letters to our governor. We have written letters to our state House and Senate representatives in the General Assembly. We have brought thousands of people to the People's House. Now we once again, by putting our bodies on the line, are asking our representatives to reconsider their assault on the poor, on the unemployed, on our many citizens without healthcare, and on our embattled public schools and public education. We're asking them to reconsider and to get on the right side of history.

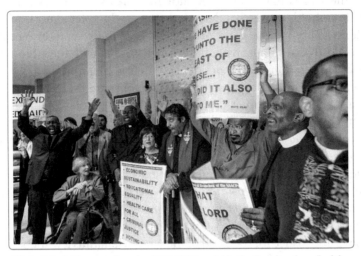

The original 17 arrested on April 29, 2013, outside the "golden doors" of the
North Carolina Legislative Building chambers *(Eric Etheridge photo)*

They've already voted and passed legislation to deny federal funds
for Medicaid to five hundred thousand poor North Carolinians. That's
shameful.

They've already voted to take unemployment benefits from one
hundred sixty five thousand North Carolinians. They've already raised
taxes on nine hundred thousand of North Carolina's poor and working
people, by ending the state-earned income tax credit, so they could
pay for a tax break for 23 multimillionaire families.

They've already voted to take over 1.6 billion dollars from public
education. And now they're trying to pass a voucher plan to pass out
public money to private schools.

They want to restart death penalty executions, even though North
Carolina has had the largest number of people exonerated from the
death penalty. They want to repeal the North Carolina Racial Justice
Act that was proven in court to be both constitutional and necessary.

And they want to codify anti-labor language in our North Carolina
Constitution. When that Constitution was written by blacks and
whites 145 years ago, it asserted that every person has the right to the
enjoyment of the fruit of their own labor. The current legislature's anti-
labor proposals are therefore unconstitutional.

And then they want to do the greatest harm, which is to roll back
voting rights. They want to pass a 21st-century version of the poll tax,
as their voter suppression bill rolls back early voting, bans Sunday

voting, and ends same-day registration. These regressive changes will cost us millions and deny so many the right to vote.

You only push these voter-suppression policies when you can't afford a big turnout because you're scared that if you don't rig the election, then a brand-new electorate will evolve. And that electorate will continue to open the cracks in the solid South and elect in a new light of justice and diversity.

We put our bodies on the line today
because we believe this is the wrong direction.
We should be going forward and not one step back!

3

"HEALTHCARE"

MORAL MONDAY RALLY 2

May 6, 2013
Arrestees: 30

Dr. Charlie van der Horst, one of a host of medical professionals arrested
in the Forward Together Moral Movement *(Phil Fonville photo)*

When we push the least of these to the margin and push
the powerful and the wealthy to the center of public policy,
we are violating our deepest moral principles from our sacred texts.

BACKGROUND

When the first 17 witnesses were arrested on April 29 in front of the locked
doors of the North Carolina Senate chambers, a national outcry broke out.

NC NAACP members in over one hundred college, youth, and adult branches across the state were ready to back their leaders. Members of churches pastored by arrestees wanted to show their support. The arrests caught the attention of doctors and other healthcare professionals, who were outraged by the rejection of health insurance for half a million poor people in North Carolina. They knew it was the same as signing a death warrant for dozens of poor and elderly people. History professors, clergy, students, and working people alike were inspired to be part of the Movement that shouted as its theme:

Forward Together . . . Not One Step Back!

People called the NC NAACP office and asked: *How can I be a witness? When is the next protest?*

So on Monday afternoon, May 6, about 80 people met at Davie Street Presbyterian Church. NAACP organizers and attorneys asked those who were willing to risk arrest to sit in the Witness Section of the sanctuary. A doctor, several NAACP leaders, the singing group The Raging Grannies, a couple of military veterans, and several young people took their designated seats to become witnesses.

These 30 witnesses on this second Monday were encouraged to make sure their consciences supported this personal decision to perform civil disobedience and risk arrest. They were informed about the process and its consequences. If they wanted to proceed, they were asked to leave their purses and other personal items with friends and family who had come to support them. A short service was conducted, with prayers and Movement songs to bless the witnesses as well as those who were being hurt by the extremists' policies. NC NAACP President Barber then called a short news conference and spoke about the urgent moral callings of the week. The 30 witnesses were invited to speak about what had caused them to take this major step in their lives, and they spoke about the vicious attacks the extremists had unleashed against the poor and the sick and the children. Some gave painful personal stories.

The Davie Street Church crowd drove to Jones Street and gathered across from the People's House on the Bicentennial Plaza across from the North Carolina Legislative Building. A support group of several hundred greeted them. There had been no organized effort to mobilize supporters. Many said they had heard about the arrests of the 17 the past Monday, and had come out just to show their support. As the 30 witnesses lined up to enter the People's House, the supporters created two lines to protect and surround them. Clergy led the 30 into the People's House through the aisle created by the supporters, who reached out and touched each witness on the shoulder as they walked by.

When the 30 witnesses got to the front of the locked Senate doors on the second floor, they displayed small signs, while a pastor blessed the occasion. The Raging Grannies sang. History professors talked about lessons from the Civil Rights Movement in the 1950s and 1960s. Doctors spoke of how the extremists' policies harmed their patients. The teach-in was disrupted by the legislative police chief's voice coming out of his bullhorn: *This is an illegal gathering. If you do not disperse, you will be arrested.*

After two more warnings, the Legislative Building police chief's officers approached the witnesses, strapped their wrists together behind their backs with plastic ties, and pulled the knot tight against their wrists. Each handcuffed witness was led to the elevator, taken to the basement, searched, and held until they were all processed by Raleigh police.

Meanwhile, hundreds of supporters waited around the rotunda inside the Legislative Building. The supporters then went outside to find where the jail bus was parked. After keeping up a steady stream of old and new songs and chants for almost an hour, the first witness appeared at the basement door, hands behind her back and sending a big smile to her supporters across the street. Then came the now-famous cheer created on the first Moral Monday for witnesses as they walked the short way to board the bus to the Wake County Detention Center. Hundreds of supporters yelled at the top of their voices:

> *Thank You. We Love You.*
> *Thank You. We Love You.*
> *Thank You. We Love You.*

"We are North Carolinians who choose nonviolent civil disobedience in the face of the avalanche of extremist policies that threaten healthcare, education, voting rights, the poor, African Americans, Latinos, women, seniors, and students.

We take no pleasure, necessarily, in going to jail. But when we see what is happening in the recesses of our General Assembly, it is uncivil, unnecessary, and unconstitutional, and it must be challenged. We come here with a deep sense of prayer, and today, another wave of protesters will go in; and we will have a pray-in and a teach-in in the halls of the General Assembly.

We do have a legal strategy. Our lawyers are planning on challenging in court many of the policies that are being passed. We do have an organizing strategy, and our organizing strategy will involve moving around the state.

We come here today standing in the deep moral tradition of constitutional law. The North Carolina Constitution, written 145 years ago in 1868, set down principles that guide us today. Some ministers were a part of putting that Constitution together; one of them was J.W. Hood, who became the bishop of the A.M.E. Zion Church in this state. These writers declared: *We hold it to be self-evident that all persons are created equal; that they are endowed by their Creator with certain inalienable rights; that among these are life, liberty, the enjoyment of the fruit of their own labor, and the pursuit of happiness.* They further proclaimed: *All political power is vested in and derived from the people; all government of right originates from the people, is founded upon their will only, and is instituted solely for the good of the whole.*

And we believe we are now seeing a state legislature that is out of control, not following its own constitutional principles that it swore to uphold. We see that they seem to be more interested in doing what is good for a few, to meet the whims of a few, than in doing what is good for the whole of the people of this state.

We stand today hoping to be faithful to the great tradition of Scripture. The Bible sets down public policy conditions in several of its texts. It does so when it asks in the book of the prophet Micah: *What doth the Lord require of [you]? ... Do justly, and to love mercy and to walk humbly with [your] God* (v. 8 KJV). That question was not pointed to an individual but to a nation. And in Matthew 25 we hear this gospel-based public policy inquiry: *When I was hungry, did you feed me? When I was sick, did you heal me? In prison, did you visit me? When I was naked, did you clothe me?* Those are admonitions not just to individuals, but to the whole nation. These two Hebrew and Christian texts are scriptural reminders that whatever a nation or state does to the least of these, it does those things unto God. And so when we don't do for the least of these, when we push the least of these to the margin and push the powerful and the wealthy to the center of public policy, we are violating our deepest moral principles from our sacred texts.

Why are we frustrated today in our moral hopes?

We wrote to our governor early on, and to the speaker of the House, asking them regardless of party to engage in a political attitude that was bigger than party, but about the people. They resisted. We brought nearly twenty thousand people here for Historic Thousands on Jones Street in 2013: this sample of North Carolinians included persons who were black, white, Latino, young, and old, as we came together to put forward a positive agenda. We did not merely curse the darkness. We said, *listen*. And for North Carolina, let's focus on economic sustainability, poverty, and jobs. Let's focus on a high-quality education for every student. Let's focus on healthcare for all, protecting Medicaid benefits offered by the Affordable Care Act. Let's focus on dealing with the injustices within our criminal justice system. And in this great state, where we have led for the last two election cycles in the number of people participating in elections, we said: *Let's expand voting rights, and let's protect them.*

Instead of accepting these recommendations, and accepting a positive move forward, our governor and our legislative leaders chose an assault on the poor, the unemployed, citizens without healthcare, and public schools. In the first 50 days of this infamous legislative session, despite our prayers, despite the people speaking, they've denied Medicaid expansion to up to half a million poor North Carolinians. Half a million. Some of them are Democrats, some of them are Republicans, some are black, some are white, some are Latino, and some are women. But five hundred thousand people.

They've taken unemployment insurance benefits from one hundred seventy thousand people. On July 1, three days before Independence Day, almost one hundred seventy thousand North Carolinians–black, white, Democratic, Republican, young, and old– will lose their unemployment checks as they are trying to dig their way out of a recession in a state that has 1.6 million poor people and six hundred thousand poor children who have come from families that are working. That's wrong. That's unconstitutional. That's immoral.

By ending the state Earned Income Tax Credit, always claimed by Republicans and Democrats alike as the best anti-poverty program in the nation, they in effect raised taxes on nine hundred thousand North Carolinians. nine hundred thousand. That's more than the total population of Charlotte and Asheville combined. They did this to save state dollars so that they could give a state tax cut to 23 millionaires.

But now they've added to that assault by trampling on voting rights. With their unnecessary voter ID requirement–more stringent than those that Alabama or South Carolina imposed–they've packed in scores of voter-suppression tactics, undoing 50 years of voting-rights expansion in our state. They want to roll back early voting and get rid of same-day registration. We must name that voter ID bills are hinged on racism. Did you hear about the North Carolina legislator who said in his reference to Sunday voting: *The blacks have six other days that they can vote.* It sickens us to see a bill where they want a test of mental competency before one can vote; where they want to charge parents $2,500 in lost tax deductions if their children vote where they go to college, as opposed to where they were born. It is infuriating to see bills that say to those who have completed prison terms or probation: *You've got to wait five years to vote again, and then after five years you can apply to three people, and then three people have to vote unanimously for you to have your voting rights.*

That is not democracy! That is not the American way! That is not the best of North Carolina! It's regressive, it's mean, and it's almost as though they passed all of these regressive bills to hurt people and to say: *Well, maybe those same people that wake up and want to vote, well, now we're going to deny them the right to vote, now we're going to undermine, now we're going to suppress their vote, because my narrow-minded agenda just might not make it in the public square if all these people use their right to vote.*

Apparently our governor and House speaker and Senate president pro tem have decided they want to be the George Wallaces of the 21st century. That they want to run a fresh Southern strategy right here in North Carolina that excludes rather than includes. And so, we stand as witnesses today, because of this avalanche, because of all of these combined policies that we see happening, and because we can see the damage that they will bring not just now but to generations, even after this moment. From the deepest place in our moral fiber, from the framework of our Scriptures and our Constitution, we make a witness. By the way, our Constitution says that as people of North Carolina, we have a right to instruct our legislators. And so we will do that now.

We are together a coalition of people of goodwill, of all different races, colors, and creeds. We are a volunteer army of love to oppose this legislature's ideologically driven agenda. And we call on people of goodwill to call this nation to prayer and to protest. We will be, in our generation, what Dr. King called *the trumpet of conscience.*

4

"EQUAL PROTECTION UNDER THE LAW"

MORAL MONDAY RALLY 4

May 20, 2013
Arrestees: 57

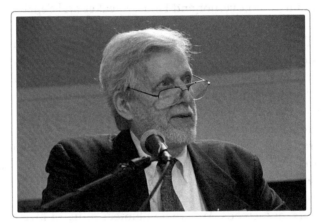

Civil rights attorney and Forward Together Moral Movement
elder Al McSurely *(Phil Fonville photo)*

The foundation of a true democracy—and more importantly,
a wholesome society—is equal protection under the law.

BACKGROUND

The size and spirit of the nearly one thousand people who rushed to Jones Street after they got off work on May 20 was overwhelming. They filled the northern half of Bicentennial Plaza, breaking the past week's count. As 57 moral witnesses prepared to enter the People's House on Jones Street, Rev. Barber inspired and encouraged everyone.

Love and Justice have never lost. They might get crucified. They might get beat down.
But at the end of the day, when the fame is over and the dust settles, Justice and Love always win. So get your head up! It's time to walk! It's time to march! It's time to say:

Forward Together . . . Not One Step Back!

After the third Moral Monday on May 13, when 49 people chose to express their concerns in civil disobedience leading to arrest, the fourth Moral Monday zeroed in on the fundamental constitutional principle of "Equal Protection Under the Law," with a special focus on ending racism in the criminal justice system and providing high-quality education for all of North Carolina's children.

The 57 witnesses included ministers, students, immigrants, and veterans. A former NAACP branch president who had been a part of the 1960 sit-in Movement in Greensboro came to bear moral witness. A county school board member and a medical doctor joined in as well. An economics professor said: *Any policy that reduces Medicaid for the poor, reduces unemployment insurance for the jobless, lowers taxes on the rich while raising them on the poor, is defaulting on our obligation.*

A 92-year-old woman decided she could not stand idly by while the North Carolina General Assembly and governor tried to take North Carolina backward. The 57 witnesses ranged in age from 18 to 92. One of the young people, Ivanna Gonzales, aroused tears and applause when she spoke in front of the locked Senate doors:

I learned a history that tells me that these attacks on women, people of color, immigrants, public workers, are tricks that have been tried before. They have been stopped before. I'm here as a student to stand by my liberal-arts education. As a woman I am here to declare this body is mine! As an immigrant I'm here to remind us that most of our families came from somewhere else. As a human being I am here because I know that the attacks on my gay friends, on immigrants in detention centers, on the housekeepers on UNC's campus are all interconnected and are attacks on the people I love.

The North Carolina Racial Justice Act was the most respected death penalty legislation in the South. For the first time, Southern courts had legal tools

Message to legislators: Power rests in the hands of the people *(Phil Fonville photo)*

to examine the obvious racism involved in so many death penalty cases involving black defendants or victims. Conservative Southern politicians, who had thrived on winning elections by being tough on black crime, hated the law.

The extremist legislature that came to power in 2010 and achieved super-power in 2012 took dead aim at a law that lived up to its name: Racial Justice. While a thousand people—white, black, and Latino—focused on the constitutional guarantee of "Equal Protection Under the Law" at the fourth Moral Monday, one state senator worked to convince other senators to repeal the Racial Justice Act. He succeeded and the bill went to Gov. McCrory. The governor rubbed salt into wounds of every victim of racial injustice by signing this act on June 19. Juneteenth, as this day is called by African Americans and other freedom-loving people, was the day the news of emancipation finally made it to Southern Texas in 1865. The governor's racially insensitive gesture in this instance is part of a pattern of arrogance shown by those who have no historical awareness and who therefore see nothing wrong with blaming poor and working people for problems caused by a conscience-less economic system.

The peaceful protestors were ordered to leave, and 57 of them who refused to leave were handcuffed and taken to the Legislative Building basement. The massive number of supporters moved to the outside for the farewell rally. Because of their numbers, the people spread their support line throughout the entire length of the block behind the People's

House. Every Monday after this one, the police moved their jail buses to the west side of the People's House, providing a larger area for supporters to sing, cheer, and get to know one another.

A pattern of support had spontaneously erupted on April 29 after the first witness action and it continued and grew all summer long, as thousands of North Carolinians came out week after week and endured the blistering heat and humidity of downtown Raleigh so they could take a visible united stand. As those arrested were processed in the basement of the Legislative Building, the crowd sang and chanted outside until all were loaded onto the buses and were taken away to the Wake County Detention Center. Then many of these same supporters drove over to the Center and stayed up all night, until the very last person was released with a paper indicating an upcoming court date for trial. They provided food and drink to those who had been arrested. Initially they spread their welcome table on counters in the lobby of the Detention Center, but arbitrary enforcement of building rules forced these allies to move their food service to whatever church hosted the Moral Monday briefing and press conference.

Volunteers also provided transportation to the church and/or to arrestees' cars after their release. State Senator Earline Parmon waited at the Detention Center each week until the last arrestee was released. She thanked each one personally for his or her participation. Supporters were on the job with this gift of presence as late as 5:00 a.m. on Tuesday mornings. Many arrestees volunteered in similar capacities on Moral Mondays subsequent to their arrests.

On this particular Monday, as the three jail buses took the witnesses away, a thousand voices chanted:

Thank you. We Love You.

And they added a new line to their chants:

You're Gonna Need Another Bus, Cause Baby, There Are More of Us!

A beautiful song flowed from the talented singer who helped a thousand people join the Moral Monday Choir:

My mind is made up
I'm on my way up
Gonna hold my head up
Walking on in love!

The next Monday fell on Memorial Day, so the NC NAACP decided to undertake a back-breaking, soul-searching 26-county Forward Together Organizing Tour. The aim was to spread the bad news about the extremist rollbacks happening in Raleigh and the good news of 158 nonviolent soldiers and thousands of supporters who had started fighting back immediately. Everywhere the tour went, people were urged to attend Mega Moral Monday when the extremists returned to their cruel rule on June 3.

❝I said earlier that I'm just leaving Mississippi after spending time with the National Board of the NAACP and with Myrlie Evers, the widow of Medgar Evers. And to think that 50 years ago there was a Movement in Mississippi and a Movement in Birmingham trying to push this nation forward. And in many ways, fighting to bring many of the rights we are fighting to hold onto.

The foundation of a true democracy—and more importantly, a wholesome society—is equal protection under the law. That's our focus today as we go to the General Assembly. Now this foundation, this principle of equal protection under the law, is as old as any picture of righteousness or justice in the Scripture. Throughout the Bible, there are warnings against unequal protection, and the Scriptures call for affirmative action to ensure equal protection.

It seems strange to us that our ultraconservative brothers and sisters, who lead the General Assembly now, always make great claims about faith and the Holy Word. And yet they seem to either deliberately dismiss from their cries of morality, or are ignorant of, the existence of the call for justice that is the primary call throughout the Scriptures. Their great claims and calls for moral principle are accompanied by silence on the moral call for equal protection, and on Scripture's clear concern for the poor and the vulnerable among us. This is, my friends, a dangerous denial and a gross form of political and religious hypocrisy.

The primary framework of the Bible is clear. Matthew 25:37-40 (NIV) says:

> *"Then the righteous will answer him, 'Lord, when did we see you hungry and feed you, or thirsty and give you something to drink? When did we see you a stranger and invite you in, or needing clothes and clothe you? When did we see you sick or in prison and go to visit you?'*

"The King will reply, 'Truly I tell you, whatever you did for one of the least of these brothers and sisters of mine, you did for me.'"

Isaiah 10:1-2 speaks of this call for equal protection when it says in The Message:

Doom to you who legislate evil, who make laws that make victims,
Laws that make misery for the poor, that rob my destitute people of
   dignity,
Exploiting defenseless widows, taking advantage of homeless children.

The primary moral framework of our state and federal Constitutions speaks to equal protection under the law. NO person shall be denied equal protection under the law. NO person shall be subjected to discrimination by the state because of race, color, religion, or national origin.

When our state Constitution was written 145 years ago, coming fresh out of the Civil War, black and white leaders joining together in a North Carolina Fusion Movement had enough sense to understand that equal protection under the law must be at the heart of any democracy. And in that same year, the federal framers of the United States Constitution decided that there needed to be an amendment, the 14th Amendment. Section 1 of that amendment says:

All persons born or naturalized in the United States, and subject to the jurisdiction thereof, are citizens of the United States and of the State wherein they reside. No State shall make or enforce any law which shall abridge the privileges or immunities of citizens of the United States; nor shall any State deprive any person of life, liberty, or property, without due process of law; nor deny to any person within its jurisdiction the equal protection of the laws.

So when people wonder why we gather, why we protest, they need to understand that what faces North Carolina is a deep moral question and a deep constitutional question. The question before us is: *Does a political supermajority give you the authority to violate the fundamental principles of the Bible and our Constitution?* That's the question before us. Equal protection is at the heart of what our democracy is supposed to be, and it must guide how those elected to serve should engage when they enact public policy. But instead of honoring the principle of equal protection, here in North Carolina we are seeing full retreat from these noble ideals. And a fast march backward toward as much inequality, and unequal treatment, as people will allow. And we are here to say: *We will not allow it, and we will not go backward!*

We are a state with 1.6 million poor people, and six hundred thousand of them are children. Thousands more can't find work or do not make a living wage. Upwards of 25 percent of North Carolinians don't have health insurance. In the face of all this, the legislature denies funds through the Affordable Care Act, refusing the federal offer of Medicaid funds for up to five hundred thousand poor North Carolinians who have no health insurance. And then after denying it, these legislators seek to privatize the delivery of Medicaid services so that fat cats can make more money off the misery of the poor.

When we see this, we know that this is cruel and unusual punishment and a fundamental denial of equal protection under the law; these actions are morally indefensible and constitutionally inconsistent.

When this leadership takes unemployment benefits from one hundred sixty-five thousand North Carolinians, (black, white, Latinos, Republicans, Democrats, Independents), and the governor gives a raise to his staff and says that these unemployment insurance cuts are a necessary evil, we recognize that this is cruel and unusual punishment, and a fundamental denial of equal protection under the law. It is morally indefensible and constitutionally inconsistent.

When this leadership raises taxes on nine hundred thousand working people by ending the state earned income tax credit for poor and working poor, so that we can give a tax cut on 23 millionaires—that, my friends, is cruel and unusual punishment, and a fundamental denial of equal protection under the law.

When this leadership wants to cut personal and corporate income tax on the wealthy in a state that ranks 13th among states in the highest percentage of population living in poverty, this is morally indefensible and constitutionally inconsistent.

They ran a campaign on lowering taxes! And now they want to expand the sales tax on food, on haircuts and hairdos, on medications, and on a host of other items and services that will raise taxes on working people—not just black people but all working people, black people and white people, and poor people, and Latino people, and those in urban areas, and those in the country.

When those who are wealthy sell working poor white people the fire of race discrimination and sell them on things that rev them up—like pretending that there is no integrity in our voting process or claiming that if you support the Racial Justice Act, you're gonna release criminals—they get folk mad and on the side of those who vote for ultraconservatives. But then once they get in office, these same politicians hurt the very working people they stirred up with their fearmongering. And it's time for ALL North Carolinians to wake up, whether you are red, black, yellow, or white. It's time to WAKE UP! WAKE UP! WAKE UP! WAKE UP! WAKE UP! WAKE UP! WAKE UP!

The truth of the matter is as old as what Dr. King said years ago: *We're either going to go forward together, or we're going to fall headlong backwards.*

This leadership crew last year removed over a billion dollars from public education and now is making plans to implement a voucher plan to hand out public money to private schools! This will increase resegregation and will force the poor into ghettoized schools for minorities and poor white children. And further, they want to reduce the eligibility of preschool for poor children, denying access to more than three hundred thousand young children. This is cruel! It's unusual! It's mean! It's extreme! And it's a denial of equal protection under the law!

When this leadership wants to restart executions and repeal the Racial Justice Act that has exposed the racially discriminatory application of the death penalty, it is cruel and unusual punishment, a denial of equal protection. This leadership wants to codify anti-labor language in our state Constitution and deny workers collective bargaining rights and participation in the wealth they make for others. They want to deny workers, white and black, decent healthcare and decent benefits and decent retirement. This is a fundamental affront to equal protection under the law!

And after doing so much damage, this leadership wants to roll back early voting, ban Sunday voting, end same-day registration, impose an unneeded poll tax, and add a voter ID that will affect five hundred thousand North Carolinians. When they want the people who have been incarcerated to wait five years, and then have to apply to a local board of election to get the rights back that were guaranteed to them since 1870; when they want to charge parents $22,500 in lost dependent tax breaks if their child votes at school rather than back at home, this is draconian!

I don't normally do this in public, but y'all can print this one: All week long I was in Mississippi, and the folk down in Mississippi had one question (I know we're in a church, but they asked it in a church): *What the hell is wrong in North Carolina?*

This is why we are engaged and why we feel, with justified discontent and righteous indignation, that this leadership wants to make our state a place of even deeper stratification and inequality. Their actions are not accidental or naïve; they're premeditated and planned. They are following the playbook of ALEC (American Legislative Exchange Council), the playbook of Civitas, the playbook of the John Locke Foundation, the playbook of the Koch brothers. But they didn't know that we were going to get in the game and stop the play!

We are in the fight now because this is in fact no trifling game. Real people's lives will be affected. Don't try to make this about black and white; this is about right and wrong! This is about justice and injustice!

They are driving us down a road backward with Old South politics, extremist politics. These are George Wallace types with their 21st-century version of interposition and nullification of equal protection laws. And as someone said years ago in Gettysburg: *We've got to make sure the government of the people and by the people is NEVER wiped away from the face of this Earth.* So if you thought you had a fight a month ago, you ain't seen nothing yet! NOTHING! We fight together!

They are making it harder for poor and working people and those who get sick to get healthcare. They are making it harder for children to get education. They are making it harder for the incarcerated to be redeemed. They are making it harder for people to vote. And then they are trying to make it easier for the wealthy to get wealthier, for the sick to get sicker, for the private schools to flourish, and to implement a flawed death penalty. And on top of all that, they are trying to make it easier to carry around guns into schools and bars and parks!

But we who walk by faith have a word. We have decided to be steadfast and unmovable, always abounding in the work of the Lord. You might have a supermajority, but we read somewhere that when you're right, one can chase a thousand, and two can put ten thousand away. You must not know who we are; we are those who were spoken of in the book of Hebrews when it says:

We do not belong to those who shrink back and are destroyed, but to those who have faith and are saved (10:39 NIV).. *Now faith is the substance of things hoped for, the evidence of things not seen*
HEBREWS 11:1 NKJV

We know that we are not afraid. The Lord is our life and our salvation. We shall not be moved, like a tree planted by the water. We shall not be moved!

5

"EDUCATION, ECONOMIC JUSTICE, AND VOTING RIGHTS"

MORAL MONDAY RALLIES 5 AND 12

Moral Monday 5
June 3, 2013
Arrestees: 155

Teachers turn out in record numbers to protest cuts to public education
(Eric Preston photo)

You know that we are in a battle for the ballot.
A war, a struggle, a clash of ideals and ideologies between a
regressive desire to take us backward and the progressive agenda that
desires to keep us moving forward toward the more perfect union.

This chapter includes the background and rally speeches for two Moral Mondays.
Between these two dates, the United States Supreme Court, in its June 25

41

Shelby v. Holder decision, sent a signal to regressive legislatures in the South and beyond that the federal Voting Rights Act would no longer require the oversight of "preclearance" before these legislatures would be allowed to change voting laws. This decision, bitterly opposed by four dissenting justices and civil rights advocates across the country, opened the door to a disastrous voter-suppression bill in North Carolina. Therefore the powerful Moral Monday 12 speech by Rev. Barber on voting rights is included here to amplify the concerns of Moral Monday 5.

BACKGROUND on MORAL MONDAY 5

After the two-week Memorial Day break, the fifth Moral Monday on June 3 promised to be big. The authorities asked the NC NAACP to move our stage and sound system to the rear of the People's House in a grassy plaza they call Halifax Mall. They were worried about the growing number of people attending Moral Mondays.

The NC NAACP was not pleased with the government's attempt to control where the people could exercise our rights to assemble peacefully and petition the same government. But as the afternoon progressed, organizers went with the new location. The planning service had to be moved from Davie Street Presbyterian Church to the larger sanctuary of Martin Street Baptist Church, pastored by Rev. Dr. Earl Johnson, to accommodate the numbers of people who had decided to be moral witnesses. The Movement was getting organized.

Former witnesses, who knew firsthand the long waits for the jail bus and up to six more hours in jail, brought snacks and water for those who might get arrested. Seventy-five green armbands for the witnesses were made, but double that number were needed in the end. Volunteers ripped each armband lengthwise in half to make 150—just enough for those who wanted to be moral witnesses against the cruel policies of the extremists. A rented bus made loops to drop people off at Halifax Mall. Martin Street Church's large sanctuary was packed. The spirit of justice and love took over the crowd, as singers led (and taught) anthems of the Civil Rights Movement of the '60s to the several hundred congregants. Organizers and attorneys briefed people on what might happen at the General Assembly. Pastors prayed for the human race. Rev. Barber gave the history of the Movement and his vision for where it was going.

When the 155 witnesses, proudly wearing their green armbands, entered the Halifax Mall, over three thousand supporters were there to welcome them. The brief program began, featuring short statements of support from community organizers, LGBTQ rights advocates, immigrants, labor leaders, and clergy. The president of the largest local union in the world, George Gresham of Service Employees International Union (SEIU) 1199, joined the witnesses to stand in solidarity with all North Carolinians.

The main themes were education, economic justice, and voting rights. The Forward Together Moral Movement—multi-issue and multiracial—presented a colorful creative counterpoint to the handful of extremist senators and representatives who, with some trepidation, made their way from the Legislative Office Building across the bridge to meet with their fellow ideologues in the backrooms of the People's House.

If they had listened, they would have heard noted national farm worker organizer Baldemar Velásquez remind the state before his arrest:

> Coming from the rural areas of North Carolina, some of the hardest working people in our state are our brothers and sisters in the immigration farm worker camps. We're here to tell our legislators they cannot say no to immigration reform.

They would have heard a woman say: *I'm a grandmother. I'm a voter. I'm here to tell you—I'm furious!*

If the extremists had taken a moment to listen to Rev. Barber's blessing of the 155 witnesses, they would have heard the answer to what they no doubt were wondering: *When will you stop?* As it was, Rev. Barber shared his response to the crowd, and media gathered instead:

> Somebody asked, When will you stop? I told them they don't need to ask us when we'll stop. Ask Tillis, Berger, and the Governor: When will they stop? When will they stop hurting children? When will they stop hurting the sick? When will they stop hurting our public schools? When will they stop hurting the economy? If they stop, then we'll stop! But we can't stop as long as people are getting hurt. We can't stop while children are being denied, as long as voting rights are being attacked. Our foreparents didn't stop. Those who died to make this nation free, they didn't stop. So we're going to walk Forward Together, as long as there is strength in our bodies and hope in our souls. We're going to walk Forward Together until justice is established and the common good is a reality.

The rally ended with a prayer and sustained chanting of our slogan: Forward Together . . . Not One Step Back. Then the supporters set up two lines and the 155 witnesses proudly walked through the glad gauntlet to the locked golden doors in the rotunda of the People's House.

Supporters waited until dawn for the last of the 155 witnesses to be released from the Wake County Detention Center. Volunteer attorneys and NC NAACP interns from NC Central University's and Campbell University's law schools processed those arrested. (Over 120 volunteer attorneys have stayed with this Movement throughout adjudication of the cases of all the arrested witnesses.) Other supporters stayed at the jail parking lot with donated food and drinks until the last witness, a pastor from Winston-Salem, was released at five in the morning.

JUNE 25, 2013
SHELBY CO. V. HOLDER SUPREME COURT DECISION
OPENED THE DOOR FOR STATE VOTER SUPPRESSION LAWS
In April 2010, Shelby County, Alabama (a largely white suburb of Birmingham) filed suit in federal court in Washington, DC asking that Section 5 of the Voting Rights Act be declared unconstitutional. Shelby County, Alabama v. Holder, No. 1:10-cv-00651 (D.D.C.).
Section 5 was originally enacted in 1965, and has proved itself to be one of the important provisions of what often has been called the most effective civil rights law enacted by Congress. Congress initially provided that Section 5 was to terminate after five years; however, Congress repeatedly has renewed Section 5, after finding that there is a continuing need for its protections.

The county asserted that Congress exceeded its constitutional authority when, in 2006, it reauthorized Section 5 for another 25 years.

On June 25, 2013, the Supreme Court ruled that the coverage formula reauthorized by Congress was unconstitutional. Section 5 requires that certain states and localities, located primarily in the South and Southwest, obtain federal preclearance for all voting changes before they may be implemented. To obtain preclearance, a jurisdiction must demonstrate that the change neither has a discriminatory purpose nor a discriminatory effect.

In its 5-4 decision, the Supreme Court held that Section 4 of the Voting Rights Act, which establishes the formula that determines which jurisdictions must comply with Section 5 preclearance, is unconstitutional and can no longer be used. In the majority opinion, Chief Justice Roberts wrote: *We issue no holding on [Section] 5 itself, only on the coverage formula. Congress may draft another formula based on current conditions.*[1]

❝First of all, let me just say, y'all look mighty good. Let me also say that God has a way of showing us some powerful, prophetic metaphors. So God let it rain. In Africa, rain is a sign of blessing. But rain is also a sign of cleansing and truly, there needs to be some cleansing in that legislative house back there! And then, despite the forecast, God let the sun come out. And maybe that is a sign that what they thought they were going to do in the darkness has been brought to the marvelous light.

We're here today because of the three pillars of our democracy: economic justice, voting rights, and educational equality. There are some principles so dear, so noble, and so true that they are to guide our public life, no matter what party holds office, no matter how much money has been spent, no matter what is your faith or your creed. They are as old as the Constitution and as sacred as the Scriptures of many faiths. Those principles in our Constitution are that we hold it to be self-evident that all persons are created equal and endowed by their Creator with certain inalienable rights, among which are life, liberty, the enjoyment of the fruits of their own labor, and the pursuit of happiness. And all political power comes from the people, and should only be used for the good of the whole.

In the Scriptures it is clear that to do justice and love mercy and walk humbly before God is a sacred principle. The Bible says: *Woe to those who make unjust laws . . . to deprive the poor of their rights* (Isaiah 10:1-2 NIV). And Jesus long ago in Matthew 25 said that everybody would be judged by this standard: *When I was hungry, did you feed me; when I was naked, did you cloth me; when I was sick, did you see about me?* If I were to contemporize that, I would say: When I was sick, did you give me healthcare; when I was hungry, did you help me have a job; when I was wrongfully in prison, did you fix the system? And then he said: Inasmuch as you've done it to the least of these, you've done it unto me.

These principles are constitutional values. Say: *Constitutional.*
And moral values. Crowd: *And moral values.*

And these values are elevated far above the confines and characterization of liberal versus conservative, and white versus black, and Republican versus Democrat. These principles—the good of the whole, doing justice, and loving your neighbor—should be at the heart of our body politic. But instead of a forward agenda, rooted in our deepest values, this crowd has turned a deaf ear to the more noble causes. They have resisted the angels of our better nature. They have closed their eyes to the history of the South and the battles that we have already fought and won. They have ignored the key goal of governing, which is the good of the whole. And that's why we have come together–black, white, Hispanic, young, old, gay, straight, people of faith, people of labor–to call this General Assembly to a better way. And we must stand up and we must wake up, right here and right now!

In a state like North Carolina, in the South:

Touch your neighbor and say: *We're in the South.* Crowd: *We're in the South.*
Tell the media, this ain't Wisconsin. Crowd: *This ain't Wisconsin.*
This is the South. Crowd: *This is the South.*
Where justice was hammered out! Crowd: *Where justice was hammered out.*
Where freedom was hammered out. Crowd: *Where freedom was hammered out.*
This is the South. Crowd: *This is the South.*

Our Southern state of North Carolina ranks 13th in the nation for the number of our people in poverty. That's 1.46 million poor people; six hundred thousand children–black children, white children, and Latino children–go to bed every night without eating. We have seen veterans living under bridges and families living in the woods! We have counties where the poverty rate has been over 20 percent for 30 years! We have the fifth highest unemployment rate in the country. Given this dreadful state of affairs, it is extreme and immoral to raise taxes on nine hundred thousand working-class people so you can give a tax cut to 23 of the wealthiest families in the state! It is extreme!

Say: *It is extreme.* Crowd: *It is extreme.*
And immoral. Crowd: *And immoral.*

It's extreme and immoral to boost an ultraconservative social agenda by using wedge issues like gay marriage to lure in poor and working people, then when elected to use their power to hurt these very same people by denying healthcare and unemployment insurance and voting rights! Somebody better wake the heaven up! Tell your neighbors:

Somebody. Crowd: *Somebody.*
Better wake the heaven up! Crowd: *Better wake the heaven up.*

It's disturbing what's going on. When you cut taxes on corporations and personal income tax, and then raise sales tax and make people pay for hairdos and haircuts and food and prescription drugs, something's wrong with that! It's deeply disturbing when you cut money from education and you save $700 million for your already wealthy friends. When you take a billion dollars out of the budget, undermine our ability to fund education and to fund infrastructure; when you refuse millions of dollars for Medicaid and rather folk be sick, then, well, something is wrong!

Crowd: *Something is wrong.*

Something is wrong when you love money that much. Something is wrong when you hate your brothers that much. Something is wrong when you are that drunk with power. For the love of money, people will steal from their mothers. For the love of money, people will lie, won't they? Won't they cheat? For the love of money, people don't care who they hurt or who they beat. For the love of money. Somebody tell your legislator:

Somebody may have bought you. Crowd: *Somebody may have bought you.*

But they ain't bought us! Crowd: *They ain't bought us.*

Last year the extremists in their misleadership, chopped over a billion dollars from education.

Say: *A billion.* Crowd: *A billion.*

And now they're making plans to defund education further. We were already at 47th in the nation in teacher pay; now they have drawn us to 49th. Now they want to give vouchers to private schools, creating more resegregation, ghettoized schools. They want to allocate that voucher money; and then they want to be the ones who build these new private schools. So they make money hand over foot! But they're not even reading the news. The Louisiana Supreme Court has already ruled that you can't give vouchers, tax dollars, to private schools. That, according to their state Constitution, using state tax dollars for private school vouchers is unconstitutional. And our state Constitution has been around 145 years and is stronger than Louisiana's.

These extremists on Jones Street are even hurting our smallest children. When they reduce eligibility to preschool for poor children, denying more than thirty thousand of them access to preschool, adding that number to the twenty thousand preschoolers already on a waiting list, that's cruel, that's unusual, that's mean, that's extreme, that's immoral, and it is time for somebody to wake up!

> Crowd: *Wake up.*
> *Stand up.* Crowd: *Stand up.*
> *Wake up.* Crowd: *Wake up.*
> *Stand up.* Crowd: *Stand up.*
> *Wake up.* Crowd: *Wake up.*
> *And speak up.* Crowd: *And speak up.*

And so here we are. Now my friends in the back, listen up: To be clear, this is why we're engaged. Nobody's coming up here for fun. Nobody likes being arrested and taken off in handcuffs. But we believe we have a constitutional right, as it says in Article 1, Section 12 of our North Carolina Constitution, to instruct our legislators. And we are doing that publicly, as is our right. Our state Constitution says secret societies are dangerous. But they meet in secret with ALEC! They meet in secret with Civitas! They meet in secret with the John Locke Foundation and with high-paid lobbyists! So according to the Constitution, they ought to arrest themselves and leave us the hell alone!

But even if they won't arrest themselves, we protest, because this set of legislators wants to make our state a place of deeper stratification. This policy of theirs is not accidental or naïve; it is premeditated. They are driving us down a road backward. This is Old South politics. This is like George Wallace standing in the schoolhouse door to block opportunity for citizens of his own state. These Old South throwbacks are using the same tools as the segregationists did back in the day: interposition and nullification. They want to nullify the Affordable Care Act, so they won't accept Medicaid expansion money that came from the pockets of people right here in North Carolina! They are making it harder for poor and working people.

> Touch your neighbor and say: *They are making it harder.* Crowd:
>   *They are making it harder.*
> *For the sick to get healthcare.* Crowd: *For the sick to get healthcare.*
> *They are making it harder.* Crowd: *They are making it harder.*
> *For children to get an education.* Crowd: *For children to get an*
>   *education.*

Harder. Crowd: *Harder.*
To attract jobs to our state. Crowd: *To attract jobs to our state.*
Harder. Crowd: *Harder.*
For the unemployed. Crowd: *For the unemployed.*
To get jobs. Crowd: *To get jobs.*
Harder. Crowd: *Harder.*
For people to vote. Crowd: *For people to vote.*

But then they want to make it easier for the wealthy to get wealthier, the sick to get sicker, private schools to flourish, businesses to get big tax breaks, and to implement a flawed death penalty, and on top of all of that, they want to make it easier to get guns.

I need to say something to you today, so you understand the moment we are in. This is not even about Republican or Democrat. No, moderate Republicans and Democrats of the past supported voting, supported economic justice, supported public education. It was Democrats and Republicans together who put together the North Carolina Rural Economic Development Fund. This crowd has zeroed that fund out in their destructive budget. This is the politics of extremism. This is the politics of classism. This is the politics of racism. Driven by the strategies of ALEC. Some of the folks in there are high on Koch:

K-O-C-H! Help me, Jesus. Some of them in there are intoxicated with tea of the Tea Party that has been spiked with racism and injustice. This is a takeover. This is an attempt to turn back. But it won't work. The people are awake now. And we have decided to stand up.

Somebody asked me the question; I think it was one of the media, one of my good friends. They said: *When will you stop?* Well, that's a question for them. Don't ask us when we'll stop. Ask Tillis and Berger and the man in the governor's mansion when will they stop! When will they stop hurting children? When will they stop hurting the sick? When will they stop hurting our public schools? When will they stop hurting our economy? Because if they stop, we'll stop. But we can't stop as long as people are being hurt. We can't stop as long as children are being denied education and preschool, as long as voting rights are being attacked; we can't stop.

Our foreparents didn't stop. Those who died to make this country free, they didn't stop. And so, if you want to know how long we are going to walk forward together, we are going to walk forward together as long as there is life in our bodies and hope in our spirit! We are going to walk forward together until justice is established, and the common good is a reality. We are going to walk forward together until we see a change come. We are going to walk forward together until valleys of despair are exalted, until places of crooked politics get straightened out, until mountains of oppression are brought down. We are going to walk forward together until:

> Somebody say: *Until.* Crowd: *Until.*
> *The lion lies down with the lamb.* Crowd: *The lion lies down with the lamb.*
> *Until.* Crowd: *Until.*
> *We all hold hands together.* Crowd: *We all hold hands together.*
> *Until.* Crowd: *Until.*
> *Black and white.* Crowd: *Black and white.*
> *Brown and black.* Crowd: *Brown and black.*
> *Gay and straight.* Crowd: *Gay and straight.*
> *People of faith.* Crowd: *People of faith.*
> *And labor.* Crowd: *And labor.*

We are going to work together and go forward until love is lifted, until justice is realized, until the Beloved Community comes into being. Don't ask us to stop because stopping is not in our DNA! Stopping is not in our vocabulary! We are a Movement! We move One Step Forward, Not One Step Back! We move One Step Forward until:

> God's dream is realized!
> Everybody is blessed!
> Everybody is taken care of!
> Everybody is lifted!
> Every child is educated!
> Every sick person is well!

I don't know about you; but I intend to stay UNTIL! And there ain't nobody, nobody, gonna stop us now!

Moral Monday 12
July 22, 2013
Arrestees: 73

BACKGROUND on MORAL MONDAY 12

After June 25, when the United States Supreme Court, by a 5-4 decision, gutted the crown jewel of the Civil Rights Movement, the Voting Rights Act of 1965, North Carolina legislative leaders went back to the drawing board. Now they could throw every voter-suppression idea imaginable into one bill. One legislator let the cat out of the bag, bragging about how the *headache* of the Voting Rights Act was finally gone. Extreme legislators rejoiced that they no longer had to hide their efforts to suppress votes. A leader of the North Carolina Republican Party in the western part of the state said it plainly on national television: the whole idea was to stop lazy blacks from voting.

On July 22, while the state Senate was considering their kitchen-sink voter-suppression bill, the NC NAACP and the Forward Together Moral Movement gathered on the grass behind the People's House for the Twelfth Moral Monday of 2013. A student leader spoke to the thousands gathered:

> *The North Carolina General Assembly is attacking one of the pillars of democracy in this state by proposing their new Voter ID law. This new bill makes it so no college IDs are acceptable. It is clear the General Assembly is scared of students in this state!*

One of the NAACP's most respected warriors and leaders, First Vice President Carolyn Coleman, reminded the gathering that many people had died fighting for the right to vote.

> *You can kill a man, but you can't kill an idea.*

Rev. Barber spoke directly to the Tillis-Berger faction inside:

> *We are going to pray for you while we fight you. But we're gonna win!*

Then Rev. Barber turned toward the people who had put on their armbands and were preparing to walk through the glad gauntlet, across the bridge and into the rotunda to bear witness against the immoral work inside. He said:

> Whenever you're in the struggle for justice, don't ever forget you have a cosmic companion. We've got to know that when our backs are against the wall, we've got some help from another corner. We've got some help from another region. We've got some help from a higher source. That's how we keep on fighting. We're going to stand in the promises of God. We're going to stand in the promises of the truth. I heard the word that said: "If God is with you, it doesn't matter if the whole world is against you." One can chase a thousand. Two can put ten thousand to flight. I wish someone would put their hands in the air and say: "It ain't over! It ain't over 'til God says it's over!" Say it with me:
>
> ### We're Not Going Back!

A dozen Moral Mondays had taken place since April 29 when 17 brave souls walked up the stairs to the rotunda in the middle of the People's House and tried to instruct their representatives at the General Assembly. All the 17 had to go on was their own moral compasses, their ethical beliefs—that the life of every human being is sacred and worthy of care.

The small number of supporters at the first Moral Monday had grown to over five thousand for each of the final weeks. When 73 more people, led by the North Carolina Association of Educators president Rodney Ellis, tried to petition their representatives peaceably in the People's House, only to be handcuffed and arrested, the total number of moral witnesses who had been arrested had reached 945.

The supermajority, super-conservative legislators packed up and went home later that week. But the Forward Together Moral Movement was just getting started. The largest Moral Monday in Raleigh was being planned for the following week.

On July 24, after the Senate passed the monster voter-suppression bill, a group of young people went to Speaker Tillis's office and remained there for a sit-in until he would hear their concerns. They asked to meet with him to discuss the voting bill with them before he brought it to the floor in the house. He had six young people arrested, bringing the total arrested since April 29 to 951.

❝You know that we are in a battle for the ballot. A war, a struggle, a clash of ideals and ideologies between a regressive desire to take us backward and the progressive agenda that desires to keep us moving forward toward the more perfect union. And if we ever needed the right to vote protected, we need it right now. One of our founders of the NAACP, W.E.B. DuBois, said of the vote that the power of the ballot we need in sheer defense. What else will save us from a second slavery? Without the full access to the ballot, we become slaves to the rule of money. Without access to the ballot, we become slaves to the rule of political meanness. Without the access to the ballot, we become slaves to the manipulation of extremism.

Last night in the wee hours, though this legislature says they don't like Sunday voting, they passed a budget on Sunday that's mean, a budget that helps the greedy, hurts the needy. They passed this budget on Sunday, a day we are supposed to remember grace, love, fairness, and justice. A budget full of voodoo economics and trickle-down failed policy that hurts teachers and hurts public education and hurts the poor and hurts the working poor. And they passed it under the cover of darkness on the Lord's Day.

But the Lord has snatched the covers off, and we can see what they are doing. And now that they've done all of these extreme things, they want to suppress the vote so that we will be slaves to their decisions, without citizens having the ability to register their discontent at the ballot box. When politicians try to suppress and subvert the right to vote, they desecrate the entire struggle for the vote to be in the hands of all people.

Touch your neighbor and say: *We know history.* Crowd: *We know history.*

The history of voting here in America is one in which our Constitution guaranteed the vote only to property-owning white men. This meant that only 16 percent of the nation's population had the right to vote. When we started this nation, even white men, if they were poor or owned no land, were not allowed to vote. The history of voting is one in which the 15th Amendment guaranteeing the right to vote to African American men and all men came only after 250 years of slavery and a bloody Civil War, and then it took another 50 years for black and white women of other races to be given the right to vote.

The right to vote is sacred and it is personal. Even after the 15th Amendment was ratified, this right had to be guarded against the attacks of Jim Crow, poll taxes, literacy tests, lynching, and the brutality of the Klan. To protect the right to vote, lawyers had to fight against the arguments of "separate but equal." To protect the right to vote, Dr. King marched, not just in 1963, but in 1957, three years after Brown versus Board of Education. He said then that all types of conniving methods were still being used to prevent Negroes from becoming registered voters. To get the right to vote, people like Medgar Evers; Schwerner, Chaney, and Goodman; a white woman named Viola Liuzzo; and many others had to die. To get the right to vote, National Guard troops had to come out. To get the right to vote, people had to march. The Voting Rights Act had to be passed to insure the enforcement of what had been passed in the 15th Amendment 95 years earlier. Black people and minorities are the only people in this country for whom the right to vote took not only a constitutional amendment but also another law to ensure the enforcement of the people's constitutional right. And when the Voting Right Act was passed, only one Republican (these Republican extremists today don't even know who they are) voted against the Voting Rights Act, and his name was Strom Thurmond.

One hundred eleven Republicans voted for the Voting Rights Act. This crowd on Jones Street doesn't even know their own history. This crowd, they are not Republicans or Democrats—they are extremists.

My own father had two master's degrees in 1960, and he did not have the protected right to vote when he came back to the South. This right is sacred. This right is personal. And our fight is just not political; it's personal.

For the sisters, all the women raise your hands. For the women, the right to vote started in Seneca Falls in 1848. And I don't know if you know it, but on July 15, 1848, Frederick Douglass, the former slave and abolitionist, joined Elizabeth Cady Stanton and the other women at Seneca Falls and endorsed the Seneca Falls Declaration. Don't let them make you think that black and white folk just started coming together to fight for what is right. And at the Seneca Falls convention, one of the resolutions resolved was that it was the duty of women of this county to secure for themselves the sacred right to vote. But after that declaration, it would take 72 years for Congress to ratify the 19th Amendment guaranteeing all American women the right to vote. And many who started the fight were dead by the time victory came in 1920.

Touch your neighbor and just say: *This right is sacred.* Crowd:
    This right is sacred.
And this fight is personal. Crowd: *This fight is personal.*

And young people didn't get the right to vote until nearly two hundred years after the founding of this country. Not until after young blood was shed in Vietnam. Only then could people under the age of 21 vote. Even though they had died in every war this country's ever fought. It was on July 5, 1971, that Richard Nixon, of all people (I told you, these Republicans don't know who they are. When they try to stop students from voting, they are going against their own history) signed the 26th Amendment, that allowed those 18 years or older to vote.

> Somebody say: *The right to vote.* Crowd: *The right to vote.*
> *Is sacred.* Crowd: *Is sacred.*
> *And this fight.* Crowd: *And this fight.*
> *Is personal.* Crowd: *Is personal.*

So we are not just standing out here in this broiling sun today just for fun. The right to vote has come from many dangerous roads of sacrifice. And that sacrifice is why any group of politicians who want to suppress the right to vote in any way is engaging in a crime against democracy. And we will fight them to maintain our sacred right to vote at any time, any place, anywhere.

Every attempt by Speaker Tillis, Senate leader Burger, Governor McCrory, and their band of merry men and women to suppress the right to vote is a crime against democracy. Every time they lie and spew untrue propaganda to the people of North Carolina about voting and voter fraud, it's a crime against democracy. When Senator Apodaca describes the Voting Rights Act as a headache, he's committing a form of dangerous disrespect against the fundamental principle of American democracy. He sounds like Strom Thurmond or George Wallace or somebody. He needs to get his head fixed and his heart regulated. Because he's thinking like he's in the 19th century.

> When you try to rig elections and deny people a free and unfettered right to vote, it's a crime against democracy.

> When you fear voters, and that makes you attempt to deny the vote for your own political advantage, that's a crime against democracy.

> When you desecrate the lives, and the struggle, and the memories of all those who fought for the right to vote, it is a crime against democracy.

When you deny health insurance to the sick and unemployment benefits to workers and raise taxes on the poor and working poor, and then you implement voodoo economics, and you try to deny public education to low-wealth communities, and after you do all that, then you want to deny the right to vote? You want to pass a voter ID that is worse than the ones even in Alabama, South Carolina, Georgia, and Indiana. And then you want to scale back and eliminate early voting and same-day registration and Sunday voting, so folk will have to endure long lines like they had in Florida and get discouraged and go home. You want to decrease and suppress voter participation, and you want to rule by default, then you want to draw racially motivated redistricting maps that segregate black voters and disallow black and white people and Latino voters from coming together to elect candidates of their choice. That's a crime against democracy! And we must fight back!

Tell somebody: *We must fight back.* Crowd: *We must fight back.*
Say it again: *We must fight back.* Crowd: *We must fight back.*

Because if we do not have the ballot, money wins.

Somebody in this crowd ought to say: *We are not for sale.*
Crowd: *We are not for sale.*

Maybe Tillis is for sale; maybe McCrory is for sale; maybe Burger is for sale. But WE are not for sale!

We've got to fight back. And I stopped by to tell you that this is no time to be calm, cool, and amenable. This is no time to accept things. We've been through too much. We learned too much. We've seen too many battles. We've waged too many struggles. It's on now. You thought it was on when you cut unemployment. It's really on now. When you mess with the right to vote, you mess with the heart of our democracy. When you mess with the right to vote, you desecrate the graves and the blood of the martyrs.

And so we need to let them know: *You think you've seen a fight, but you ain't seen nothing yet!* We will fight over the right to vote, oh yes, we will; because nobody gave us the right to vote. Our grandmamas cried for it. Our grandfathers died for it. Our parents sacrificed for it. Our soldiers died for it. And our young people bled for it. And if you think we are going to allow any group of politicians to take or suppress the right to vote without a fight, you must be out of your doggone minds! No, we will fight for the full unabridged, unfettered, unhindered, undenied right to vote and not only will we fight, we're going to win. Because the 14th Amendment still guarantees equal protection under the law. We're going to win. The 15th Amendment still says you can't deny or abridge the right to vote. We're going to win. The 24th Amendment says you can't make me pay a poll tax to vote. We're going to win. Our Constitution says that all elections must be free. We're going to win. Our state Constitution says that the only qualification for voters is that they be 18, born or naturalized in these United States. We're going to win. We've never had to test some of this before in the court because we've never had a legislature since the 19th century that was foolish enough to vote against the Constitution. But because you get so crazy, we're going to help you get some sense. We're going to win. We're going to test everything they do in the courts. And we are going to fight either because we went through it or because we heard Mickey Michaux and Dr. Turner talk about it. We know what racism looks like. We know what suppression looks like. We know what it smells like. We know how it walks, no matter how it is wrapped up. And so every obstacle they try to put up, we will overcome. Because this right to vote and the fight for it is not just political; it's personal.

Somebody shout: *It's personal.* Crowd: *It's personal.*

The whole world can see through your lies, legislature. The whole world can see through your lies about voter fraud and voter integrity. Twenty million votes cast and only one instance of fraud was found, and you claim you are protecting the integrity of the vote! I said at the church, *at least you should be like Jesse Helms, at least he was bold enough to be honest.* But instead of being honest about their pedigree from the Old South, you instead try to play around and try to come up with cute ways to make what is wrong seem right. We know what you are up to. Maybe you are stuck in the 19th century, but we're not. Maybe you are stuck in Jim Crow and the Old South, but we're not. And we have come to serve notice that we will unleash every political, legal, and moral strategy that we can to create the New South. We will not go back.

The more you try to suppress the right to vote, the more we will register and vote. You can't stop the people. We will win. You can't stop the flow of democracy. You can't take government of the people, by the people, from the people. You can't stop truth. You can't stop justice. You can't stop right. We will rise up. It's on now.

Our best lawyers will fight you. Our best organizers will fight you. Our best preachers will declare the truth. Our best rabbis will tell the story. But we will not go back. We've come too far; we stand on the shoulders of the martyrs. We've been baptized in the blood of those who have gone before us. We won't go back. We walk in the power of the God of justice. We move in the spirit of the Lord of righteousness. This land is our land. North Carolina will be a state where the weak grow strong and the strong grow great. All elections will be free.

You cannot suppress our right to vote. And you may ask yourselves: *How are we going to win?* And you've got the temporary votes right now. I'm going to tell you how we are going to win. Because we are reading a different history book. We might not win every vote, but we are going to win the battle, because when I look back at how we got over, Lord, help me here, our parents won with less than we have today.

With less, they beat slavery. I wish I had a witness here.
With less, they beat Jim Crow.
With less, they beat lynching.
With less, they beat the Ku Klux Klan.
With less, Harriett Tubman got five hundred out of slavery.

She didn't have email. She didn't have Twitter. She didn't have textbooks. She didn't have a car. All she had was faith in God. Trust in God when she had epilepsy. She had a .38 pistol on her side. She had moss on the north side of a tree and the North Star in the middle of the night. If she could win then, surely we're going to win now!

Thurgood Marshall beat the Supreme Court. He had less than we have.
Martin Luther King beat racism. He had less than we have.
Nelson Mandela beat apartheid when he had less than we have.

So we will beat you! Oh, you might win a vote. You might gloat for a season. But it does not matter what you do; we are going to win ultimately. Because we are going to use our voices to speak truth to power. We are going to use our feet to march for justice. We are going to use our hands to write our choices at the ballot box. We are going to use our pulpits to sound the alarm. We are going to use our organizations to get the people together. We are going to turn loose our lawyers in the courts. We are going to trust God in everything we do. We are going to pray for you while we fight you. But we're going to win. You may try to stop the people; but it won't work. You may tell lies, but it won't work. Your distortions will be exposed. Your efforts will come to naught.

And so turn to your neighbor and say, *Let us not despair.*
Crowd: *Let us not despair.*

I use to hear my daddy say before he died: *Whenever you are in the struggle for justice, don't ever forget you have a cosmic companion.* I know some of you struggle with that thought, and that's okay, our brothers and sisters, but some of us have been through enough hell that we've got to know there is a God in heaven. We've got to know that when our backs are against the wall, we've got some help from another quarter. We've got some help from another region. We've got some help from a higher source. That's how we keep fighting. Moses beat Pharaoh because God showed up. David beat Goliath because God showed up. Jesus beat death because God showed up. What they mean for evil will be turned to good because God has shown up. No weapon formed against us will prosper because God is with us. The Lord is our light and our salvation. Whom shall we fear? We are going to stand in the promises of God. We are going to stand in the promise of the truth. The Lord is with us.

I need somebody that knows the word and worth of prayer to say: *The Lord is with us.*
Crowd: *The Lord is with us.*
We've been here before. Crowd: *We've been here before.*
But God has always shown up. Crowd: *But God has always shown up.*
And made a way. Crowd: *And made a way.*
Somehow through the storm. Crowd: *Somehow through the storm.*
We're going to make it. Crowd: *We're going to make it.*
Somehow. Crowd: *Somehow.*
Through this crazy legislature, we're going to make it. Crowd: *We're going to make it.*
Somehow. Crowd: *Somehow.*
Through this money, we're going to make it. Crowd: *We're going to make it.*

I heard a word that when God is with you, it does not matter if the whole world is against you. One can change a thousand. Two can put ten thousand to flight.

Would somebody lift your hands and say: *I believe.* Crowd: *I believe.*
Say: *It ain't over.* Crowd: *It ain't over.*
It ain't over. Crowd: *It ain't over.*
Until God says it's over! Crowd: *Until God says it's over.*
We're going forward.

And there is one thing that we are not going to do. We're not going back!

Barber and crowd: *We are not going back.*
We are not going back. We are not, we are not!
We are not going back!
We are not going back!
We are not going back!
We are not going back!

6

"LABOR, WOMEN, AND ECONOMIC JUSTICE"

MORAL MONDAY RALLY 8

June 24, 2013
Arrestees: 121

Longtime national labor leader Roz Pelles, Interim Executive
Director, North Carolina NAACP *(Phil Fonville photo)*

For us, this is bigger than Democrat or Republican;
for us, this is bigger than liberal versus conservative;
for us, this is about what is right and what is wrong.

BACKGROUND

The eighth Moral Monday came a week before the extremists' law that stripped seventy thousand North Carolina families of their federally granted long-term unemployment insurance went into effect. The ideologues argued that jobless people were lazy. The ideologues conveniently overlooked the historical fact that the Great Recession was caused by millionaire speculators' gambling and greed. The ideologues had convinced themselves that if the seventy thousand were stripped of their insurance, they would become so desperate they would work for slave wages. Men and women who had lost their jobs because of the Recession refuted these arguments. They took to the Moral Monday stage to describe their desperate circumstances and dared legislators to come to Moral Mondays and listen.

At the same time their policies were having a devastating effect on working families, the extremists unleashed a new set of ideologically driven policies against women's right to control their bodies. Hundreds of women dressed in pink joined the NC NAACP and the Forward Together Moral Movement on this day, creating a living testimony of the power of reaching across false divisions and building friendships and political alliances. Dozens joined the other people who had announced at the planning service that they were ready to be arrested, if necessary, to bear witness to their opposition to the immoral policies of the extremists. In all, 121 new people came forward wanting to stand for the rights of the poor, women, and those who had been pushed to the margins of our society.

From the sound stage on Halifax Mall, Rev. Barber told the thousands gathered that afternoon:

> No single policy proposed by this General Assembly would have alone produced the outpouring of thousands upon thousands coming to the People's House to witness and stand in defense of the poor in North Carolina. But this legislature and the governor overreached, and they overreached rapidly. Yet in doing so, they gave people of faith and people of goodwill a gift of insight. They exposed and solidified our common purpose.

Rev. Barber introduced to the crowd the 92-year-old Movement icon, Rosanell Eaton. As she began talking, the often-talkative crowd became respectfully quiet. People who were greeting old and new friends

Labor leaders Saladin Muhammad, Ajamu Dillahunt, and Angaza Laughinghouse with Sauuda Eshe in Legislative Building *(Eric Preston photo)*

stopped to hear her—our Rosa Parks, our Sojourner Truth. She told the story of how she was forced to recite the preamble of the U.S. Constitution before the county Board of Elections would allow her to vote—70 years ago. She led the thousands in the Moral Monday cheer:

Forward Together   Not One Step Back!

James Andrews, president of the North Carolina AFL-CIO, walked through the glad gauntlet to the People's House and spoke to the crowds in the rotunda and the balcony just before he was handcuffed and taken off to jail. He helped connect the women's rights and the labor rights movements as a common struggle for human dignity in an economic system that values some bodies and certain types of work over others. Mr. Andrews led the 121 witnesses and the hundreds of other supporters who crowded into the rotunda in the Labor Movement's anthem, "Solidarity Forever."

Outside, in front of thousands of supporters waiting for the moral witnesses to leave on buses, a dozen runners from the Tobacco Trail Church were fulfilling their vow to run around the People's House seven times, as in the biblical story of Jericho, to show their support for the burgeoning Movement.

It was becoming clearer each week that all of our issues intersected and that the Fusion Movement demanded continuing mutual support across formerly separate interest areas and organizations. You could feel the energy rising despite the oppressive summer heat.

❝❝Today, on this Moral Monday, our focus is on labor and workers' rights and treating the unemployed right. And also our focus is on women's rights. But I want you to know and all those who gather, wherever you are, that in North Carolina we've come together–black, white, Hispanic and Native American, poor, wealthy, people of faith, labor, and young and old–to fight against the dangerous agenda of extremist laws by the ultraconservative Tea Party right wing. For us, this is bigger than Democrat or Republican; for us, this is bigger than liberal versus conservative; for us, this is about what is right and what is wrong.

The reality is, it is extreme. It's immoral. It's an attack on democracy. And it is just wrong to make it impossible for some and harder for others to vote. It's just wrong. It's an attack on democracy. It's just wrong because you cannot just arbitrarily cut Medicaid for more than five hundred thousand people, and many of them are children.

It's extreme. It's immoral. It's an attack on democracy. It's just wrong to raise taxes on nine hundred thousand poor and working people in order to cut taxes for 23 wealthy families. It's just wrong. It's wrong to raise taxes on 95 percent of North Carolinians, create flat taxes which allow the wealthy to pay less and the working poor to pay more, just so you can give a tiny percentage of the people a tax break. It's just wrong.

It's extreme, and it's immoral, and it is an attack on democracy. It is just wrong to cut unemployment benefits and end them altogether for one hundred seventy thousand people who have lost their jobs through no fault of their own.

It is extreme, immoral, and wrong to resegregate our schools and to defund and deconstruct public education, and to kick thirty thousand low-income children from preschool programs that research has proven can help them get a leg up in society. It's just wrong. It's wrong to set up a system where you can sell judges to the highest bidder. And it is wrong to knowingly allow the racial bias to exist in the court system.

Somebody shout: *It's just wrong!* Crowd: *It's just wrong.*
It's extreme. Crowd: *It's extreme.*
It's an attack on democracy. Crowd: *It's an attack on democracy.*

And that is why we are praying. That's why we are demonstrating. That's why we are engaging in direct-action civil disobedience, risking arrest to stop the immoral, extreme policies that are being modeled here. The governor and the current leaders of our legislature want North Carolina, for the past 50 years known as a progressive Southern state, to be seen across the nation as a crucible for their extremist Tea Party policies. They want to show that if they can do it here, they can spread their platform across the rest of the South. But it must stop here, and it must stop now.

We have to look at public policy through the moral lens of justice for all and the constitutional principle of the common good. So we created here a Movement, not a Moment. Moral Monday didn't just spontaneously grow up. It grows out of organizing that has been going on with our Historic Thousands on Jones Street annual marches to the People's House by the People's Coalition. These HKonJ rallies have called both Democrats and Republican leaders to accountability for the common good and our 14-Point People's Agenda.

Our concern is the moral fabric of our society. It's about a deep vision of society that says we must look at two guiding stars. The first is our state and national Constitutions, with their insistence on the common good, the good of the whole, and establishing equal justice under the law. And the second guiding star comes from the best of all our moral and ethical traditions, loving your neighbor and doing justice. It is from these two perspectives that the public policy ought to be developed.

And so in North Carolina, I know the ones in charge now don't like us being together to proclaim these two guiding stars of our constitutional rights and the demand for love and justice from our many united faith traditions. But there ain't no changing us now!

You can't push people but so hard. You can't push people down but so much. After a while, folk stand up. And we're here to stand up, because the greatest myth of our time is the notion that some of our ultraconservative friends suggest: that if you cut certain programs, you're going to hurt only certain people. And so they use racial code words to claim that we must cut *entitlements*, and take needed healthcare and educational and unemployment benefit programs away from people who do not deserve it, i.e., black people, i.e., Latino people, i.e., poor white people.

What we've got to do is unpack the truth. The truth is that when you cut Medicaid and cut unemployment and raise taxes on the working poor and the poor, you hurt everybody. You hurt white people. You hurt black people. You hurt Latino people. You hurt everybody. You hurt the whole society.

We're not wrong; we're right. We're right because the Constitution of our United States says: *We the People of the United States, in Order to form a more perfect Union, establish Justice, insure domestic Tranquility, provide for the common defense, promote the general Welfare, and secure the Blessings of Liberty to ourselves and our Posterity.*

We're not wrong; we're right. We're right because the North Carolina Constitution says in Article 1: *We hold it to be self-evident that all persons are created equal; that they are endowed by their Creator with certain inalienable rights; that among these are life, liberty, the enjoyment of the fruits of their own labor, and the pursuit of happiness.*

We're not wrong; we're right. Section 2 of Article 1 of our North Carolina Constitution, which concerns the sovereignty of the people, says: *All political power is vested in and derived from the people; all government of right originates from the people, is founded upon their will only, and is instituted solely for the good of the whole.* We're not wrong; we're right.

And I keep telling my conservative friends, when they want to put their hands on a Bible and read parts of it and push an agenda while they hide the rest of it, that they are ignoring the Bible's main moral concerns for the widow, the orphan, the poor. But there are some folks in this crowd who KNOW what the Book says.

Do I have a witness here? Crowd: *Yes!*

We know we are right; because the Book says in James 5:1-4 (*The Message*):

A final word to you arrogant rich: Take some lessons in lament. You'll need buckets for the tears when the crash comes upon you. Your money is corrupt and your fine clothes stink. Your greedy luxuries are a cancer in your gut, destroying your life from within. . . . All the workers you've exploited and cheated cry out for judgment. The groans of the workers you used and abused are a roar in the ears of the Master Avenger.

We know what the Book says. Isaiah 58 gets to the point. If you want to know what God is interested in, break the chains of injustice, get rid of exploitation in the workplace, free the oppressed, cancel the crushing burden of debt, share your food with the hungry, invite the homeless into your house, put clothes on the naked. Do this and the lights will turn on. Do this and your nation will turn around. Do this and righteousness will prepare your way. Do this and God will hear your prayers. Do this and you shall be called repairers of the breach. Do this, and when you call, God will answer.

Tell somebody: *We're not wrong.* Crowd: *We're not wrong.*
We're right. Crowd: *We're right.*

Because treating people with loving care is always right. Doing justice is always right. Making the world better is always right. It doesn't matter what the critics say; we're right. It doesn't matter how many times they call us outsiders; we're right. Because we are outsiders. Oh yeah, we're outsiders. We're outside the politics of meanness, but we're inside the politics of love and the politics of Jesus.

Tell your neighbor: *We're right.* Crowd: *We're right.*

It doesn't matter how many times they paste our mug shots from our arrests all over the Internet. They can do that if they want to, but we know we're right. And that's why we are going to keep right on standing, keep right on marching, keep right on coming, keep right on gathering, keep right on praying, keep right on demanding. North Carolina, you ain't seen nothing yet!

It would have been better for them to leave us alone; but we're awake now. We know what is happening now. We're on the move now. We're in the game now. We ain't going away now.

Am I right about it? Crowd: *Yes!*
Am I right about it? Crowd: *Yes!*

7

"UNITED FOR WOMEN"

MORAL MONDAY RALLY 11
(MONDAY AFTER THE TRAYVON MARTIN CASE VERDICT)

July 15, 2013
Arrestees: 98

North Carolina NAACP's Mother Carolyn Coleman *(Eric Preston photo)*

But the reality is that in this country, all great Movements
have happened because there was a deep moral center.
And a center based on constitutional values.

BACKGROUND

When you strike a woman, you strike a rock! Those were the words of South African women when the apartheid government forced them to carry an ID card restricting where they could live, where they could work, and where they could be. Tea Party extremists in the North Carolina General

Assembly struck the same rock when they tried to restrict the rights of North Carolina women to control their own bodies by passing a sneak amendment to an unrelated bill about motorcycle safety after midnight on Sunday. Their midnight amendment not only struck a rock but it opened the floodgates of women's resistance to the far right's agenda. But this alliance between women's rights and NAACP priorities was not new.

Many in the women's Movement had been with and in the NC NAACP for a long time. A Planned Parenthood leader said at the rally:

> Don't believe for a minute that we are here just because of their sneak attack last week. We have been here every week. We know that when you work on suppressing the vote, you hurt women. Sixty-six percent of eligible voters without a photo ID are women. And when you eliminate unemployment benefits, you hurt women. Over thirty thousand women lost their unemployment benefits last Monday. So we know what's at stake.

But the midnight motorcycle amendments energized thousands of new protestors. To harness and focus these newly energized people, women leaders asked the NC NAACP to focus its next Moral Monday, on July 15, on Women's Rights. NC NAACP President Barber readily agreed and told them that he and other leaders from the State Conference would be in Orlando, Florida, for the National NAACP Convention in Orlando that week.

On Saturday night, July 13, 2013, a Florida jury found George Zimmerman not guilty of the murder of Trayvon Martin. As were many Americans, the national NAACP leaders, including Rev. Barber, were mightily angry and discouraged. Rev. Barber has a 17-year-old son— the same age as Trayvon. He found it difficult to explain the decision to his son. After staying up all night Saturday discussing the decision with the young NAACP activists, Rev. Barber decided he wanted to return to North Carolina and attend the women's Moral Monday, to emphasize women's goals and to share his parental concerns at this particular historical moment.

The rally leaders invited him to join them on the stage before one of the largest gatherings ever seen on Halifax Mall. Rev. Barber spoke about how hurtful the Zimmerman verdict was to every parent and how he decided to come back to be a part of the hope and love of Moral Mondays. The large crowd was quiet, experiencing a breakthrough in understanding the universality of human problems as they struggled for justice, wondering, how can we all raise our kids and heal the racial and gender divisions in our societies? The answer was there—in the midst of the large, loving sea of humanity.

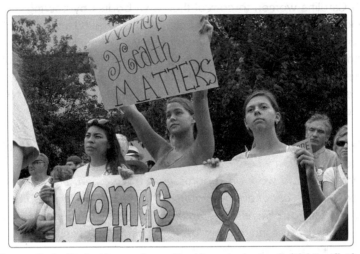

Women rally for Medicaid expansion and healthcare justice for all *(Phil Fonville photo)*

The women's rights messages were about the struggles of poor and working women. They spoke to every woman and man who was there or who watched the gathering on television and the internet. The 98 people—mainly women—who risked arrest trying to instruct and petition their representatives made a powerful witness. A mountain woman told the supporters packed in the rotunda, just before being handcuffed:

> *My brother and I cannot find work. We just lost our unemployment checks. My niece and nephew are disabled and are losing their Medicaid insurance.*

She stopped for a moment and then asked the haunting question: *What are we supposed to do? Then she was taken off to jail.*

Rev. Barber returned to Florida the next morning, working with national civil rights leaders seeking an answer to the mountain woman's question. The women's leaders talked in jail, and they talked the next day and every day since, trying to answer the mountain woman's question. All who were there were pushed to a higher ground, trying to answer her prayer:

> *What are we supposed to do?*
> *What are we supposed to do?*

"Thank you all for being here today. Turn to your neighbors and just bless them by putting your hands on them and telling them, *I am so glad to be at Moral Monday with you today.*

I want to say something from the outset because the longer something goes on, the more clarity and direction you may have to give. Some of the signs I see out there are inappropriate for this gathering. This is Moral Monday. We don't have to curse people to be right. We don't have to call people animals to be right. When you are in a Moral Movement, you hope that your enemies will become your friends. This is a rally based on our moral faith, but that does not mean we're anti-anybody. We preach to people of faith, people wrestling with faith, and people who've lost their faith. I have struggled with my own faith over time. But the reality is that in this country, all great Movements have happened because there was a deep moral center. And a center based on constitutional values. And so we come as a people of prayer; we come recognizing all faiths. But I also have learned that never again will we allow the so-called *right* to define the most important moral categories in the public square.

This Moral Monday is dedicated to women's rights. It's dedicated not just to a particular issue or bill but more broadly to women raising their voices and putting their bodies in action against all of the extreme immoral policies and decisions of the current leadership of our governor, our House speaker, and the Senate leader.

Nobody made the sisters come today. Nobody made them stand up. And we must be careful, particularly because the media are here and because we've read some reports where the media said that it's the anti-abortion bill that snuck through the Senate that made the women show up. A group of men who've never been pregnant tried to ram through some legislation. Our opponents are saying the only reason thousands of sisters have joined our Movement is because they are temporarily upset with their abortion-restriction bill that was cut, pasted, and emailed to them by their national right-wing allies called ALEC: A-L-E-C, the American Legislative Exchange Council.

But the truth is, when we started the HKonJ People's Assemblies seven years ago, women were there and in the center of the leadership. All the sisters who've been in HKonJ, raise your hands. Look all around. When we brought nearly eighteen thousand people to the seat of state government this year for the People's Assembly to bring our concerns, women were at the center of that leadership. When we started Moral Mondays, the women were at the front lines. In fact,

I walked in there with Barbara Zelter, my sister. And for those of us who know the Book called the Bible, women have always been there. There were women who took on Pharaoh. There was a woman named Deborah in the Hebrew tradition who led when the men were too scared! A woman preached the first resurrection sermon. My Momma is a woman, and she has been fighting all her life.

So get the story right, my friends in the media. The sisters have been here in the spirit of Susan B. Anthony, who said: *Cautious and careful people always casting about to preserve their reputation or social status can never bring about reform.* The sisters are here in the spirit of Marian Wright Edelman, who said: *My faith has been the driving thing of my life, and I think it is important that people who are perceived as liberals not be afraid of talking about moral and community values.* The sisters have been here in the spirit of Eleanor Roosevelt, who said: *Nobody can make you feel inferior without your consent, so don't ever give it.*

The sisters are here, the sisters have been here, and the sisters are here to stay. And it's a pro-choice decision. Nobody told them to come. They chose to say NO to extremists. They chose to say NO to the attacks on our children. They are choosing to say NO to the attacks on education and attacks on the sick and attacks on the poor and attacks on voting rights. They are here by choice because the sisters in this crowd are the real pro-life advocates in our state and in our nation.

You see, our opponents, their strategy is always one of division. They want us to think we live in silos, not communities, not the Beloved Community, not as human beings. The idea of community to us is the notion of we. The idea of community to them is us *versus them.* That's their strategy—division along lines of race and class. They've tried, and it's worked for a long time in the South especially, but a change has come.

No longer will we be divided. We're all connected, all tied together. We care about the common good, the good of the whole. We are determined to love our neighbor and to promote the general welfare. A change has come.

So I stop by this evening, not to speak for the sisters, but to stand in solidarity as we say to the extremists: *You don't get it.*

Say that with me: *You just don't get it.* Crowd: *You just don't get it!*

We've been having weekly camp meetings down here at Halifax Mall. We're learning afresh how to be human beings, how to act like God's children. We're all the human family. We don't come into the human community and then start fighting among ourselves. We're trying to figure out how we work together, and so we come here every Monday to say:

> You mess with the poor, you mess with all people. We care about justice.
>
> If you mess with voting rights, you mess with all people who care about justice.
>
> If you mess with education, you mess with all people who care about justice.
>
> If you mess with labor rights, you mess with all people who care about justice.
>
> And when you mess with women's health, you mess with ALL people who care about justice.

We come here because we are our brothers' AND our sisters' keeper. DON'T TOUCH my sisters' rights. Because when you mess with them, you're messing with all of us! I didn't have any physical sisters, but I got a whole lot out here, so when you mess with them, you mess with me. When you mess with one sister, you actually unify us and bring us together.

But there is a larger, more strategic reason we gather here today. The reason is this: That when black and white and Latino and Native people and people of faith and gay and straight people and women and old and young people begin working to repair the breach in God's human family, we are powerful! When we refuse to let the dividers divide us and deprive us, when we refuse to let them do their dirty work on God's human family in the dark, and when we come together to glorify our diversity and creativity, all things are possible, if only we believe!

That's why hundreds of women of all colors have gone to jail over the last 10 weeks. Our sisters tell us that when they get put in jail, they come out more committed and more unified.

Now let me be personal for a minute and tell you why I came back to this rally even though I had planned to stay out of town today for the NAACP national convention. In case you don't know, the NAACP is a 104-year-old organization that started out fighting against the peculiar form of Southern "justice," lynching–the murder of black men for no reason other than that they're black. The NAACP's first major campaign was to stop this lynching. W.E.B. DuBois, our first national director, and our first chair, a white woman, Mary White Overton, would hang a poster out of the NAACP office in New York each day, announcing the number of black men who were just lynched. Soon there were massive marches and civil disobedience against this form of domestic terrorism. It took many years, but finally, without one black legislator being in the Congress, the NAACP won the passage of an anti-lynching bill. They won because they dared in the public square to raise the moral issue of lynching.

Let me be personal and somewhat vulnerable for a moment. I was in my hotel room on Saturday night for the convention with one of my three sons. My sons are tall, big boys, strong boys. I carry my children with me as much as I can because I want them to learn what I'm learning every day about humanity. And I need them to know why their father's on the road all the time.

This past Saturday night, I was only 30 miles down the road from a Florida town named Sanford when the verdict came down about the murder of Trayvon Martin. After two days of talking among themselves, the jury in this Florida trial decided that Mr. Zimmerman—who had concealed weapons and who had stalked and killed Trayvon Martin, a young man in a hoodie—was not guilty of anything. He was declared not guilty of second degree murder, not guilty of manslaughter. Mr. Zimmerman was upset by Trayvon's looks. He profiled this child with curse words that you can hear on the 911 tape. He engaged Trayvon, got him in a confrontation somehow, and took it upon himself to dispense some Southern justice somehow. Now, my friends, I'm a preacher, and I'm a civil rights man, and God knows I work hard to be nonviolent. And I ask for God's help. I've tried to follow all the rules of society. I've got three degrees from the best universities in this country. I have a wonderful church. I help run a community development corporation. I hope to have some grandchildren one of these days. I turn 50 in August, two days after the 50th anniversary of the 1963 March on Washington.

But when I learned—I'm just letting y'all be my family for a minute—how the wheels of Southern justice have allowed this lynching of an unarmed young man, who had left his father's home to get a bag of candy and was walking back home, I got sick. When Trayvon Martin caught Mr. Zimmerman's eye, the next thing we know, Mr. Zimmerman shot and killed him. It hurt. I was angry, mad, and depressed all at the same time. My first thought was the safety of my three sons. One was back in North Carolina, but two were with me, and I cried, worrying about them.

I knew that if Emmett Till had tried to fight back against the men who dragged him out of his house in Mississippi in 1955, those men would have argued under the current law that they had killed that child in self-defense. Southern justice would have winked and said: *Yes, the murderers had a right to stand their ground.*

Now I'm on the national leadership team of the NAACP, and I knew that the collective wisdom and history of our organization would think it through when we all settled down. But I was hurting. And last night, we heard our chairwoman preacher, Roslyn Brock, say to thousands and to the nation: *In 1955, a young man in Money, Mississippi, went to the store to buy some candy, and 57 years later, another black man in Sanford, Florida, did the same thing, and both trips led to murder. It wasn't right in 1955, and it isn't right in 2012.* And then she said, *But we shall not be moved,* and she talked about how the young people had gathered together and decided to start a petition calling on the Justice Department to open a civil-rights case. And we now have word that they have, too.

But also, we decided that we would mount a campaign to repeal Stand Your Ground laws all over this country. And then we decided that we would mount a campaign to pass anti-racial profiling laws all over this country. And this must be about black and white, not about black, because the precedent they have set up now is if a white kid was in a community that happened to be predominantly black, and someone black profiled him as a thug, that person could then engage him, get in a fight, shoot him, kill him, and then claim self-defense. We want Stand Your Ground laws banned for everybody. And our young people and others at this national NAACP convention decided to channel our anger into a plan that whether we are on the South Side of Chicago or in Goldsboro, North Carolina, or in a gated community in Sanford, we must end gun violence. We must stop the violence.

And so I left the convention floor last night and went back to my room and cut on the TV. I had to watch my oldest boy well up in tears and grab his fists, because when we happened to turn the TV on, it was on Fox, and he heard the Fox commentator make this statement: *Trayvon is not a hero; he was a young man whose life ended way too soon because he decided to confront a man he believed was showing him disrespect.* My son turned to me and said, *Dad,* with tears in his eyes. I could see the tears and the anger. He said: *Dad, they want to emasculate us all. They want to take our voting rights. They want to hurt the poor. They want to take away education. Then they want to even take away the ability for us to defend ourselves.*

And then I thought about how this legislature we are confronting has gone gun crazy. Right here they are passing bills that will allow concealed weapons on college campuses, in bars and restaurants where they serve alcohol, and wherever there are assemblies, parades, or funerals. They want freedom to use guns more than they want citizens to express ourselves in the People's House!

And the one thing that became clear to me through the hurt and the anger that I was feeling last night for the low value that the racialized Southern culture places on black life, is that I needed to come home to talk to my other kids, and I needed to be here with you all at this Moral Monday. Because when you are hurting, you need to be around some people who still believe in the possibility of our being one people united together.

So as this is the Moral Monday about women and sisters, I asked them if they would be willing to let me come back home and testify today. In my tradition, you don't just testify when you're feeling good. You testify when you're hurting, and you say to somebody who knows the words and the worth of prayer, *Pray for me.*

So I ask you all here, in a week when it seems like our young people don't matter: *Pray for me.* When we devalue life in the midst of this race-hating and class-baiting legislature and policies: *Pray for me.* Last night and today I didn't need to be around that anemic faith preached in far too many houses of worship that remains disconnected to the cause of justice; I needed to come to church on Moral Monday! I needed to be back here today for my own personal renewal! I know some of y'all that clapped at me, but today, I needed you, because we ALL need a Movement that keeps us centered in the midst of the shifting Earth beneath us.

WE NEED A MOVEMENT that can somehow keep our eyes open in the midst of the ugly realities of meanness and injustice. When Trayvon dies, we all die a little.

I came back from Florida this morning to be with you all at this women's Moral Monday for three reasons. Number One: to honor our sisters, and to tell every one of you women here: *We love you, we are with you, and when they mess with you, they mess with us, and we will never go back.* Number Two: I came to tell you that people all over the country are applauding your work here in North Carolina. Everywhere I have gone this year, folks from all 50 states were talking about Moral Mondays, and many of them were talking about doing Moral Mondays in their own states!

But I also came back for reason Number Three, to say to all of us: *Let's stand our ground.* This is our ground. This is sacred ground! THIS IS JUSTICE GROUND! THIS IS FREEDOM'S GROUND! THIS

IS DOING RIGHT'S GROUND! This is where we are working to repair the breach in God's human family. Tell anyone who would try to malign us rather than answer our moral critique, anyone who would force and ram through immoral and extreme legislation, this message: *You might be able to pass this mess now, but you can't break our spirit!* NO! Sometimes we do get discouraged, but then the Holy Spirit comes! Then we get around each other and it REVIVES our souls again. We stand on our ground.

We understand what Coretta Scott King meant when she said: *Poverty produces a kind of violence.* A starving child is violence. Suppressing people is violence. Neglecting school children is violence. Discriminating against working people is violence. Ghettos are a form of violence. Ignoring healthcare is violence. Even the lack of willpower to help your fellow brother or sister is a form of violence.

So we need a Movement that doesn't ask what is Republican or what is Democrat, but rather asks: *What is right?* We will stand our ground. We need a Movement that troubles the conscience of this nation and troubles the conscience of this state. We will stand our ground. We need a Movement that stands in the vision of this prayer attributed to Saint Francis:

> *May God bless you with discomfort at easy answers, hard hearts, half-truths, and superficial relationships.*
> *May God bless you so that you may live from deep within your heart where God's Spirit dwells.*
> *May God bless you with anger at injustice, oppression, and exploitation of people.*
> *May God bless you so that you may work for justice, freedom, and peace.*
> *May God bless you with tears to shed for those who suffer from pain, rejection, starvation, and war.*
> *May God bless you so that you may reach out your hand to comfort them and turn their pain into joy.*

We need a Movement that will tell us to stand our ground. We need a Movement that calls the people to go back to their communities and turn on the light of truth. We will stand our ground. We need a Movement that stands against violence without being violent, and that stands against meanness without being mean and that stands against hate without being hateful. A Movement that stands against injustice without being unjust, and stands against destruction without being destructive, and stands against those who do not care without becoming uncaring. We need a Movement that stands against evil without being evil ourselves. We need a Movement where people still believe in a more perfect union, who believe in justice, and who will stand our ground.

And so I just came back to say: *Thank you sisters.* Thank you for letting this country preacher testify so I can properly minister to my own sons; and so that I won't lose the hope in the midst of the fight. And thank you today, for being modern-day Esthers. The biblical Esther lived in ancient times of bad public policy and sinister schemes of rulers against her kinfolk. Nevertheless, she decided to be brave and to stand her ground to defend her people.

Somebody say: *We must stand our ground.* Crowd: *We must stand our ground.*

Yeah, we gotta love each other. We must stand our ground! Crowd: *We must stand our ground.*

We've got to fight for the poor. We MUST stand our ground! Crowd: *WE MUST STAND OUR GROUND!*

And fight for education. WE MUST STAND OUR GROUND! Crowd: *WE MUST STAND OUR GROUND!*

And fight for the sick to have healthcare. WE MUST STAND OUR GROUND! Crowd: *WE MUST STAND OUR GROUND!*

And fight for labor rights and the unemployed. WE MUST STAND OUR GROUND! Crowd: *WE MUST STAND OUR GROUND!*

And fight for voting rights. WE MUST STAND OUR GROUND! Crowd: *WE MUST STAND OUR GROUND!*

I believe when I look at you out there that we will stand our ground. WE HAVE TO STAND OUR GROUND! WE MUST STAND OUR GROUND! AND LIKE A TREE PLANTED BY THE WATER, WE SHALL NOT BE MOVED! WE SHALL NOT BE MOVED! WE SHALL NOT BE MOVED! STAND YOUR GROUND!

8

"THIS IS THE DAY"

MORAL MONDAY RALLY 13

July 29, 2013
[No civil disobedience]

North Carolina NAACP's Public Policy and Legal Coordinator Jamie
Phillips-Cole and Field Secretary Rob Stephens *(Phil Fonville photo)*

This is the day that we believe there is still a better way.
All our children can be educated.

All of our sick can have health insurance.
All of our workers can be protected. The poor can be lifted.

And all people, regardless of who they are, can be loved and accepted.

BACKGROUND

A few days after the last legislator went back to his or her home district, having wreaked havoc on poor and working people's lives across North Carolina, the Forward Together/Moral Monday Movement had the last word. The 13th Moral Monday had two hundred times more participants than when the first 17 people and their supporters walked into the People's House to directly petition their representatives for redress of their grievances.

Led by many of the same people of faith—although this time the faith leadership swelled at the front of the march—a flock of over ten thousand joined Rev. Barber on this day. They marched from the back of the empty People's House, South on Salisbury Street to well past the Capitol, and then worked their way back up Fayetteville Street for a giant rally outside the State Capitol.

Inspired by their North Carolina Association of Educators (NCAE) leaders, who had been arrested the week before for peacefully petitioning at the General Assembly, hundreds of NCAE members and their fellow teachers—all wearing bright red shirts—were conspicuous in the throng of old and new activists on the beautiful summer evening. The extremists' policies toward public school teachers could not have been crueler. They passed, and Gov. McCrory signed, anti-education laws that included:

Ending teacher tenure, thus punishing our most experienced teachers;

Stripping incentives for newer teachers to improve their skills and knowledge by earning graduate degrees;

Loosening accountability for scores of new charter schools, and thus siphoning off higher-income students and much-needed funds from our struggling public schools;

Refusing to give even the tiniest raise to teachers for the fifth straight year, dropping North Carolina to 46th in teacher pay in the nation, and 50th in the amount teacher pay had increased over the past decade.

Just before they returned to their home districts, extremists rammed through the most restrictive voter-suppression bill in the nation. The bill included:

Moral Monday Rally 13 served as a sort of dress rehearsal for the Mass Moral March in Raleigh on February 8, 2014. Above, news media and thousands of marchers attend the Mass Moral March. *(Phil Fonville photo)*

Cutting a week from early voting time;

Cutting same-day voter registration;

Forcing the elderly and others without driver's licenses to spend time and their already stretched resources to gather the documents needed to go to the DMV and obtain a photo ID;

Stopping pre-registration of 16 and 17-year olds at high schools;

A profusion of other provisions designed to suppress minority voting.

This Moral Monday on the Fayetteville Street Mall in front of the Capitol was a dress rehearsal for the combined eighth annual Historic Thousands on Jones Street /Moral March on Raleigh set for February 8, 2014. Rev. Barber and other NC NAACP leaders spelled out the Next Steps for the Movement from August 2013 through February 2014:

1. We would take Moral Mondays on the road, and the legislators who thought they could get away from the people (and the voters) in Raleigh were going to have to deal with local Moral Mondays in their own home counties.

2. We would hire buses to take people to Washington for the 50th anniversary of the 1963 March on Washington that would be held on the Saturday before the actual anniversary on August 28.

3. We would put our main energy into following Dr. King's advice 50 years ago and bring the Movement back home. We would bring

it to the Sandhills of North Carolina, to her foothills, her mountains, and to her impoverished black belt and coastal plains. *In short,* said Rev. Barber, *big rallies in D.C. are fine, but for the real social change, we must organize at the courthouse levels.* So on August 28, we would organize 13 simultaneous protests in the 13 US Congressional Districts to honor Dr. King's instructions.

4. The NC NAACP would file a major lawsuit to stop the race-based voter-suppression bill before it took effect. The multiracial Forward Together Movement was just getting started, and everyone could be proud of the Movement built by that summer.

Rev. Barber used this occasion to recapitulate the history of struggle in the nation, and to bolster the crowd to press on, to seize the day, to maintain their hope.

With the teachers in their red shirts; the diverse men and women of faith bringing their mission of love and justice to thousands of people on the street; the thousands of black, white, and Latino working families soaking in the fellowship of the summer evening; and the fresh marching orders, there was a unified spirit. We chanted *Forward Together* again and again and *Not One Step Back* again and again. People hummed freedom songs as they walked away.

———

Sometimes, my brothers and sisters, we must look back from whence we have come to understand how we must stand and fight in the current moment. A hundred and forty-five years ago, at the end of a brutal Civil War, blacks and whites coming out of the ugly and dehumanizing vestiges of slavery came together to imagine a new South and to build a new world. Together they began to forge a new faith in a new kind of South and society, and to be a new kind of people. Together they envisioned a new North Carolina.

Together, black and white, they guaranteed public education. Together, they guaranteed equal protection and fairness in the courts and free and fair and unrestricted elections for all males regardless of race or income. This occurred right here in North Carolina one hundred years before the Civil Rights Movement. A hundred and forty-five years ago, they dreamed of a world where we would work together and stand together and educate our children together.

Why do we gather as people of faith? Because people of faith drove this vision of unity as the 1868 North Carolina Constitution was formed. Two pastors in particular were at the center of forging this vision and empowering this dream. One of them was an African American preacher, the Rev. J.W. Hood. The other was a white Congregationalist named Reverend Samuel Ashley.

But you should know, my friends, that though this vision of justice and fairness was noble, and though togetherness and unity are great things, enemies abounded then like they abound now. Wherever there are those who want to move forward, there are always those who despise moving forward. They would rather live in the darkness of inequality, the darkness of injustice and inhumanity toward others. For economic gain they push to preserve their privileges built on the pain of others. For every move forward, there's always been a fight to push backward.

So what did these forces of inequality do 145 years ago? They formed an immoral strategy they called the Redeemers Movement. Sounds like something good, doesn't it, but as my grandfather once said, not everyone who says "Lord, Lord" is with the Lord! They called it the Redeemers Movement, but underneath it was a devilish movement because the foundation of that movement was to redeem the South from what they saw as the sinful influence of black and white and brown working together as equals and using that unity power to influence politics! They fought to go back to strict white supremacy by forming terrorist groups like the Red Shirts and the Ku Klux Klan, paramilitary groups of men who hid under masks to intimidate and keep blacks and whites and Jews and Catholics from working together. They fought to go back by changing election laws and rigging elections. They fought to go back by working to stack the courts so activist judges would roll back the power of the new constitutional rights represented by the 14th Amendment and the 15th Amendment. And then after they cheated, they used their power to pull federal troops out of the South in 1877, so that those who wanted to go backward would have no force to stop them, and those desiring to go forward would have no force to protect them.

They fought to go back by going to the United States Supreme Court in 1896 to win the infamous Plessy versus Ferguson case in which the Klan's notion of "separate but equal" was declared constitutional. Out of the entire Supreme Court, only one justice, a white justice from Kentucky, dissented in this decision that African Americans were not complete people, complete citizens with equal rights under the law.

They fought to go back right here in North Carolina with a violent coup d'état against blacks and whites in Wilmington in 1898. In that white supremacist coup d'état they cold-bloodedly ran duly elected black and white officers out of office and out of town. This opened the doors for the election of a governor named Charles B. Aycock, a U.S. Senator named Furnifold Simmons, and other regressive legislators who together pushed in an avalanche of regressive Jim Crow policies intent on stopping forever the vision of us moving together as people of the South. Then they gloated and they boasted of what they had done.

But in the midst of this dastardly action to go back, something happened: In February of 1900, a resistance movement was reborn. At a segregated public school, James Weldon Johnson and his brother, on Abraham Lincoln's birthday, had the students in that school sing for the first time a song that would become the anthem and hymn of the new Movement of blacks and whites and brown and poor and rich and people of faith who would mount a resistance and fight back against the enemies of justice and equality. And so in the midst of the setbacks and the gloating of the enemies of progress and the forces of extremism and the forces of immorality and regressivism, they began 113 years ago to sing and strengthen themselves for a Movement to fight back. I don't know if you all know it, but some of us know what they sang. In the midst of that pain, they sang:

(Rev. Barber in unison with the crowd)

> *Lift every voice and sing*
> *Till earth and heaven ring,*
> *Ring with the harmonies of Liberty;*
> *Let our rejoicing rise*
> *High as the listening skies…*

And then they said when you're hurting:

> *Sing a song full of the faith that the dark past has taught us,*
> *Sing a song full of the hope that the present has brought us,*
> *Facing the rising sun of our new day begun*
> *Let us march on till victory is won.*

And then they sang:

> *Stony the road we trod,*
> *Bitter the chastening rod,*
> *Felt in the days when hope unborn had died;*
> *Yet with a steady beat,*
> *Have not our weary feet*
> *Come to the place for which our fathers sighed?*

And then they closed it with the refrain of faith:

> *God of our weary years,*
> *God of our silent tears,*
> *Thou who has brought us thus far on the way;*
> *Thou who has by Thy might, led us in to the light,*
> *Keep us forever in the path, we pray.*
> *Lest our feet (God Almighty!) stray from the places, our God,*
> *where we met Thee,*
> *Lest, our hearts drunk with the wine of the world, we forget Thee;*
> *Shadowed beneath Thy hand,*
> *May we forever stand.*
> *True to our God,*
> *True to our native land.*

They sang. Crowd: They sang.

And by faith refused to give in. They sang. Crowd: *They sang.*

And by faith they built a new Movement. They sang. Crowd: *They sang.*

And by faith they organized an army of resistance. They sang. Crowd: *They sang.*

And believed that America would someday be America to all of us. They sang! Crowd: *They sang!*

And believed that the South would not forever be bound in the shackles of hate and discrimination. They sang! Crowd: *They sang!*

And organized when they didn't have the votes. They sang! Crowd: *They sang!*

And they organized when the legislature was against them. They sang! Crowd: *They sang!*

And they organized their lawyers to think in new ways. They sang! Crowd: *They sang!*

Kept the faith moving forward despite being beaten and killed and lynched. They sang! Crowd: *They sang!*

And with faith they went into the courts and went into the streets and went into pulpits believing that someday things would change. They sang. Crowd: *They sang.*

And by faith they were in the Supreme Court in 1954. They sang and prayed in. They moved presidents. They moved the leaders, Republicans and Democrats, with their moral stamina. They sang!

And faith with faith, they beat back the John Birch Society and the Dixiecrats and the Sovereign Commission and the Ku Klux Klan right here in North Carolina! They sang! And by faith they reversed the course of history. And this, my friends, is our legacy and it is calling once again today.

Yes, we have seen an immoral and regressive legislature.

Yes, in six months, one hundred and eighty days, they have turned this state one hundred and eighty degrees in the wrong direction.

Yes, they have attacked the poor and attacked the sick and attacked our children and attacked teachers and attacked non-heterosexuals and have attacked labor.

Yes! They have hurt us. And what they have done is mean, is hurtful, and is wrong!

But, we are the children of a Movement, of a multiracial, multicultural Movement. We know how to sing! And fight, oh, we know how! We are a Movement of deep faith and values and vision. We are the Movement. We are the children of those who have always fought back, pushed forward, had courage, and who have refused to be moved.

And so now is our calling, now is our time to take up the mantle and plant our feet one more time. Elijah brought us here! But we are Elijah now. Moses brought us here! But we are Joshua now! And once again, we must sing the vision of freedom and justice, and by faith we must go forward. We've been here before, and if slavery didn't kill us, if the oppression of women didn't kill us, surely no weak legislature with 86 votes is gonna kill us!

We know who we are! We are the sons and daughters of those who won against incredible odds. We are the sons and daughters of those who had hope when hope unborn had died. We are the sons and daughters of those who refused to become drunk with the wine of the world, drunk with the wine of racism, drunk with the wine of injustice, drunk with the wine of power, and drunk with the wine of inequality.

We *know* who we are! Now it won't be easy; it won't be an easy fight, but it will be a fight. We know how to fight. In fact, while nonviolent in strategy, we live for this kind of fight. Don't make no mistake, North Carolina. This is no momentary hyperventilation or momentary protest. This is a Movement, not a moment. We've got a reputation to uphold. My Momma is depending on us! My Daddy looking down from the portals of heaven is depending on us! Rosa Parks is depending on us! Medgar Evers is depending on us! Viola Liuzzo, a white woman who was killed for her voting rights activism, is depending on us!

For we who believe in freedom cannot rest. Yes, we've got a governor who's decided to be on the wrong side of history. Oh, yes, we've got a legislature bragging and boasting about its power and legislating on the basis of lies and discrimination. But though they have temporary power, the future does not belong to them! Injustice does have its moments, but the future does not belong to injustice; because, always, there comes a day when people rise up. And this, my friends, is that day. Always!

Somebody say: *Always.* Crowd: *Always!*
A new day comes. Crowd: *A new day comes.*
Always! Crowd: *Always!*
The morning follows the dark night. Crowd: *The morning follows the dark night.*

I'm so pleased to stand here today with rabbis. Oh, yes, joy comes in the morning. That great text of Psalm 118, known as a "Song of Victory," says almost painfully words along these lines: *Out of my distress I called on the LORD; the LORD answered me and set me in a broad place. With the LORD on my side I do not fear. What can mortals do to me? The LORD is on my side to help me; I shall look in triumph on those who hate me* (vv. 5-7 NRSV). Then the psalmist feels his help coming and he says: *It is better to take refuge in the LORD than to put confidence in mortals. It is better to take refuge in the LORD than to put confidence in princes* (vv. 8-9). Then the psalmist speaks of a new day; he says: *[In the middle of the distress] the stone that the builders rejected has become the chief cornerstone. This is the LORD's doing; it is marvelous in our eyes. This is the day that the LORD has made; let us rejoice and be glad in it* (vv. 22-24).

Now I came by here—I ain't nothing but a country preacher—to announce that *this* is the day that the Lord has made. This is a moment in history that the Lord has made, and we shall rejoice and be glad in it. Through this pain, through this abuse, this despicable day, the Lord, as my grandmama said, *the Lord has brought us together. The spirit of the times,* or *zeitgeist* as the German theologians would say, *has brought us together. The Great Spirit,* as my Tuscaroran ancestors would say, *has gathered us under the wing of the eagle and called us together.* God has called the stones that the builders rejected to come together. We are the stones that this legislature has rejected, that the governor has rejected. And this is the day for all of us to fight for this state to do right. This is the day when we announce we will not go back.

Look around for a moment and see what the Lord has done. Just take a look. Could nobody but the Lord start with 17 and then fill up

Fayetteville Street. Look at what the Lord has done. All they do to keep us divided, yet here we are all races, all colors, all sexualities, all communities, and all incomes.

> I wish somebody would shout: *This is the day!* Crowd: *This is the day! That the Lord has made!* Crowd: *That the Lord has made!*

And so my friends, don't you get discouraged. Oh, no, no, no. Claim the power of this moment, and let us prove once again that what men mean for evil, God can turn into good. Let us prove again, that when the stones that the builder rejected get together, a new day has arrived. I know without a doubt when I look out on you, the stones that have been rejected, that this state will be a state where we grow strong and the strong grow great because this is the day that the Lord has made.

I *know* when I look out on you that no weapon formed against us will prosper because this is the day that the Lord has made! I *know* when I look out on you that our one-blood God has made all people because this is the day that the Lord has made! *Look around,* and see what the Lord has done. *Look around,* and see North Carolina's new future right out here on the street. *Look around,* and see a new South. *Look around,* and see a new America!

There was a time when we wouldn't be together like this. There was a time the right wing would have kept us from holding strong together, but look at us now holding hands together, educators fighting along with the unions, and unions fighting for civil rights, and people of faith fighting along with the children, and environmentalists coming together with the health workers, and doctors standing on the side of the sick, and millionaires standing with the unemployed, and straight folk standing with gay folk, and people of faith standing with those wrestling with their faith. *Look at what the Lord has done!*

This, this is the day when we remind this governor and every governor that comes after him, that being elected does not give you the authority to govern for a few. We believe ultimately that the people have veto power over every political bully. THIS is the day that we say to Governor McCrory: *You better get on the right side of history. Haven't you read? Didn't you pass History? And if you didn't, get one of these teachers to give you an extra course.* This is the day that we remind Governor McCrory: *George Wallace lost! Lester Maddox lost! You're on the wrong side of history!*

This is the day that we say to this power-drunk extreme legislature that justice will prevail over your trickery and your temporary victory. That's why you rushed to do your dirt and then ran out of town, 'cause you know inside yourself: it ain't gonna stand. You know inside yourself: it's just temporary. What you have done will not stand the test of time, the scrutiny of the Constitution, or the power of the people.

This is the day that we believe there is still a better way. All our children can be educated. All of our sick can have health insurance. All of our workers can be protected. The poor can be lifted. And all people, regardless of who they are, can be loved and accepted.

This is the day that we refuse to go backward. This is the day. Somebody plant your foot. Just pick the right one up and plant it. This is the day we plant our feet. This is the day we are saved by hope. This is the day that we renew our faith, that they that wait upon the Lord shall renew their strength, shall climb up on eagles' wings.

This is the day that we believe that God is for us. It doesn't matter who's against us. *This* is the day that we declare in the face of this puny human power that the Lord is our light and salvation.

This is the day that we recognize there's no greater force than the power of love. There's no greater force than the power of truth, and there's no nobler cause than that of justice for all. This is the day that we believe: greater is the spirit in us than the spirit in the world. What men mean for evil, God works for the good.

Uh-oh! Instead of depressing us, they have made us determined to fight!

Uh-oh! Instead of defeating us, they've made us defiant!

Uh-oh! Instead of dividing us, they've united us!

Uh-oh! Instead of scaring our lawyers, they've made our lawyers ready to fight!

Uh-oh! Instead of discouraging our young people, they put a fire in them and raised up a new generation of warriors for the battlefield!

Uh-oh! Instead of doing their dirt in the darkness, now the whole world can see them.

Uh-oh! Instead of making themselves more popular, less than one out of five North Carolinians agree with the shenanigans of this legislature. But Moral Monday is the talk of the state and the talk of the nation and the talk of the world. Uh-oh!

Uh-oh! Oh God! Some of us would've stayed in our pulpits, but now they've gone and messed up; they've got rabbis and imams and preachers coming out of their congregations and pulpits, getting out in the street!

Uh-oh! Even the Pope said yesterday: *It's time to act up!* Uh-oh!

Uh-oh! Instead of making us go home, they motivated us to come out together for 12t straight weeks, 84 days, to pray together, sing together, go to jail together!

This is the day that the Lord has made! We will organize from Asheville to Nags Head, from Elizabeth City to Wilmington, from Greensboro to Charlotte, from the I-40 corridor to the back roads of eastern North Carolina, from Raleigh to Rockingham, we will fight! We will fight!

This is the day! We will not bow our heads or allow our spirits to be broken. *This* is the day that the Lord has made, and we will work in this day until the day comes that we are one nation, one state, one people, one community, under God, indivisible, indivisible, with liberty and justice for all! And when we get to that day, oh my God! When we get to that day, we gonna shout together, we gonna say *hallelujah* together, we gonna thank God together. Because when we all see justice, what a day, what a day, what a day, when we *all* see justice! What a day! *What a day! What a day! I'm rejoicing!*

9
"TAKING THE DREAM HOME"

FIFTIETH ANNIVERSARY OF
MARCH ON WASHINGTON RALLY

upon the 50th anniversary of the
1963 March on Washington
August 28, 2013

Freedom Summer 2014 Youth organize to keep the dream alive *(Phil Fonville photo)*

Go back to Mississippi, go back to Alabama, go back to
South Carolina, go back to Georgia, go back to Louisiana,
go back to the slums and ghettos of our northern cities,
knowing that somehow this situation can and will be changed.

THE REV. DR. MARTIN LUTHER KING JR.,
AUGUST 28, 1963, MARCH ON WASHINGTON

BACKGROUND

On August 28, 1963, the Rev. Dr. Martin Luther King Jr. shared with the world a radical and revolutionary dream of social and economic justice. What many observers forget is his insistence that the marchers *go back* to their homes and organize, that they fight and *continue to work with the faith that unearned suffering is redemptive!*

After traveling to Washington, D.C. for the 50th anniversary of the March on Washington on Saturday, August 24, Moral Monday and Forward Together Moral Movement organizers brought the dream back to North Carolina. In an unprecedented show of the growing strength of the re-emerging Southern Freedom Movement in North Carolina, North Carolinians of all walks of life in every corner of the state held 13 simultaneous Take the Dream Home rallies in each of the state's U.S. congressional districts.

The goal of the Take the Dream Home campaign was twofold: (1) to educate North Carolina's citizenry on the legislative session that had just ended—one of the most disastrous in the history of the North Carolina General Assembly, and (2) to rally support to demand that the United States Congress renew Section 4 of the Voting Rights Act and reinstate protections for marginalized communities in states like North Carolina with a long history and reality of racial discrimination.

The scope of the campaign made it so that some communities that had not seen civil rights protests since the 60s and 70s found themselves in the middle of the largest social Movement the state has seen in a long time.

❝Tomorrow we remember the historic March on Washington 50 years ago and claim again the power of its witness and its relevance for today, so let us make sure we do so properly. A lot of people have glamorized that day, but the truth is, it had a lot of drama, frustrations, and fears. The truth is, even Dr. King, the preacher, struggled, as did all who participated.

He and others had to stand that day and challenge the most powerful nation in the world, in the midst of threats and hatred. This was no TV preaching like we see so much today: preaching for mere performance with no prophetic substance that speaks to the issues of justice. Preaching that merely puts a good song on the front end, a performance about personal prosperity in the middle, and then raising an offering for a Rolls Royce at the end. This was prophetic preaching, the kind of word that speaks to the death of the times, that takes on injustice and wrong with a word and a commitment to action. That declares that the nightmares promulgated by evil forces of oppression do not and will not have the last say.

The March on Washington tomorrow must be seen as a witness for truth over lies. An event where we declare that we will not give up on what is right. Those who journey toward freedom will not rest. And the nightmares of wrong and injustice will not have the last word, the final say, or the final victory.

It was in this space that Dr. Martin Luther King Jr. wrestled with what he'd say to the thousands of people who would gather at the Lincoln Memorial in the summer of 1963 for the March on Washington. One adviser urged him to give a political speech. Another suggested a more scholarly lecture. Others said he ought to preach like the black Baptist preacher he was.

Dr. King wrestled with his own fears; you know President Kennedy didn't want the march to happen. He wrestled with his own inadequacies, like his youth: he was 33. He wrestled with potential danger. An FBI report after the speech said of King: *We must mark him now, if we have not done so before, as the most dangerous Negro of the future in this nation from the standpoint of communism, the Negro, and national security.*

Historian Gary Younge notes that the night before the March on Washington in 1963, Dr. King asked his aides for advice about the next day's speech. One of his closest said: *Don't use the lines about I have a dream; it's trite, it's cliché. You've used it too many times already.*[1]

With all three television networks offering live coverage of the march for jobs and freedom, as it was called, this speech would be his oratorical introduction to the nation. How frightening. After a wide range of conflicting suggestions from his staff, King left the lobby at the Willard hotel in D.C., to put the final touches to a speech he hoped would be received, in his words, *like the Gettysburg address. I am now going upstairs to my room to counsel with my Lord,* he told them. *I will see you all tomorrow.*[2]

It must have been a miraculous consultation. When Dr. King stood at the Lincoln Memorial on August 28, 1963, he gave voice to a vision nurtured since the days of slavery. His rich prophetic language, rooted deep in the black South, was also bright with the vision of a new day. It had been a violent and astonishing spring and summer, and the blues and the gospel had both grappled within him to express it. As the end of the summer drew near, it was hard to say what had been won and lost. And now two hundred fifty thousand people had gathered in what King called *the greatest demonstration for freedom in the history of our nation*. In front of him on the podium lay a speech he had labored on for four long days with the help of half a dozen of his aides. Gripping the podium, he started out reading the text of the speech.

Toward the end of the prepared speech he said: *Go back to Mississippi, go back to Alabama, go back to South Carolina, go back to Georgia, go back to Louisiana*. And then, behind him, Mahalia Jackson—who sung often with him and sensed the need for something more—cried out: *Tell 'em about the dream, Martin*. She could see what God saw and she said it to Dr. King.

Dr. King continued: *Go back to the slums and ghettoes of our northern cities, knowing that somehow this situation can and will be changed.* Jackson shouted again: *Tell 'em about the dream!* She could see what God saw.

King: *Let us not wallow in the valley of despair. I say to you today, my friends.*
Jackson: *Tell them about the dream, Martin!*

Nobody knows whether he heard her or not, but Dr. King left his prepared text entirely and began to improvise from a set piece he had first delivered in Rocky Mount, North Carolina, almost a year before, a piece Mahalia had heard in Detroit. And so began the only part of that speech that anyone ever remembers: *So even though we face the difficulties of today and tomorrow, I still have a dream.*

It is crucial that we remember not only that voice but the voices from offstage and the chorus of the ancestors that beat within him and the thousands of people of people who organized the Movement in local communities across the South, that made the Movement take on legs. This is not just about Dr. King.

Like Dr. King, once again we here are being called to tell this nation and world about the dream. Yes, there are some difficult days ahead, and yes, those who live in and love the nightmares of injustice are trying to dominate the conscience of our nation. But like Dr. King we must be realistic. We must be fearless to stand up to:

Those who are trying to steal, segregate, and suppress our right to vote.
Those who would dare trample on the graves and walk through the blood of the martyrs.

Those who would desecrate the sacrifice of Medgar Evers, Viola Liuzzo, and the three young murdered Freedom Summer workers: Schwerner, Chaney, and Goodman.

Those Supreme Court justices who like those on the Plessy versus Ferguson court of 1896 who misinterpret the Constitution for the mean and menial benefit of the far right.

Those who would see the Shelby decision (Supreme Court repeal of Section 5 of the Voting Rights Act) just like the radical racists saw the removal of the federal troops from the South in 1877: open season to assault and attempt to nullify our most precious rights.

Those who would kill our children like Trayvon and criticize us for standing up for our babies, our sons and daughters, and then in our face turn justice upside down and let the killer go. If a black man or woman stands his or her ground against attackers, the black man or woman goes to jail. If someone else makes a claim of standing ground against us, even when it's not true, he or she goes free.

Oh yes.

Those anti-union forces and anti-worker exploiters who force the laborers of this nation to make some kind of life without a living wage, while some greedy corporate leaders take more and more and more.

Those people sick in spirit and mind who purport the sick idea that there is a crime in providing healthcare insurance to all Americans. What kind of sickness is it that you get elected by the people and by virtue of your election, you prevent the people who elected you from having the same benefits you enjoy?

Those who fight harder to get more guns and less funding for public education and who care more about guns than about equal rights for everybody. Who fight more for guns than for addressing issues of poverty and economic disparity.

Yes, there are those who, rather than working in cooperation with President Obama, spend night and day hating him, despising his skin color, working to *other* him and make him something other than American. These folk live off of their psychotic hatred and would drive this country down to take our president down.

Yes, there are even those who use the Bible and our faith in their attempt to twist morality and righteousness into tools of oppression and subjugation rather than instruments of truth, love, and liberation.

Because these nightmares abound, we must hear the call once again, tell our people about the dream. God told Ezekiel to stand up and speak. We must hear what the wise one said in Proverbs, that when there is no vision, the people perish. Vision will cause people to stand up and steady their spines and refuse to give in to the nightmares.

Don't you hear Mahalia? Don't you hear the ancestors, the cloud of witnesses? Don't you hear the people all over the world stirring up the strong power of truth and saying: *Tell them about the dream?*

Don't accept living by what the enemy sees; he's a liar.

Don't sniff the propaganda of the Koch brothers; tell them about the dream.

Don't get drunk on the tainted and racist brew of the Tea Party.

Don't let your view be shaped by the immoral extremist views and diatribes of the Rush Limbaughs and the Bill O'Reillys or governors and legislators in your state. They are on the wrong side of history. They are reading from the playbook of George Wallace and Strom Thurmond and Bull Connor, and like them they will lose. Their nightmare will end.

Our job is to tell the nation about the dream.

This dream is God's dream that said: *Let justice roll down like water and righteousness like a mighty stream.*

This dream is the dream of Jesus, who said the Spirit of the Lord is upon the earth and that he was anointed to preach good news to the poor, recovery of sight to the blind, healing to the brokenhearted and liberty to the bruised; he was to bring deliverance to the captives and to proclaim the acceptable year of the Lord.

This is the kind of dream that causes the enslaved to stand up in his or her spirit and declare: *Before I'll be a slave I'll be curing in my grave and go home and be free.*

This dream is the dream on paper that we have yet to complete: We the people of the United States are to form a more perfect union and establish justice.

This dream is the dream of A. Philip Randolph of the Brotherhood of Sleeping Car Porters. Twenty-one years before the 1963 March on Washington, at a 1942 union policy conference, he declared: *We have come to set forth our goals, declare our principles, formulate our policies, plan our program and discuss our methods, strategy, and tactics.*[3] This kind of envisioning is the job of every Movement that seeks to map out clearly the direction in which it is going.

Thus our feet are set in the path toward equality—economic, political, social, and racial. Equality is the heart and essence of democracy, freedom, and justice. Dr. King said that without equality of opportunity in industry, in labor unions, schools and colleges, government, politics, and before the law, without equality in social relations and in all phases of human endeavor, the Negro is certain to be consigned to an inferior status. There must be no dual standards of justice, no dual rights, privileges, duties, or responsibilities of citizenship. No dual forms of freedom.

Once again we are being summoned by history, and this is the moment to tell folk about the dream. Tell the nation's enemies and friends about the dream.

We are being called to never give up.

We are being called to resist being drunk with the wine of the world and instead to see what God sees.

We are being called to prophetic vision, vision that comes from revelation by God. Vision and dreams that are not afraid of the enemy, vision and dreams that do not know how to fail or how to give up. The kind of vision that makes you run on and see what the end will be. The kind of vision and dream that keeps us from perishing, from letting go, from bowing down, from living in depression.

We are being called to tell them about the dream:

The kind of dreaming that makes you determined to fight.

The kind of dream that as Paul Tillich said, gives you the *courage to be.*

Prophetic dreaming is the kind of vision that comes in the midst of nightmares. Yes, there are some nightmares, but the dream of justice is greater! The dream of truth is greater!

I need to tell you about the dream that is unfolding down in North Carolina right now. We have a Movement called the Forward Together Moral Movement. Thousands of ordinary people are mobilizing now each week to confront our General Assembly on their regressive, extremist bills and laws. These powerful convergences are called

Moral Mondays, and this phrase is now a household name around the nation. Seeing us out there every week, the forces of the nightmare are twisting in their spirits.

A few weeks ago I was invited to Mitchell County in the far west of North Carolina. The county is 99 percent white and 89 percent Republican. The extreme policies of our Tea Party legislature and governor have hurt the people of Mitchell County. These politicians believe the way to run a state is to blame the poor for their poverty, to give the wealthy more, to cut public education, to deny Medicaid coverage granted by the Affordable Care Act, to attack voting rights, and then to give people the right to carry guns into bars, schools, and parks. This kind of nightmarish vision has hurt people all over our state.

So we went to the mountains, in Republican territory, armed not with guns but with the dream. I went there and told them about our dream vision:

Economic sustainability, jobs, and labor rights.
Educational equality.
Healthcare for all, including protecting the environment.
Protecting and expanding voting rights.

Before we left, we were all singing the hymn, "Blest Be the Tie That Binds." They let it be known that the Republican Chair had renounced the party. His daughter was organizing a local Moral Monday, and the next day they joined a crowd of more than ten thousand in nearby Asheville, claiming: *Forward Together . . . Not One Step Back!* This is not about Republicans and Democrats; this is about justice, about what's right!

I tell you the dream is right. But not only that. The dream is renewing; it will give you hope even in the midst of difficult situations.

But finally I need to tell you that the dream also is a resource for defiance. In North Carolina we have had to file suit against the worst voter-suppression legislation in the country. Our lead plaintiff is Rosanell Eaton, 92 years old. She is up here with us today. She made history working for voting rights back in the day. And she is still in the fight, now that our state is rolling back all the victories she fought so hard to attain.

A few weeks ago, Ms. Eaton committed civil disobedience at our Legislative Building on a Moral Monday and submitted herself to arrest. She is 92! In the rally before we entered the building, she spoke to a crowd of thousands and lit us on fire. The other day Ms. Eaton and I were on a radio show together, and the reporter asked her about her life. She said: *I got concerned at 10. I didn't have parents to help, but I had heard about the dream of my grandfather, who fought to get out of slavery.* She said: *When I started on this journey, God gave me what I needed. I kept my eye on his way and his purposes and God gave me what I needed.* Then the interviewer asked: *Why would you do this at 92?* And she said: *We are called by God to work 'til the day is done. We don't ever stop working on God's plans. It's disgusting what people are trying to do now to our rights and our dreams. But I'm too old not to be steadfast. And I intend to do so until my day is done and God will give me and us what we need.*

Go back and tell people about the dream. Don't be afraid of those who create nightmares. We are the children of the dream! And God takes care of God's dreamers.

Yes, God can bring God's own dream to pass.

Moses dreamed and defied the nightmare.
David dreamed.
Shadrach, Meshach, and Abednego dreamed.
Esther dreamed.
Jesus dreamed.
Harriet Tubman dreamed.
Frederick Douglass dreamed.
Rosa Parks dreamed.
Young people dreamed.
Fannie Lou Hamer dreamed.
Nelson Mandela dreamed.
Barack Obama dreamed.

Go back home and tell them about the dream. March. Organize. Go to court. Go to jail. Don't just talk about want they did back then. Fight for the dream now!

Notes from the Simultaneous Rallies in Honor of the 50th Anniversary of the March on Washington

CABARRUS COUNTY

The Cabarrus County NAACP led a coalition of educators, community activists, labor leaders, and others for a powerful rally in Concord, near Charlotte, a town in the eighth congressional district. A local high school principal spoke to the crisis of public education in North Carolina, created by years of funding neglect by the General Assembly. A representative from the local International Brotherhood of Electrical Workers union told stories of workers under attack due to the array of actions by the General Assembly.

FORSYTH COUNTY
This Triad-area Twin City served as host for the famous twelfth congressional district during the Taking the Dream Home protest. Partially due to the historical and current hyper-segregation of the city, Winston-Salem produces some of the most regressive and some of the most progressive representatives to the North Carolina General Assembly and to the U.S. Congress. The rally brought roughly a thousand people to downtown Corpening Plaza. Rabbi Fred Guttman of Greensboro gave the keynote address. Linda Sutton of Democracy NC, one of the moral witnesses during the 13 Moral Mondays in Raleigh and a longtime voting rights activist, spoke about the extreme attacks on minority voters. Families and NAACP members lingered for hours; it was a vibrant evening of music and testimony.

GUILFORD COUNTY
In Greensboro, an epicenter of 1960s student civic action, college students led a massive march from Bennett College, where the original sit-ins were planned in 1960, to a downtown park. Greensboro NAACP branch president Rev. Dr. Cardes Brown summed up the message of the day: *Those who are with us are more than those who are against us!* The Beloved Community Center, one of our strongest coalition partners, supported the local branch in organizing the historic day.

HARNETT COUNTY
Under the leadership of NC NAACP Second Vice President Carolyn McDougal, Harnett County hosted another impressive and diverse protest in its county seat of Dunn. With freedom songs blaring from the sound system, the rally began from the steps of the Town Hall. Nancy Shakir of Democracy NC spoke to the power of the vote, and NCAE president Rodney Ellis spoke on behalf of all teachers in North Carolina who are being denied the resources and respect to do their best to educate our precious children.

JACKSON COUNTY
In the far west town of Sylva in Jackson County, Forward Together Moral Movement supporters and environmental activists worked with the nearby Henderson County branch of the NAACP to bring the dream home to the 11th U.S. congressional district. In this rural town, five hundred mountain people showed up to take a stand. In a new

phenomenon for the NC NAACP, mostly white Jackson County is now in the process of forming its own NAACP branch!

LINCOLN COUNTY

Rev. Barber surprised people gathered in Lincolnton when he showed up in Congressional District 10 for their rally outside the Lincoln County Courthouse. Despite alleged threats of right-wing disruption from the blogosphere and reported pressure on public employees not to attend, churches led the way to organize a successful rally in a difficult part of the state to organize. A youth member of the Dream Defenders out of Florida rode with Rev. Barber, speaking about their Movement spawned in response to the murder of Trayvon Martin, resulting in a 31-day sit-in at the Florida governor's office to demand an end to Stand Your Ground laws in their state.

MECKLENBURG COUNTY

After speaking in Lincolnton, Rev. Barber traveled to Charlotte, where only nine days earlier, local organizers had mobilized thousands for the Charlotte Moral Monday. Undaunted by the organizing challenge, another energized crowd showed up for the second rally in Marshall Park.

NEW HANOVER COUNTY

Deborah Maxwell, president of the New Hanover branch of the NAACP, who was arrested on Mega Moral Monday on June 3 at the General Assembly while trying to tell her representatives how devastating their extreme agenda would be for her community, helped lead the organizing effort for the Taking the Dream Home Rally in Wilmington. She was joined by NC NAACP Third Vice President, Rev. Dr. T. Anthony Spearman, who gave the keynote address. Well-known Duke University historian Bill Chafe, author of *Civilities and Civil Rights* among many other publications, and who was arrested during the second Moral Monday on May 6, gave a history lesson to provide context to the Forward Together Moral Movement. Over four hundred people attended this coastal Carolina rally.

ORANGE COUNTY

Meanwhile in Chapel Hill, protestors filled the Peace and Justice Plaza in front of the downtown post office and courthouse. The turnout exceeded organizers' expectations, and the police were forced to close down one. lane of traffic on Franklin Street to accommodate the overflow crowd. The Raging Grannies led everyone in freedom songs as Rev. Jimmy Hawkins, pastor of Covenant Presbyterian Church, and NC NAACP Field Secretary Laurel Ashton keynoted the event.

PASQUOTANK COUNTY

The Pasquotank County branch of the NAACP, led by Keith Rivers, joined area branches and coalition partners for a rally in Elizabeth City in North Carolina's first congressional district. The rally drew over five hundred people. Bob Hall of Democracy NC spoke to a crowd largely made up of students from Elizabeth City State University (ECSU). An ECSU student was running for local office and was stymied by the new voting restrictions of the North Carolina General Assembly. An NAACP lawsuit upheld his cause, and the student now serves as a town council representative. Students left the gathering with their marching orders to continue building the Forward Together Moral Movement.

PITT COUNTY

The Pitt County branch of the NAACP, led by NC NAACP Branch President of the Year Calvin Henderson, organized several hundred defenders of justice for what turned out to be a rainy Taking the Dream Home rally in eastern North Carolina. NC NAACP organizer and Forward Together cultural leader Yara Allen traveled to Greenville to join youth and community speakers. Ms. Allen, the Bernice Johnson Reagon of the Forward Together Moral Movement, inspired and engaged the dedicated crowd outside the Pitt County Courthouse with full-throated freedom songs.

WAKE COUNTY

Back at our state's capital city, the Raleigh-Apex branch of the NAACP and labor leaders including the AFL-CIO of North Carolina held down the fort in downtown Raleigh while the rest of the Movement fanned out across the state.

WATAUGA COUNTY

In the Appalachian State University town of Boone, also many hours from Raleigh, students and community members packed an inside theater. The high-energy rally was forced inside due to a strict outside-sound town ordinance that would have limited what promised to be a spirited evening. Over the summer in Boone, Moral Monday supporters who were not able to make it to Raleigh held weekly solidarity protests in a shopping center parking lot. Watauga County is also now in the process of chartering a new NAACP branch.

10

"THE CALL TO HIGHER GROUND"

HISTORIC THOUSANDS ON JONES STREET RALLY 8

A Moral Movement for the Nation
February 8, 2014

At Riverside Church in New York on Palm Sunday, 2014, preaching on
"Higher Ground" *(Eric Preston photo)*

*These are troubling times. Corporations are treated like people.
People are treated like things. Some members of the Supreme Court have
become legal enablers of those who would conspire to buy our democracy.
We must know there is a better way. In the midst of these changing times,
we must know there is a standard that never changes.*
*This nightmare of regressive public policy and mean, oppressive politics
are taking us in the wrong direction. These backward policies and
oppressive politics want us to accept an anemic faith and sell out to the
highest bidder. But we must not!*

BACKGROUND

When upwards of eighty thousand people showed up in Raleigh in the dead of winter for the Historic Thousands on Jones Street Rally 8, it represented the largest civil rights and social justice march since the one to Selma in 1965. Rev. Barber sought to summarize and clarify the work that had been building over the past eight years. In light of the fresh energy around the Movement of the past two years, he contrasted the competing ideologies in North Carolina with one low road leading to destruction, and the other as a pathway to higher ground.

Not long after this February 2014 speech, Rev. Barber received an invitation to carry that same message to the nation, as he was invited by the Rev. Dr. James Forbes to preach on Palm Sunday at Riverside Church in New York, a sacred space of historic prophetic proclamation for social justice. The message here built on and expanded the one brought to the eighty thousand in Raleigh at the march. Dr. Barber called both North Carolina and the nation to embrace a "Fusion coalition" for the purposes of building a Moral Movement rooted in the principles of equal justice for all.

What follows is the entire text shared with the capacity crowd at Riverside Church in New York City on Palm Sunday.

▟▌When Jesus came into history, much of the religious and political structure cults had hijacked the moral and righteous standards of our faith, adjusting the faith to serve the few, the wealthy, the privileged. And so in his first public sermon, recounted in verse 16 of Luke 4, Jesus–God's own son, God's own self–opens God's own word. Not a Bible with indices or a concordance, but a simple, unmarked scroll.

Deliberately, despite all of the passages available, Jesus anchors his ministry's focus in the prophets, specifically, in Isaiah 61.

> *The spirit of the Lord GOD is upon me, because the LORD has anointed me; he has sent me to bring good news to the oppressed, to bind up the brokenhearted, to proclaim liberty to the captives, and release to the prisoner, to proclaim the year of the LORD's favor (vv. 1-2 NRSV).*

Jesus says, in the words of our younger generation: *Don't get it twisted.* The vocation of faith, as it has always been for those whom God calls, is to engage in the work of liberation of the poor, the blind, the captive, the oppressed, and the outcast.

What is significant is that this is normative preaching of the gospel. This central focus is at the heart, not at the margins, of the gospel. As Philip Esler notes in his book *Community and Gospel in Luke-Acts,* the programmatic function of the church is rendered heretical if we do not honor the pride of place in the inaugural preaching of Jesus given to the poor and others who are at risk and vulnerable within the world.

As Dr. Forbes suggests in his book *The Holy Spirit and Preaching,* God's anointing produces the ability to address the death of our times. Anointing produces prophets who will not merely serve the culture, but who will call for a counterculture in Jesus' name. Anointing produces prophets to save the church from being a mere consecrated club, and instead makes it a prophetic community.

Jesus said this in the midst of Roman domination, in the face of all its pomp and power and precedence that allowed religion as long as it did not challenge the state, or the state of things.

How extraordinary it must have sounded to a crowd in a Greco-Roman city for the Lucan Jesus to begin his public ministry by specifying beggars and a number of other groups at the very bottom of the social register as the primary recipients of the gospel, the good news for the common people.

Now this first public sermon almost got Jesus killed that day, and it set his march toward Calvary and made him an enemy of the status quo. In Matthew 23, Jesus is on his way to be crucified, and he is still preaching, still challenging both the religious cults and the political arena that had formed an unholy alliance to limit morality to the performance of piety, while it overlooked and often sanctioned political and social injustice following a pattern laid down by Jeremiah centuries before when he prophesied:

This is what the LORD says: Go down to the palace of the king of Judah and proclaim this message there: Hear the word of the LORD to you, king of Judah, you who sit on David's throne—you, your officials and your people who come through these gates. This is what the LORD says: Do what is just and right. Rescue from the hand of the oppressor the one who has been robbed. Do no wrong or violence to the foreigner, the fatherless or the widow, and do not shed innocent blood in this place.

JEREMIAH 22:1-3 (NIV)

Jesus heads toward Jerusalem to weep, wail, and woe over what he sees:

> *Woe to you, scribes and Pharisees, hypocrites! For you pay tithe of mint and anise and cummin, and have neglected the weightier matters of the law: justice and mercy and faith. These you ought to have done, without leaving the others undone.*
>
> MATTHEW 23:23 NKJV

One commentator says that this fifth woe speaks against scrupulosity in trifles and the neglect of weighty duties. Jesus challenged political and recessive leaders who were careful and observant in their perspective on personal piety to the point of even going beyond the requirements, for public display, but they were cunning and oppressive in their politics to the point of fostering deception and domination.

Worthless and hypocritical are all outward observances when justice (*tan krisis* in Greek), acting equitably to one's neighbor and hurting nobody by word or deed, is neglected.

When mercy—loving kindness in conduct, as in the case of the widow, the stranger, and the debtor—is neglected, when faith in God's way is neglected, Jesus' moral critique is rendered to those who want "fashion-show" religion that covers and dismisses the connection between faith and social justice and that refuses to speak truth to power. Both Jeremiah and Matthew remind us in riveting ways of the real call of righteousness. And I believe we need a revival of a Movement of sustained moral critique and dissent in our current time.

Jesus' example made it our burden, our calling, to be mindful of the poor, the weak, and those on the sidelines of life. And we cannot escape this call. Walter Wink's *Engaging the Powers* noted that Jesus, by the Spirit, puts forth a different value than the value of the world's atmosphere. Our society assigns a unique value to money that has made wealth the highest value. But people of faith cannot be seduced into considering people like the world considers people. God desires to save us from anything that oppresses us—racial injustice, economic injustice, and anything that works against the solidarity of the human community.

In *Jesus and the Disinherited*, Howard Thurman writes:

> *This is the position of the disinherited in every age. What must be the attitude toward the rulers, the controllers of political, social, and economic life?*

True spirituality calls us to be suspicious of concentrations of wealth and privilege and power, and to mistrust ideological rationalism that justifies subordinating persons. We are called to be sensitive to the poor, the disenfranchised, the stranger, and the outsider.[1]

When we have had what Dr. William Turner, my mentor and professor of preaching and theology at Duke Divinity School calls *a crisis experience of conversion,* our active orientation to life is shifted. In other words, when the Spirit moves and we are saved, born again, changed, filled, however you describe it, what follows is a challenge to the way things are. Being moved by the Spirit necessitates a *quarrel with the way things are in the world.*

If the church speaks of Christ but defends the powerful and says nothing and more importantly *does* nothing about social forces that ravage men's lives, the claim of being in the Spirit must remain suspect.

I thought I might admit something here at Riverside this morning on this Palm Sunday. I am a theological conservative. I have to blame my grandmother, from whom I learned applied theology. And my father is to blame. He took his faith in God more seriously than anyone I knew. And my mother, who sang and played the old hymns to me as a boy, before what they call contemporary hymns. I'm talking about:

O, for a faith that will not shrink,
Though pressed by every foe,
That will not tremble on the brink
Of any earthly woe![2]

My grandmother once told me, *Son, remember that which the Lord has said. The Lord meant it, whether we like it or choose to follow it or not!*

My father—a preacher/justice activist—would often leave home to help persons who were victims of racism and oppression and injustice, with literally no money in his pocket, sometimes no transportation, depending only on his thumb to hitch a ride. I once asked how he could move with such faith. And he said to me: *God never changes, and since his name is Jehovah Jireh, which means "I will provide," who am I not to trust and believe what God has said?*

So I'm a born-and-bred conservative. Which is to say, I have deep struggles with those who tend to call themselves ultraconservatives today, who liberally resist and ignore so much of God's character. They say so *much* about what God says so *little,* and so *little* about what God says so *much.* How can you be conservative if you dismiss, downplay, and almost have a disdain for the weightier matters of the law, like justice and love and mercy and caring for the least of these and challenging the social and political powers of domination?

And I believe if we ever needed a Moral Movement in the nation to challenge much of our current hypocrisy, we need it now!

I know there are those who say our concern as the people of God should be private soul-saving, private devotion, private praise, and private personal morality that addresses issues of the inner man only. Those who would limit the voice of the faithful to the categories of abortion, homosexuality, prayer in school, and execution in a way that violates the ultimate requirement of God that we love one another. I know there are those who espouse some kind of weird theology that places God on the side of private ownership at the expense of the poor. Mass gun ownership and support of the death penalty divinely sacrificial. They say the church faithful should have no real voice in social/cooperative liberation. But there must be a Moral Movement that challenges these fallacies that dismiss too liberally so much of what God says! And the truth is that at various moments of our history, we have always needed the revival of a sustained prophetic Moral Movement.

Abolitionist William Lloyd Garrison once was rescued from being lynched by a pro-slavery mob, when the mayor of Boston had him thrown into jail. While incarcerated, Garrison wrote on the wall of his cell:

Wm. Lloyd Garrison was put into this cell Wednesday afternoon, October 21, 1835, to save him from the violence of a "respectable and influential" mob, who sought to destroy him for preaching the abominable and dangerous doctrine that "all men are created equal." [3]

Henry David Thoreau in his book *Walden* and essay "On the Duty of Civil Disobedience," said: *And if I repent of anything it is very likely to be my good behavior (in the face of injustice).* In 1896, United States Supreme Court Justice John Harlan provided a vote of moral constitutional dissent as the only justice to stand against the majority decision in the shameful Plessy versus Ferguson case:

There is no caste here. Our constitution is colorblind, and neither knows nor tolerates classes among citizens. In respect of civil rights, all citizens are equal before the law. The humblest is the peer of the most powerful. [4]

Harry Emerson Fosdick said from this pulpit in a sermon: *Mankind needs the sense of community.*

A single look at the world reveals how deplorably we are split into fragmentary and conflicting individuals and groups. We often say that this is a crazy world, and in the literal meaning of that word it is true, for crazy comes from the French écrasé, which means broken and shattered. We human beings ought to be in cooperative community, using the resources of this planet for the common good, and we are not.

For so many of us morality is merely group consensus. In our modern sociological lingo, the mores are accepted as the right ways. We have unconsciously come to believe that right is discovered by taking a sort of Gallup poll of the majority opinion. How many are giving their ultimate allegiance to this way of thinking?

The Christian owes his ultimate allegiance to God, and if any earthly institution conflicts with God's will, it is our Christian duty to take a stand against it. We must never allow the transitory evanescent demands of manmade institutions to take precedence over the eternal demands of the Almighty God. God never intended for one group of people to live in inordinate wealth, while others live in abject deadening poverty. In 1967 from this very pulpit, Dr. Martin Luther King Jr. bellowed out: *A time comes when silence is betrayal. That time has come for us in relation to Vietnam.*

After the murder of Dr. King, our nation understood a brief sharing Movement. It was a time when there was some moral commitment to lift the poor. People struggled for and won programs like Head Start, Medicare. They pushed for expansion of Social Security benefits to those left out when the program began. They won the Civil Rights and Voting Rights Acts, federal funding for K-12, and Pell grants for higher education. All of these programs went on to enjoy broad public support.

Russell Sage breaks the programs of the War on Poverty into three parts. The first part was designed to boost wages through education and job training. The second was to provide income support, particularly for single mothers and the elderly. And the third was to bring a system of government healthcare to the elderly and the poor.

This was a time to address racism in public policy. One of the lesser known benefits of the War on Poverty was its linkages with the Civil Rights Movement. For instance, Medicare funds were withheld from hospitals if they didn't comply with the Civil Rights Act, which in turn led to the desegregation of Southern hospitals and a drop in black infant mortality rates.

Addressing racism and poverty were spoken of as moral imperatives. Education opened up, voting rights opened up, election opportunity opened up.

In 1960, before we launched the War on Poverty, 35 percent of American seniors lived in wrenching poverty, as did 30 percent of the nation's kids. By 1975, 15 years later, child poverty had been cut in half and poverty among seniors was reduced by over 60 percent! We didn't lose the War on Poverty; we abandoned the field!

The moral imperative was removed. The progress once popular was racialized and disorganized by intentional efforts like the so-called "White Southern Strategy."

Signs and wonders are now showing us the need for a revised Movement. Last year Supreme Court Justice Ruth Bader Ginsburg became the voice of moral and constitutional dissent when she wrote about the terrible Voting Rights Act (VRA) decision by the majority in the Shelby County versus Holder case that removed protections against race-based voter suppression in the South and wherever else it occurred. Ginsburg wrote:

> *Hubris is a fit word for today's demolition of the VRA...throwing out preclearance [the Section Four formula] when it has worked and is continuing to work to stop discriminatory changes is like throwing away your umbrella in a rainstorm because you are not getting wet.*[5]

But she also reminded the court of the Bloody Sunday campaign for voting rights in Selma, Alabama, and quoted Martin Luther King Jr.'s hopeful determination when he said: *The arc of the moral universe is long, but it bends toward justice.* Ginsburg also quoted Shakespeare, telling the Court that what's past is prologue, and the Spanish-American poet and philosopher George Santayana, who said *those who cannot remember the past are condemned to repeat it.* Her words.

John Kasich, governor of Ohio and a Republican in a Movement of moral epilepsy, said as he sat at the head of a burnished table as members of his cabinet lingered after a meeting: *I'm concerned about the fact there seems to be a war on the poor, that if you're poor, somehow you're shiftless and lazy.* He added: *You know what? The very people who complain ought to ask their grandparents if they worked for the Works Progress Administration.*[6] Signs and wonders! Everywhere there are signs that we need a deep structured, substantive prophetic Moral Movement in America now.

Across our nation, across our world, these are tough times. Driven by the false worship of market morality, we've seen an implosion of our economy that we haven't seen since the Great Depression. There are some who want us to have pity on the billionaires. They want us to inflict more pain on the poor. We have politicians who claim they are being faithful, claim that safety net programs provide a hammock for the poor and make them lazy, and seemingly suggest America will be great if we deny them a net. Never before in history has so much money been spent to resist the struggle for equality; we need a deep, structured, sustained prophetic Moral Movement.

These are troubling times. Corporations are treated like people. People are treated like things. Some members of the Supreme Court have become legal enablers of those who would conspire to buy our democracy. We must know there is a better way. In the midst of these changing times, we must know there is a standard that never changes.

This nightmare of regressive public policy and mean, oppressive politics is taking us in the wrong direction. These backward policies and oppressive politics want us to accept an anemic faith and selling out to the highest bidder. But we must not!

Two years ago the Forward Together Moral Movement called for Putting a Face on Poverty, a tour that traveled across the state of North Carolina. One day on the tour we were invited to walk down a path into the woods. We were confronted with the fresh reality of man's inhumanity to man. As we walked along the path, we saw baby dolls and toys, eerie signs that there were children amidst all our affluence, amidst all our wealth, amidst all our national claim to be one nation; there were children living like animals under and beneath the trees and brushes of the woods. When we got to the community in the middle of the woods, we met God's family—black, brown, and white; male and female.

I was brought to uncontrollable tears when our new friends welcomed us. They swept the dirt and made space for us among the grass and the weeds. They told us of how often the authorities would come out to their small community and run them out of the woods because the city did not want to acknowledge its level of devastating poverty. And yet, in that same city, like so many other places, politicians open their meetings with prayers unto God. Good church folk come to service and ask God for more personal abundance and more personal prayers. Standing in those woods, it seems like I heard God talking like Isaiah did in his 58th chapter: *You want to know why it is that you fast and I don't look your way? That you humble yourselves and I don't even notice?*

Well, here's why:

> *The bottom line on your "fast days" is profit.*
> *You drive your employees much too hard.*
> *You fast, but at the same time you bicker and fight*

You fast, but you swing a mean fist.
The kind of fasting you do won't get your prayers off the ground!

Do you think this is the kind of fast day I'm after:
a day to show off humility?
To put on a pious long face
and parade around solemnly in black?
Do you call that fasting,
a fast day that I, GOD, would like?

This is the kind of fast day I'm after:
to break the chains of injustice,
Get rid of exploitation in the workplace,
free the oppressed,
cancel debts.

ISAIAH 58:3-6, THE MESSAGE

Seems like I heard God's voice saying to the nation and even to the church: *Come out of the exile of false religion. Come out of the exile of the religions of idolatry and self-worship, that only sustain oppression, rather than alleviate it. Get your focus on the weightier matters!*

A political economist from the University of Maryland, in an article called "America Beyond Capitalism," said:

> *What we're really beginning to experience is a process of slow decay, punctuated by a recurring economic crisis, one in which reforms achieve sporadic gains. But the long term trends of growing inequality, economic dislocation, failing democratic accountability, deepening poverty, ecological degradation, greater invasions of liberty and growing imprisonment especially of minorities, continues to slowly and quietly challenge the belief in the capacities and moral integrity of the overall system and its governing elite.*[7]

MIT Professor Otto Scharmer said: *There is a blind spot in American economic theory today. It is called "consciousness." Our refusal to have an economic theory that looks and sees that we are all integrated and we all really need each other.*[8]

Right now, this evening, in the richest nation on earth, the richest nation ever, we have more poor people than at any other moment in our country's history. Our poverty numbers, especially child poverty numbers, are far higher than any other advanced western democracy.

We add to that, now, the greatest gaps between rich and poor since we began collecting data five decades ago. Our income inequality is documented to be the highest in the advanced world. We've also become the least economically mobile. So if you're born poor here, you are more apt to stay that way than in other advanced countries. And, of course, if you're born rich you're more likely to stay that way.

The South where I come from is the native home of American poverty, where we have more poor people, and more political leaders that are utterly untroubled by it, than the rest of the land. Ten of the country's poorest 12 states are Southern. Though about 15 percent of Americans live in poverty generally, in Mississippi it's 23 percent, Louisiana 22 percent, Arkansas 20 percent, Georgia 19.1 percent, South Carolina 19 percent, and Texas 19 percent. The former Confederate states set the gold standard in American economic deprivation.

We also lead the nation in those without healthcare coverage of any kind. Here, Texas paves the way—with an astonishing 25 percent. But Louisiana (21 percent), Florida (21 percent), South Carolina (20 percent), Georgia (almost 20 percent) and Mississippi (19 percent) are close runners-up. Oddly, we're the states most strongly opposed to stimulus funding, to healthcare reform, to the expansion of Medicaid. We would benefit the most from such programs, of course.

A Movement of moral dissent is necessary now. Somebody must stand and say it doesn't matter what party is in power, who has a political supermajority. There are some things that transcend political majorities and mere majority politics and the narrow categories of liberal versus conservative. There are some things that must be challenged because they are wrong, extreme, and immoral. We must heed the call of the songwriter:

> *Will justice be demanded*
> *By ten million righteous men?*
> *Make them hear you*
> *Make them hear you*

We need a Moral Movement across the nation. An indigenously homegrown, state-based, state government-focused, deeply moral, deeply constitutional, anti-racist, anti-poverty, pro-justice, pro-labor, transformative, Fusion Movement. A Movement that is about the moral fabric of our society guided by a deeply moral and constitutional vision of what is possible. Where we build relationships that are long-term, not based on one issue or campaign. Where we challenge the greatest myth of our times, that extreme policies only hurt a small subset of people, such as people of color. These policies harm us all. We need a Moral Movement with Southern context that understands if you want to challenge America, think states, Southern states. A Movement that understands we cannot afford to be ahistorical. Anti-racism and anti-poverty work must always remain at the heart of our struggle.

We need a Moral Movement guided by our deeper faith tradition and values:

    A Movement of grassroots organizing across every state
    A Movement of civil disobedience strategy when needed
    A Movement of voter registration and education
    A Movement of strong constitutional legal strategy
    A Movement of transformative long-term coalition relationships

Yes, it is a necessity for the destiny of our democracy that we realize we have to look at policy through the moral lens of justice for all and through the constitutional principle of the common good.

Keeping millions of poor people from seeing a doctor when they are sick is not just bad policy; it is immoral and hypocritical in the face our deepest faith values and constitutional dream. Kicking hard-working people who lost jobs through no fault of their own off of unemployment benefits to give tax cuts to the very wealthy is not just bad policy; it's immoral. Trying to undermine public education and give tax dollars to private school owners is immoral and hypocritical in the face of our deepest faith values and constitutional dreams. It's immoral to deny workers a living wage and to destroy the right to collective bargaining. It's immoral to sing *America, America, God shed his grace on thee*, but then to deny that grace to women, immigrants, those who want marriage rights, and those whose families are being torn apart by poverty.

This brings us to Forward Together Moral Movement in North Carolina, where we are building a Movement of moral dissent. We recognize that dissenters help destroy the myths of delusion and domination. And so I'm glad today to be a part of this generation of moral dissenters! I'm glad to be among those who give voice and spirit and bodies to the cause of justice! I'm glad because it's our turn now! Others have come before us and they fought the fights of their day. It's our time now to focus on the weightier matters of justice and compassion and faith. The nightmare of regressive public policy and mean oppressive politics takes us in the wrong direction. We are dissenters because we know there is a better way. It's our time now! It's our time to:

1. Secure pro-labor, anti-poverty policies that ensure economic sustainability.
2. Provide well-funded, quality public education for all.
3. Promote healthcare for all, including affordable access, the expansion of Medicaid, protections for women's health, and the assurance of environmental justice in every community.
4. Address the continuing inequalities in the criminal justice system and ensure equality under the law for every person, regardless of race, class, creed, documentation, or sexual orientation.
5. Protect and expand voting rights, women's rights, LGBT rights, immigrants' rights and the principle of equal protection under the law.

It's our time, as Walter Brueggemann says, to *restore prophetic hope and imagination*. It's our time to remind ourselves and our society of the question raised in Micah 6:8 (NRSV): *What does the LORD require of you but to do justice, and to love kindness, and to walk humbly with your God?* It's our time to recall Isaiah 10:1-2 (NIV): *Woe to those who make unjust laws . . . to deprive the poor of their rights.* It's our time to remember the standard Jesus raised for righteousness in Matthew 25-35 (NIV): *"For I was hungry and you gave me something to eat, I was thirsty and you gave me something to drink, I was a stranger and you invited me in, I needed clothes and you clothed me, I was sick and you looked after me, I was in prison and you came to visit me."*

And it's time for us to dust off the broken principle of our Constitution: *We the People of the United States, in Order to form a more perfect Union, establish Justice, insure domestic Tranquility, provide for the common defense, promote the general Welfare, and secure the Blessings of Liberty.*

If we will be great in the things God desires, we must resist the low road of hypocrisy and seek higher ground where:

If we follow God's values, we can use global technology and targeted economics for infrastructure investment, total access to education, and job-creation strategies for a green economy, to address the ugly realities of poverty.

If we follow the enduring ethic of love, we can beat our swords of racism into the plows that will till the new soil of brotherhood and sisterhood. We can go to higher ground.

If we see the poor as our neighbors, if we remember we are our brother's keeper, then we shall put the poor, rather than the wealthy, at the center of our agenda.

If we hold on to God's values, the sick shall have good healthcare. The environment shall be protected. The injustices of our judicial systems shall be made just. We shall respect the dignity of all people. We can love all people. We can see all people as God's creations.

We can use our resources to develop our minds and economy, rather than build bombs, missiles, and weapons of human destruction.

Do we want to keep pressing toward God's vision? Do we want a just, wholesome society, or do we want to go backward? This is the question before us. And I believe that in this sanctuary and still in the world at this time there is somebody who wants what God wants. Somebody who wants higher ground. Somebody who understands that there are some things with God that never change. There are still some prophetic people that have not bowed, who as a matter of faith know that love is better than hate. Hope is better than despair. Community is better than division. Peace is better than war. The good of the whole is better than the whims of a few. God wants everybody—red, yellow, black, brown, and white—taken care of. God wants true community, more togetherness—not more separateness. God wants justice, always has, always will.

We are people who see and seek the higher ground:

There is a higher ground where we can pay hard workers living wages and ensure their basic human right to form unions and collectively bargain for fairness on the job.

There is higher ground where we can use global technology, green economy, and targeted tax cuts for economic and infrastructure investment in underserved communities.

We are on higher ground when we reject hate and division and mean attempts to write people out of their due constitutional protections because of their race, their creed, or their sexual orientation.

We are on higher ground when we support education and job-creation programs that fully address the ugly realities of poverty.

If we see the poor as our neighbors, and if we remember we are our brother's keeper, then we shall put the poor, rather than the wealthy, at the center of our agenda.

We will know we are on higher ground when the moral calling of our state and nation is not to look down on and disdain the poor, but to weave strong safety nets to lift up the poor.

Those of us who love freedom and justice are being called to take this nation from the low lands of injustice and division to higher ground! Higher ground! To get there, we will:

March.
Mobilize.
Organize.
Pray.
Speak truth to power.
Protest.
Go to court.
Stand up.
Vote like never before.
March for justice and love.
March in the humility of God.
Just do God's work.

We who believe in freedom can't settle for anything less than higher ground!

No matter which governor is in office,
What the Congress does,
Or what the Tea Party says we can't be.

The extremists say:

You didn't have enough political power to vote us away,
Enough insults to talk us away,
Enough money to buy us away.

But we are still here! We have not and will not give up on getting to higher ground, on building a better North Carolina, a better South, and a better America. We are going to move Forward Together and we refuse to take one step back!

We are the children who have been born for such a time as this, and there is no way we will ever abdicate our birthright. It is our time now—our time to work to see that:

Every child is educated,
The sick receive healthcare and are healed,
The poor are lifted up and not pushed down,
And voting rights are secured.

We want a democracy that protects the rights of *everyone*:

Where we are truly one nation under God with liberty and justice for all,
Where all of God's children are seen as special, and loved, and important,
Where the powerful seek to serve and not be served.

Higher ground! That's what we deserve! Is there anybody here that still believes in higher ground? Too many tears have been cried, and too many people have sacrificed, bled, and died for us to settle for anything less than higher ground.

We cannot wallow in this valley of injustice. We know our politics can reach higher ground...

Can be Moral!
Merciful!
Kind!
Loving!
Just!
Fair!
Equal!

We declare that this land is your land and my land! We refuse to live low down! We refuse to accept anything but higher ground! We refuse to believe the myths of domination, and the falsehood of inequality! We are better than meanness and domination! America, we are better than this. World, we are better than this. Our deepest moral values are better than this.

Yes we are,
Yes we are,
Yes we are.

Tell your neighbor it's time—to dig a little deeper, work a little harder. Organize better—it's Movement Time! I heard somewhere that the moral arc of the universe is long but bends toward justice. If we help the poor and stop exploitation in the workplace, we will be called repairers of the breach. They that serve the Lord shall mount upon wings as eagles. I heard if God be for us, doesn't matter who is against you! One can chase a thousand; two put ten thousand to flight! The Lord is my light. God can pick you up turn you around, set your feet on solid ground. Weeping may endure for a night but joy comes in the morning!

So no matter how tough things are, no matter how antithetical things are to the values of God, remember that God is the same yesterday, today, and tomorrow. Hold on to faith. Hold on. Trust that God is not impotent. God and God's ways shall still be exalted. *Thus saith the Lord* still carries weight. God's Spirit that anoints is still able to strengthen and sustain us. Know that, because God never changes.

Weeping may endure for a night. Mean politicians may endure for a night. But joy still comes in the morning! We will never lose our faith. We might have some dark Fridays, crucified Fridays, dark Fridays, socially dark, politically dark, economically dark Fridays. But we will not lose our faith. Because we know, we know that dark Fridays have to give way to bright Sunday morning resurrections.

We shall overcome.
We shall survive.
God's vision, God's dream will win out.
We shall be called repairers of the broken places.
We will see higher ground!
Lord, lift us up, and let me stand by faith on Canaan's land;
A higher plane than I have found, Lord, plant my feet on higher ground.
Plant New York!
Plant America!
Plant our politics on higher ground!

11

"A LOOK BACK"

OUR ALLIANCE WITH LGBT RIGHTS

Equality NC Gala
November 9, 2012

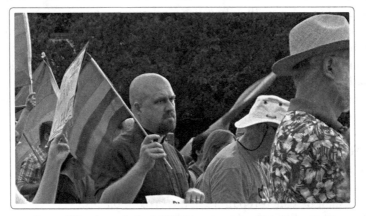

Forward Together rally for LGBTQ human rights *(Eric Preston photo)*

*As we work together now, one of our lessons is that we cannot
buy into the regressive ultra-right strategy to build a wedge between the
African American community and the LGBT community.*

BACKGROUND

One cannot understand the power of a progressive Fusion Movement
without understanding the main weapon of regressive right-wing
extremism: the divide-and-conquer strategy. One of the most toxic lies

of this strategy is the assertion that LGBT rights and marriage equality are objectionable to African Americans. That black folk don't support gay folk.

This lie is especially pervasive in the South, where solidarity across differences petrifies the forces of regression, the ones who want to maintain white supremacy and heterosexual privilege, to go backward as the nation is moving forward to greater and greater inclusion. They think that if they frame African Americans as a solid bloc of religious right gay-bashers, they can drive a wedge to break solidarity among blacks and the LGBT rights movement.

This lie is not only nefarious but it is illogical. Black persons are the same as people of all ethnicities and cultures when it comes to sexual orientation and identity—African Americans embody the full range of human dimensions and cannot be boxed into a corner as gay-rights opponents to serve divide-and-conquer objectives.

We include this speech because our goal is to reveal all the lies that divide and to be repairers of the breach that breaks us into different human communities. To this end, Rev. Barber has taken leadership in expressing support for the campaigns for LGBT rights and marriage equality in North Carolina and has urged the national NAACP to also be clear in its stance on these issues. The two texts here convey that effort.

The first is Rev. Barber's address to North Carolinians who gathered for an Equality NC gala in Greensboro after the shameful passage on May 8, 2012, of what was popularly known on the ballot as Amendment One, which enshrined discrimination into our state Constitution. The second is the historic decision made by the national NAACP Board of Directors on May 19, 2012.

■■We all have lessons to learn in life. As we work together now, one of our lessons is that we cannot buy into the regressive ultra-right strategy to build a wedge between the African American community and the LGBT community. We have to be careful of our own description of the politics. I had to challenge some of my friends during the marriage amendment fight who would say that whether the amendment passed or failed was on the backs of the black community. First of all, this is not empirically true. According to the documented voting statistics, black precincts did not support the amendment. Second, to blame any single group for discriminatory law against lesbian, gay, bisexual, transgender, or queer-identified persons is a waste of time and creates unnecessary divisions. Instead, what we should do is seek to organize and find allies in every community, thereby creating a new, broader, and more diverse electorate.

Another lesson we must learn—and progressives and liberals in particular need to learn this lesson—is not to throw away the moral high ground and walk away from religious discourse. Progressives must not assume that the majority of people who confess faith do so along the same ultraconservative so-called religious right evangelical frame. The truth is, and some of you might be shocked when I say this tonight: I am a Christian evangelical and consider myself conservative. I believe that many of those who claim to be conservative are actually quite liberal. Because while they talk religion, they liberally leave out any mention of the centerpieces and the heart of biblical faith; they leave out any mention of love for all people, which in practice requires a deep commitment to justice and fairness in the public square.

If we are to broaden and deepen the electorate, we must recognize that there are friends and allies of the LGBT community who may not religiously or culturally endorse what they would call a particular lifestyle, but their non-endorsement is not rooted in meanness or hatred. In fact, when the issue is framed along the lines and requirements of loving all humanity and seeing all people as brothers and sisters; when the issue is framed as a fundamental constitutional right to guarantee equal protection under the law for every person regardless of race, creed, class, gender, or sexuality; they will stand beside and defend the LGBT community every day and every time.

We must also have a deep commitment to building and strengthening what I call 21st -century Fusion politics. Through Fusion politics in 1868, right after the Civil War and during the First Reconstruction, blacks and whites together created a new political electorate in the South and rewrote the North Carolina Constitution. Together they guaranteed voting rights, equal protection under the law, and expanded labor rights. Together they pushed for progressive tax reform to address the economic injustices created by slavery.

Again in the 1960s, during the Second Reconstruction, it was Fusion politics throughout the South that took on Jim Crow and segregation. Blacks and whites; Protestants, Jews, and Catholics; and students and labor unions united to create a new kind of politics with a deep moral center. Together they stood with great hope and faith and a vision of possibility, believing that they could reconstruct the nation toward her paper promise of a more perfect union where all people were endowed with inalienable rights.

The energy and ethic of this Civil Rights Movement was not only to tear down Jim Crow, but in the face and viciousness of what some thought were impossible odds—to reconstruct the heart of America's jurisprudence system. Stalwart activists won the Brown versus Board of Education decision. They expanded the promise of Social Security for those who had been left out of its original framework. They created a political atmosphere that enabled the passage of the 1964 Civil Rights Act, which made illegal discrimination not only for African Americans but for women and the disabled. The energy and ethic of this movement created political space for the War on Poverty, the establishment of Medicaid and Medicare, and the passage of the Voting Rights Act of 1965, which mandated that not only African Americans but women be allowed to serve on juries, and which expanded representation from the houses of Congress to state houses to courthouses all over the United States.

The power of Fusion politics produced the 1968 Fair Housing Law. It helped us finally gain in 1971 voting rights for 18- to 21-year-olds. Now, each of these Fusion-driven movements was greeted with mean, nasty backlashes. But my point is that despite the regressive pushback against every push for greater equality under the law, Fusion politics always makes America a little more beautiful and helps her to mend her flaws of injustice and inequality.

In 2006 the NC NAACP embarked upon a journey to build a 21st-century Fusion Movement. We joined with allies and came together around a 14-Point People's Agenda. We said it was time to inject a new politics into the veins of our public square. The coalition won same-day registration and early voting in North Carolina. And this Fusion coalition is still bearing fruit.

That fruit is our united stand against regressive Voter ID laws and challenging our General Assembly last year when they passed an unconstitutional budget that hurt sixty-four thousand poor children who were made ineligible for the More at Four program. That fruit appears in court. The NC NAACP and Democracy NC and the North Carolina League of Women Voters and the A. Philip Randolph Institute together brought a court challenge to the race-based redistricting plan passed by the General Assembly. And that fruit also appeared in our united campaign against what was known as Amendment One, which when passed in 2012 enshrined our current discriminatory law against marriage equality into our state Constitution. Though we lost that fight, we were able to help change the national dialogue on this critical issue, and to move the national NAACP to state publicly for marriage equality when that fight emerged in Maryland. The Fusion Movement won in that state, which enjoys marriage equality as of January 1, 2013.

Our North Carolina Third Reconstruction Fusion Movement saw over fifteen thousand people gather in front of our General Assembly in 2013. This has been the most diverse coalition of its type ever to appear in the South, representing over 140 organizations: black, white, Latino, labor, gay, and straight all holding hands together. That's why there has been so much national right-wing extremist money flowing into North Carolina to go backward. That's why the Tea Party leadership has spent so much energy trying to shame and divide us. A tree is known by the fruit it bears. The visible fruit of our Fusion Movement has forced the leaders of regression to see us.

Now they are betting we are going to become despondent because of the way the gerrymandered elections turned out here in North Carolina in 2010 and 2012, but I would dare challenge this room tonight that this is no time to be despondent in North Carolina or in America! We have seen President Obama elected twice by the most diverse electorate in the history of the country. His election means that the Supreme Court will not be getting any more ultraconservative judges any time soon. His election proves that black people and Latino people are not fooled by wedge issues like gay marriage and will not follow the paid preachers of the far right.

Even though President Obama lost in our state in 2012 by a scant one hundred thousand votes, the extremist right knows something is afoot because with our Fusion Movement on the rise. We must look deeper, not become despondent. Here's why. More than one million North Carolina African Americans and Latinos engaged in early voting in 2012, and African Americans made up more than 23 percent of the total North Carolina electorate; just think about that for a minute. That 23 percent is only part of the Fusion unity that we have now! So if we work together, stay in coalition together, and don't become despondent in building this Fusion Movement, we will get to 51 percent, despite their gerrymandering! Progressive whites, Latinos, labor, and the LGBT community can make up that other 28 percent to get us to a majority of 51 percent!

My friends, it is no time to wring our hands, but it is a time to keep building! Time to keep strengthening and building the ties that bind us. They push back, so we must push forward with even more strength. We must believe that in the long arc to full justice, political defeats are only temporary. Righteousness never ultimately loses. Weeping may endure for a night, but joy still comes in the morning! I come from a faith tradition that believes that life can be redirected out of death and that pain can produce power and that mountains of despair can be molded into stones of hope! That truth outweighs lies and that love is still and always more powerful than hate.

And so this is no time to be despondent; it's time to believe a little deeper. It's time to dig the foundation of our coalition a little deeper; it's time to love one another a little deeper. And as my grandmother said, *It's time to dig a little deeper down in your soul, to steady your spine and declare: I ain't gonna let nobody, nobody turn us around!*

I was born August 30, 1963, three days after the March on Washington. Bayard Rustin was an openly gay march organizer. He and Dr. King and the others pressed forward together to make that stunning event happen even against a president not wanting them to march, against vicious racists not wanting them to march, and even against some in their own community not wanting to believe it could make a difference. Despite all the daunting and frightening odds, they came together; Fusion politics took place and changed America. It did.

Echoing some words that they declared: *I still have a dream; I still believe.* They did it then; we can do it now! One of my favorite passages of Scripture says that the stone that the builder rejected has become the chief cornerstone. In the words of Scripture, we can use the rejected to produce the revival. And I know in this room there are those who have known rejection. Rejection because of sexuality, rejection because of who you love, rejection because of how you were born. Rejection because somebody decided in their own ideology that they had a right and mandate to demean your humanity and my humanity given to us by God. But I want you to know that the stones that the builders rejected are now the cornerstone of this experiment we call America.

I want you to know that when the rejected get together, we can in fact redeem America from hate and discrimination! When hands that once picked cotton join Latino hands, and join progressive white hands, and join faith hands, and join labor hands, and join Asian hands, and join Native American hands, and join poor hands, and join wealthy hands, and join gay and lesbian and bisexual and transgender and straight hands, then those who have been rejected become instruments of redemption. And these instruments can and will guarantee that the common good and the promise of life, liberty, the pursuit of happiness, and equal justice under the law can never be taken away or forfeited for anybody, anywhere, at any time.

The Historic Decision of the NAACP National Board of Directors

On May 19, 2012, at its regular quarterly meeting, Chair Roslyn Brock and President Benjamin T. Jealous asked the national board of the NAACP to take up the issue of marriage equality under the law. The NAACP has had a longstanding position on fundamental equality. The NAACP had once before addressed the issue of marriage equality when an interracial couple, the Lovings, prevailed over the state of Virginia in 1967, invalidating Virginia and all other states' laws banning interracial marriage because those laws violated the 14th Amendment. More recently the NAACP has publicly opposed state and federal efforts to ban the rights and privileges of LGBT citizens. The NAACP strongly opposed California's Proposition 8, the Defense of Marriage Act, and the amendment to the North Carolina Constitution to prohibit same-sex marriage.

Chair Brock asked the Rev. Dr. William Barber, the president of the North Carolina NAACP, to present to the NAACP Board at this May meeting the lessons learned from the recent North Carolina constitutional struggle. The full statement below contains much of Dr. Barber's presentation to the board. After his presentation, the board engaged in a robust discussion. As the 64-member board began to reach consensus, Chair Brock, former Chair Julian Bond, Director of the Washington NAACP Office Hillary Shelton, and Board members Carolyn Coleman, Lenny Springs, and Dr. Barber crafted a resolution to clarify the thinking of the full board. Dr. Barber introduced the proposed resolution:

> *The NAACP Constitution affirmatively states our objective to ensure the political, educational, social and economic equality of all people. Therefore, the NAACP has opposed and will continue to oppose any national, state, local policy or legislative initiative that seeks to codify discrimination or hatred into the law or to remove the constitutional rights of LGBT citizens. We support marriage equality consistent with equal protection under the law provided under the Fourteenth Amendment of the United States Constitution. Further, we strongly affirm the religious freedoms of all people as protected by the First Amendment.*

The board approved the policy statement almost unanimously. Chair Brock summed up the meaning of the policy: *The mission of the NAACP has always been to ensure the political, social and economic equality of all*

people. We have and will oppose efforts to codify discrimination into law.
President and CEO Jealous cited the solid constitutional and historical
footing of the policy: *Civil marriage is a civil right and a matter of civil law.
The NAACP's support for marriage equality is deeply rooted in the Fourteenth
Amendment of the United States Constitution and equal protection of all people.*
Two days later, on May 21, 2012, Dr. Barber presented this statement
back in North Carolina.

Statement on the Need for NAACP Support for LGBT Equality

The NAACP does not have or hold a position on same-sex marriage
from a personal, religious, or moral perspective. We did not endorse
biracial marriage in the 1960s. We don't endorse heterosexual marriage
or people living together outside of marriage, and we don't endorse
same-sex marriage. What we do endorse is a stance against any attempt
to codify discrimination or hate in the law. What we do endorse is
same-sex marriage equality, as protected by the 14th Amendment. We
endorse the right under the Constitution for citizens of this country
to have equal protection in the lifestyle they choose. We endorse
and defend the rights of citizens that should never be taken away or
tampered with in our democracy. And we further endorse and defend
the right of religious institutions under the First Amendment to decide
their theological positions on these matters. Therefore, the question
regarding the equality of rights for the LGBT community and same-
sex couples is not a question for black America, but for America itself.
When we say *we the people*, when we say *equal protection under the law* for
all people, does that mean only those who we agree with personally
and religiously? Do we mean some people, and not others? And if this
is the case, we then render the noble sentiments of our democracy and
the lofty language of inclusion to be painfully hypocritical.

The strength and clarity of this position grows partly out of our
organization's discernment as to the forces promoting various agendas.
The campaign to discriminate against the LGBT community and same-
sex couples has been led nationally by groups such as the National
Organization for Marriage, whose own internal secret documents,
recently unsealed by a judge, revealed their goal is not so much to
promote morality but to split the LGBT and black communities. Also
the Family Research Council, listed as a hate group by the Southern
Poverty Law Center, has been active in the discriminatory campaign.

The far religious right has, since the nation lost the moral leadership of Dr. King, worked diligently over the last 40 years to turn the moral discussions of our nation from the prophetic social justice issues of equality, economic justice, racism, worker's rights, and educational equality to personal and social wedge issues, such as abortion and homosexuality.

Theologically, and from a Bible-centric perspective of the Judeo-Christian faith, the issues that should dominate the public square ought to pertain to how we treat the poor, the sick, children, women, those on the margins, and the unaccepted. The reality is, when you examine voting records and public policy positions carefully, the same forces fighting us on voting rights, educational equality, economic justice, racial disparities in the criminal justice system, etc., are the same ones behind the current attacks on the LGBT community. Remember, as one writer said: *The states' rights and ultraconservative religious critiques, when attempted in our democracy in the past, were also used to justify slavery and segregation.*

The same forces often provide pseudo-religious cover for those who, even today, continue to vigorously oppose the gains of the Civil Rights Movement, the women's Movement, and the continuation of New Deal and Great Society programs like Social Security, Medicare, and Medicaid, as they push for regressive budgetary actions to cut social programs. These forces advocate for reducing taxes for the wealthy and increasing the burdens on the poor. They advocate strict criminal laws while ignoring racial disparities in the justice system; they want to underfund public education and support draconian legislative activities that would curb voting rights and reinstate 21st-century forms of Jim Crow and James Crow, Esquire, through voter photo ID bills and race-based redistricting.

On the other hand, the prophetic religious tradition, particularly the Christian form as practiced by Dr. King and a growing number of black, white, and Latino preachers and theologians, has, as one writer stated, played a key role in securing democracy's future by emphasizing the worth and dignity of all citizens. It has done this with a liberal reading of the Bible in tandem with the Constitution and Declaration of Independence.

In our recent fight against the discriminatory Amendment One in North Carolina, we learned that once the NAACP and our allies properly framed and contextualized the issue, the people quickly grasped how the treatment of LGBT citizens is an issue of civil rights and human rights. Look at the results at the polls.

In each of North Carolina's five largest cities, voters in majority-black precincts rejected the measure: Charlotte (52 percent), Raleigh (51 percent), Greensboro (54 percent), Winston-Salem (55 percent), and Durham (65 percent). Durham's results were dramatic: Not a single majority-black precinct supported the amendment. Several crushed it by margins of 3-to-1 and even 4-to-1. Yes, even rural North Carolina had islands of resistance. The amendment failed 2-to-1 on the African-American side of Scotland Neck.[1]

As a matter of law, we are afforded the protection of the U.S. Constitution's First Amendment, which provides for and guarantees the freedom of, and from, religion. The First Amendment of the U.S. Constitution states:

Congress shall make no law respecting an establishment of religion, or prohibiting the free exercise thereof; or abridging the freedom of speech, or of the press; or the right of the people peaceably to assemble, and to petition the Government for a redress of grievances.

Our Constitution also guarantees equal protection for all persons, with no restrictions based on race, creed, color, income, gender, or sexual orientation. The 14th Amendment states in Section 1:

All persons born or naturalized in the United States, and subject to the jurisdiction thereof, are citizens of the United States and of the state wherein they reside. No state shall make or enforce any law which shall abridge the privileges or immunities of citizens of the United States; nor shall any state deprive any person of life, liberty, or property, without due process of law; nor deny to any person within its jurisdiction the equal protection of the laws.

Within our democracy, because of the First Amendment, we have a right to disagree or agree on issues of personal and religious morality. However we do not, because of the 14th Amendment, have the license to enact laws that, because of our religious or private convictions, force a particular lifestyle or remove equal protection of the law from any citizen. This is a critical point.

The 14th Amendment was passed in the aftermath of slavery and the Civil War to address America's original sin of writing discrimination, division, and hate into the Constitution, costing our nation and our people 250 years of slavery, one hundred years of Jim Crow, and the institutional racism and other residual effects we still must eliminate. This is why the NAACP stands against all forms of discrimination–race, age, gender, income, and sexual orientation.

The NAACP understands that issues of marriage rights for same-sex couples are sensitive issues for many. People of goodwill have heartfelt differences of opinion about it. We respect these differences. This is exactly why the government has no business taking away the rights of some because others don't like them.

Many in our community know that you can be religiously and culturally heterocentric without being legally and constitutionally homophobic. The African American church has never, in large part, asked the government to address issues of private and religious morality. We have understood the difference between sacraments and church doctrines on one hand, and civil and contractual rights on the other hand. We have understood that the former are protected by the First Amendment, and should not be debated or voted on in the public square. We have embraced the faith which says the mandates of Christian love invalidate any license to hate. We recognize that we mere human beings cannot exclude those whom God still includes in his constitutional covering that spreads over every human being. We know that whether God agrees or disagrees with us, he still allows everybody to benefit from the air, the sun, the rain, his grace, his mercy, and his love.

We deeply respect differences of personal conscience on the religious definition of marriage, and we strongly affirm the religious freedoms of all as protected by the First Amendment. As I mentioned earlier, the NAACP does not have or hold a position on same-sex marriage from a personal, religious, or moral perspective. We did not endorse biracial marriage in the 1960s. We don't endorse heterosexual marriage or people living together outside of marriage. We don't endorse same-sex marriage.

What we do endorse is a stance against any attempt to codify discrimination or hate in the law. What we do endorse is same-sex marriage equality, as protected by the 14th Amendment. We endorse the right under the United States Constitution for citizens of this country to have equal protection in the lifestyle they choose. We endorse and defend the rights of citizens that should never be taken away or tampered with in our democracy. And we further endorse and defend the right of religious institutions under the First Amendment to decide their theological positions on these matters.

The NAACP has always opposed any custom, tradition, practice, law, or constitutional amendment that denies any right to any person. The NAACP has a long history of opposing any proposal that would alter a federal or state Constitution for the purpose of excluding any group or individuals from guarantees of equal protection under the law. Our opposition is based on our mission statement, which calls for the *equality of rights of all persons*. Regardless of one's opinion for or against same-sex marriage on religious or personal grounds, which is protected by the First Amendment of the Constitution, the NAACP knows that we must stand firm on the principle that we will never support attempts to codify or legalize discrimination, division, or hate.

The issue of how one feels religiously or personally about same-sex marriage is a private matter of conscience, a matter of religious or moral perspective, not a public matter of constitutional and civil law. It should be worked out within one's conscience, within one's faith, and within one's own heart and faith community. We don't vote on private morality or individual religious points of view. Now to be sure, there have been times when the NAACP has had to raise the conscience of the nation but it has always been around issues of fairness, justice for all, common good, general welfare, and the ideals of life, liberty, and the pursuit of happiness for every citizen.

The issue for the NAACP is equal protection under the law. The African American community and the LGBT community are not separate communities. LBGT African Americans are members of our families, our communities, and our churches. Affirmation of the equal protection under the law for LGBT individuals and marriage equality in civil law is an affirmation of the full range of African American families.

Stop for a minute and remember the history of amending the United States Constitution. Our nation had to fight a long and bloody civil war in order to amend our Constitution, on paper at least, and to begin to expand its protections to all persons. The 13th Amendment abolished slavery; the 14th Amendment guaranteed all persons equal protection under the law; the 15th Amendment provided voting rights regardless of race or previous condition of servitude; the 19th Amendment guaranteed voting rights for (white) women; the 23rd Amendment provided voting rights in presidential elections for residents of the District of Columbia; the 24th Amendment eliminated discriminatory poll taxes in federal elections; and the 26th Amendment provided voting rights for younger Americans. No other amendment ever restricted the rights of any persons, except the two that established and then repealed prohibition of the sale of alcoholic beverages. When we look at the history of our United States, there has never been an amendment to narrow protections to liberty, but only ones to expand protections to all persons, and to remedy past injustices.

The real insult to the civil rights movement is that the very same regressive forces—who sued to overturn the 1965 Voting Rights Act, who are resegregating and robbing our public schools of valuable resources, who are blocking workers' rights to organize, who are suppressing voting rights by cutting back on the time and opportunities to vote and by forcing many to get photo IDs, and who are refusing to deal with racial disparities in the criminal justice system—now somehow think the sons and daughters of the civil rights movement cannot see through their Trojan horse trick when they try to use their wedge issues to seduce us into being a part of their scheme to deny LGBT citizens fundamental rights. Not on our watch!

No matter our color. No matter our faith tradition. Those who stand for love and justice are not about to fall for their trick. No matter how you feel personally about same-sex marriage, no one—especially those of us whose forebears were denied constitutional protections and counted as three-fifths of a vote for their slave masters, and mere chattel property for other purposes in the original Constitution—none of us should ever want to deny any other person constitutional protections!

Within this framework, the question is: *Do you believe discrimination should be codified and legalized constitutionally?* We in the NAACP believe this should never happen. No persons, regardless of race, gender, or sexuality, should be rendered second-class citizens. Rights under the Constitution should never be denied or abridged. We believe in the equality of rights for all persons. We believe the members of the LGBT community and same-sex couples are afforded those rights just as all other citizens. Any attempt to fundamentally remove those rights, regardless of how you feel personally or religiously, undermines the principals of justice and equality throughout our democracy and places all of our rights at risk.

Therefore, the question regarding the equality of rights for the LGBT community and same-sex couples is not a question for black America, but for America itself. When we say *we the people*, when we say *equal protection under the law* for all people, does that mean only those who we agree with personally and religiously? Do we mean some people, and not others? And if this is the case, we then render the noble sentiments of our democracy and the lofty language of inclusion to be painfully hypocritical.

12

"COMING TOGETHER TO GO BEYOND"

OUR ALLIANCE WITH LABOR UNION RIGHTS

"Coming Together for Higher Ground"
Coalition of Black Trade Labor Unions Convention
May 25, 2014

MaryBe McMillan, Secretary-Treasurer, North Carolina AFL-CIO
(Phil Fonville photo)

*Today, I humbly stand on Dr. King's broad shoulders and update
his logic and his requests. Labor and Civil Rights are one and the same
in the South, and I believe you can't have one without the other.*

*We are all trade unionists. We are all civil rights activists.
We can win against extremism.*

133

BACKGROUND

There can be no real Movement in the South, or for that matter, in America, that pushes forward a moral agenda without unity between labor and civil rights. Worker rights are civil rights. Just before the 2013 NAACP National Convention began in Houston, during the summer before the presidential election, Rev. Barber was asked to deliver the convention's annual Labor Luncheon Speech. More than one thousand people were in attendance, including labor leaders from across America. He delivered the speech about one hour after then-presidential candidate Romney had addressed the full convention. Rev. Barber chose at that time to lift up some of the points Dr. King had made years earlier about labor and civil rights and their relevance to our 21st-century context.

Later, many weeks into the Forward Together Moral Movement campaign of 2013-2014, Rev. Barber was invited by longtime civil rights and union movement veteran Bill Lucy to address the Coalition of Black Trade Unionists at their annual convention in Atlanta. At that time, Dr. Barber revived the call he had made to the national NAACP during the Houston speech. One unique difference about context was that Rev. Barber just a few weeks earlier, along with Mary Kay, the president of the Service Employees International Union (SEIU), marched in Chicago with thousands of fast-food workers who demanded a living wage. Those workers had publicly noted that much of their inspiration came from following North Carolina's Forward Together Moral Movement.

Below is Rev. Barber's address to the national convention of the Coalition of Black Trade Unionists, followed by his article in *Sojourners* magazine, "Why I Marched on McDonald's."

❝❝In his book, *Why We Can't Wait*, Dr. King looked at the historical denial, exploitation, and humiliation of the Negro and the poor down through the centuries. He said some form of payment needed to be made. Dr. King proposed, 50 years ago, that America should launch a broad-based, gigantic Bill of Rights for the disadvantaged and a Marshall Plan for the poor and the hurting. Way back then, he was talking about a *stimulus*. Dr. King said:

> *While Negroes form the vast majority of America's disadvantaged, there are millions of poor whites who would also benefit from this kind of massive, bottom-up stimulus. He said: The moral justification for*

the special measures for the Negroes is rooted in the robberies by the institution of slavery. But many poor whites were the derivatives of the victims of slavery. As long as labor was cheapened by the involuntary servitude of the black man, the freedom of white labor, especially in the South was little more than a myth.

We must develop a federal program of public works, retraining in jobs for all so that none, white or black, will have cause to feel threatened. At the present time, thousands of jobs a week are disappearing in the wake of automation and other production efficiency techniques. Black and white will all be harmed unless something grand and imaginative is done. The unemployed, poverty-stricken white man must be made to realize that he is in the very same boat as the Negro.[1]

That's Dr. King! Together, he said, we must exert massive pressure on the government to get jobs for all! Together, we must form a grand alliance! Together, we must merge all people for goodwill! Dr King went on to explain:

The two most dynamic Movements that reshaped the nation the past three decades are the labor and civil rights Movements. Our combined strength is potentially enormous. We have not used a fraction of it for our own good or for the needs of society as a whole. If we make the war on poverty a total war; if we seek higher standards for all workers for an enriched life, we have the ability to accomplish it, and our nation has the ability to provide it. If our two Movements unite their social pioneering initiative, thirty years from now people will look back on this day and honor those who had the vision to see the full possibilities of modern society and the courage to fight for their realization. On that day, the brotherhood of man, undergirded by economic security, will be a thrilling and creative reality.[2]

It's not some easy-kind-of-coming-together, Dr. King said in 1961, speaking to a group just like this. It just might be the only group that could form the massive reconstruction of the American society—a massive coalition of blacks, poor whites, progressive whites, working-class folks, and even recipients of welfare. This may be the only coalition that could shift America's economic architecture and make the profound changes necessary to care for all her people.

This kind of social and political strategy is born out of a serious assessment of the history of injustice and its contemporary reality. And these words, spoken from Dr. King's prophetic imagination of a just community, have just as much relevance and application today. Dr. King said America needed a Stimulus Plan 50 years ago! His stimulus plan called for a *bottom-up* approach, not a *banker-down* approach. If we had only listened back then, we would not be in the trouble that we're in now. Wall Street can't drive a just society. Capitalism can be driven crazy by greed. If you ignore the poor, if you ignore those on the bottom, there will eventually be an implosion!

In fact, when you think about it, we've been talking about this whole current economic crisis wrong. The fact of the matter is we've had a Silent Depression that has caught up with us. A political economist from the University of Maryland said in an article called "America Beyond Capitalism":

> *What we're really beginning to experience is a process of slow decay, punctuated by a recurring economic crisis, one in which reforms achieve only sporadic gains. But the long term trends of growing inequality, economic dislocation, failing democratic accountability, deepening poverty, ecological degradation, greater invasions of liberty and growing imprisonment, especially of minorities, continues to slowly and quietly challenge the belief in the capacities and moral integrity of the overall system and its governing elite.*[3]

MIT Professor Otto Scharmer said: *There is a blind spot in American economic theory today. It is called "conscience." Our refusal to have an economic theory that looks and sees that we are all integrated and we all really need each other.*[4]

And when you add the race critique, you find that not only do we have income inequality but injury inequality, where the long-term and historic injury to black and brown people is much worse. In this environment, the Koch-brother, Tea-Party extremist environment that is poisoning our public life: those who would keep inequality in place are not so much winning as they are merely taking advantage of our discord and our lack of commitment to the moral vision and strategy Dr King laid out.

And I believe, my friends, the reason we are seeing such an all-out attack on voting rights, labor rights, public education, and fair-tax policy is because the extremist adversaries of democracy see what the psalmist said in Psalm 78, that we in fact have everything we need to win, if we just fight. They see and fear, just as on the day of Pentecost, what can happen if we come together: a fresh wind of justice will blow and change things in America.

I along with others believe we are on the threshold of the Third Reconstruction Movement. The First Reconstruction, built by a multiracial Southern Fusion Movement, was crushed by the nation's acceptance of Jim Crow, by Plessy versus Ferguson, and within the next decade or so by a series of white terror attacks such as the murderous coup d'état in Wilmington, North Carolina, in 1898.

The Second Reconstruction can be traced to that glorious day in May, 60 years ago, when nine white men in black robes said "No" forever to the evil system of Jim Crow. For the next 14 years, young and old, white and black, rich and poor, Southern people risked their lives, their fortunes, and their sacred honor to repair the breach in God's human race. In 1968, with the murder of Dr. King, the destruction of the organizational infrastructure of the Southern Freedom Movement, and a clever propaganda campaign with barely disguised racist appeals to white Southern voters, the extremists had betrayed Mr. Lincoln's vision and turned their backs on people of color. This strategic effort ended the Second Reconstruction. Tim Wise notes that this strategy was not new, per se. In a starkly revealing interview, former GOP strategist Lee Atwater boldly described how the Southern strategy worked to undermine Fusion type political Movements through a 40-year effort to dismantle the gains of the Second Reconstruction.

> *You start out in 1954 by saying, 'Nigger, nigger, nigger.' By 1968, you can't say 'nigger;' that hurts you. Backfires. So you say stuff like forced busing. State's rights and all that stuff. You're getting so abstract now [that] you're talking about cutting taxes, and all these things you're talking about are totally economic things and a by-product of them is [that] blacks get hurt worse than whites.[5]*

The target of the Southern strategy was all of the Southern states of the old Confederacy, with the goal of developing a solid South that ensured the majority of Southern whites would resist and repel any Fusion political alliances with African Americans.

Now, we are at the threshold of the Third Reconstruction Movement. The electorate that brought Barack Obama to the presidency messed up the political predictability of the so-called solid South. The changing demographics scare the "ba-Jesus" out of extremists who have sold the myth of extremism to particularly Southern whites for years. Their world is breaking apart. That's why the American Legislative Exchange Council (ALEC) came to our Tea Party state legislature. It's why they have a coordinated strategy to attack voting, redistricting, labor, public health, LGBT rights, and more. Because they know if the people ever come together and understand the "intersectionality" of our issues, if we ever get the civil rights community fighting for labor rights, labor rights fighting for education and standing up for healthcare, women's rights, and LGBT and immigrant rights, we are unstoppable.

In order to address this, we must have a talk about labor with a Southern touch. In order to address this, we must have the right kind of Fusion Movement. I want to talk about labor, the labor Movement and the larger Moral Movement with a Southern drawl for a moment.

Since the early days of the First Reconstruction from the mid-1860s through the present day, labor's most difficult challenge has been to organize Southern workers. Every generation or so, enough people in labor's leadership in New York, Pittsburgh, Cleveland, Washington D.C., and other northern cities figure out that the racist grip of the solid South congressional caucus must be addressed if there is going to be any long-term effective strategy for labor rights in America.

Remember in the late 1800s, the Knights of Labor and other white labor unions reached across the color line in North Carolina. The realities of racism drove them, sometimes reluctantly, always desperately, to finally imagine African American workers as their allies. When they did, the resulting black-white Fusion Movement won every statewide election in North Carolina. The Fusionists won the governor's mansion and swept the legislature. This black-white alliance could have won every organizing drive. It could have helped the South rise again, this time as a place where working people would be treated with the respect we are due.

This experiment in interracial democracy was so strong, it could not be stopped at the polls. Nor in the plants. It could only be stopped by race-baiting conservatives who overthrew the government with violence, by fraud, and by revoltingly vilifying black men as a threat to white womanhood. The ex-planters and new corporation owners paid poor white men to put on red shirts and bring their guns and a Gatling machine gun mounted on a wagon to the streets of Wilmington, North Carolina. In a bloody daylight terrorist attack, the Red Shirts killed more people per capita than the 9/11 attack of 2001. The Red-Shirt terrorists murdered scores of black people in the streets on November 10, 1898, a day that will live in infamy. And hundreds of black and white Fusionists were exiled from Wilmington, never to return.

Labor's ill-fated efforts to organize the South sometimes were frustrated by Northern white chauvinism and paternalism. Northern organizers often came south with the naive assumption that the community would be at least neutral, if not favorable, to their efforts. They would neglect doing the necessary community work *before* the organizing drive started. They would only come to black community leadership *after* realizing that every organizing drive in the South must deal with the wide disparities that exist between white working people and their black sisters and brothers. What we know is when unions worked hard and worked early to educate its white members about race-baiting and red-baiting, such tactics failed. And labor won. When the union did not confront the fears and ignorance of its white members early on about black people, labor lost.

When the Congress of Industrial Organizations (CIO) came south after World War II in its first Operation Dixie, race proved to be its Achilles heel. Dixie's Jim Crow way of life proved inscrutable and insurmountable for the CIO.

There was one exciting exception—Local 22 of the Food, Tobacco, and Agricultural Workers in Winston-Salem. This union did not turn and run when the bosses began their race and red-baiting. Local 22 organized interracially in a workplace with heavy African-American presence. Not only did Local 22 win their union at R.J. Reynolds Tobacco but its members elected the first black elected official in the South since the fall of the Fusion Movement, a city alderman in Winston-Salem. While the bosses labeled them Reds and Blacks, union members saw through these lies, rose above their differences, and won. This is the only winning recipe for labor victories in the South—black and white, unite and fight.

We learned this same lesson again a few years back. The North Carolina NAACP decided to provide serious solidarity with the decades-old labor organizing drive of the United Food and Commercial Workers Union at the largest hog slaughterhouse in the world, in Tar Heel, North Carolina, owned by Smithfield. Working closely with the UFCW's Don Cash and Robin Williams, who took the issue of racism against the large Latino and black workforce in the more than five-thousand-worker plant near Fayetteville, we fought side by side with the workers. We worked hard to educate our black sisters and brothers to stand up for their brown co-workers from Latin America, against efforts to divide black from brown. Despite many efforts to buy us off and scare us off, I am happy to report that the union was recognized, a good contract was negotiated, and we have had strong ties with the UFCW ever since. They bring scores of workers to our rallies, and provide a positive example of black and brown unity. I want to suggest that if labor is serious, we must change America by thinking of organizing in terms of states, especially Southern states, and together with the civil rights community we must build a Fusion Movement.

In 1961, Dr. King's adviser and friend, A. Philip Randolph, was the leader of the Negro American Labor Council within the AFL-CIO. Mr. Randolph had repeatedly asked AFL president George Meany to support the growing Civil Rights Movement in the South. And Meany had repeatedly put Mr. Randolph off. Randolph had not organized the Brotherhood of Sleeping Car Porters without learning persistence, and he kept after Mr. Meany. Finally Meany, hoping it might get Mr. Randolph and the AFL-CIO's growing caucus who understood the need for strong solidarity with the Southern Civil Rights Movement to get off his back, finally invited Dr. King to speak before a convention of the AFL-CIO in Florida on December 11, 1961. Dr. King's theme was "If the Negro Wins, Labor Wins." He said to the assembled union members:

> Our needs are identical with labor's needs: decent wages, fair working conditions, livable housing, old-age security, health and welfare measures, conditions in which families can grow, have education for their children, and respect in the community. That is why Negroes support labor's demands and fight laws which curb labor. That is why the labor-hater and labor-baiter is virtually always a twin-headed creature spewing anti-Negro epithets from one mouth and anti-labor propaganda from the other mouth. The duality of interests of labor and Negroes makes any crisis which lacerates you, a crisis from which we bleed. And as we stand on the threshold of the second half of the twentieth century, a crisis confronts us both.[6]

Furthermore, 53 years ago, in words in this same speech, Dr. King asked the national AFL-CIO convention to take two steps to plow the ground for successful labor organizing in the South. First, labor must join the fight to root out racism both within its ranks and within the general community. Fighting for the rights of black people must be part of a great crusade for labor. And secondly, Dr. King said, labor has organizing experience we need, it has an apparatus unparalleled in the nation, and it has financial resources. Dr. King reminded the hundreds of delegates at the convention that only five years before, in 1956, shortly after the successful Rosa Parks-inspired Montgomery bus boycott had captured the imagination of the nation, labor's top leaders projected a $2 million campaign to assist grassroots black people struggling against the horrible conditions for black people in the

South. But as of 1961, five years later, only $10,000 of this $2 million projection had been forthcoming, a grant made by the Garment Workers Union of New York City.

Dr. King closed his inspirational talk with a simple request that every union ask its members to tax themselves one dollar each to make democracy real for millions of deprived American citizens. *If you would do these two things now in this convention, Dr. King said, resolve to deal effectively with discrimination and provide financial aid for our struggle in the South, this convention will have a glorious moral deed to add to an illustrious history.*[7]

Today, I humbly stand on Dr. King's broad shoulders and update his logic and his requests. Labor and civil rights are one and the same in the South, and I believe you can't have one without the other. We are all trade unionists. We are all civil rights activists.

We can win against extremism. Yes, we are in tough times. But it's not worse than what the slavery abolitionists faced. Not worse than what women faced when Elizabeth Cady Stanton and Sojourner Truth got together.

Don't forget that Franklin Delano Roosevelt had polio when he declared the right to a minimum wage against Republicans and Democrats and the Supreme Court and big business. It's not worse than apartheid in South Africa. It's not worse than the legal segregation and violence that civil rights leaders faced 50 years ago, when young people put their very lives on the line.

Why am I so sure we can win? Well, in North Carolina for seven years we have to come together, to revive Fusion politics. Moral voices are coming together!

Those of faith, those wrestling with faith, black and white, Latino, Native American, Asian:
   Coming together!
Gay and straight, unemployed and righteous business people:
   Coming together!
Teachers and students, women and men, even people of different political parties:
   Coming together to resist extremism and fight against a dangerous agenda of extremist deconstruction by the ultra-conservative right wing.

Our vision has been to build an indigenously led, state-based, state government-focused, deeply moral, deeply constitutional, anti-racist, anti-poverty, pro-justice, pro-labor, transformative, Fusion Movement. And a transformative Fusion Coalition.

> We understand the connectivity between the issues that each partner focuses on and embrace them as our own. We build relationships that are long-term, not based on one issue or campaign. The greatest myth of our times is that extreme policies only hurt a small subset of people, such as people of color. These policies harm us all.

> The Movement in North Carolina is about the moral fabric of our society and we are called by a deeply moral and constitutional vision of what is possible. We look at public policy through a moral lens of justice and history for all and through the constitutional principle of governing for the good of the whole. We point out how extremist policy is morally indefensible, constitutionally inconsistent, and economically insane.

> In a Southern context, we have worked to bring together a diverse coalition that takes seriously the issue of race. Where whites openly address the issue of race and institutional racism because we cannot afford to be ahistorical. Anti-racism and anti-poverty must be at the heart of our struggle. We understand that organizing the changing demographics in the South—the increase in black and Latino voters and the increase in young voters who vote their futures, not their fears—is connected to the extremist attack we are facing.

We organize around a hopeful, intersecting agenda:

1. Pro-labor, anti-poverty policies that insure economic sustainability;
2. Educational equality by ensuring every child receives a high-quality, well-funded, constitutional, diverse public education;
3. Healthcare for all by ensuring access to the Affordable Care Act, Medicare and Medicaid, Social Security, and by providing environmental protection.
4. Fairness in the criminal justice system by addressing the continuing inequalities in the system for black, brown, and poor white people.
5. Protect and expand voting rights, women's rights, LGBT rights, immigrant rights, and the fundamental principle of equal protection under the law.

We have found that somebody must stand and say that it doesn't matter what party is in power, who has a political supermajority. There are some things that transcend political majorities and mere majority politics and the narrow categories of liberal versus conservative. There are some things that must be challenged because they are wrong, extreme, and immoral: we need language to break through the code words and fear of the confining Southern strategy. To these ends, we have found 12 necessary steps:

1. Engage in indigenously-led grassroots organizing across the state.
2. Use moral language to frame and critique public policy through our deepest moral and constitutional values, regardless of who is in power.
3. Demonstrate a commitment to civil disobedience that follows the steps of the Movement and that is designed to change the public conversation and consciousness.
4. Build a stage from which to lift the voices of everyday people impacted by immoral, extremist policies, not a stage for partisan politics.
5. Build a coalition of moral and religious leaders of all faiths.
6. Intentionally diversify the Movement with the goal of winning unlikely allies.
7. Build transformative, long-term coalition relationships rooted in a clear agenda that doesn't measure success just by electoral outcomes and that destroys the myths of extremism.
8. Make a serious commitment to academic and empirical analysis of policy (activist scholars).
9. Utilize social media coordination in all forms: video, text, Twitter, Facebook, etc.
10. Engage in voter registration and education.
11. Pursue a strong legal and court strategy.
12. Resist the One Moment Mentality. We are building a Movement!

And what has happened using this strategy? So far, 941 of us have been arrested for lifting up this moral call of God's vision. In the state Legislative Building on April 29, we went in because God said go in. Our legislature is under the leadership of extremists who attack poor sick children, the unemployed, LGBT people, women, and even voting rights. We went in hoping that we could speak to their conscience. Instead of listening, they ordered us arrested. Our arrest sheet says arrested for praying, singing, and talking loud, or in other words, for preaching!

One year ago in North Carolina we began something that's come to be known as Moral Mondays. We started having what some say was *church* at the General Assembly's legislative building. Some said it wouldn't make a difference. Some said it was a waste of time. Some said the legislators in control wouldn't listen. And they were right, partially. But since April 29, daring to speak God's truth and love and vision of community, the dry bones have and are coming together!

> From 17 moral witnesses on April 29 to over fifteen thousand witnesses and supporters by July.
> Hundreds of thousands of others have joined in by social media–people from all over the country and all over the world!

The extremists played the politics of deconstruction but we are the Third Reconstruction. We have everything to win if we just fight.

Let's update Dr. King's request. Let's build a Moral Movement. Let's find a way to generate an Organizing Fund to fund labor and civil rights organizers in the former Confederate states for as long as necessary. Let's conduct on the 51st anniversary of the March on Washington for Jobs and Justice, a seven-day direct action campaign in every state capital. In North Carolina we have already put out the call, with Roz Pelles and Al McSurely leading the effort.

We must do this because labor rights are moral causes; education, healthcare and voting rights are moral causes. Way before Dr. King's speech to labor, the Book had God declaring in Deuteronomy 24:14-15 (ESV):

> *You shall not oppress a hired worker who is poor and needy, whether he is one of your brothers or one of the sojourners who are in your land within your towns. You shall give him his wages on the same day, before the sun sets (for he is poor and counts on it), lest he cry against you to the LORD, and you be guilty of sin.*

Jeremiah 22:13 (ESV) says:

> *Woe to him who builds his house by unrighteousness,*
> *and his upper rooms by injustice,*
> *who makes his neighbor serve him for nothing*
> *and does not give him his wages.*

James 5:1-4 (NRSV) says:

Come now, you rich people, weep and wail for the miseries that are coming to you. Your riches have rotted, and your clothes are moth-eaten. Your gold and silver have rusted, and their rust will be evidence against you, and it will eat your flesh like fire. You have laid up treasure for the last days. Listen! The wages of the laborers who mowed your fields, which you kept back by fraud, cry out, and the cries of the harvesters have reached the ears of the Lord of hosts.

In fact, two thousand six hundred years ago, God gave us the right message for the nation. Yes, labor rights have an *economic* message. Yes, labor rights have an *American* message. But everything that has ever changed America or the world, for the better, had to have a *moral* message. A message rooted in the righteousness of God. Hospitals were formed when somebody sounded the alarm of what was right in the sight of God. Libraries and schools to educate the minds were formed when somebody sounded what was right in the sight of God. Civil rights and voting rights laws did not make their way into the framework of America until somebody sounded the alarm of what was morally right in the sight of God.

Don't let the religious ultraconservatives dictate the moral message of our time! God has a vision for working men and women. Labor rights and fair wages are moral rights in the sight of God. God has love, deep love, for working men and women. Moses was a builder of government buildings. Noah was a shipbuilder and an expert in transit. Nehemiah built walls. David worked in livestock and the meat business. One of the psalmists was a janitor, a doorkeeper in God's house. Ruth was a farmhand. Peter worked in the fishing industry. Paul worked in the textile industry, and Jesus was trained as a carpenter. God has great love for working men and women.

Two thousand six hundred years ago, through his prophet Isaiah, God laid out his vision for working men and women. His vision for justice in Isaiah 58 is still relevant today.

"Shout! A full-throated shout!
Hold nothing back—a trumpet-blast shout!
Tell my people what's wrong with their lives,
face my family Jacob with their sins!
They're busy, busy, busy at worship,
and love studying all about me.

To all appearances they're a nation of right-living people—
   law-abiding, God-honoring.
They ask me, 'What's the right thing to do?'
   and love having me on their side.

But they also complain,
   'Why do we fast and you don't look our way?
   Why do we humble ourselves and you don't even notice?'

"Well, here's why:

"The bottom line on your 'fast days' is profit.
   You drive your employees much too hard.
You fast, but at the same time you bicker and fight.
   You fast, but you swing a mean fist.
The kind of fasting you do
   won't get your prayers off the ground.
Do you think this is the kind of fast day I'm after:
   a day to show off humility?
To put on a pious long face
   and parade around solemnly in black?
Do you call that fasting,
   a fast day that I, GOD, would like?

"This is the kind of fast day I'm after:
   to break the chains of injustice,
   get rid of exploitation in the workplace,
   free the oppressed,
   cancel debts.
What I'm interested in seeing you do is:
   sharing your food with the hungry,
   inviting the homeless poor into your homes,
   putting clothes on the shivering ill-clad,
   being available to your own families.
Do this and the lights will turn on,
   and your lives will turn around at once.
Your righteousness will pave your way.
   The GOD of glory will secure your passage.
Then when you pray, GOD will answer.
   You'll call out for help and I'll say, 'Here I am.'

"If you get rid of unfair practices,
  quit blaming victims,
  quit gossiping about other people's sins,
If you are generous with the hungry
  and start giving yourselves to the down-and-out,
Your lives will begin to glow in the darkness,
  your shadowed lives will be bathed in sunlight.
I will always show you where to go.
  I'll give you a full life in the emptiest of places—
firm muscles, strong bones.
You'll be like a well-watered garden,
  a gurgling spring that never runs dry.
You'll use the old rubble of past lives to build anew,
  rebuild the foundations from out of your past.
You'll be known as those who can fix anything,
  restore old ruins, rebuild and renovate,
  make the community livable again."

vv. 1-12 *The Message*

If we come together, then we can save the soul of our democracy, beat back the influence of immoral money, and cleanse the veins of the nation from the poisonous intoxication of Tea Party division. We can move this nation a little closer to the more perfect union we were declared to be. Then we can move from the low roads of political destruction to higher ground.

Higher ground.
I'm pressing on the upward way,
New heights I'm gaining every day.
Still praying as I'm onward bound,
Lord, plant my feet on higher ground.
Lord, lift me up and let me stand,
By faith, on Heaven's tableland,
A higher plane than I have found;
Lord, plant my feet on higher ground.
Lord, use us to lift a blessed nation.

Lord, use us to lift a blessed nation.

"Why I Marched on McDonald's"[8]

As I travel the country, I see more and more evidence that we are
on the threshold of the Third Reconstruction Movement.

Recently, I marched with McDonald's workers from three dozen cities to the company's corporate headquarters outside of Chicago. After they refused to leave the corporate campus of the fast-food giant with its $5.6 billion in profits last year, 101 workers were arrested.

I knew I had to come when the workers invited me to share some of the lessons we have been learning in North Carolina about civil disobedience – and moral support.

I watched my new friends sit down. I watched the police gather. I prayed with the McDonald's workers as the police looked on and then slapped plastic handcuffs on more than one hundred of the workers and arrested them.

I could not help but think of the historic arc of the Civil Rights Movement. For all the gains we have been making, the treatment of low-paid workers by some of the most profitable corporations in the world ranks high in the more significant causes of the growing inequalities in the U.S.

I have helped lead the fight against backward laws passed by an extremist group of legislators that, three years ago, took power in North Carolina. Last year, national media discovered us, calling us the Moral Monday protesters. In fact we have been organizing and protesting for eight years. The fight for living wages and the right to collectively bargain for all workers are key parts of the 14-point agenda we developed in 2006 along with dozens of progressive partner organizations. We know money in the hands of low-wage workers lifts our economy.

But helping workers collectively fight for better wages is central to our movement and the right thing to do. All great religions instruct their followers on how employers should treat their workers. Living wages are at the center of our deepest moral and faith traditions.

Consider Deuteronomy 24:14: *You shall not oppress a hired servant who is poor and needy, whether he is one of your brothers or one of the sojourners who are in your land within your towns. You shall give him his wages on the same day, before the sun sets (for he is poor and counts on it), lest he cry against you to the Lord, and you be guilty of sin.*

Or Jeremiah 22:13: *Woe to him who builds his house by unrighteousness, and his upper rooms by injustice, who makes his neighbor serve him for nothing and does not give him his wages.*

As I travel the country, I see more and more evidence that we are on the threshold of the Third Reconstruction Movement. The First Reconstruction, built by a multiracial Southern Fusion Movement in the wake of the Civil War, was crushed when the nation legalized segregation and two-tier employment, housing, education and health system. Jim Crow laws were driven deep into the Southern economic and political system, setting back the human race in the struggle to repair the breach caused by racism.

The Second Reconstruction can be traced to that glorious day in 1954 when nine white men in black robes said no to Jim Crow. Over the next 14 years, young and old, white and black, rich and poor risked their lives, their fortunes, and their sacred honor to repair the breach. In 1968, with the murder of the Rev. Martin Luther King Jr., the destruction of the organizational infrastructure of the Southern freedom movement, and a clever propaganda campaign relying on thinly disguised racist appeals to white Southern voters, extremists betrayed President Lincoln's vision and his party. They turned their back on people of color. And they have become willing accomplices to a 40 year effort to dismantle the gains of the Second Reconstruction.

Now we believe we have come to the threshold of the Third Reconstruction. The McDonald's employees take their honored places in the front lines of this movement. Injustice cannot be met with silence. We must listen to workers like Cherri Delesline, mother of four from South Carolina, who makes the same $7.35 an hour she made on her first day at McDonald's 10 years ago. Hear the voice of Adriana Alvarez, a single mother from Chicago, who makes pennies above minimum wage at McDonald's and has to rely on public assistance to care for her son.

You cannot see injustice and say nothing. You cannot see exploitation and say nothing. You cannot see systematic poverty and say nothing. You cannot see one human being abuse another human being, God's creation, and say nothing. At every time, in every age, we need dissenters, who speak out about injustice.

In North Carolina, we say "Forward Together . . . Not One Step Back." We salute the McDonald's workers. They are in the front ranks of the Third Reconstruction—the fight of our time.

13

BEYOND PROTEST TO VOTER MOBILIZATION

Moral Monday
June 23, 2014
[Arrestees: 15]
(The total number of arrests is now over one thousand)

Ms. Rosanell Eaton, age 92, voting rights activist who faced Jim Crow
barriers, still active for voting rights for all *(Rob Stephens photo)*

If you are fired up, you better register and vote.

BACKGROUND

On June 23, 2014, the Forward Together Moral Movement kicked off its
Moral March to the Polls with widespread enthusiasm and a dedicated
commitment to voter mobilization as thousands of people flooded the

North Carolina General Assembly to hold a Sit-In, Teach-In, Plan-In and Pray-In. Filling every corner of the People's House, North Carolinians led by dozens of Team Leaders made concrete commitments for what they were willing to do to build the Moral March to the Polls.

More than thirty-five hundred North Carolinians rallied in Raleigh for this final Moral Legislative Building protest for the North Carolina General Assembly short session of 2014. Carrying signs, waving flags and sporting T-shirts with such slogans as "We Love Public Schools" and "Love Conquers Hate," they challenged this General Assembly's regressive policy agenda.

For the Sit-In, Pray-In, Stand-In, Teach-In, Plan-In segment of the rally, hundreds of people, outfitted with poster-sized paper, markers and voter registration forms, poured into the building. They set up small workshops throughout the first and second floors, including near Senate Leader Berger's and Speaker Tillis' closed office doors.

After an hour of discussing how to take the Movement back home to their communities, the crowd reassembled in the rotunda between the North Carolina House and Senate chambers to sing, chant, and listen to the stirring personal testimonies of people who have been harmed by these destructive public policies.

This rally marked 60 weeks of Moral Mondays organizing and protest, including more than 120 actions statewide and over one thousand arrests for civil disobedience. This Moral Monday marked a pivot towards the polls, with Moral March to the Polls activities planned in local communities across the state.

Fifteen moral witnesses were later arrested inside the Legislative Building after the Moral Monday Sit-In for expressing their dissent against the legislature's punitive budget and bills. Two leading Greensboro pastors stood strong outside the golden doors of the North Carolina Senate despite having recently left the hospital for serious medical issues. Beside them stood Pattie Meegan, who had recovered from a stroke just a few weeks ago prior and whose husband was in the hospital with late-stage cancer.

A leader in the LGBTQ rights community spoke about the intersectionality of our Movements: *I am here because poverty is an LGBTQ issue; healthcare is an LGTBQ issue. But more importantly, I am here because voting rights is a North Carolina issue.*

The building authorities quickly moved to tamp down the protest, and hundreds complied with their request to move onto the third floor. There, they stood in silence but in solidarity with the 15 moral witnesses who refused to budge from their position outside the North Carolina Senate doors. Holding banners high that read "Public Education," "Voting Rights," and "Expand Medicaid," the group sang, chanted, and continued to tell their stories as the building police began to make arrests.

Rick Rapfogel, one of the moral witnesses from faraway Boone, North Carolina, had to speak through another witness who could raise his voice loudly enough to reach the third floor.

I may have lost most of my voice to cancer, Rapfogel said, *but I am not going to lose my right to vote or my voice as a citizen of North Carolina.*

When the Legislative Building police finally asked everyone to leave the entire building, the crowd began chanting *Whose House? Our House!* and *The people united will never be defeated!* as they began to march out to Bicentennial Mall. As the last of the crowd trailed through the doors to head back and mobilize their communities, the words *Ain't gonna let nobody turn me around!* rose up the stairs to the third floor where the Senate and House chambers sat empty.

❝*"Shout! A full-throated shout! Hold nothing back—a trumpet-blast shout!*
Tell my people what's wrong with their lives, face my family Jacob with their sins!
They're busy, busy, busy at worship, and love studying all about me.

To all appearances they're a nation of right-living people—law-abiding, God-honoring.
They ask me, 'What's the right thing to do?' and love having me on their side.

But they also complain, 'Why do we fast and you don't look our way? Why do we humble ourselves and you don't even notice?'

Well, here's why:

The bottom line on your 'fast days' is profit.
You drive your employees much too hard. You fast, but at the same time you bicker and fight.
You fast, but you swing a mean fist.
The kind of fasting you do won't get your prayers off the ground.
Do you think this is the kind of fast day I'm after: a day to show off humility?
To put on a pious long face and parade around solemnly in black?
Do you call that fasting, a fast day that I, GOD, would like?

"This is the kind of fast day I'm after:

To break the chains of injustice, get rid of exploitation in the workplace, free the oppressed, cancel debts.

What I'm interested in seeing you do is: sharing your food with the hungry, inviting the homeless poor into your homes, putting clothes on the shivering ill-clad, being available to your own families

Do this and the lights will turn on, and your lives will turn around at once.
Your righteousness will pave your way.
The GOD of glory will secure your passage.
Then when you pray, GOD will answer.
You'll call out for help and I'll say, 'Here I am.'

"If you get rid of unfair practices, quit blaming victims, quit gossiping about other people's sins,
If you are generous with the hungry and start giving yourselves to the down-and-out,
Your lives will begin to glow in the darkness, your shadowed lives will be bathed in sunlight.
I will always show you where to go.

I'll give you a full life in the emptiest of places—firm muscles, strong bones.
You'll be like a well-watered garden, a gurgling spring that never runs dry.
You'll use the old rubble of past lives to build anew, rebuild the foundations from out of your past.

You'll be known as those who can fix anything, restore old ruins, rebuild and renovate, make the community livable again."
ISAIAH 58:1-12 *THE MESSAGE*

Today we begin our Moral March to the Polls! Today we move inside the legislative building to plan how every one of us will mobilize the vote back at home, all over North Carolina. We know our five goals:

1. Secure pro-labor, anti-poverty policies that ensure economic sustainability.
2. Provide well-funded, quality public education for all.

3. Promote healthcare for all, including affordable access, the expansion of Medicaid, protections for women's health, and the assurance of environmental justice in every community.
4. Address the continuing inequalities in the criminal justice system and ensure equality under the law for every person, regardless of race, class, creed, documentation, or sexual orientation.
5. Protect and expand voting rights for people of color, women, immigrants, LGBT persons, the elderly, and students.

We believe in strong public schools.
We believe in mercy for the poor, especially children.
We believe in economic fairness, common sense, and economic progressivism.
We welcome people as neighbors.
We believe in greater access to the ballot for all eligible voters.

In North Carolina, we have come together to fight against a dangerous agenda of extremist laws by the ultraconservative right wing: policies that are constitutionally inconsistent, morally indefensible, and economically insane.

They deride us and deflect our questions because they can't debate on the issues. They can't make their case on moral and constitutional grounds.

We know who we are. We are black, white, Latino, Native American. We are Democrat, Republican, and Independent. We are people of all faiths, and not of faith but who believe in a moral universe. We are natives and immigrants, business leaders and workers, doctors and the uninsured, gay and straight, students and retirees. We stand here—a quilt of many colors, faiths, and creeds. We stand united in our full color against our state government's current attack on the most vulnerable. We stand together to lift up the most sacred principles of our democracy, of our faiths, and of our Constitution.

And we are winning and shifting the center of political gravity!

While we don't judge justice by polls alone, every poll on our issues shows that the extremists are out of line with the noble values of most North Carolinians. Last week poll numbers came out and they show that only 17 to 18 percent of North Carolinians agree with the Tillis-Berger budget and policies!

The extremists lie and distort the facts and say that our priorities would ruin our state economy. They are wrong! The North Carolina

Justice Center's Budget and Tax Center has run the numbers and said that our Moral Budget would in fact be revenue neutral and would actually add surplus dollars to our state!

We've now been at this Forward Together Moral Movement for 60 weeks straight and we have held over 120 actions, if you count the Historic Thousands on Jones Street People Assemblies we've held every February since 2007. Since HKonJ and the Forward Together Moral Movement began, over eighty thousand North Carolinians have come out and joined together to say there is a better way! Young people engaged like never before! And we now have Moral Freedom Summer Program, with youth organizers in 50 counties—that's half our state!

Our Moral Movement has drawn people from the mountains to the coast, from the borders of Virginia and South Carolina. Over one thousand of us have made moral witness and been arrested for raising our voice.

Over one thousand clergy of all faiths have engaged this cause.

Labor union members and civil right activists have come back each week.

Champions of the environmental, women's, LGBT, and immigrant rights have come out like never before.

You all have made our state movement a national issue. Our Fusion Movement has inspired similar movements in nine other states and is growing as we gather here today! Why is this happening?

Because you built a Movement, not a Moment! We is the most important word in the justice vocabulary.

> *We* worked to keep the 60-year-old Pungo Hospital on the coast in Belhaven from closing after the extremists refused to accept the Affordable Care Act's Medicaid expansion funds!
>
> *We* won a court injunction against the extremist plan to use public dollars to fund private schools and undermine public education!
>
> *We* won the challenge to end teacher tenure and due process for our school teachers!
>
> *We* won a federal court Voter ID lawsuit, when the court struck down a legislative immunity motion the extremists wanted so they could hide their stunts!
>
> *We* won an injunction against the new Legislative Building rules they rewrote just to keep us quiet!
>
> *And we* headed to court in two weeks to ask for a full injunction against their voter suppression law!

So now we take all of this, and we move to the next phase: the Moral March to the Polls. We don't judge our movement by elections alone but voter education, registration, and election participation is and must be a part of our work. Today we move into that part, and we will go back inside the Legislative Building for a Pray-In, Sit-In, Teach-in, and Plan-In.

In every quadrant of the People's House we will gather in groups of 25 to 30 people. Each will have a team leader, and we will plan what we will do in the March to the Polls when we leave here.

If you're fired up about attacks on teachers, register and vote!

If you care about public education, healthcare, the unemployed, working people, poor people, the environment, gay people, immigrants, young people, students, register and vote!

If you stand against the power of greed and the pornographic sums of money being spent to rob and buy our democracy, register and vote!

It's time for a Forward Together Moral March to the Polls campaign! Which side are you on? We're on the side of the people and our North Carolina Constitution guarantees us our rights! Article 1 is our Declaration of Rights. It includes these guarantees:

Section 2. Sovereignty of the people.

All political power is vested in and derived from the people; all government of right originates from the people, is founded upon their will only, and is instituted solely for the good of the whole.

Section 9. Frequent elections.

For redress of grievances and for amending and strengthening the laws, elections shall be often held.

Section 10. Free elections.

All elections shall be free.

Article VI of our North Carolina Constitution concerns suffrage and eligibility of office and describes further guarantees:

Section 1. Who may vote.

> *Every person born in the United States and every person who has been naturalized, 18 years of age, and possessing the qualifications set out in this Article, shall be entitled to vote at any election by the people of the State, except as herein otherwise provided.*

Article XI expresses our core value to guarantee the well-being and common good of all.

Section 4. Welfare policy; board of public welfare.

> *Beneficent provision for the poor, the unfortunate, and the orphan is one of the first duties of a civilized and a Christian state. Therefore the General Assembly shall provide for and define the duties of a board of public welfare.*

If you are fired up, you better register and vote. If we ever need to vote, we sure do need to vote now!

14

LESSONS FROM THE MOVEMENT

We must remind those who make decisions regarding
public policy what the prophet Isaiah said:
Woe unto those who legislate evil, who rob the poor of their rights,
who make children and women their prey.

BACKGROUND

As the Moral Monday protests in North Carolina grew increasingly visible in the media, Rev. Barber and the North Carolina Conference of the NAACP received a growing number of requests to explain their formula for success in our state's Third Reconstruction fusion movement. Rev. Barber has traveled across the South to assist organizers in several states launch their own moral movements around their own concerns. Leaders from around the country have come to North Carolina to participate in Forward Together Movement actions and to learn from them.

Each state's history, social dynamics, and political situations are unique, yet basic alignments of race and class are similar across the South and beyond, in the age of growing income inequality and political polarization. Therefore Rev. Barber and the NC NAACP have worked to summarize basic lessons from the movement here.

Rev. Barber was contacted by the Rev. Jim Wallis of *Sojourners*, who said that he was greatly supportive of the goals and works of the Forward Together Moral Movement in North Carolina. He requested that Rev. Barber write a descriptive message that would be circulated nationally and internationally through *Sojourners*. Below is Rev. Barber's summation of the Forward Together Moral Movement's principles and practices, for those in other states and communities who share the same values and who may hope to build similar Fusion coalitions for social justice.

We Are In a Crisis—A Moral Crisis[1]

❝I believe that deep within our being is a longing for a moral compass. For those of us who are moved by the cries of our sisters and brothers, we know that, like justice, the acts of caring for the vulnerable, embracing the stranger, healing the sick, protecting workers, welcoming and being fair to all members of the human family, and educating all children should never be relegated to the margins of our social consciousness. These are not just policy issues; these are not issues for some left versus right debate; these are the centerpieces of our deepest traditions of our faiths, of our values, of our sense of morality and righteousness.

We must remind those who make decisions regarding public policy what the prophet Isaiah said: *Woe to those who make unjust laws, . . . deprive the poor of their rights, . . . making widows their prey and robbing the fatherless.* (Isaiah 10:1-2 NIV).

Martin Luther King Jr. said 46 years ago in one of his last sermons that if you ignore the poor, one day the whole system will collapse and implode. The costs are too high if we don't address systemic racism and poverty. It costs us our soul as a nation. Every time we fail to educate a child on the front side of life, it costs us on the back side—financially *and* morally.

Every time we deny living wages, leaving whole communities impoverished, it costs us on the back side. Every time we fail to provide healthcare on the front side of life, it costs us on the back side. Every time we attempt to suppress the right the vote, it tears at the heart of our democracy and the necessary foundations to establish justice.

The greatest myth of our time is the notion that extreme policies harm only a small subset of people, such as people of color. These extreme policies harm us all.

What we have witnessed here in North Carolina and other parts of our nation are wealthy extremists playing on the fears of working class white people. We have seen ultraconservative politicians and their financial backers adopt a divide-and-conquer strategy, intentionally causing many people to vote against their own interests.

Our job is to unpack the truth about these extreme policies and show how they adversely affect all people. We approach this necessary task with two hopes. We hope that those forces who promote these extremists ideas and policies will be redeemed and find a new way. And, if this redemption is not to be, we hope there will be a mass Movement of moral dissent spreading across the nation, changing the actions and consciousness of all the people.

Building this Forward Together Moral Movement to take on the extremist forces requires, I believe, an indigenously led, state-based, state-government focused, deeply moral, deeply constitutional, anti-racist, anti-poverty, pro-justice, pro-labor, transformative, Fusion Movement.

This Fusion framework has its roots in the successes of the structure of Southern Fusion Movements that grew out of necessity from 1868-1898, or what we call the first Reconstruction. And these same roots were watered again during the massive changes the South underwent from 1954-1968, when the civil rights movement confronted Jim Crow directly, or what we call the second Reconstruction.

Today, as we pick up the plow of justice and equality one more time, beginning the difficult task of the Third Reconstruction, the relationships we develop with our coalition partners must be transformative, not transactional. We must build an understanding of the connectivity between the issues that each coalition partner focuses on and embrace their issues as we do our own. Our agenda, by necessity, is based on hope not fear. It emphasizes:

1. Pro-labor, anti-poverty policies that create economic sustainability by fighting for employment, living wages, the

alleviation of disparate unemployment, a green economy, labor rights, affordable housing, targeted empowerment zones, strong safety net services for the poor, fair policies for immigrants, infrastructure development, and fair tax reform;

2. Educational equality by ensuring every child receives a high quality, well-funded, constitutional, diverse public education as well as access to community colleges and universities and by securing equitable funding for minority colleges and universities;

3. Healthcare for all by ensuring access to the Affordable Care Act, Medicare and Medicaid, Social Security and by providing environmental protection;

4. Fairness in the criminal justice system by addressing the continuing inequalities in the system and providing equal protection under the law for black, brown, and poor white people;

5. Protecting and expanding voting rights, women's rights, LGBT rights, immigrant rights, and the fundamental principle of equal protection under the law.

With this agenda we have seen hundreds willing to engage in civil disobedience to take on extremism and tens of thousands willing to mobilize over and over. The moral narrative that puts a face on the pain caused by extremism and at the same time points us to higher ground is a necessity at this time in American history. We mobilize in the streets, at the polls, in the halls of the state legislature, and in the courtroom. In the Forward Together Moral Movement, a dozen do's seem helpful to our success:

1. Engage in indigenously led grassroots organizing across the state and nation;

2. Use moral language to frame and critique public policy, based on our deepest moral and constitutional values, regardless of who is in power;

3. Demonstrate a commitment to civil disobedience that follows the steps of the movement and that is designed to change the public conversation and consciousness;

4. Build a stage from which to lift the voices of everyday people affected by immoral, extremist policies—not a stage for partisan politics;

5. Build a coalition of moral and religious leaders of all faiths;

6. Intentionally diversify the movement with the goal of winning unlikely allies;

7. Build transformative, long-term coalition relationships rooted in a clear agenda that doesn't measure success just by electoral outcomes and that destroys the myth of extremism;

8. Make a serious commitment to academic and empirical analysis of policy;

9. Use social media coordination in all forms: video, text, Twitter, Facebook, etc.;

10. Engage in voter registration and education;

11. Pursue a strong legal strategy; and

12. Resist the "One Moment Mentality"–We are building a movement!

EPILOGUE

People sometimes ask me and those of us in the Forward Together Moral Movement: *What are you all actually accomplishing with your demonstrating and getting arrested and all?*

Let me here give you some very clear answers to this question, based on our realities here in North Carolina and across the country.

CONVERSATION SHIFT

The center of political gravity and discussion has shifted due to the 70+ Forward Together Moral Movement actions began in April 2013. Polls show that more and more people feel represented by our Movement, as fewer feel represented by our governor and legislative leaders.

MOBILIZATION

Fifty years after the first Freedom Summer in 1964, bolstered by a week of training by noted civil rights icons at the historic Bennett College, 37 young people from many cultures spanned out for more than 10 weeks working in over 40 North Carolina counties from the far western counties to the coast, to educate, register, and mobilize voters to the polls. This is kind of sustained and trained youth organizing for social justice has not happened since the 1960s. These young people are finding respect and success even in areas of the state generally proudly conservative, as they engage our effort for the Moral March to the Polls.

HEALTHCARE ORGANIZING ACROSS POLITICAL LINES

The majority leaders in our state of North Carolina, like those in many other states, rejected the offer to expand Medicaid coverage from President Obama's Patient Protection and Affordable Care Act. This decision to deny national dollars for state needs has generated horrific results in our state and elsewhere. One dire result of the rejection of Medicaid expansion money is the closure of rural hospitals.

Our movement was called to the rural coastal town of Belhaven, North Carolina, where a hospital was being closed due to our state's rejection of Medicaid expansion funding. What our regressive leaders meant for bad turned to good in our North Carolina Forward Together Fusion Movement, as a Republican mayor, a self-declared conservative, sent for us to help stand against the closure of Pungo Hospital, a lifeline for over 25,000, mostly poor, people of all races, creeds, and colors in eastern North Carolina.

We partnered with the Belhaven community and have engaged in litigation and mobilization to keep their local hospital open. We supported the Belhaven mayor's 273-mile justice walk to Washington, D.C., to call attention to the devastation in rural America because of the ideological denial of Medicaid expansion by extremist leaders in our own state and across the country.

The rural hospital and healthcare situation underlines how the Forward Together Moral Movement crosses political lines to engage in a debate of Right versus Wrong. All people deserve healthcare justice.

THE NEW SOUTHERN STRATEGY: UNITING FOR THE COMMON GOOD

On August 19, 2014, the North Carolina NAACP hosted a national call, which was the result of our traveling and sharing the foundations and formulas of the Forward Together Moral Movement model. We had announced in North Carolina that we were doing seven Days of Moral Action and Jericho March around our state capitol during the week of August 22-28, which was the 51st anniversary of the week of the March on Washington in 1963. This idea was generated in Selma, Alabama, at the 49th anniversary of the march across Edmund Pettus Bridge, during which I had been invited by Faya Rose and State President Bernard Simulton to speak about the principles of our Movement. During that time I imagined during a speech: *What would it look like if the Southern states particularly would have seven days of unified moral action?* To this proposal there was a resounding Yes and Amen.

Not only did the participants affirm this idea in words; they went home, took the principles, and began to form coalitions. And on August

19, 2014, we announced on a national call that was attended by the *Washington Post, Huffington Post, U.S. Religion News, Associated Press,* the Raleigh *News & Observer,* just to name a few, that the following states would join our efforts, using their own creativity, but in solidarity with both our agenda and our organizing strategies and moral framework during the seven days: Mississippi, Alabama, Georgia, Wisconsin, Tennessee, Virginia, Arkansas, Maine, and Ohio.

As I write this final note, others have also called to request training, including pastors and leaders on the ground in St. Louis and Ferguson, Missouri.

Perhaps the only way to conclude this piece is to say we have learned that there is a deep hunger for the recovery of our moral compass, for language in the political debate that is not bound by the restraints of mere left and right, Democrat and Republican; that many people still desire to see the light of justice; and that the prophetic clarion call can also sometimes awaken those who thought they were your enemies to be your friends in the struggle.

Therefore we seek to Keep the Faith, to reside in the Place of Hope, even in the midst of despair. We seek to run on and see what the end will be. We hope to make a continuing declaration like a tree standing beside the water: to never be moved. We are not those who shrink back unto destruction, but we are those who persevere unto the salvation of the soul. *Faith is the substance of things hoped for, the evidence of things not seen* (Hebrews 11-1, KJV).

ACKNOWLEDGMENTS

The poet and cleric John Donne said, "No man is an island, entire of itself." It is also true with a book project that there can be no completion by oneself.

In all of life, families matter most. Yet when one is engaged in civil rights and activism, it's one's spouse and family members who stand by and sacrifice their family time for a cause to ensure the well-being of others. So I here deeply honor my wife, Rebecca, and our children, Andrew, Benjamin, Rebekah, William III, and Sharrelle. They are my soul's home. My wife has held my hand and walked this journey with me since our days in college, and my children continue to inspire me with their laughter, their loving critiques, and their brilliance.

As I now look back over my life, I must in memory thank my father, Elder William Joseph Barber, Sr., who taught me that there was no possible way to be true to my Christian faith without being committed to love, justice, and social engagement. My mother, Eleanor P. Barber, spent a lifetime of action for justice, and her example and presence shine in my life even now, as I consider how she and my father helped integrate North Carolina public schools. My beloved parents serve as an ongoing reminder of why we must still fight today. Like my parents, the Rev. Dr. William Turner, professor of theology, shaped my life with his teaching and his demand for my theological formation.

My travels are many, my schedules are demanding, my pace is fast, and only an extremely dedicated person can assist me with a smile, sensitivity, and sincerity. Whenever and wherever I have shown up and was prepared, it was because of the constancy, generosity, and partnership of Ms. Charmeine (Turner) Fletcher.

The people of Greenleaf Christian Church in Goldsboro have taught me, have expanded and deepened my ability to preach, and have sustained my family for over 21 years, with their constant love and support.

After this close circle, I give thanks and honor to the multitude of people and organizations that have helped make the Forward Together Moral Movement, its message, and its momentum a force for positive progressive change in the face of entrenched regressive extremism in North Carolina and beyond. There is no way to thank them all, but some of the true heroes of this movement are the over 1000 persons, who by putting their bodies on the line in civil disobedience, shifted the center of moral debate and political gravity in North Carolina and across the nation. They wear not a badge of shame, but a badge of honor.

We cannot mention contributions to this movement without recognizing the host of young people who gave their energy, time, and ability, and who placed themselves at the center of our movement.

The North Carolina NAACP has been the foundation for the movement described in this book. Every North Carolina NAACP member and branch president must be applauded for enlivening local branches to take leadership in our work from the coast to the mountains of North Carolina.

A President of the NAACP is not a lone leader, but a servant leader in the midst of other leaders. I am thankful for the support and wisdom of every member of our Executive Committee, which is made up of District Directors and other special appointees. There must be a special note of appreciation for our State Vice Presidents, which include Carolyn Q. Coleman, Carolyn McDougal, Courtney Patterson, Meta Knight-Nzongola, the Rev. Dr. T. Anthony Spearman, and also Dominique Penny, our youth and college president. Furthermore, I am thankful to those who guided financial and personnel matters, and strategic organizing planning—Joyce Johnson, Keith Corbett, Sylvia Barnes, Avie Lester, Reuben Blackwell, Daphne Holmes-Johnson, O'Linda Gillis, Rena McNeil, and Debra Tyler Horton. Also let us recognize our hard-working staff team: Laurel Ashton, the Rev. Kojo Nantambu, Ashley Marshall, William Barber III, Maya Hunter, and the Rev. Curtis Gatewood, who have assisted in coordinating our coalition partners, our religious leaders, and our youth organizing, and our branch field work for HKonJ events and the Moral Monday movement.

Our Moral Monday rallies and Forward Together mass events require hosting, moving, and directing hundreds and sometimes thousands of people. This staging and security management is not easy, and the role of those who handle these tasks cannot be dismissed. Let me here thank the coordinating team of Peter Anlyan, Frank Jones, Leroy Lewis, Gary McFadden, Terrence Muhammad, and Charles Cooke. Special thanks to Martin Street Baptist Church, Christian Faith Baptist Church, Davie Street Presbyterian Church, and Pullen Memorial Baptist Church, which host almost all of the Moral Monday organizing meetings.

A core strength of our moral message has been our community of clergy representing the many faith traditions, leaders who have accepted the clarion call to be prophetic instruments and voices in these times. Along with appreciation for our tradition's leaders like the Rev. Drs. Nelson Johnson, Nancy Petty, Cardes Brown, Rodney Sadler, Gregory Moss, John Mendez, and Earl Johnson, and the Reverends Jimmy Hawkins and Jay Leach, we also thank our interfaith partners Rabbi Lucy Dinner and Rabbi Fred Guttman, and Manzoor Cheema.

There are so many partner clergy to note here that this list is woefully incomplete, but we greatly appreciate them all.

We cannot engage this world of public policy without those who help us wade through the facts and penetrate the implications of policy, so let me thank Bob Hall, Melinda Lawrence, Rob Schofield, Gene Nichol, Jarvis Hall, Stella Adams, Michelle Laws, Derrick Smith, Alexandra Forter Sirotta, Adam Linker, Dennis Gaddy, and Andrea Harris and many unnamed others, for being ready with timely data, policy news, and interpretation.

Every civil rights and social justice effort needs movement lawyers. The work we do would not be possible without the support of the Advancement Project, led by Penda Hair, along with her host of attorneys and communication staff. We also have to acknowledge the great work of Anita Earls and the skilled legal team at the Southern Coalition for Social Justice. Attorneys Scott Holmes, Irvin Joyner, Geeta Kapur, and Al McSurely have notably taken on the burden of representing the thousand-plus people who were arrested for exercising their civic voice in protest; we are most grateful for the freely given time and expertise of these and over 120 other attorneys who have worked pro bono for our cause. Special commendation goes to Jamie Phillips-Cole; who has the enormous task of coordinating our public policy and legal activities.

Three men have been indispensable in recording the history of the Southern freedom movement, making sure that our own work honors that strong tradition. It should be known that every Jeremiah movement needs its Baruch. Thanks go to our own Baruchs: Dr. Timothy Tyson, Rob Stephens, and Attorney Al McSurely.

Al McSurely has earned special notice because his historical vision has lent the frame for our Moral Movement. Since the movement's inception in 2006, Al has spent many hours with me helping to formulate strategy and believing that a true fusion peoples' coalition could be built upon a race and class critique. He kept hope that with this analysis and a moral voice, we could reenergize discouraged activists and inspire ordinary folk of all ages and cultures across the South. He was right. And Al has offered his wisdom and historical perspective with the most profound humility, and a willingness to be what I would call the "elder" and guiding spirit of the movement.

Every successful human rights movement must have a rhythm-and-music interpretation that provides strength, stamina, and joy. Ms. Yara Allen and her sister Sauuda Eshe have been for us what the Book of Kings calls "minstrels"; they are the cultural artists of our movement. Together they have ensured that the arts play a central role in cementing our coalitions. Yara and her sister have also drawn others into our movement events: the Love Music Army, the Raging Grannies, Freddy Green Street Genie, and many others.

On the line of cultural talent, Eric and Andrea Preston of Fusion Films dropped into the life of our movement offering the gift of videography. Many of you have seen Eric's capturing of each and every Forward Together event in YouTube clips—history caught in the making. Deep thanks to Eric and Andrea for bringing our work to viewers around the world.

Similarly, documentarians Annabel Park and Eric Byler of *Story of America* have honored us all by listening to our North Carolina stories and turning them into provocative pieces of persuasive film about real life at this historical time.

The photos you see in this book are also a gift, from Phil Fonville, who follows most every Forward Together event with his keen eye and offers all his photography to us free of charge. We also thank Cam Choiniere for her graphic design contributions to our work.

One other quiet contributor deserves special mention. Wally Myers took upon himself the onerous task of audiotaping and then transcribing a majority of my Moral Monday and HKonJ speeches, capturing the spontaneity that was not in my roughly prepared notes. This allowed us to have a record of lived events; thank you, Wally.

There is a phrase that the Lord always provides. Roz Pelles was the one God provided, when she came out of retirement because she was inspired by the movement and wanted to offer her years of organizing expertise to what we were doing. Let me also thank Bob Zellner, who was the first white person to work as staff of the Student Nonviolent Coordinating Committee; he heard about our movement and humbly came to offer his valuable insight.

This book would not have been possible without my friend and sister whom I met years ago through the North Carolina Council of Churches, Barbara Zelter, whose brilliance is indisputable and whose commitment to justice is without question. At the first Moral Monday, seventeen of us walked into the North Carolina Legislative Building without knowing what the Spirit would do with our pray-in and teach-in of civil disobedience. It was Barbara's hand that I held as a sign of solidarity that day. Her hand shaped and edited this book, in continuing solidarity for the Forward Together Moral Movement vision.

Finally, some may be surprised that I acknowledge God at the end, but there is a tradition with my faith that says, *My soul looks back and wonders how I go over.* My soul looks back with wonder at all these people and memories that have led to the mass movement of hope captured in this book. When I look back at what God has done, it makes me want to look FORWARD, never going backward, and see what the end shall be....

NOTES

WELCOME
1. From www.winwisdom.com/quotes/author/sir-francis-bacon-8.aspx.

CHAPTER 1: HISTORIC THOUSANDS ON JONES STREET RALLY 7
1. From Dr. King's sermon "The Three Dimension of a Great Life," in *A Knock at Midnight: Inspiration from the Great Sermons of Reverend Martin Luther King, Jr.*, ed. Clayborne Carson and Peter Holloran (New York: Warner Books, 1998).

2. Statistics shared at Moral Mondays came from NC Justice Center (ncjustice. org), NC Policy Watch (ncpolicywatch.com), and Center for Work, Poverty, and Opportunity at UNC (www.law.unc.edu/centers/poverty/).

CHAPTER 5: MORAL MONDAY RALLIES 5 AND 12
1. Summary is adapted from Lawyers Committee for Civil Rights Under the Law, www.lawyerscommittee.org/projects/voting_rights/page?id=0073.

CHAPTER 9: FIFTIETH ANNIVERSARY OF MARCH ON WASHINGTON RALLY
1. Gary Younge, "Martin Luther King: the story behind his 'I have a dream' speech," *The Guardian* (Aug. 9, 2013), available online at www.theguardian.com/world/2013/aug/09/martin-luther-king-dream-speech-history.

2. Ibid.

3. From www.aasp.umd.edu/chateauvert/mowmcall.htm.

CHAPTER 10: HISTORIC THOUSANDS ON JONES STREET RALLY 8
1. Howard Thurman, *Jesus and the Disinherited* (Boston: Beacon Press, 1976), 23.

2. William H. Bathhurst, 1831.

3. Nick Fauchald, *William Lloyd Garrison, Abolitionist and Journalist* (Minneapolis: Compass Point Books, 2005), 68–69.

4. Plessy v. Ferguson, 163 U.S. 537 (1896)

5. From www.supremecourt.gov/opinions/12pdf/12-96_6k47.pdf

6. From www.statenet.com/capitol_journal/11-04-2013/html#governors.

7. Gar Alperovitz, *America beyond Capitalism: Reclaiming Our Wealth, Our Liberty, and Our Democracy* (Hoboken, N.J.: John Wiley and Sons, 2005).

8. From www.ottoscharmer.com/docs/articles/2009_SevenAcupuncturePoints 5.pdf.

CHAPTER 11: OUR ALLIANCE WITH LGBT RIGHTS
1. Barry Yeoman, "On North Carolina's Amendment One, the fault line was not racial–it was urban-rural," *The Prospect*, available online at http://prospect.org/article/town-and-country.

CHAPTER 12: OUR ALLIANCE WITH LABOR UNION RIGHTS

1. Martin Luther King Jr., *Why We Can't Wait* (1964; rep. Boston: Beacon Press, 2010).

2. Speech given to the state AFL-CIO in Springfield, Illinois, on Oct. 7, 1965, available online at www.aflcio.org/content/download/2511/24271/King's =Speeches+to+Labor.pdf.

3. Gar Alperovitz, *America beyond Capitalism: Reclaiming Our Wealth, Our Liberty, and Our Democracy* (Hoboken, N.J.: John Wiley and Sons, 2005).

4. From www.ottoscharmer.com/docs/articles/2009_SevenAcupuncturePoints 5.pdf.

5. From www.thenation.com/article/170841/exclusive-lee-atwaters-infamous-1981-interview-southern-strategy.

6. Speech given to the AFL-CIO Fourth Constitutional Convention in Miami Beach on December 11, 1961, available online at www.aflcio.org/content/download/2511/24271/King's=Speeches+to+Labor.pdf.

7. Ibid.

8. This was previously published in the May 21, 2014 edition of *Sojourners* magazine.

CHAPTER 14: LESSONS FROM THE MOVEMENT

1. This was previously published in the May 13, 2014 edition of *Sojourners* magazine.

INDEX

A

A. Philip Randolph Institute, 123
Abernathy, Ralph, 22
abortion, 71, 108
Affordable Care Act, 12, 30, 38, 48, 98, 142, 155, 161, 163
AFL-CIO, 63, 102, 140
Allen, Yara, 63, 102
Alvarez, Adriana, 149
"America Beyond Capitalism," 112, 136
American Legislative Exchange Council (ALEC), 40, 48, 49, 71, 137
Andrews, James, 63
Anthony, Susan B., 72
anti-abortion bill, 71
anti-education laws, 80
anti-lynching bill, 74
anti- povery, 2, 8, 30, 113, 114, 115, 142, 153, 160
anti-racial profiling laws, 75
anti-racism, 2, 8, 113, 114, 141, 142, 160
Apodaca, Tom, 54
Ashley, Samuel, 6, 83
Ashton, Laurel, 102
Atwater, Lee, 137
Aycock, Charles B., 84

B

Bacon, Francis, viii
Barber, William, 27, 33, 42, 43, 52, 60, 62, 69–70, 126, 127, 134, 158–59
Baker, Ella, 10
Beloved Community, 10, 22, 50, 72
Beloved Community Center, 100
Berger, Phil, 43, 49, 41, 151, 154
biracial marriage, 127, 130
Bond, Julian, 126
Brock, Roslyn, 75, 126
Brotherhood of Sleeping Car Porters, 96, 140
Brown, Cardes, 100
Brown v. Board of Education (1954), 3, 54, 123
Brueggemann, Walter, 115

C

Cabarrus County, 99–100
Cash, Don, 139
Chafe, Bill, 101
Chaney, James, 54, 95
charter schools, 80
    . *See also* educational equality
Civil Rights Act (1964), 109, 123
Civil Rights era (1960's), 3, 10, 18, 42, 51, 104, 109–10, 122–23, 140
Civitas, 40, 48
classism, 11, 13, 49
Coalition of Black Trade Unionists, 133
Coleman, Carolyn, 51, 126
collective bargaining, 39, 114

REV. DR. WILLIAM J. BARBER II

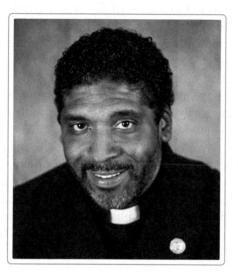

- Pastor Greenleaf Christian Church (Disciples of Christ), Goldsboro
- President of N.C. Conference of 100 adult, youth and student NAACP
- Branches in the largest State Conference in the South
- Architect of the Moral Monday-Forward Together Movement.
- Convener of the Historic Thousands on Jones Street (HKonJ) Coalition
- Chair of the Political Action Committee of the National NAACP Board

Rev. Dr. Barber was born in Indianapolis two days after the 1963 March on Washington. His parents moved him from Indiana's integrated kindergarten to the segregated kindergarten in his father's home in Washington County, a conscious act to desegregate NC's dual school systems. His father was one of the first black teachers of physics, and his mother was the first black office manager in a Washington County high school. **He earned his bachelor's degree in political** science and public administration at NC Central University, his master's from Duke University, and his doctorate from Drew University in public policy and pastoral care.

Civil Rights and Progressive Movement-Building: In 2005, Rev. Dr. Barber was elected President of the North Carolina NAACP. He quickly began the difficult job of transforming the NAACP into one of the largest membership-based progressive organizations in the state. In 2006, he gathered leaders of 16 progressive North Carolina organizations to hammer out a 14-Point People's Agenda; in February 2007, he convened the first Historic Thousands on Jones Street (HKonJ) Peoples Assembly to approve the Agenda and post it in front of the North Carolina General Assembly on Jones Street. The original sweet 16 has now grown to over 200 partners of all races, creeds, faiths, political affiliations, classes, sexualities and locations. For more than eight years, under Dr. Barber's leadership, the Forward Together Moral Movement continued to effectively fight *with* (and sometimes *against*) Democratic Party leaders in the General Assembly to win key victories for the people of North Carolina, including, for example Same-Day Registration, the Racial Justice Act, and cross-racial unity in the marriage equality fight.

Moral Mondays: Dr. Barber, the NC NAACP and the Forward Together Moral Movement were ready to challenge the newly-arisen regressive extremism that wanted to take North Carolina backward.

In late April 2013, Rev. Dr. Barber, along with 16 other ministers and activists, peacefully petitioned their representatives on Jones Street to stop the regressive attack. The General Assembly leaders had their police arrest the peaceful moral witnesses. Almost twice as many witnesses came the next Monday, and they too were thrown in jail. For 12 Mondays, the number of arrests grew and the number of supporters who came to sing, pray, and cheer them on grew. By the end of the legislative session, 944 people had been arrested and about 25,000 people had participated in the Moral Mondays. Upwards of 80,000 people participated in the eighth HKonJ - Moral March on Raleigh in early 2014, the largest civil rights march ever in the South. The movement has held more than 117 events since 2013 in North Carolina alone. By June 2014–after 62 straight weeks of mobilizing–the number of arrestees reached 1,004, the most ever in the history of the country arrested for civil disobedience at a state legislature.

The Movement in North Carolina is about the moral fabric of our society, and we are called by a deeply moral and constitutional vision of what is possible. We look at public policy through a moral lens of justice for all and through the constitutional principle of governing for the good of the whole. Our work points out how these extremist policies are morally indefensible, constitutionally inconsistent, and economically insane.

Agenda of the Movement is

1. **Secure pro-labor, anti-poverty** policies that insure economic sustainability by fighting for employment, living wages, the alleviation of disparate unemployment, a green economy, labor rights, affordable housing, targeted empowerment zones, strong safety net services for the poor, fair policies for immigrants, infrastructure development and fair tax reform.

2. **Educational equality** by ensuring every child receives a high quality, well-funded, constitutional, diverse public education as well as access to community colleges and universities and by securing equitable funding for minority colleges and universities.

3. **Healthcare for all** by ensuring access to the Affordable Care Act, Medicare and Medicaid, Social Security and by providing environmental protection.

4. **Fairness in the criminal justice system** by addressing the continuing inequalities in the system and providing equal protection under the law for black, brown and poor white people.

5. **Protect and expand** voting rights, women's rights, LGBT rights, immigrant rights and the fundamental principle of equal protection under the law.

Rev. Dr. Barber practices what he preaches: He led the Greenleaf Christian congregation in analyzing and then buying the two-mile circle surrounding the church as well as in investing $1.5 million into building more than 60 homes for low-income families, a 41-unit senior citizens' residence, a 90-student pre-school, an academic after-school, a computer lab for youth and adults, an HIV information and testing center and a Second Chance program for training formerly incarcerated men and women in the culinary arts, landscaping, and technical jobs.

Honors, (a small number mentioned)

- Honorary doctorate—North Carolina Central University, Durham, NC
- Featured on several MSNBC talk shows, including the "Melissa Harris Perry Show," "All in with Chris Hayes" and "The Last Word with Lawrence O'Donnell"

- 2013 Person of Year for several NC news outlets
- the Paul Wellstone Citizen Leadership Award–Campaign for America's Future
- Named first of the "14 Faith Leaders to Watch in 2014" by the Center for American Progress
- The Martin Luther King Award–the National Education Association.
- Rev Barber was awarded and named among the top 100 grassroots leaders in the nation for 2013 from NBC's Grio Blog.
- Selected to serve as a MIT CoLab Mel King Fellowship
- Invited to preach a Moral Message to the Nation at the Historic Riverside Church, Harlem NY

"To hear Rev. Dr. Barber at one of the Moral Monday gatherings is to witness our nation's greatest emerging prophet at work. We usually study great movements after they have run their course. In this book, Dr. Barber ushers us into the center of our nation's most exciting and promising social justice movement as it is developing. We can walk with Dr. Barber week by week as he weaves together a profound prophetic faith vision with skillful grassroots organizing, challenging and engaging the raw, ugly and crushing political extremism that swept across North Carolina in 2013. The growing Forward Together Moral Movement has already inspired, educated, and united hundreds of thousands in a most amazing diversity of preachers, rabbis, imams, laborers, Republicans and Democrats, gay and straight, mountain Whites, Latinos, African Americans, and youth to fight together for a better North Carolina. The Forward Together Moral Movement is taking root across the South and drawing attention around the nation. This book is a must-read for all seeking hope and direction for the future of our country." *—Nelson Johnson, Executive Director of Beloved Community Center of Greensboro, NC*

"This is a must read for anyone desiring to bring working people in our country together. The Forward Together Moral Movement makes a demand for the values upon which this country was created. It is one of the most diverse movements in our country—North, South, East, or West." *—George Gresham, President, 1199SEIU United Healthcare Workers East*

"What does the Lord require? This book, as well as the life and leadership of Dr. Barber, is a gift to the world that clearly articulates the answer to this question. I have been blessed to hear and be shaped by the messages written on these pages from the pulpit of Greenleaf Christian Church. It is virtually impossible to read this book and not be stirred to act justly and to love mercy and to walk humbly with your God." *—Gladwyn Uzzell, Greenleaf Christian Church, Goldsboro, North Carolina*

"The Forward Together Moral Movement is one of the most significant approaches to the struggles for social, economic, and political fairness that our country has had to confront. Congratulations to the followers for their commitment and to the Rev. William Barber II for his vision." *−William Lucy, Former Secretary-Treasurer, American Federation Of State, County, and Municipal Employees, AFL-CIO*

"The Forward Together Moral Movement and Rev. Barber changed my life as a pastor and as a person of faith. I first encountered the words of this book as living, transforming, inspiring, and breath-taking prophetic words at Moral Mondays. I have been a personal witness to how the *Moral Movement* has transformed individual lives, the heart of North Carolina, and the soul of our nation. This book is an inspiration and guidebook for every pastor committed to social justice. And it is a prophetic call to all people of faith." *−Nancy E. Petty, Pastor of Pullen Memorial Baptist Church*

"From the architect and leader of the most significant social movement of the day, we hear the collective voices of past, present, and future change agents. The words of Rev. William Barber tell us that change should take place, that it can take place, and that it will take place. Thus, if you believe in and want to be a part of change—I mean real change—then do yourself a service and read this book." *−Jarvis A. Hall, Institute for Civic Engagement and Social Change, North Carolina Central University*

"Rev. William Barber is truly an extraordinary leader. Knowing him has given me an understanding of what it must have been like for the rabbis with whom many of us grew up to have had the privilege and the opportunity to know Rev. Martin Luther King and the other great civil rights leaders of that era." *−Rabbi Fred Guttman, Temple Emanuel, Greensboro, North Carolina*